discover
CALIFORNIA

BETH KOHN, ALEX LEVITON
ALEXIS AVERBUCK, AMY C BALFOUR, ANDREW BENDER, SARA
BENSON, ALISON BING, NATE CAVALIERI, JOHN A VLAHIDES

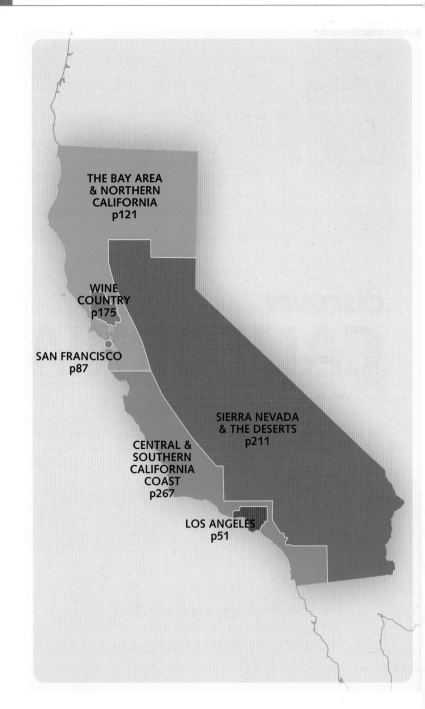

THE BAY AREA
& NORTHERN
CALIFORNIA
p121

WINE
COUNTRY
p175

SAN FRANCISCO
p87

SIERRA NEVADA
& THE DESERTS
p211

CENTRAL &
SOUTHERN
CALIFORNIA
COAST
p267

LOS ANGELES
p51

DISCOVER CALIFORNIA

Los Angeles (p51) Not just sunny beaches and air-kissing celebs, but cool culture, diverse neighborhoods and hipster haunts.

San Francisco (p87) Uncover Fog City's unique DIY flavor and ecoconsciousness, especially for outdoors lovers and foodies.

The Bay Area & Northern California (p121) Delve into redwood forests, rocky shorelines and wild spaces.

Wine Country (p175) Take a spin through rolling hills and vineyard valleys and sample some of the state's best cuisine.

Sierra Nevada & the Deserts (p211) Explore powdery mountain peaks, prickly desert plateaus and oak-dotted foothills.

Central & Southern California Coast (p267) The surf's always up on California's most sought after sun-kissed beaches.

↘CONTENTS

⬎ THIS IS CALIFORNIA   10

⬎ CALIFORNIA'S TOP 25
   EXPERIENCES   13

⬎ CALIFORNIA'S TOP
   ITINERARIES   31

⬎ PLANNING YOUR TRIP   39

⬎ LOS ANGELES   51

LOS ANGELES HIGHLIGHTS   54
LOS ANGELES' BEST…   58
THINGS YOU NEED TO KNOW   59
DISCOVER LOS ANGELES   60
Information   60
Dangers & Annoyances   60
Sights   60
Activities   74
Tours   75
Sleeping   76
Eating   78
Drinking   81
Entertainment   82
Shopping   84
Getting There & Away   84
Getting Around   85

⬎ SAN FRANCISCO   87

SAN FRANCISCO HIGHLIGHTS   88
SAN FRANCISCO'S BEST…   92
THINGS YOU NEED TO KNOW   93
DISCOVER SAN FRANCISCO   94
Orientation   94
Information   94
Dangers & Annoyances   94
Sights & Activities   98
Tours   107
Festivals & Events   107
Sleeping   108
Eating   110
Drinking   114
Entertainment   114

Shopping   116
Getting There & Around   119

⬎ THE BAY AREA &
   NORTHERN CALIFORNIA   121

THE BAY AREA & NORTHERN
CALIFORNIA HIGHLIGHTS   122
THE BAY AREA & NORTHERN
CALIFORNIA'S BEST…   126
THINGS YOU NEED TO KNOW   127
THE BAY AREA & NORTHERN
CALIFORNIA ITINERARIES   128
DISCOVER THE BAY AREA
& NORTHERN CALIFORNIA   130
BERKELEY   130
Information   130
Sights & Activities   130
Sleeping   133
Eating   133
Drinking   134
Entertainment   134
Shopping   135
Getting There & Away   135
SOUTH TO PESCADERO   135
Sleeping & Eating   136
MARIN COUNTY   137
Marin Headlands   137
Sausalito   140
Tiburon   143
The Coast   143
NORTH COAST   147
Coastal Highway 1   147
Inland Highway 101   155
Southern Redwood Coast   156
Northern Redwood Coast   168
Mt Shasta & Around   170

⬎ WINE COUNTRY   175

WINE COUNTRY HIGHLIGHTS   176
WINE COUNTRY'S BEST…   180
THINGS YOU NEED TO KNOW   181
WINE COUNTRY ITINERARIES   182
DISCOVER WINE COUNTRY   184

Getting There & Away 184
Getting Around 184
Tours 185
NAPA VALLEY 186
Napa Valley Wineries 186
Napa 188
Yountville 191
St Helena 192
Calistoga 194
Around Calistoga 196
SONOMA VALLEY 197
Sonoma Valley Wineries 197
Sonoma & Around 199
RUSSIAN RIVER AREA 202
Russian River Area Wineries 202
Guerneville 205
Santa Rosa 207
Healdsburg 208

**◢ SIERRA NEVADA &
THE DESERTS** 211

**SIERRA NEVADA & THE DESERTS
HIGHLIGHTS** 214
**SIERRA NEVADA & THE DESERTS'
BEST...** 218
THINGS YOU NEED TO KNOW 219
**SIERRA NEVADA & THE DESERTS
ITINERARIES** 220
**DISCOVER THE SIERRA NEVADA &
THE DESERTS** 222
SIERRA NEVADA 222
Lake Tahoe 222
Yosemite 229
Sequoia & Kings Canyon 236
Eastern Sierra 241
GOLD COUNTRY 247
Auburn State Recreation Area 248
Marshall Gold Discovery State
Historic Park 248
Sacramento 248
THE DESERTS 250
Palm Springs & Coachella Valley 250
Joshua Tree National Park 256

Anza-Borrego Desert State Park 258
Mojave National Preserve 260
Death Valley 261

**◢ CENTRAL & SOUTHERN
CALIFORNIA COAST** 267

**CENTRAL & SOUTHERN
CALIFORNIA COAST HIGHLIGHTS** 270
**CENTRAL & SOUTHERN
CALIFORNIA COAST'S BEST...** 274
THINGS YOU NEED TO KNOW 275
**CENTRAL & SOUTHERN
CALIFORNIA COAST ITINERARIES** 276
**DISCOVER CENTRAL & SOUTHERN
CALIFORNIA COAST** 278
MONTEREY BAY 278
Santa Cruz 278
Monterey 282
Pacific Grove 288
Carmel-by-the-Sea 291
BIG SUR 292
SAN LUIS OBISPO 296
SANTA BARBARA 300
ORANGE COUNTY 306
Disneyland Resort 306
Laguna Beach 312
SAN DIEGO 314

◢ CALIFORNIA IN FOCUS 333

ARTS & POP CULTURE 334
BEACHES & OUTDOOR ACTIVITIES 338
CALIFORNIA CUISINE 344
FAMILY TRAVEL 351
HISTORY 355
LAND & WILDLIFE 363
SHOPPING 366
SUSTAINABLE TRAVEL 369
THE WAY OF LIFE 372
WINE & MICROBREWS 374

**◢ DIRECTORY &
TRANSPORTATION** 377

DIRECTORY 378
Accommodations 378

Activities   379
Climate Charts   379
Courses   379
Dangers & Annoyances   379
Discount Cards   382
Festivals & Events   382
Gay & Lesbian Travelers   382
Holidays   383
Insurance   383
International Visitors   383
Internet Access   385
Legal Matters   386
Maps   386
Pets   387
Time   387
Tourist Information   387
Tours   387
Travelers with Disabilities   388
Women Travelers   389
TRANSPORTATION   **389**
Getting There & Away   389
Getting Around   390

↘ **BEHIND THE SCENES**   395

↘ **INDEX**   404

↘ **MAP LEGEND**   416

THE BAY AREA
& NORTHERN
CALIFORNIA
p121

WINE
COUNTRY
p175

SAN FRANCISCO
p87

CENTRAL &
SOUTHERN
CALIFORNIA
COAST
p267

SIERRA NEVADA
& THE DESERTS
p211

LOS ANGELES
p51

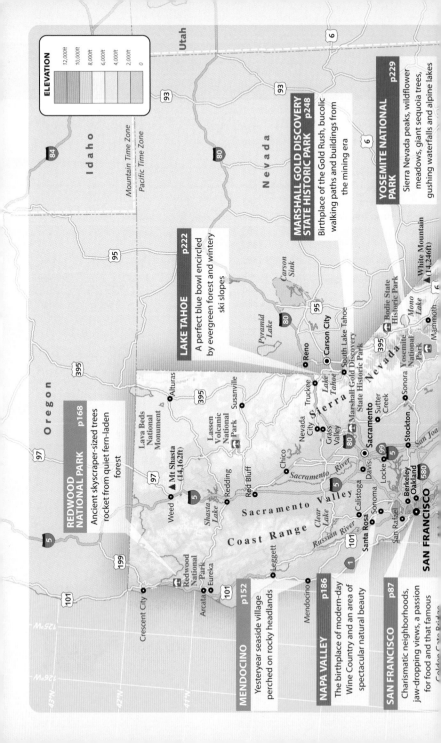

ELEVATION

	12,000ft
	10,000ft
	8,000ft
	6,000ft
	4,000ft
	2,000ft
	0

Mountain Time Zone
Pacific Time Zone

Utah

Idaho

Nevada

Oregon

REDWOOD NATIONAL PARK p168
Ancient skyscraper-sized trees rocket from quiet fern-laden forest

MENDOCINO p152
Yesteryear seaside village perched on rocky headlands

NAPA VALLEY p186
The birthplace of modern-day Wine Country and an area of spectacular natural beauty

SAN FRANCISCO p87
Charismatic neighborhoods, jaw-dropping views, a passion for food and that famous
Golden Gate Bridge

LAKE TAHOE p222
A perfect blue bowl encircled by evergreen forest and wintery ski slopes

MARSHALL GOLD DISCOVERY STATE HISTORIC PARK p248
Birthplace of the Gold Rush, bucolic walking paths and buildings from the mining era

YOSEMITE NATIONAL PARK p229
Sierra Nevada peaks, wildflower meadows, giant sequoia trees, gushing waterfalls and alpine lakes

Carson Sink

Pyramid Lake

Carson City

Reno

South Lake Tahoe

Lake Tahoe

Truckee

Nevada City

Grass Valley

Marshall Gold Discovery State Historic Park

Sacramento

Sutter Creek

Stockton

Sonora

Yosemite National Park

Bodie State Historic Park

Mono Lake

Mammoth

White Mountain (14,246ft)

Alturas

Susanville

Lava Beds National Monument

Lassen Volcanic National Park

▲ Mt Shasta (14,162ft)

Weed

Redding

Red Bluff

Chico

Sacramento River

Shasta Lake

Sierra Nevada

San Joa

Crescent City

Arcata

Eureka

Redwood National Park

Leggett

Mendocino

Santa Rosa

Russian River

Clear Lake

Calistoga

Sonoma

Davis

Locke

Berkeley

Oakland

San Rafael

Coast Range

Sacramento Valley

SAN FRANCISCO

125°W

126°W

42°N

41°N

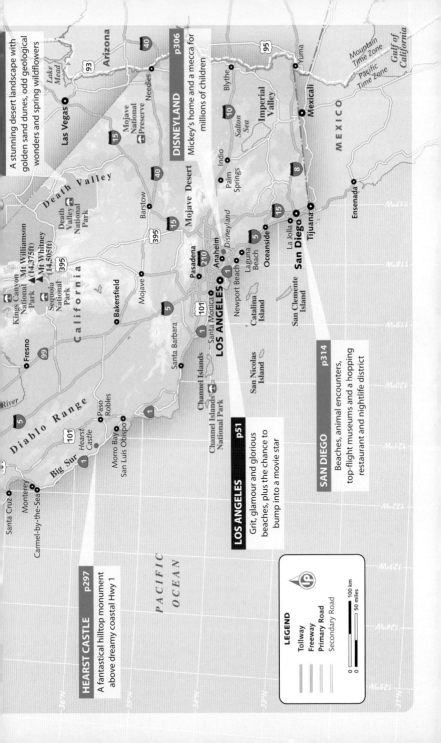

A stunning desert landscape with golden sand dunes, odd geological wonders and spring wildflowers

DISNEYLAND p306

Mickey's home and a mecca for millions of children

HEARST CASTLE p297

A fantastical hilltop monument above dreamy coastal Hwy 1

LOS ANGELES p51

Grit, glamour and glorious beaches, plus the chance to bump into a movie star

SAN DIEGO p314

Beaches, animal encounters, top-flight museums and a hopping restaurant and nightlife district

LEGEND

Tollway
Freeway
Primary Road
Secondary Road

0   100 km
0   50 miles

PACIFIC OCEAN

MEXICO

Gulf of California

Mountain Time Zone
Pacific Time Zone

↘ THIS IS CALIFORNIA

It's said that trends in California take 10 years to catch on in the rest of the country. A pioneer of technology, politics and ideas, California has a bohemian spirit, a proudly multicultural population and a die-hard passion for the good life.

Even if you've seen it on TV, California still comes as a shock to the system. The Venice Beach skateboarders, San Francisco same-sex-wedding planners, Santa Cruz wild-mushroom hunters, Rodeo Drive–pillaging trophy wives and cheerful San Diego doomsday cult members aren't on different channels. They all live here.

A detailed mosaic of the old and the new, California's cities have more flavors than a jar of jellybeans. Start in San Francisco, equal parts earth mother and geek chic, or Los Angeles, where nearly 90 independent cities are rolled into one, then drift down to Southern California's blond, botoxed enclaves or across the San Francisco Bay to radical, hippie-dippie Berkeley.

And California's landscape seems to have it all: snowy mountains, endless beaches, raging rivers, vast deserts, and forests where black bears roam. But to make the most

of this all-natural bounty, you've got to put a little sweat into it. Play hard outdoors, like the locals do.

You'll notice that no matter where you go in California, vineyards never seem far away. World-beating wines are waiting to be tasted, alongside all the other sundry regional pleasures, such as an afternoon cycling along country roads, past biodynamic farms and ranches that supply fresh produce to risk-taking restaurants.

California's nickname of the 'Golden State' comes from its 19th-century pioneer mining history, but on sunny days when the coastal fog lifts, it might as well describe the state's more than 1100 miles of Pacific beaches. Whether you swim, surf or just ramble the sands, don't miss these shoreline spots.

> 'Even if you've seen it on TV, California still comes as a shock to the system'

So take a serendipitous route from San Francisco to SoCal, ascend the Sierra Nevada, detour into soul-searching deserts, cruise rural heartland valleys and lose yourself on the northern Redwood Coast. Wherever you go, California will soar beyond your expectations.

↘ CALIFORNIA'S TOP 25 EXPERIENCES

1

❱ ANCIENT REDWOOD FORESTS

Towering redwood giants are iconic California. It's possible to drive past them, or even through them, but there's nothing like wandering among these ancient trees at places such as **Redwood National Park** (p168), one of California's most spectacular natural areas. Ditch the cell phone and hug a tree.

🢆 CALIFORNIA CUISINE

2

The shining glory of the Golden State remains the same: **California flavor** (p344). You'll find that California cooks are generous about sharing credit for a memorable dish with the stellar ingredients brought to them by local producers – many cheesemakers, wineries, farms, ranches and fisheries are credited by name on California menus.

🢆 PACIFIC COAST HIGHWAY

3

Take your time as you travel along this roller coaster of urban and natural delights. Although CA Hwy 1 runs almost the entire length of the state, it's the official 'PCH' stretch from Orange County north into Los Angeles past Santa Monica and on to **Malibu** (p60) that gets rave reviews for its oceanfront views.

1 WOODS WHEATCROFT; 2 JERRY ALEXANDER; 3 EDDIE BRADY

1 Lady Bird Johnson Grove, Redwood National Park (p168); 2 Local specialties include crab cakes with mango salsa; 3 The Pacific Coast Hwy winds its way through Big Sur (p292)

◥ TOUR WINE COUNTRY

4

Pack a picnic basket and spend some time tasting your way through California's premier wine-growing regions of **Napa Valley** (p186), **Sonoma Valley** (p197) and the **Russian River area** (p202). Though wine growing has become more upscale, it still has the uniqueness of *terroir*, with sun-dappled vineyards surrounded by pastoral ranchlands.

5

◥ DISNEYLAND

Pop culture comes to life at **Disneyland** (p270), one of the most-visited attractions on the planet. At two side-by-side theme parks, kids can hug roaming Disney characters, teens can scream on fast roller coasters, and the whole family can marvel at the nightly fireworks show. Perennial favorite rides include the Haunted Mansion and Pirates of the Caribbean.

↘ YOSEMITE NATIONAL PARK

Explore what naturalist John Muir called his 'high pleasure-ground.' Meander through Yosemite's (p214) wildflower-strewn meadows and glacier-carved valleys, stare up at its mammoth granite domes, and find a quiet corner to contemplate the passing of time. Glacier Point is sublime by the light of the full moon.

6

4 WES WALKER; 5 ©DISNEY ENTERPRISES, INC; 6 DOUGLAS STEAKLEY

4 Cabernet vines, Napa Valley (p186); 5 'it's a small world' attraction, Disneyland (p270); 6 El Capitan, Yosemite National Park (p229)

↘ EXPLORE GOLDEN GATE PARK

You could spend years in **Golden Gate Park** (p88) and still not find all its nooks and crannies. Take tea in the Japanese garden, rent a paddleboat or visit a paddock of beefy bison. For a bird's-eye view, take the elevator to the observatory at the **MH de Young Fine Arts Museum** (p102).

7

CALIFORNIA'S TOP 25 EXPERIENCES

8

⌅ HOLLYWOOD

Historic movie palaces bask in restored glory and some of LA's hottest nouveau-hipster haunts have sprung up in a recently revitalized **Hollywood** (p67). Even 'Oscar' has found a permanent home in the Kodak Theatre, part of the vast Hollywood & Highland shopping and entertainment complex.

⌅ DEATH VALLEY NATIONAL PARK

9

It's not all doom, gloom and scorched animal carcasses in **Death Valley** (p261), especially if your car has good air-conditioning. But be sure to brave the elements outside of your car so that you can feel the heat in your lungs, dodge wild burros and tumble down giant sand dunes.

7 JOHN ELK III; 8 CHRISTINA LEASE; 9 WITOLD SKRYPCZAK

7 Japanese Tea Garden (p103), Golden Gate Park, San Francisco; 8 Hollywood Walk of Fame (p67), Los Angeles; 9 Death Valley National Park (p261)

CALIFORNIA'S TOP 25 EXPERIENCES

⬎ SAN DIEGO ZOO & BALBOA PARK

10

Residents of San Diego always seem to take it easy – and who can blame them, with their close-to-perfect year-round climate? Do as they do, and take an extended stroll through the gardens, promenade and museums of **Balboa Park** (p317), and visiting the denizens of its world-famous **zoo** (p318).

⬎ MONTEREY BAY AQUARIUM

11

Trippy jellyfish, tangly kelp-forest creatures, graceful rays and boisterous sea otters enliven the awesome **Monterey Bay Aquarium** (p286). Make a point of stopping by the tanks during feeding times, when divers hand-feed the sharks, and nattily plumed penguins waddle and jostle.

⬊ LAGUNA BEACH

12

If you've ever wanted to step into a painting, a sunset stroll through Laguna Beach (p312) might be the next best thing. But hidden coves, romantic cliffs and azure waves aren't the only draw; public sculptures and arts festivals imbue the city with an artistic sensibility you won't find elsewhere in SoCal.

13

⬊ SANTA BARBARA

Just a 90-minute drive north of LA, Santa Barbara (p300) basks smugly in its near-perfection. Tucked between the Santa Ynez Mountains and the ocean, the city's red-tiled roofs, white-stucco buildings, Spanish mission and Mediterranean vibe have long given credence to its claim to the title of the American Riviera.

14

↘ GOLDEN GATE BRIDGE

You can drive, sashay or bicycle across this iconic **bridge** (p99), the dramatic golden gateway to San Francisco. Spy on cargo ships threading through the pylons and drink in panoramic views of the rugged Marin Headlands, the far-off skyscrapers downtown and the speck that is Alcatraz Island.

↘ FEAST ON MEXICAN FOOD

From the East LA taco trucks hawking tacos *al pastor* (with marinated, fried pork) to the bulky *carne asada* (grilled meat) or vegetarian burritos of San Francisco's Mission District and the seafood-infused dishes in close-to-the-border San Diego, Mexican food is ubiquitous across California.

15

14 ORIEN HARVEY; 15 JOHN HAY

14 Golden Gate Bridge (p99), San Francisco; 15 An array of Mexican staples – beef, tortillas, black beans, rice, sour cream, salsa and guacamole

⬐ SURF'S UP

The de facto state sport, **surfing** (p339) ranks as an obsession across the coast. From the many-millimeter wetsuits of chilly, kelp-draped Santa Cruz to the fiercely guarded sweet spots of SoCal, the Pacific Ocean dishes out both powerhouse surf breaks and gentle bodysurfing swells.

16

17

◥ COAST BY AMTRAK

California's biggest cities are not as public-transportation friendly as they could be, but you can reach almost all of them via **train** (p394). Amtrak's *Coast Starlight* and *Pacific Surfliner* are stunningly beautiful coastal routes, at times passing through scenic spots that are otherwise off-limits to the public.

◥ MISSIONS

18

In the 18th century, Spain planned to colonize the USA. For the glory of God – and to fill its tax coffer – 21 missions were built across the state by conscripted Native Americans. Some of the remaining missions can be visited in **Santa Barbara** (p303) and **Carmel** (p291).

16 CHRISTER FREDRIKSSON; 17 STEVE SHUEY/ALAMY; 18 EDDIE BRADY

16 Surfing the breaks around San Diego (p314); 17 Amtrak's *Pacific Surfliner* (p394) passing through Del Mar; 18 Mission Santa Barbara (p303)

⬀ GOLD COUNTRY

Churn through a frothing whitewater river or try panning for gold among rolling hillsides dotted with historic towns, sun-soaked terraces and the rusting relics of long-gone miners. Gold Country (p247) also attracts woodsy adrenaline junkies looking to bomb down single-track mountain-bike lanes or plunge into icy swimming holes.

19

20

↘ NORTH BEACH, SAN FRANCISCO

Scale the heart-stopping stairway streets in a neighborhood that has at-tracted bebop jazz musicians, civil rights agitators, topless dancers and Beat poets. With its tough climbs and giddy vistas, North Beach (p108) is a place with more sky than ground, an area that was civilized but never entirely tamed.

19 WITOLD SKRYPCZAK; 20 STEPHEN SAKS

19 Gold Country (p247); 20 North Beach (p108), San Francisco

CALIFORNIA'S TOP 25 EXPERIENCES

21

↘ HEARST CASTLE

Swan to the hilltop roost of Hearst Castle (p297), a phenomenal and over-the-top homage to material excess. Suppress envy as you tour the sprawling mansion and endless estate, with heaving citrus trees you can't pick from and inviting pools sadly bereft of swimmers.

↘ BEACH LIFE IN MALIBU

22

Elbow your way to the sand, dodging the territorial surfers and camera-shy celebrities that flock to the shores of Malibu (p60). You don't have to be a starlet, big-screen action hero or tousle-topped surfer dude to check out the wave riding at Surfrider Beach or to dine by the sea.

⬎ LA JOLLA

For a camera-worthy beach stroll, take the half-mile bluff-top path that winds above the La Jolla (p324) shoreline. For an airborne thrill, try a tandem launch into the sea breezes on a hang glider or paraglider, jumping off the high cliffs of Torrey Pines.

⬎ JOSHUA TREE NATIONAL PARK

Chalk up your hands and try not to look down as you tackle the boulders of Joshua Tree National Park (p256). The longest climbs are not much more than 100ft or so, but there are many challenging technical routes, and most can be easily top-roped for training.

21 JOHN ELK III; 22 ARIADNE VAN ZANDBERGEN; 23 EDDIE BRADY; 24 RUTH EASTHAM & MAX PAOLI

21 Neptune Pool, Hearst Castle (p297); 22 Malibu Beach (p60); 23 Hang gliding off Torrey Pines, La Jolla (p324); 24 Joshua Tree National Park (p256)

↘ LAKE TAHOE

No matter what season you visit, **Lake Tahoe** (p222) is an all-weather adventure zone. At this beautiful, blue Sierra Nevada mountain lake, you can swim, paddle a canoe, hike, mountain-bike, ski and snowboard (but not all in one day!).

25

25 LEE FOSTER

25 Snowboarding at Northstar, Lake Tahoe (p222)

A TALE OF TWO CITIES

FIVE DAYS LOS ANGELES TO SAN FRANCISCO

With five days, you can compare and contrast California's two rival cities. Spend three days taking the pulse of eclectic LA, then fly one hour north to roam the famous hills and fog of San Francisco. Tack on a few days to drive the coastal route.

❶ LOS ANGELES

Get acquainted with 'the Industry' by taking a star-emblazoned stroll down the **Hollywood Walk of Fame** (p67) and stopping at **Grauman's Chinese Theatre** (p67) along revitalized Hollywood Blvd. For a backstage look at what's being filmed today, catch a **Universal Studios Tour** (p72), then check out **Griffith Park** (p67), America's largest urban park, where you'll also find the iconic **Hollywood sign** (p67). Bring in the night at one of the city's hot **bars** (p82) or **live music venues** (p82). On your next day, dig deeper into LA culture on a literary or city history tour with **Esotouric** (p75), wander through the colorful stalls of Downtown LA's **Grand Central Market** (p80), and visit either the **Los Angeles County Museum of Art** (p72) or the hilltop **Getty Center** (p66).

❷ PACIFIC COAST HIGHWAY

Day three is an exploration along LA's coast, starting along the **Santa Monica Pier** (p61) and then poking along the canals and boardwalk in **Venice** (p61). Continue north along the Pacific Coast Hwy to **Malibu** (p60) to take your pick of celebrity-studded restaurants and watch the feats of fearless surfers.

Hollywood Walk of Fame (p67), Los Angeles

LOU JONES

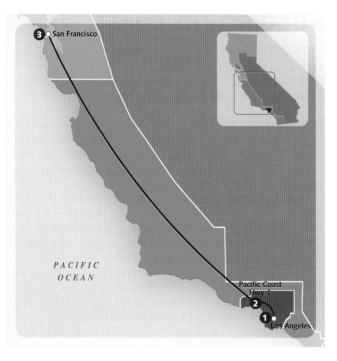

❸ SAN FRANCISCO

On your fourth day, consider the San Francisco Bay from all angles, starting with a taste test through the Ferry Building farmers market (p120), along the Embarcadero near the Bay Bridge. Hop a streetcar north to Fisherman's Wharf (p103) to ogle the raucous resident sea lions at Pier 39, and set sail for the ascetic former prison and thriving bird habitat at Alcatraz Island (p100). Cap off the day with a windy ramble across the dramatic Golden Gate Bridge (p99) before spending the evening at the theater (p116). The following day, check out the city's biggest green space and some of its best museums in Golden Gate Park (p88), and do some shopping (p116) in the nearby Haight neighborhood or in downtown's Union Square. Swim the tide of humanity on the frenetic sidewalks of Chinatown (p108) and then settle in for a quiet coffee in North Beach (p108). Book dinner at one of the city's destination restaurants (p110), and shake it 'til dawn at one of the city's many clubs (p114).

HUGGING THE COASTLINE

TEN DAYS SAN DIEGO TO SANTA CRUZ

Can't avert your eyes from the hypnotic surf of the Pacific Ocean? Embark on this classic road trip from San Diego, tracing the coast 500 miles north to Santa Cruz.

❶ SAN DIEGO

Give yourself two days to soak up the sun and sights in this pleasant SoCal city. Start with some animal spectaculars and rides at SeaWorld (p322), and let the kids go nuts at the petting pools. Then go wiggle your toes around in the hot sand at Mission Beach (p323) and try to stay standing during a surfing lesson. Budget most of the following day for the museums, gardens and the overall atmosphere of Balboa Park (p317), making certain to see some of the 3000 animals at its world-famous zoo (p318). Pass the evening enjoying the nightlife in downtown's Gaslamp Quarter (p315).

❷ LAGUNA BEACH

Continue north to artsy Laguna Beach (p312), the quintessential California beach town. Stop by the Laguna Art Museum (p313) and peruse the galleries on S Coast Hwy. For swimming, Main Beach (p313) is your best bet.

❸ SANTA BARBARA

Also vying for the coveted Southern California beauty prize is Santa Barbara, where you should meander along Stearns Wharf (p301) and take a dip in one of its many beaches. Spend the night in its

Sunrise over the bay, San Diego (p314)

WITOLD SKRYPCZAK

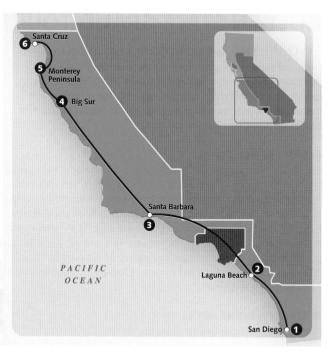

Mediterranean-style downtown, visiting the **Mission Santa Barbara** (p303) as you leave town.

❹ BIG SUR

On your way to the fabled stretch of shoreline called **Big Sur** (p292), take a gander at the opulent hilltop pleasure dome of **Hearst Castle** (p297) before strolling Pfeiffer Beach and staying at a nearby inn or campground.

❺ MONTEREY PENINSULA

Stop by Carmel to tour its exquisite Spanish **mission** (p291) and for coastal views of dramatic Monterey pines. Visit John Steinbeck country at Monterey's restored **Cannery Row** (p283), and allow a few hours to marvel at the marine life of the **Monterey Bay Aquarium** (p286). Overnight here so you can go **whale-watching** (p285) the next day.

❻ SANTA CRUZ

End your journey with a fistful of cotton candy and a scream down the wooden roller coaster at the Santa Cruz **boardwalk** (p280). Inspect a shark-munched surfboard at the cliffside **surfing museum** (p280) and rekindle your respect for those who paddle out to sea.

GOLDEN STATE GRAND TOUR

TWO WEEKS SAN FRANCISCO TO LOS ANGELES

Jump off for a whirlwind tour of this sprawling state, drinking in a taste of its landscapes and cultures. You'll experience its two most exciting cities, wildlife-rich coastline, high granite mountains, a patchwork quilt of vineyards, and a desiccated desert wilderness.

❶ SAN FRANCISCO

Take a bell-clanging trip aboard the city's fabled **cable cars** (p119) and traipse the creaky wooden floors at **City Lights** (p94) bookstore. Wander through the **Ferry Building** (p98) and grab lunch, then check out the latest show at the spacious **San Francisco Museum of Modern Art** (p100), and admire the gilded dome and elegant marble rotunda at **City Hall** (p101). Explore Golden Gate Park and survey amazing plant life inside the steamy **Conservatory of Flowers** (p103). Cap off the day by crossing the bay to dine at Berkeley's renowned **Chez Panisse** (p134) restaurant.

❷ MARIN & POINT REYES

Head north over the Golden Gate Bridge into the heart-stopping hills of Marin, calling at the headlands viewpoint of **Point Bonita Lighthouse** (p140) and the hushed redwood grove at **Muir Woods** (p144). Continue north to the **Point Reyes National Seashore** (p146), a must for nature lovers. It's an animal-spotting bonanza, from the migrating whales spouting just off the lighthouse, to the tule elk preserve at Tomales Point and marine mammals sunning themselves in

Drink in the city views at a San Francisco bar (p114)

SABRINA DALBESIO

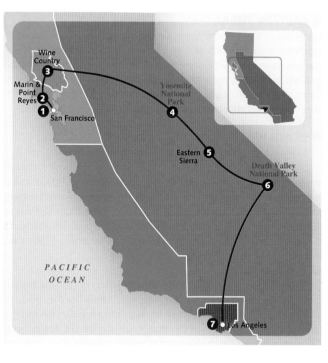

hidden coves. Drop by the nearby town of **Point Reyes Station** (p145) to fill your picnic basket with some of the best cheese in the state.

❸ WINE COUNTRY

Put all your senses into play with a seaweed wrap and a hot-spring bath in the spa town of **Calistoga** (p194) and book a meal to re-member at one of the destination restaurants in **Yountville** (p191) or **Healdsburg** (p208). Naturally, don't think of missing the opportu-nity to go wine tasting in **Napa Valley** (p186) and the other regional wineries. Budget two days.

❹ YOSEMITE NATIONAL PARK

Descend into **Yosemite Valley** (p231), and you'll understand the lure of this landscape to so many. Give yourself at least two days to explore Yosemite's trails, splash in the Merced River and romp through soaring groves of **giant sequoias** (p232). Splurge for an overnight stay or a meal at the historic **Ahwahnee Hotel** (p235) to experience its clas-sic grandeur, and reserve campsites almost six months beforehand.

❺ EASTERN SIERRA

Continue to the Eastern Sierra along Hwy 120, losing elevation to reach the haunting vista of Mono Lake (p242), then head south on the mountain-hemmed Eastern Sierra Scenic Byway, with a stop at the geological curiosity of Devils Postpile National Monument (p246). Complete the day in Lone Pine (p246), watching the sunset seep into steely silver mountains and ginger-orange hills.

❻ DEATH VALLEY NATIONAL PARK

Detour east to feel a wall of heat and witness the unusual geology of Death Valley National Park (p261). Drive around its odd array of mineral deposits and consider the novelty of playing golf (p265) at the lowest-elevation course in the world. Learn about the area's mining history and then overnight at one of the accommodation options in Furnace Creek (p265), and cool off in a spring-fed pool. The following day, make sure to tour Scotty's Castle (p264), an ornate 1930s villa.

❼ LOS ANGELES

Ditch the car to ramble along the South Bay Bicycle Trail (p74), then gawk at LA's prehistoric past at the gooey La Brea Tar Pits (p73). In Downtown LA, Frank Gehry's Walt Disney Concert Hall (p65) and the collection at the Museum of Contemporary Art (p65) are highlights. Good shopping (p84) can be done in neighborhoods across the city.

DAVID PEEVERS

Venice Beach (p61), Los Angeles

PLANNING YOUR TRIP

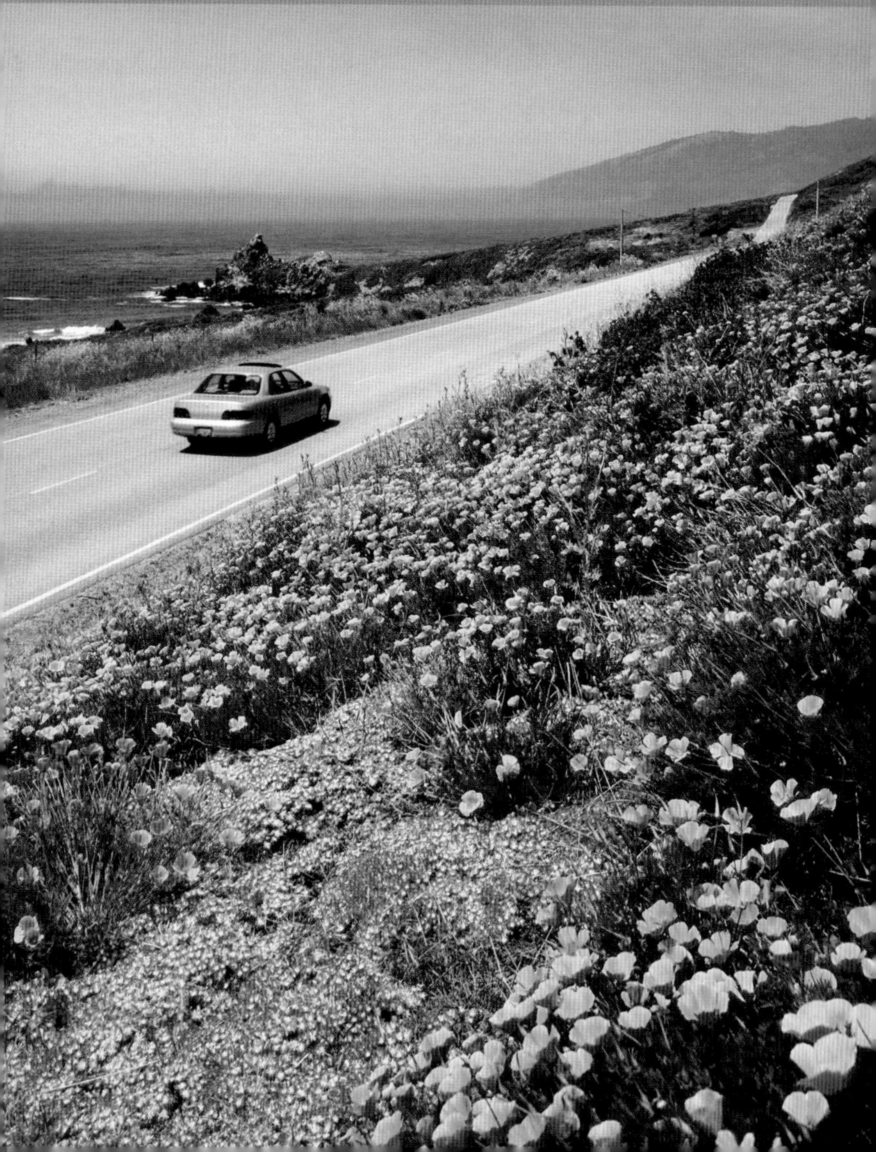

CALIFORNIA'S BEST...

🔽 DINING SPOTS

- **Chez Panisse** (p134) Taste the revolution Alice Waters started at her small Berkeley restaurant.
- **Ferry Building Farmers Market** (p120) The mother of all farmers markets.
- **Geoffrey's** (p78) From braised tofu to foie gras risotto, with the Pacific Ocean as your backdrop.
- **La Petite Rive** (p152) Romantic French dining in Elk.
- **Farmhouse Inn** (p193) Half the ingredients on the menu come from within 30 minutes of the restaurant.

🔽 DAY HIKES

- **Half Dome** (p231) A very strenuous day (or two-day) hike, including steep climbs with cables and plenty of crowds, but worth every second.
- **Griffith Park** (p67) Hike for spectacular views of Los Angeles and the Hollywood sign.

- **Julia Pfeiffer Big Sur State Park** (p293) Bring the kids along on this easy hike to beachfront waterfalls.
- **Point Lobos State Reserve** (p291) Watch as the wildflowers come out in May and June.
- **Muir Woods** (p144) Just a quick drive (or bus ride) from downtown San Francisco and you're in the redwoods.

🔽 DESSERTS

- **Franny's Cup & Saucer** (p150) Throw your next tea party here.
- **Osteria Stellina** (p145) A remote dessert outpost with equally delectable dinners.
- **Urth Caffé** (p81) Healthy, all-natural desserts (including vegan) and the occasional celebrity.
- **Sojourner Café** (p305) Go healthy with strawberry rhubarb cobbler made with stevia, or go straight to the fudge cake.

LEFT: SABRINA DALBESIO; RIGHT: GLENN VAN DER KNIJFF

Left: Ferry Building Farmers Market (p120), San Francisco; Right: Half Dome (p231), Yosemite National Park

- Mission Pie (p113) Delish sweet and savory pies, with a side of San Francisco–style social justice.

DRIVES

- Foxen Canyon Wine Trail (p306) Hidden canyons among oak-covered hills tucked between San Luis Obispo and Santa Barbara.
- Mt Shasta (p170) Take the Everitt Memorial Hwy almost to the top of the mountain.
- Tioga Road (p231) Hwy 120 E goes through the best of Yosemite's back country; passable only in summer.
- 17-Mile Drive to Big Sur (p289) From ritzy Pebble Beach, past a dozen state parks in chilled-out Big Sur.
- Avenue of the Giants (p157) A 32-mile detour through the heart of redwood country.

HISTORIC ARCHITECTURE

- San Juan Capistrano (p314) The architectural gem of California's Spanish missions.
- Hearst Castle (p297) Take a tour of the largest private residence ever built in the US.
- Los Angeles Union Station (p64) The last of the grand railroad stations in the USA, built in 1939 in a combination of Spanish Mission and art deco style.
- Ahwahnee Hotel (p235) Yosemite's swank lodge is a national historic landmark.

- Old Town (p319) Twinned with the nearby Gaslamp Quarter, two eras a few miles apart.

MARITIME MUSEUMS

- Monterey (p285) See a historic 19th-century Fresnel lens up close, along with hundreds of other artifacts spanning California's history.
- San Diego (p317) The 1863 *Star of India* and the USS Midway aircraft carrier are the highlights here.
- Santa Barbara (p301) Hands-on exhibits and virtual reality make this a fabulous destination for kids.
- Point Arena Lighthouse (p150) One of the only lighthouses on the West Coast you can still enter, with a museum of local maritime history.
- USS Pampanito (p103) Tall folks will want to watch their heads climbing aboard this WWII submarine.

UNIQUE EXPERIENCES

- Kinetic Sculpture Museum (p160) If you miss the race in May, check out some of its former champion kinetic contraption entries.
- Mystery Spot (p280) Travel back in time for optical illusions and campy good fun.
- Palm Springs Follies (p255) Broadway revue meets off-color humor, performed by stars from the good ol' days.
- Madonna Inn (p300) Is it possible to get tooth decay from a hotel?
- Alcatraz Island (p100) Sure, everyone goes, but it's a prison. On an island. In the middle of the bay.

PLANNING YOUR TRIP

THINGS YOU NEED TO KNOW

 # THINGS YOU NEED TO KNOW

⬑ AT A GLANCE

- **ATMs** Available everywhere
- **Credit cards** Accepted almost universally
- **Currency** US dollar
- **Electricity** 220-volt
- **Language** English
- **Tipping** 15-20% in restaurants, 10-15% for taxis, bars $1 per drink, porters $2 per bag
- **Visas** Not required for most Europeans; check for elsewhere

⬑ ACCOMMODATIONS

- **B&Bs** Every coastal town has at least a dozen; quaint and romantic but can be quite pricy.
- **Camping** Extremely popular, from luxury tents to barebones primitive national park sites.
- **Hostels** Both independent hostels and HI are popular, especially along the coast in larger cities.
- **Hotels** The pricier the lodging, the more amenities and services.
- **Motels** Chains are ubiquitous along highways or in heavily visited areas.
- **Resorts** From swish lodges to casual outdoorsy spots.
- **Spas** Many Wine Country hotels now double as spas.

⬑ ADVANCE PLANNING

- **Two months before** Shop for airfares online; book accommodations in popular areas.
- **One month before** Set up special tours of film studios; make reservations at in-demand restaurants.

- **One week before** Buy Disneyland tickets if you don't want to stand in line; choose from a mountain of options and plan a rough itinerary.

⬑ BE FOREWARNED

- **Driving distances** Driving from the northern tip to the Mexico border would take you about 18 to 20 hours. LA to San Francisco is about seven hours, and it's another five or six hours to the redwoods.
- **Earthquakes** Small tremors happen daily, but are rarely felt. If you're in a large earthquake, get away from glass and move under a doorway or the sturdiest place you can find.
- **Smog** On hot days, smog and heat can make an unhealthy combination. Watch for reports for advice on staying inside.
- **Weather** On the same day in July, Death Valley might be 124°F while San Francisco, Monterey or Carmel might top out at 56°F (before wind chill). Dress and pack with this in mind.

⬑ COSTS

- **$100 per day** Hostels or roadside motels, sandwiches or tacos, lots of days on the beach or hiking.
- **$100-250 per day** B&Bs or good-value hotels, rental car, splurge lunches, a concert.
- **More than $250 per day** High-end hotels, wine-tasting tours, Disneyland.

EMERGENCY NUMBERS

- Police/fire/ambulance/accidents (☎ 911) A trained operator will connect you with the right services.

GETTING AROUND

- Air Inexpensive flights between LA and San Francisco save time.
- Boat Ferries ply the San Francisco Bay for Sausalito, Tiburon, Angel Island and Alcatraz.
- Bus Greyhound and Amtrak run inexpensive options between most major towns; trips can be lengthy.
- Car Required in Napa Valley and throughout much of the coast and eastern backcountry.
- Train Runs only between Los Angeles, Santa Barbara, San Luis Obispo, Salinas (near Monterey) and Oakland/East Bay.

GETTING THERE & AWAY

- Air The largest airports are in San Francisco, Los Angeles, San Jose, Oakland and Burbank.
- Bus From another state, it would take at least a day's journey to get to California.
- Train Usually more expensive than flying, but also more romantic.

WHAT TO BRING

- Clothing Dress to impress in LA, bring hiking boots or good walking shoes for the rest of the state.
- ID Required to rent cars or use internet services.
- Insurance Obtain international insurance for renting a car.
- Sun protection Bring sunscreen, sunglasses and hats for long days at the beach or at amusement parks.

PLANNING YOUR TRIP

THINGS YOU NEED TO KNOW

ANDERS BLOMQVIST

Madonna Inn (p300), San Luis Obispo

◥ WHEN TO GO

- **Best months** March through May. It's probably colder where you're from in March through May, plus you can still ski, spot whales and view early sprouting wildflowers.

- **Second-best months** August through October. The Bay Area and Northern California sees their 'summer' start in late August and go through October.

- **Worst month** January. Not much happens in January as most folks are in a post-Christmas hibernation.

LEFT: RICHARD CUMMINS; RIGHT: JERRY ALEXANDER

Left: California poppy fields, near San Diego (p314); Right: Hot-air ballooning (p188), Napa Valley

GET INSPIRED

BOOKS

- **A Heartbreaking Work of Staggering Genius** (2000) Dave Eggers' memoir of raising his brother in San Francisco.
- **Cannery Row** (1945) Before you visit Monterey, read John Steinbeck's true-to-life account.
- **LA Confidential** (1990) James Ellroy's detective novel about the seedy world of 1950s Los Angeles.
- **My First Summer in the Sierra** (1911) Find out why John Muir felt passionate enough to found the Sierra Club.
- **Slouching Towards Bethlehem** (1968) Musings on California by Joan Didion.
- **Tripmaster Monkey** (1989) Maxine Hong Kingston writes about the Chinese-American immigrant community in San Francisco's turbulent 1960s.

MUSIC

- **California** (Joni Mitchell) Songstress' dreamy ballad about the Golden State.
- **California Love** (2Pac and Dr Dre) The rappers' ode to California, from Long Beach to Sacktown.
- **Californication** (Red Hot Chili Peppers) Anthony Kiedis' journey to the dark side of Hollywood.
- **Los Angeles** (X) Exene Cervenka and John Doe's post-punk homage to their city.
- **Sittin' on the Dock of the Bay** (Otis Redding) Written on a houseboat in Sausalito.

- **Surfin' USA** (Beach Boys) Reads like a page out of a Southern California beach-town atlas.

FILMS

- **Dirty Harry** Do you feel lucky enough to see San Francisco on the big screen? Do you, punk?
- **Fast Times at Ridgemont High** Every LA high school in the '80s had its own version of Jeff Spicoli.
- **LA Story** Steve Martin drives 25ft to his neighbor's house.
- **Lost Boys** Before vampires became the rage, they ate it up in Santa Cruz.
- **Sideways** An Oscar-winning bachelors' romp through the Santa Barbara wine country maligns merlot and scores points for pinot.
- **Vertigo** The quintessential 'San Francisco meets Alfred Hitchcock' classic.

WEBSITES

- **www.discoverlosangeles.com** Find where to surf, dine and sun.
- **www.onlyinsanfrancisco.com** Official info about the city's unique offerings.
- **www.parks.ca.gov** Learn about all of California's state parks.
- **www.parksconservancy.org** The extensive network of Golden Gate National Parks covers the Bay Area.
- **www.sandiego.org** Amusement parks, historic neighborhoods and microbreweries.
- **www.visitcalifornia.com** Read about the entire state in one go.

PLANNING YOUR TRIP

GET INSPIRED

CALENDAR

JAN　FEB　MAR　APR

ROBERTO GEROMETTA

Chinese New Year celebrations, San Francisco

◥ JANUARY & FEBRUARY

TOURNAMENT OF ROSES
Famous New Year's Day parade, with flower-coated floats, marching bands and equestrians, held in the LA suburb of Pasadena; see www.tournamentof roses.com.

CHINESE NEW YEAR
Held in late January/early February with firecrackers, parades, lion dances and lots of food; the biggest celebrations are in San Francisco and LA.

◥ MARCH & APRIL

SAN DIEGO LATINO FILM FESTIVAL
Screens films from throughout Latin America and the US in mid-March; see www.sdlatinofilm.com.

TOYOTA GRAND PRIX OF LONG BEACH
This weeklong auto-racing spectacle through city streets draws world-class drivers to LA in mid-April; see www. gplb.com.

SAN FRANCISCO INTERNATIONAL FILM FESTIVAL
California's longest-running film festival, held from late April to early May; see www.sffs.org.

◥ MAY & JUNE

BAY TO BREAKERS
Thousands run costumed, naked and/ or clutching beer from Embarcadero to Ocean Beach on the third Sunday in May; see www.baytobreakers.com.

| MAY | JUN | JUL | AUG | SEP | OCT | NOV | DEC |

KINETIC GRAND CHAMPIONSHIP

Over Memorial Day weekend, quirky human-powered contraptions of all sorts ride from Arcata to Ferndale in the North Coast's wackiest event; see http://kineticgrandchampionship.com.

SAN FRANCISCO PRIDE

USA's biggest lesbian, gay, bisexual and transgender pride parade attracts more than one million participants in late June; see www.sfpride.org.

↘ JULY

FESTIVAL OF ARTS & PAGEANT OF THE MASTERS

Exhibits by hundreds of artists and a pageant of art masterpieces 're-created' using real people in July and August in Laguna Beach, Orange County; see www.foapom.com.

US OPEN SANDCASTLE COMPETITION

Amazing sandcastle competition held in mid-July at Imperial Beach, south of San Diego; see www.usopensand castle.com.

MENDOCINO MUSIC FESTIVAL

Orchestral, chamber, opera, jazz and world music concerts on the North Coast headlands, with children's matinees and open rehearsals, in mid-July; see www.mendocinomusic.com.

↘ AUGUST

REGGAE ON THE RIVER

Draws huge crowds for reggae and world music, arts-and-craft fairs, camping and swimming outside Garberville in NorCal in early August; see www.reggaeontheriver.com.

DAVID PEEVERS

Festival of Arts & Pageant of the Masters, Laguna Beach

PLANNING YOUR TRIP

CALENDAR

 # CALENDAR

| JAN | FEB | MAR | APR |

OLD SPANISH DAYS FIESTA

A celebration of early rancho culture with parades, rodeo, crafts exhibits and shows in Santa Barbara in early August; see www.oldspanishdays-fiesta.org.

STEINBECK FESTIVAL

Celebrates California's literary Nobel laureate with films, theater, storytelling and tours in Salinas in early August; see www.steinbeck.org.

◥ SEPTEMBER

SAN FRANCISCO FRINGE FESTIVAL

This theater marathon happens in mid-September and attracts a variety of performers from around the world; see www.sffringe.org.

MONTEREY JAZZ FESTIVAL

This big-name festival takes place in mid-September and celebrates both traditional and modern styles of jazz; see www.montereyjazzfestival.org.

FLEET WEEK

US military shows its might with a parade of ships, air shows and concerts in San Diego from mid-September through early October; see www.fleetweeksandiego.org.

SIMON RODIA WATTS TOWERS JAZZ FESTIVAL

This music festival features jazz, gospel, R&B and other sounds in the shadow of LA's Watts Towers, usually on the last weekend of September; see www.parks.ca.gov.

◥ OCTOBER

SAN FRANCISCO JAZZ FESTIVAL

Features live performances by established and new artists throughout the Bay Area from early October through to early November; see www.sfjazz.com.

JUDY BELLAH

Kinetic Grand Championship (p161), Ferndale

| MAY | JUN | JUL | AUG | SEP | OCT | NOV | DEC |

San Francisco Jazz Festival

IMAGEBROKER/VOX

WORLD CHAMPIONSHIP PUMPKIN WEIGH-OFF
In Half Moon Bay, south of San Francisco, this competition among West Coast pumpkin growers takes place in mid-October; see www.miramar events.com.

LITQUAKE
Author readings, discussions and literary events such as the legendary pub crawl; held in San Francisco in mid-October; see www.litquake.org.

◣ NOVEMBER

DÍA DE LOS MUERTOS
Party to wake the dead on November 2, with costume parades, sugar skulls and fabulous altars, including in San Francisco's Mission District and across SoCal; see www.dayofthedeadsf.org.

HOLLYWOOD CHRISTMAS PARADE
Features celebrities waving at the fans lining LA's Hollywood Blvd, plus classic cars, floats and marching bands. Held on the first Sunday after Thanksgiving; see www.hollywoodchristmasparade. org.

◣ DECEMBER

CHRISTMAS BOAT PARADE
A parade of 150 or so brightly illuminated boats, including multimillion-dollar yachts, floating at Orange County's Newport Beach; see www. christmasboatparade.com.

FIRST NIGHT
Alcohol-free New Year's Eve street festivals, featuring dance, theater and live music suitable for families, take place in many coastal cities.

LOS ANGELES

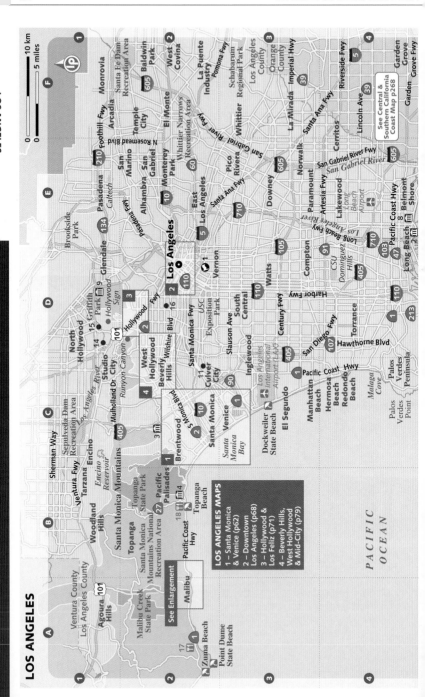

0 ──────── 10 km
0 ──────── 5 miles

LOS ANGELES MAPS

1 – Santa Monica
& Venice (p62)
2 – Downtown
Los Angeles (p68)
3 – Hollywood &
Los Feliz (p71)
4 – Beverly Hills,
West Hollywood
& Mid-City (p79)

See Central &
Southern California
Coast Map p268

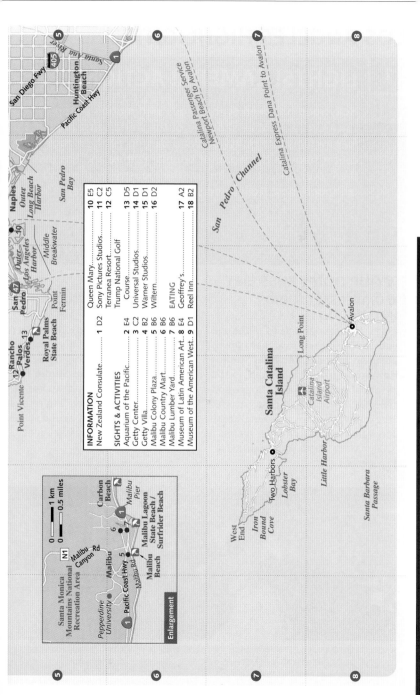

INFORMATION		
New Zealand Consulate	1	D2
SIGHTS & ACTIVITIES		
Aquarium of the Pacific	2	E4
Getty Center	3	C2
Getty Villa	4	B2
Malibu Colony Plaza	5	B6
Malibu Country Mart	6	B6
Malibu Lumber Yard	7	B6
Museum of Latin American Art	8	E4
Museum of the American West	9	D1
Queen Mary	10	E5
Sony Pictures Studios	11	C2
Terranea Resort	12	C5
Trump National Golf Course	13	D5
Universal Studios	14	D1
Warner Studios	15	D1
Wiltern	16	D2
EATING		
Geoffrey's	17	A2
Reel Inn	18	B2

LOS ANGELES HIGHLIGHTS

LOS ANGELES

1 LIGHTS! CAMERA! ACTION!

Hollywood has been synonymous with motion pictures since Cecil B DeMille shot one of the world's first full-length feature films in a Hollywoodland barn in 1914. LA took center stage in the world of popular culture and has been there ever since. Lucky for us, 'the Industry' is alive and well (although most Hollywood studios aren't anymore).

LOS ANGELES HIGHLIGHTS

↘ OUR DON'T MISS LIST

❶ UNIVERSAL STUDIOS HOLLYWOOD

Rides, film sets and Jaws. Although you won't see much actual filming going on anymore, **Universal Studios Hollywood** (p72) theme park is still all about entertainment, Hollywood style. Get up close and personal with Shrek, the Simpsons and King Kong, and learn how the computer graphics (CGI) masters create your favorite film experiences.

❷ WARNER BROS STUDIO TOUR

Want to trade in 3-D and roller coasters for a more authentic film experience? Visit one of the working studios, including the **Warner Bros Studio Tour** (p75). Like most working studios, it's not in Hollywood anymore, but you will see backlots and props, sound stages and possibly even a few celebrities.

Clockwise from top: Hollywood Walk of Fame (p67); Grauman's Chinese Theatre (p67); Lucy and Ethel from *I Love Lucy*, Universal Studios Hollywood (p72)

CLOCKWISE FROM TOP: CHRISTINA LEASE; DAVID PEEVERS; DAVID PEEVERS

❸ SHOPPING ON ROBERTSON BOULEVARD

You can't swing a leopard-print Armani scarf on this **shopping street** (p84) in Beverly Hills and West Hollywood without hitting at least one celebrity. Shop alongside J-Lo buying OshKosh overalls or watch as Lindsay Lohan backs into a car. Then do lunch at **The Ivy** (p81), if you can get past the paparazzi.

❹ GRAUMAN'S CHINESE THEATRE

In 1927 Sid Grauman opened his dream **theater** (p67) with none other than Cecil B DeMille's 'The King of Kings.' Ten decades of premiers later, his theater is one of LA's 10 most visited sites. Come watch celebrities walk the red carpet, or on nonpremier days, mere mortals can enter the temple of film for a VIP tour or to watch a movie.

❺ STROLL THE HOLLYWOOD WALK OF FAME

More than 2000 celebrities have been memorialized as 'official' stars on this 1.7-mile-long **path** (p67) of Hollywood history. Awarded in up to five categories, immortalized stars include the likes of Ronald Reagan, Winona Ryder, Winnie the Pooh, Tony Danza and Mary-Kate and Ashley Olsen.

↘ THINGS YOU NEED TO KNOW

Studio tours Book tours two weeks in advance; prices range from $50 to $200; film aficionados might want the upgrade **Celebrity-spotting tip** Keep an eye out for packs of photographers **Transportation** Metro Rail's Red Line follows Hollywood Blvd; alight at Hollywood/Vine or Hollywood/Highland

LOS ANGELES HIGHLIGHTS

↘ SOUTH BAY BICYCLE TRAIL

This **two-lane beach thoroughfare** (p74), known in LA as 'The Strand,' mixes LA's two favorite things: freeways and looking good. Hundreds of bikini-clad bicyclists and oiled-up rollerbladers glide along a flat, pothole-free 'street,' which runs along the beach from Will Rogers State Beach to Torrance Beach. Go ahead, just try to make the 22-mile-long journey without singing Randy Newman's 'I Love LA.'

↘ GETTY CENTER & GETTY VILLA

One of the top museums for European art in the US, the **Getty Center** (p66) isn't just about the art. Plan on spending a day soaking up the sun on the lawn, wandering the garden maze or enjoying one of the special events (film noir movies, traveling Da Vinci exhibits etc). If you can't get to the ancient world, you can make it to the **Getty Villa** (p66), a Roman-, Greek- and Etruscan-filled treasure trove.

LOS ANGELES

LOS ANGELES HIGHLIGHTS

↘ GRIFFITH OBSERVATORY

Cosmically informing Angelenos since 1935, the **observatory** (p69), located in gigantic Griffith Park, underwent a $100 million refurbishment last decade. Check out its out-of-this-world astronomical exhibits. To see the best foliage and views in all of Griffith Park, ramble the two-mile trail from the Fern Dell area to the observatory.

↘ THIRD ST PROMENADE

The best window-shopping in LA is along Santa Monica's open-air **Third St Promenade** (p61). Dozens of street performers/aspiring actors entertain shoppers with balloon animals, juggling or comedy routines. Still not entertained? Head three blocks to the **Santa Monica Pier** (p61) to ride the carousel or visit the aquarium.

↘ VENICE BEACH BOARDWALK

Dodgy glass-pipe vendors, exorbitant parking fees, thong bikinis, steroid-laden muscle men with their pit bulls...what isn't there to love about **Venice Beach** (p61)? Perhaps nowhere on earth are folks more inclined to let their freak flag fly high. More kid-friendly are the **Venice Canals** (p64), just two blocks east of the beach.

2 JOHN BORTHWICK; 3 RICHARD CUMMINS; 4 EDDIE BRADY; 5 WITOLD SKRYPCZAK; 6 DAVID PEEVERS

2 South Bay Bicycle Trail (p74); 3 Getty Center (p66), designed by architect Richard Meier; 4 Griffith Observatory (p69); 5 Third St Promenade (p61), Santa Monica; 6 Venice Beach Boardwalk (p61)

LOS ANGELES' BEST...

⤵ STREET MARKETS

- **Santa Monica** (p61) Wednesday is generally less crowded.
- **Mid-City LA** (p73) LA's 'original' farmers market, started in 1934.
- **Grand Central Market** (p80) Packed and lively, with permanent restaurants and booths.
- **Olvera St** (p64) Mexican market at LA's original European settlement site.

⤵ PLACES TO TAKE YOUR KIDS

- **Hollywood & Highland** (p67) Redeveloped mall replaces grit with campiness in downtown Hollywood.
- **Santa Monica Pier** (p61) Rides, games, souvenirs, all along a fabulous beach.
- **La Brea Tar Pits** (p73) Kids will love this giant fossil sandbox.
- **Griffith Park** (p67) Hiking trails, picnic spots and a kid-friendly observatory and zoo.

⤵ BEACHES

- **Hermosa Beach** (p70) Old-school LA beach city vibe.
- **Manhattan Beach** (p70) Glamorous condos, swank shops and surfers.
- **Zuma Beach** (p61) Stunningly gorgeous Malibu's even more stunningly gorgeous beach.

⤵ PLACES TO SEE ART

- **Los Angeles County Museum of Art** (p72) Ancient art through to Kandinsky, with Friday evening jazz.
- **Getty Center** (p66) A billion-dollar architecturally impressive art museum with equally impressive gardens and city views.
- **Getty Villa** (p66) Head back in artistic time 2000 years for Roman, Greek and Etruscan examples.
- **Annenberg Space for Photography** (p73) LA's newest space for photographic excellence.
- **Museum of Contemporary Art** (p72) Art as modern as LA.

LEFT: RAY LASKOWITZ; RIGHT: STEPHEN SAKS

Left: Fruit for sale, Olvera St (p64); Right: Women's Beach Volleyball Team, Manhattan Beach (p70)

THINGS YOU NEED TO KNOW

⬊ VITAL STATISTICS

- **City population** 3.9 million
- **County population** 9.9 million
- **Area codes** ☎Downtown 213; ☎Central Los Angeles 323; ☎Coast 310/424; ☎Long Beach area 562; ☎San Fernando Valley 747/818

⬊ NEIGHBORHOODS IN A NUTSHELL

- **Santa Monica & Venice** (p61) Affluent beachfront properties line LA's active seaside.
- **Downtown LA** (p64) Nobody walked in (downtown) LA until a revitalization effort in the '90s.
- **Hollywood, Los Feliz & Silver Lake** (p67) The young and hip own these streets.
- **Beverly Hills & Brentwood** (p73) The most famous zip code in the US: 90210.
- **Malibu** (p60) If you had Jennifer Aniston's money, you'd want to live on the beach here, too.

⬊ ADVANCE PLANNING

- **Two months before** See which TV shows are taping; call or email for free audience tickets.
- **One month before** Sign up for VIP studio tours.
- **Two weeks before** Book your hotels and make restaurant reservations.

⬊ RESOURCES

- **Discover Los Angeles** (www.discoverlosangeles.com) Official information.
- **LA Weekly** (www.laweekly.com) Complete listing of Southern California's events and entertainment.
- **Los Angeles Times** (www.latimes.com) One of the top newspapers in the country.
- **Sig Alert** (www.sigalert.com) Real-time traffic information for LA area freeways.
- **US Geological Survey** (earthquake.usgs.gov) Up-to-the-minute earthquake updates.

⬊ GETTING AROUND

- **Bus** LA buses: not just for the pre-teen or desperate anymore.
- **Car** An extension of your very existence in LA. Santa Monica to Hollywood can take 45 minutes to an hour.
- **Metro** Not nearly comprehensive enough but an impressive effort.
- **Walking** Best within neighborhoods: Santa Monica, Silver Lake, Venice.

⬊ BE FOREWARNED

- **Drugs** Venice Beach, Hollywood and downtown LA see their fair share of shady behavior.
- **Freeways** Traffic is ubiquitous during rush 'hour,' which runs from 5am to 9am and 3pm to 7pm.

LOS ANGELES

THINGS YOU NEED TO KNOW

DISCOVER LOS ANGELES

Ah, Los Angeles: land of starstruck dreams and Tinseltown magic, and perhaps the most resented place in California. You may think you know what to expect from LA: earthquakes, traffic, Paris (and Perez) Hilton. Done? Good.

Now here are some other things you should know: LA is America's largest county in terms of population (it would be the eighth-largest state on its own), it's an economic powerhouse, it has the hemisphere's largest port and, oh yes, it's the world's entertainment capital. So, Angelenos philosophize, you take the challenges along with the good.

And there *is* a lot of good: the beaches, the mountains and loads of culture, food and sheer style. Though you may well find surgically enhanced blonds and Hollywood honchos weaving lanes at 80mph, LA is intensely diverse and brimming with fascinating neighborhoods and characters that have nothing to do with 'the Industry.' You owe it to yourself to see LA with your own eyes. You won't need much to act out your own LA story. Credit card, wheels, beach towel, and you're golden. But please leave your preconceptions at home.

INFORMATION

Downtown LA Visitors Center (Map p68; ☎ 213-689-8822; http://discoverlosangeles.com; 685 S Figueroa St; ☼ 8:30am-5pm Mon-Fri)

Hollywood Visitors Center (Map p71; ☎ 323-467-6412; Hollywood & Highland complex, 6801 Hollywood Blvd; ☼ 10am-10pm Mon-Sat, 10am-7pm Sun)

Santa Monica (☎ 310-393-7593, 800-544-5319; www.santamonica.com) Visitors Center (Map p62; 1920 Main St; ☼ 9am-6pm); Information Kiosk (Map p62; 1400 Ocean Ave; ☼ 9am-5pm Jun-Aug, 10am-4pm Sep-May)

DANGERS & ANNOYANCES

Despite what you may see in the movies, LA is generally safe, especially in the areas covered in this book. Downtown LA, Santa Monica and Venice are home to numerous homeless folks, who generally leave you alone if you do the same.

SIGHTS

We've organized LA County's neighborhoods and towns in geographical order, beginning along Santa Monica Bay. Ritzy Malibu kicks things off to the north, followed by Santa Monica and Venice. Then we head inland to the transit and culture hub of Downtown LA and Hollywood, and curve west again toward the coast, via Mid-City, West Hollywood and Beverly Hills.

MALIBU

Malibu, which hugs 27 spectacular miles of Pacific Coast Hwy, has long been synonymous with surfing, stars and a hedonistic lifestyle, but actually looks far less posh than the glossy mags make it sound. Still, it's been celebrity central since the 1930s when money troubles forced landowner May Rindge to lease out property to her Hollywood friends. Leo, Brangelina, Streisand, Cher and other A-listers have homes here and can often be spotted shopping at the village-like **Malibu Country Mart** (Map p52; 3835 Cross Creek Rd; Ⓟ), the new and super-chichi **Malibu Lumber Yard** (Map p52; 3939 Cross Creek Rd; Ⓟ) and the more utilitarian **Malibu Colony Plaza** (Map p52; 23841 W Malibu Rd; Ⓟ).

Despite its wealth and star quotient, Malibu is best appreciated through its twin natural treasures: the **Santa Monica Mountains National Recreation Area** (Map p52) and the beaches, including **Point Dume**, **Zuma** (this one especially is packed on weekends) and **Surfrider**, a world-famous surf spot. Parking fees vary but average around $8, if you don't strike gold and find a spot on the highway.

SANTA MONICA

The quintessential LA beach town, Santa Monica melds big-city sophistication with a laid-back, politically progressive, environmentally aware ethos. Bronzed women toting yoga mats share the sidewalk with skateboarding scruffians. It boasts a pleasure pier, pedestrian-friendly Downtown and miles of sandy beaches.

The most recognizable landmark is the **Santa Monica Pier** (Map p62; ☎ 310-458-8900; www.santamonicapier.org; admission free; ♿), the oldest amusement pier in California (1909), with a vintage **carousel** and the small **Pacific Park** (Map p62; unlimited ride pass adult/child under 7yr $20.95/12.95; ♥ daily in summer, Fri-Sun rest of yr), complete with solar-powered Ferris wheel, a roller coaster and other rides. The city's main **farmers market** (Map p62; Arizona Ave at 3rd St; ♥ 8:30am-1:30pm Wed & Sat) is hugely popular and widely considered one of the best in the country.

Meandering under the pier is the 22-mile paved **South Bay Bicycle Trail**. Bike or in-line skate rentals are available on the pier and at beachside kiosks.

The car-free **Third St Promenade** – between Wilshire Blvd and Broadway – is a great place for a stroll and a spot of people-watching. Jugglers, street musicians and Bible-thumpers share space with dinosaur topiaries and (mostly) high-end chain stores such as Anthropologie and Abercrombie & Fitch. For more local flavor, head to celeb-frequented **Montana Ave** (Map p62) or down-home **Main St** (Map p62), the neighborhood once nicknamed Dogtown and birthplace of skateboard culture.

Art-lovers should head inland about 2 miles to the **Bergamot Station Arts Center** (Map p62; 2525 Michigan Ave; ♥ 10am-6pm Tue-Sat; Ⓟ), a former rail yard now home to more than 30 avant-garde galleries, including the **Gallery of Functional Art** where clever gifts can be had. To get there, go northeast on Olympic Blvd, turn right on Cloverfield Blvd and then left on Michigan Ave.

VENICE

Venice began as the dream of eccentric tobacco heir Abbot Kinney (1850–1920). Where others saw swampland, he envisioned an amusement park and seaside resort called 'Venice of America' and in the early 1900s carved out canals for Italian *gondolieri* to pole tourists about. Venice faded from the radar until the 1950s and '60s, when its funky vibe drew beatniks and hippies like Jim Morrison. Venice is still a cauldron of creativity, peopled by karmically correct new-agers and a few celebs, including Dennis Hopper and Julia Roberts.

The seaside **Venice Boardwalk** (actually an asphalt beachside strip; Map p62) is a freak show, a human zoo, a wacky carnival and an essential LA experience. Get your hair braided, your karma corrected or a *qi gong* back massage. Encounters

SANTA MONICA & VENICE

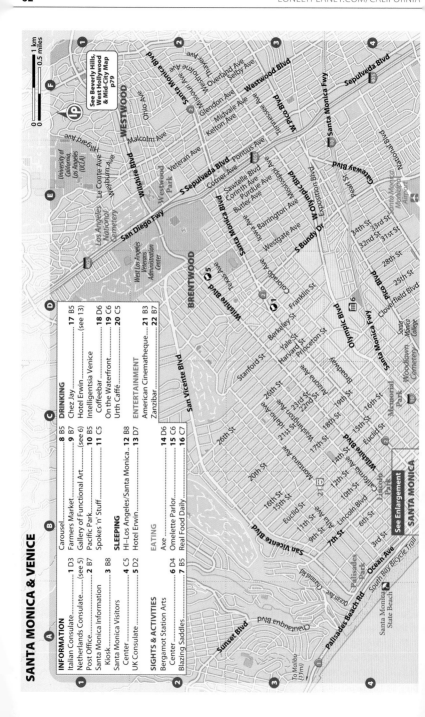

INFORMATION
Italian Consulate	1 D3
Netherlands Consulate	(see 5)
Post Office	2 B7
Santa Monica Information Kiosk	3 B8
Santa Monica Visitors Center	4 C5
UK Consulate	5 D2

SIGHTS & ACTIVITIES
Bergamot Station Arts Center	6 D4
Blazing Saddles	7 B5
Carousel	8 B5
Farmers Market	9 B7
Gallery of Functional Art	(see 6)
Pacific Park	10 B5
Spokes 'n' Stuff	11 C5

SLEEPING
HI–Los Angeles/Santa Monica	12 B8
Hotel Erwin	13 D7

EATING
Axe	14 D6
Omelette Parlor	15 C6
Real Food Daily	16 C7

DRINKING
Chez Jay	17 B5
Hotel Erwin	(see 13)
Intelligentsia Venice	18 D6
Coffeebar	19 C6
On the Waterfront	20 C5
Urth Caffé	

ENTERTAINMENT
American Cinematheque	21 B3
Zanzibar	22 B7

See Beverly Hills, West Hollywood & Mid-City Map p79

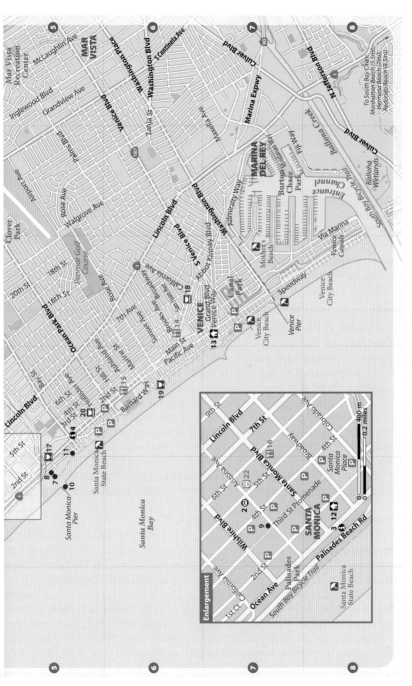

with wannabe Schwarzeneggers, hoop dreamers, a Speedo-clad snake charmer or a roller-skating Sikh minstrel are pretty much guaranteed, especially on hot summer afternoons. Alas, the vibe gets a bit creepy after dark.

To escape the hubbub, meander inland to the **Venice Canals** (Map p62), a vestige of Abbot Kinney's dream. Today, ducks preen and locals lollygag in row boats along the serene, flower-festooned waterways.

The hippest shopping strip on LA's west side is funky-sophisticated **Abbot Kinney Blvd** (Map p62), a palm-lined mile of restaurants, yoga studios, art galleries and eclectic shops selling midcentury furniture and handmade perfumes.

There's street parking around Abbot Kinney Blvd and parking lots ($6 to $15) on the beach.

DOWNTOWN LA

Downtown is LA's historic core and main business and government district, though for decades it sat empty at night and weekends. A bevy of new cultural, transit and housing options is changing that.

Start by immersing yourself in LA's Spanish Mexican roots, where the city began, at **El Pueblo de Los Angeles**. The 1818 **Avila Adobe** (Map p68; ☎ 213-628-1274; Olvera St; admission free; ☼ 9am-4pm) sits on **Olvera St**, a festive tack-o-rama where you can chomp on tacos and stock up on handmade candy and folkloric trinkets. Nearby the 1939 **Union Station** (Map p68;

LOS ANGELES IN...

One Day

Fuel up at the **Omelette Parlor** (p78), then rent bikes at Santa Monica Beach to ride the 22-mile **South Bay Bicycle Trail** (p61) along the oceanfront before the weekend hordes get there (it's least crowded Monday to Friday). Now that you've reached your fitness quota for the day, indulge at one of the fabulous beaches of **Malibu** (p60) or the amusement park of the century-old **Santa Monica Pier** (p61) and lunch at the **Reel Inn** (p78). Midafternoon, head south to the **Venice Boardwalk** (p61) to see the seaside sideshow, then walk inland to **Abbot Kinney Blvd** (above) where the fascinating shops compete with tantalizing restaurants, or take a relaxing stroll around the **Venice Canals** (above). Watch the sunset or the stars over the ocean at High, the rooftop bar at **Hotel Erwin** (p76).

Two Days

Venture inland to explore what makes LA a world city. Dim sum breakfast at **Empress Pavilion** (p78) is a trip to Hong Kong sans passport. The 'overseas' trek continues at **El Pueblo de Los Angeles** (above). Then catapult to the future at **Walt Disney Concert Hall** (right) and **Cathedral of Our Lady of the Angels** (right). Have lunch at the new entertainment center **LA Live** (p66), and take in the **Grammy Museum** (p67). From here, it's a short drive to the **Hollywood Walk of Fame** (p67) and **Grauman's Chinese Theatre** (p67) along revitalized Hollywood Blvd. Up your chances of spotting actual celebs by hitting the fashion-forward boutiques on paparazzi-infested **Robertson Blvd** (p84) and having dinner at **The Ivy** (p81).

800 N Alameda St) is a glamorous edifice of Spanish mission and art deco design.

The centerpiece of the **Grand Avenue Cultural Corridor** is Frank Gehry's 2003 **Walt Disney Concert Hall** (Map p68; ☎ 323-850-2000; www.laphil.com; 111 S Grand Ave), a gravity-defying sculpture of curving and billowing stainless steel and home of the Los Angeles Philharmonic, now under the baton of Venezuelan phenom Gustavo Dudamel. Tours are available subject to concert schedules.

Rounding out the cultural corridor are the **Museum of Contemporary Art** (MOCA; Map p68; ☎ 213-626-6222; www.moca.org; 250 S Grand Ave; adult/child under 12yr/student/senior $10/free/5/5, 5-8pm Thu free; ☾ 11am-5pm Mon & Fri, 11am-8pm Thu, 11am-6pm Sat & Sun) and the world-famous stages of the **Dorothy Chandler Pavilion, Mark Taper Forum** and **Ahmanson Theater**. Diagonally across from the Ahmanson, architect José Rafael Moneo mixed Gothic proportions with bold contemporary design for his 2002 **Cathedral of Our Lady of the Angels** (Map p68; ☎ 213-680-5200; www.olacathedral.org; 555 W Temple St; admission free; ☾ 6:30am-6pm Mon-Fri, 9am-6pm Sat, 7am-6pm Sun).

Other ethnic enclaves Downtown include **Little Tokyo**, with a contemporary mix of traditional shops, Buddhist temples and restaurants. An increasingly lively **Arts District** (www.ladad.org) is emerging just southeast of Little Tokyo, with some 1200 artists living and working in studios above abandoned warehouses and small factories. **Chinatown** is a few blocks north along Broadway and Hill St, crammed with

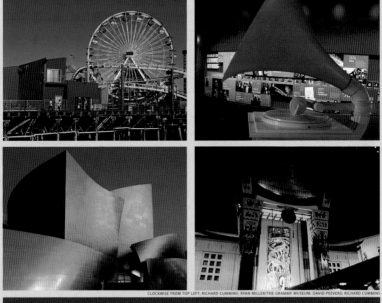

CLOCKWISE FROM TOP LEFT: RICHARD CUMMINS; RYAN MILLER/THE GRAMMY MUSEUM; DAVID PEEVERS; RICHARD CUMMINS

Clockwise from top left: Pacific Park, Santa Monica Pier (p61); Grammy Museum (p67); Grauman's Chinese Theatre (p67); Walt Disney Concert Hall (p65), designed by architect Frank Gehry

dim sum parlors, herbal apothecaries and curio shops. On **Chung King Rd**, an edgy contemporary art-gallery scene lures hipsters from around town.

Downtown's newest draw is the $1.7 billion dining and nightlife complex **LA Live** (Map p68), which opened in 2008 at Downtown's southern end, near the con-

The Getty Center, designed by architect Richard Meier

GETTY CENTER & GETTY VILLA

The hilltop **Getty Center** presents triple delights from its perch above the 405 Fwy: a stellar art collection from the Renaissance to David Hockney; Richard Meier's fabulous architecture; and Robert Irwin's seasonally changing gardens. On clear days, add breathtaking views of the city and ocean. Even getting to the 110-acre 'campus' aboard a driverless tram is fun, though you can walk it in 20 minutes.

The paintings collection is strongest when it comes to pre-20th-century Europeans, including famous canvases by Van Gogh, Monet, Rembrandt and Titian. Tours, lectures and interactive technology, including audioguides ($5), make the art accessible to all. Visit in the late afternoon when the crowds have thinned, and you can watch the sunset while enjoying a picnic or a snack from a kiosk or the self-service cafe. Also check the Getty's cultural events calendar, which includes fabulous concerts, lectures and films (all free). Reach the Getty Center via MTA bus 761.

West from the Getty Center, Malibu's cultural star is the **Getty Villa**, a hillside replica of a Roman villa that's a fantastic showcase of Greek, Roman and Etruscan antiquities, with stunning sightlines to the shimmering Pacific. Admission is by timed ticket (no walk-ins). MTA bus 534 goes to the villa; be sure to get your ticket punched by the bus driver for admission to the museum.

Things you need to know: Getty Center (Map p52; ☎ 310-440-7300; www.getty.edu; 1200 Getty Center Dr; admission free, parking $15; ☽ 10am-6pm Sun & Tue-Thu, 10am-9pm Fri & Sat); Getty Villa (Map p52; ☎ 310-440-7300; www.getty.edu; 17985 Pacific Coast Hwy; admission free, parking by reservation only $15; ☽ 10am-5pm Thu-Mon)

vention center. The **Grammy Museum** (Map p68; ☎ 213-765-6800; www.grammymuseum. org; 800 W Olympic Blvd; adult/child 6-17yr/child under 6yr/senior over 65yr/student $14.95/10.95/free/11.95/11.95; 🕑 11:30am-7:30pm Sun-Fri, 10am-7:30pm Sat) offers mind-expanding interactive displays on the history of American music and plenty of listening opportunities. Discounted tickets are available through the museum's website. The 7100-seat **Nokia Theatre** (Map p68) hosts the MTV Music Awards and *American Idol* finals. LA Live also includes live-music clubs, a movie megaplex and a dozen restaurants. Across the street, the flying saucer-shaped **Staples Center** (Map p68; ☎ 213-742-7340; www.staplescenter. com; 1111 S Figueroa St) is a sports and entertainment arena with all the high-tech trappings and headliners including the Lakers basketball team and major concert events.

HOLLYWOOD, LOS FELIZ & SILVER LAKE

First things first: Hollywood the neighborhood is not where one generally goes these days to see stars in the flesh. But even the most jaded visitor may thrill in the famous forecourt of the 1927 **Grauman's Chinese Theatre** (Map p71; ☎ 323-464-6266; 6925 Hollywood Blvd), where generations of screen legends have left their imprints in cement: feet, hands, dreadlocks (Whoopi Goldberg) and even magic wands (the young *Harry Potter* stars). Actors dressed as Superman, Marilyn Monroe and the like pose for photos (for tips).

Grauman's is on the **Hollywood Walk of Fame** (Map p71), which honors more than 2000 celebrities with stars embedded in the sidewalk between La Brea Aveand Vine St. Real-life celebs sashay along the red carpet for the Academy Awards at the **Kodak Theatre** (Map p71; ☎ 323-308-6363;

www.kodaktheatre.com; tours adult/child 3-17yr/child under 3yr/senior over 65yr $15/10/free/10; 🕑 10:30am-4pm Jun-Aug, 10:30am-2:30pm Sep-May, closed irregularly), open via pricey tours.

The spark plug for the neighborhood's rebirth was **Hollywood & Highland** (Map p71; ☎ 323-467-6412; www.hollywoodandhighland. com; 6801 Hollywood Blvd; admission free; 🕑 24hr), a multistory mall marrying kitsch and commerce. Its plaza is designed to frame views of the **Hollywood Sign** (Map p52).

Following Hollywood Blvd east beyond Hwy 101 (Hollywood Fwy) takes you to the neighborhoods of Los Feliz (lohs *fee*-liss) and Silver Lake, both boho-chic enclaves with offbeat shopping, funky bars and a hopping restaurant scene, as well as resident cool kids such as Beck and Flea.

The Metro Red Line (p85) serves Hollywood (Hollywood/Highland station) and Los Feliz (Vermont/Sunset station) from Downtown LA.

GRIFFITH PARK

America's largest urban park, **Griffith Park** (Map p71; ☎ 323-644-6661; admission free; 🕑 6am-10pm, trails close at dusk; P 🔁) is a playground for all age levels and interests. Five times the size of New York's Central Park, it has an outdoor theater, zoo, observatory, museum, antique trains, golf, tennis courts, playgrounds, bridle paths, 53 miles of hiking trails, Batman's caves and even the Hollywood Sign. The **Ranger Station** (4730 Crystal Springs Dr) has maps. Trails include the 3-mile **Mt Hollywood Hiking Trail**, with a spectacular view of the sign.

The **Museum of the American West** (☎ 323-667-2000; www.autrynationalcenter.org; 4700 Western Heritage Way; adult/child 3-12yr/student/senior over 60yr $9/3/5/5, free 2nd Tue each month; 🕑 10am-5pm Tue-Sun, to 8pm Thu Jun-Aug; P 🔁) exhibits the good, the bad and the ugly of America's westward

DOWNTOWN LOS ANGELES

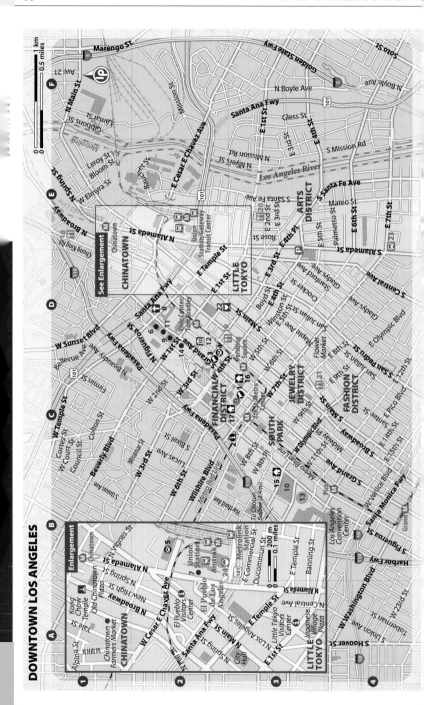

INFORMATION					
Canadian Consulate	**1** C3	Mark Taper Forum	**11** D2	Grand Central Market	**19** D2
Downtown LA Visitors Center	**2** C3	Museum of Contemporary		LA Live	(see 10)
Japanese Consulate	**3** D2	Art	**12** D2	R-23	**20** E3
Post Office	**4** D2	Nokia Theatre	(see 10)	Tiara Café	**21** C3
Terminal Annex Post Office	**5** B2	Staples Center	**13** B3		
		Union Station	(see 24)	DRINKING	
SIGHTS & ACTIVITIES		Walt Disney Concert Hall	**14** D2	Edison	**22** D2
Ahmanson Theater	**6** D2				
Avila Adobe	**7** B2	SLEEPING		ENTERTAINMENT	
Cathedral of Our Lady of the		Figueroa Hotel	**15** B3	Conga Room	(see 10)
Angels	**8** D2	Millennium Biltmore Hotel	**16** C3		
Dorothy Chandler Pavilion	**9** D2	Standard Downtown	**17** C3	TRANSPORT	
Grammy Museum	(see 10)			Greyhound Bus Terminal	**23** E4
LA Live	**10** B3	EATING		Union Station/Gateway	
		Empress Pavilion	**18** E1	Transit Center	**24** B2

expansion. Star exhibits include an original stagecoach, a large Colt firearms collection and a nymph-festooned saloon.

On the southern slopes of Mt Hollywood, the 1935 art deco **Griffith Observatory** (Map p71; ☎ 213-473-0800; www.griffithobservatory.org; 2800 Observatory Rd; admission free, planetarium shows adult/child 5-12yr/senior over 60yr $7/3/5; ☽ noon-10pm Tue-Fri, 10am-10pm Sat & Sun; ℗ 🏃) has renovated exhibition halls, cutting-edge planetarium technology, shows in the Leonard Nimoy Event Horizon Theater, and opportunities for you to play junior astronomer in its high-power telescopes.

Access to the park is easiest via the Griffith Park Dr or Zoo Dr exits off I-5.

WEST HOLLYWOOD

Rainbow flags fly proudly over Santa Monica Blvd. Celebs keep the gossip rags happy by misbehaving at the clubs on fabled Sunset Strip and browsing sassy and chic boutiques on Robertson Blvd. Welcome to the city of West Hollywood (WeHo), 1.9 sq miles of pure personality.

WeHo's also a hotbed of cutting-edge design for furniture and furnishings, particularly along the **Avenues of Art & Design** (Map p79) around Beverly Blvd

DAVID PEEVERS

Replicas of the area's Ice Age animals, La Brea Tar Pits (p73)

LOS ANGELES

and Melrose Ave. Some 130 showrooms fill the monolithic 'blue whale' and 'green whale' of the **Pacific Design Center** (PDC; Map p79; ☎ 310-657-0800; www.pacificdesign center.com; 8687 Melrose Ave; ☺ 9am-5pm Mon-Fri), though most sales are to the trade only. A 'red whale' was under construction as we went to press, and there's a small

SIGHTS

CHRISTINA LEASE

Sunset at Hermosa Beach

↘ IF YOU LIKE...

If you like the casual, ritzy beaches of **Malibu** (p60) or the gritty beachiness of **Venice** (p61), we think you'll like these other towns:

- **Palos Verdes** A certain Mr Trump added a bit of pizzazz to the sleepy peninsula where peacocks roam and kids still ride horses to McDonalds. Drive along clifftop Palos Verdes Drive (Map p52) to **Trump National Golf Course** (Map p52; ☎ 310-303-3260; 1 Ocean Trails Drive, Rancho Palos Verdes) for dinner at one of its two restaurants and stay a night to admire the sunset at next door's **Terranea Resort** (Map p52; ☎ 310-265-2800; 6610 Palos Verdes Drive S, Rancho Palos Verdes; r from $240).

- **Hermosa Beach** (Map p52) Beachfront bars, surf tournaments, hippie clothing shops and vegetarian burritos rule this oceanfront town. Walk Second St's shops on your break from a day at the beach, or stay the night to drink margaritas at a beachfront bar or watch an up-and-coming comic at the Comedy and Magic Club.

- **Manhattan Beach** (Map p52) Geographically and financially north of Hermosa Beach, this is the most upmarket of the South Bay beach cities (Redondo, Hermosa and Manhattan). Manhattan has exploded recently, with $2-million condos and haute-couture boutiques, but surfers still rule the waves.

- **San Pedro** The gritty cousin south of the South Bay, Pedro (known as Pee-dro, even by its large Latino population) is the northern half of the Los Angeles/Long Beach harbor. The area has been revitalized recently and hipster salty dogs populate its vintage shops and trendy restaurants.

HOLLYWOOD & LOS FELIZ

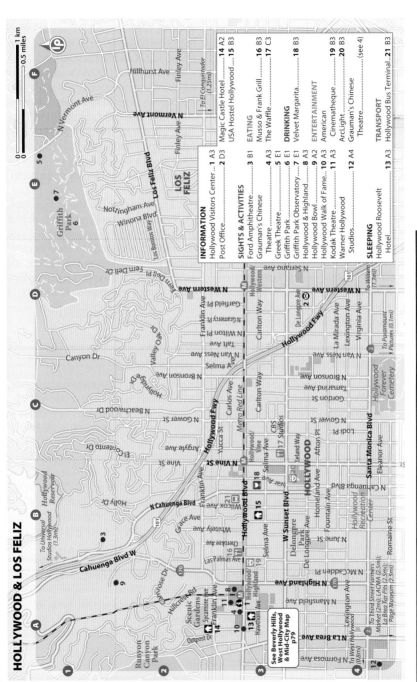

INFORMATION
Hollywood Visitors Center.....1 A3
Post Office.....2 D3

SIGHTS & ACTIVITIES
Ford Amphitheatre.....3 B1
Grauman's Chinese Theatre.....4 A3
Greek Theatre.....5 E1
Griffith Park.....6 E1
Griffith Park Observatory.....7 E1
Hollywood & Highland.....8 A3
Hollywood Bowl.....9 A2
Hollywood Walk of Fame.....10 A3
Kodak Theatre.....11 A3
Warner Hollywood Studios.....12 A4

SLEEPING
Hollywood Roosevelt Hotel.....13 A3

Magic Castle Hotel.....14 A2
USA Hostel Hollywood.....15 B3

EATING
Musso & Frank Grill.....16 B3
The Waffle.....17 C3

DRINKING
Velvet Margarita.....18 B3

ENTERTAINMENT
American Cinematheque.....19 B3
ArcLight.....20 B3
Grauman's Chinese Theatre.....(see 4)

TRANSPORT
Hollywood Bus Terminal.....21 B3

offshoot of the **Museum of Contemporary Art (MOCA; Map p79; admission free;** noon 11am-5pm Tue-Fri, 11am-6pm Sat & Sun) behind PDC's main buildings. Parking is $4.50 per hour.

MID-CITY

Among LA's dozens of great museums, some of the best line Museum Row, a short stretch of Wilshire Blvd just east of Fairfax Ave.

Los Angeles County Museum of Art (LACMA; Map p79; ☎ 323-857-6000; www.lacma. org; 5905 Wilshire Blvd; adult/child under 17yr/ student/senior $12/free/8/8, 'pay what you wish' after 5pm, 2nd Tue of each month free; noon-8pm Mon, Tue & Thu, noon-9pm Fri, 11am-8pm Sat & Sun) is one of the country's top art museums and the largest in the western USA. A major 2008 revamp masterminded by Renzo Piano brought the three-story **Broad Contemporary Art Museum** (B-CAM), whose collection includes seminal pieces by Jeff Koons, Roy Lichtenstein, Andy Warhol and Richard Serra.

Elsewhere on LACMA's campus are millennia of paintings, sculpture and decorative arts: Rembrandt, Cézanne and Magritte; ancient pottery from China, Turkey and Iran; photographs by Ansel Adams and Henri Cartier-Bresson; and a jewel box of a Japanese pavilion. There are often headline-grabbing touring exhibits. Parking is $7.

A four-story ode to the automobile, the **Petersen Automotive Museum** (Map p79; ☎ 323-930-2277; www.petersen.org; 6060 Wilshire Blvd; adult/child 5-12yr/senior over 62yr/ student $10/3/5/5; 10am-6pm Tue-Sun;) exhibits shiny vintage cars galore, plus a fun LA streetscape showing how the city's growth has been shaped by the automobile. Parking is $8.

DETOUR: UNIVERSAL STUDIOS HOLLYWOOD

Universal Studios (off Map p71; ☎ 818-622-3801; www.universalstudioshollywood.com; 100 Universal City Plaza; admission over/under 48in $67/57; hours vary;) first opened to the public in 1915 when studio head Carl Laemmle invited visitors at a quaint $0.25 each (including a boxed lunch) to watch silent films being made. Nearly a century later, Universal remains one of the world's largest movie studios, even if today's visitors are directed to a movie-based theme park where your chances of seeing an actual movie shoot are approximately nil.

Nonetheless, generations of visitors have had a ball here. Start with the 45-minute narrated **Studio Tour** aboard a giant, multicar tram that takes you past working soundstages and outdoor sets such as *Desperate Housewives* (when there's no filming). Also prepare to survive a shark attack à la *Jaws* and an 8.3-magnitude earthquake. It's hokey but fun.

Of Universal's thrill rides, top billing goes to the **Simpsons Ride**, a motion-simulated romp 'designed' by Krusty the Clown. **Special Effects Stages** give a glimpse into the craft of movie-making. **Water World** may have bombed as a movie, but the live action show based on it is a runaway hit, with stunts including giant fireballs and a crash-landing seaplane.

While Universal is generally kid-friendly, Disneyland (p306), Legoland (p326) and SeaWorld (p322) are more targeted to the single-digit set.

Parking is $12, or arrive via Metro Red Line.

RICK GERHARTER

Los Angeles County Museum of Art (LACMA)

Between 10,000 and 40,000 years ago, tar-like bubbling crude oil trapped saber-toothed cats, mammoths, dire wolves and other Ice Age critters, still being excavated at **La Brea Tar Pits** (Map p79). Check out their fossilized remains at the **Page Museum** (Map p79; ☎ 323-934-7243; www.tarpits.org; 5801 Wilshire Blvd; adult/child 5-12yr/senior/student $7/2/4.50/4.50; 🕑 9:30am-5pm; 🚻). An active staff of archaeologists works behind glass. Parking is $6.

Nearby, the **Original Farmers Market** (Map p79; 6333 W 3rd St; 🅿 🚻) has plenty of food stalls for a fill-up before hitting the adjacent **Grove** (Map p79), an open-air shopping mall with a musical fountain.

BEVERLY HILLS & BRENTWOOD

The mere words 'Beverly Hills' conjure images of Maseratis, manicured mansions and megarich moguls. Stylish and sophisticated, this is indeed a haven for the well-heeled and famous. See Tours (p76) for guided peeks at stars' homes.

It's pricey and pretentious, but no trip to LA would be complete without a saunter along **Rodeo Drive** (Map p79), the famous three-block ribbon of international style from Armani to Zegna, in killer-design stores.

TV and radio addicts can indulge their passion at the **Paley Center for Media** (Map p79; ☎ 310-786-1000; www.paleycenter.org; 465 N Beverly Dr; suggested donation adult/child under 14yr/senior/student $10/5/8/8; 🕑 noon-5pm Wed-Sun), a mind-boggling archive of TV and radio broadcasts going back to 1918. Pick your faves, grab a seat at a private console and enjoy.

Several city-owned garages offer two hours of free parking in central Beverly Hills.

Just west of Beverly Hills, in the skyscraper village known as Century City, the **Annenberg Space for Photography** (Map p79; ☎ 213-403-3000; www.annenbergspace forphotography.org; 2000 Ave of the Stars, No 10; admission free; 🕑 11am-6pm Wed-Sun) opened in 2009 as the region's first museum of photography, presenting changing shows including the Pictures of the Year exhibit.

Aquarium of the Pacific, Long Beach

LEE FOSTER

Parking is $3.50, or $1 on weekends and after 4:30pm daily.

LONG BEACH

Long Beach's 'flagship' is the grand (and supposedly haunted) British ocean liner **Queen Mary** (Map p52; ☎ 562-435-3511; www.queenmary.com; 1126 Queens Hwy; adult/child/senior from $25/13/22; ☺ 10am-6pm), permanently moored here. Larger and fancier than the *Titanic*, it transported royals, dignitaries, immigrants and troops during its 1001 Atlantic crossings between 1936 and 1964. Now visitors can tour its decks, state rooms and dining rooms, and enjoy a meal on board at one of its numerous restaurants. Parking is $12.

Kids will probably have a better time at the **Aquarium of the Pacific** (Map p52; ☎ 562-590-3100; www.aquariumofpacific.org; 100 Aquarium Way; adult/child 3-11yr/senior over 62yr $24/12/21; ☺ 9am-6pm; ☺), a high-tech romp through an underwater world where sharks dart, jellyfish dance and sea lions frolic. Its 12,500 creatures hail from tepid Baja California, the frigid northern

Pacific, coral reefs of the tropics, and local kelp forests. It's also the only facility in the world that has successfully bred the Seussian-looking weedy sea dragon. Parking is $7. Queen Mary/Aquarium combination tickets cost $35 per adult and $19 per child aged three to 11.

A short ride away, the **Museum of Latin American Art** (Map p52; ☎ 562-437-1689; www.molaa.org; 628 Alamitos Ave; adult/child under 12yr/student/senior $9/free/6/6, Sun free; ☺ 11am-5pm Wed-Sun; P) is the only museum in the western USA specializing in contemporary art from south of the border. The permanent collection highlights spirituality and landscapes, and special exhibits are first rate.

ACTIVITIES
CYCLING & IN-LINE SKATING

Skate or ride the paved **South Bay Bicycle Trail** that parallels the beach for 22 miles, from Pacific Palisades (north of Santa Monica) to Torrance in the South Bay. Rentals cost around $7.50 per hour and $18 per day for in-line skates and $22 for bicycles. There are numerous rental shops along the beaches, including the following:

Blazing Saddles (Map p62; ☎ 310-393-9778; Santa Monica Pier, Santa Monica)

Spokes 'n' Stuff (Map p62; ☎ 310-395-4748; 1750 Ocean Front Walk, Santa Monica) On the paved boardwalk behind Loews Hotel.

HIKING

For a quick ramble, head to **Griffith Park** (p67) or **Runyon Canyon** (trailhead Fuller St at Franklin Ave). You'll have fine views of the Hollywood Sign, the city and, particularly at Runyon Canyon, eye candy of fitness-obsessed locals and their dogs.

Malibu Creek State Park (Map p52) has a great trail leading to the set of the TV series *M*A*S*H*, where an old jeep and other relics rust in the sunshine. The trailhead is in the park's main parking lot on Malibu Canyon Rd, which is called Las Virgenes Rd if coming from Hwy 101 (Ventura Fwy). Parking is $12.

SWIMMING & SURFING

Top beaches for swimming are Malibu's **Zuma** (Map p52), **Santa Monica State Beach** (Map p62) and **Hermosa Beach** (p70).

'Endless summer' is, sorry to report, a myth, so much of the year you'll want to wear a wet suit in the Pacific. Water temperatures become tolerable by June and peak at about 70°F (21°C) in August and September. Water quality varies; for updated conditions check the Beach Report Card at www.healthebay.org.

Good surfing spots for nonbeginners include **Malibu Lagoon State Beach** (Map p52), aka Surfrider Beach, and the **Manhattan Beach** (Map p52) pier. Surfing novices can expect to pay about $125 for a two-hour private lesson or $75 for a group lesson, including board and wet suit. The following schools have several beachside locations:

Learn to Surf LA (☎ 310-920-1265; www.learntosurfla.com)

Surf Academy (☎ 877-599-7873; www.surfacademy.org)

TOURS

Esotouric (☎ 323-223-2767; www.esotouric.com; bus tours $58) Hip, offbeat, insightful and entertaining tours themed around

TOURING THE STUDIOS

Half the fun of visiting LA is hoping you'll see stars. Up the odds by being part of the studio audience of a sitcom or game show, which usually tape between August and March. For free tickets contact **Audiences Unlimited** (☎ 818-260-0041; www.tvtickets.com) or stop by its booth inside Universal Studios Hollywood (p72).

For an authentic behind-the-scenes look, take a small-group tour by open-sided shuttle at **Paramount Pictures** (off Map p71; ☎ 323-956-1777; 5555 Melrose Ave, Hollywood; tours $35, minimum age 12yr; ☼ Mon-Fri) or **Warner Bros Studios** (Map p71; ☎ 818-972-8687; www2.warnerbros.com/vipstudiotour; 3400 Riverside Dr, Burbank, San Fernando Valley; tours $45, minimum age 8yr; ☼ 8:30am-4pm Mon-Fri, longer in spring & summer) or walking tours of **Sony Pictures Studios** (Map p52; ☎ 323-520-8687; 10202 W Washington Blvd, Culver City; tours $25; ☼ tours at 9:30am, 10:30am, 12:30pm, 1:30pm & 2:30pm Mon-Fri; Ⓟ). All show you around sound stages and backlots (outdoor sets) and into such departments as wardrobe and make-up. Reservations are required; bring photo ID.

famous crime sites (Black Dahlia), literary lions (Chandler to Bukowski) and historic neighborhoods.

Los Angeles Conservancy (☎ 213-623-2489; www.laconservancy.org; tours $10) Thematic walking tours, mostly of Downtown LA, with an architectural focus.

Red Line Tours (☎ 323-402-1074; www.redlinetours.com; tours $25) 'Edutaining' walking tours of Hollywood and Downtown using headsets that cut out traffic noise.

Spirit Cruises (☎ 310-548-8080; www.spiritmarine.com; adult/child $12/6) One-hour boat tours of LA harbor from Long Beach and San Pedro, including shipping terminals and Terminal Island Federal Prison, whose A-list inmates included Al Capone and Timothy Leary.

Starline Tours (☎ 323-463-333, 800-959-3131; www.starlinetours.com; tours from $39) Narrated bus tours of the city, stars' homes and theme parks.

SLEEPING

Your choice of lodging location can be a big part of the LA you experience.

For coastal life, base yourself in Santa Monica, Venice or Long Beach. Coolhunters and party people will be happiest in Hollywood or WeHo, and city-slicker culture-vultures in Downtown. Rates are pretty steep (highest in summer) and further swelled by a lodging tax of 12% to 14%; always ask about discounts.

SANTA MONICA & VENICE

HI-Los Angeles/Santa Monica (Map p62; ☎ 310-393-9913; www.lahostels.org; 1436 2nd St, Santa Monica; dm members/nonmembers $28/31, r with shared bathroom from $104; ✂ 💻 🛜) This 260-bed hostel is in an architecturally interesting building, but it's the killer location – between the beach and Third St Promenade – that really makes it. Rates include linens and continental breakfast.

Hotel Erwin (Map p62; ☎ 310-452-1111; www.jdvhotels.com; 1679 Pacific Ave, Venice; r from $169; ✂ 💻 🛜) Finally, a Venice hotel worthy of the neighborhood. Rooms aren't the biggest and in most there's a low traffic hum, but it's hard to complain when you're steps from the beach and your room fea-

The skyline of Downtown LA

WITOLD SKRYPCZAK

tures graffiti- or anime-inspired art and honor bar containing sunglasses and '70s-era soft drinks. Its lobby restaurant and rooftop bar are respectively called Hash and High (*nudge, nudge*); the latter boasts spellbinding coastal vistas. Parking is $25.

DOWNTOWN LA

Millennium Biltmore Hotel (Map p68; ☎ 213-624-1011, 800-245-8673; www.thebiltmore.com; 506 S Grand Ave; r $119-399, ste $460-3000; 🔀 🖳 🛜 🖳) Drenched in tradition and gold leaf, this palatial hotel has bedded stars, presidents and royalty since 1923, although some rooms lack elbow space. The gorgeous art deco health club takes the work out of workout. Parking is $40.

Figueroa Hotel (Map p68; ☎ 213-627-8971, 800-421-9092; www.figueroahotel.com; 939 S Figueroa St; r $134-164, ste $225-265; 🔀 🖳 🛜 🖳) A rambling 1920s oasis across from LA Live, the Fig welcomes guests with a richly tiled Spanish-style lobby segueing to a sparkling pool and buzzy outdoor bar. Rooms are furnished in a world-beat mash-up of styles (Moroccan, Mexican, Japanese…) and are comfy but varying in size and configuration. Parking is $12.

Standard Downtown (Map p68; ☎ 213-892-8080; www.standardhotel.com; 550 S Flower St; r from $165; 🔀 🖳 🛜 🖳) This 207-room design-savvy hotel in a former office building goes for a young, hip and party-happy crowd – the rooftop bar fairly pulses – so don't come here with kids or to get a solid night's sleep. Mod, minimalist rooms have platform beds and peek-through showers. Parking is $31.

HOLLYWOOD

USA Hostel Hollywood (Map p71; ☎ 323-462-3777, 800-524-6783; www.usahostels.com; 1624 Schrader Blvd; dm incl breakfast & tax from $30-37, r from $70-85; 🖳 🛜) Not for introverts, this energetic hostel puts you within

steps of Hollywood's party circuit. Make new friends during staff-organized BBQs, comedy nights and tours, or during free pancake breakfasts in the guest kitchen.

Magic Castle Hotel (Map p71; ☎ 323-851-0800, 800-741-4915; www.magiccastlehotel.com; 7025 Franklin Ave; r from $164; 🔀 🖳 🛜 🖳) Walls are thin, but this renovated former apartment building around a courtyard boasts contemporary furniture, attractive art, comfy bathrobes and fancy bath amenities. Most rooms have separate living room. For breakfast: fresh-baked goods and gourmet coffee on your balcony or poolside. Ask about access to the namesake private club for magicians. Parking is $10.

Hollywood Roosevelt Hotel (Map p71; ☎ 323-466-7000, 800-950-7667; www.hollywood roosevelt.com; 7000 Hollywood Blvd; r from $399; 🔀 🖳 🛜 🖳) This venerable hotel has hosted elite players since the first Academy Awards were held here in 1929. It pairs a palatial Spanish lobby with sleek Asian contemporary rooms, a busy pool scene and rockin' restaurants. Marilyn Monroe shot her first commercial by the pool. Parking is $30.

WEST HOLLYWOOD, MID-CITY & BEVERLY HILLS

our pick **Farmer's Daughter Hotel** (Map p79; ☎ 323-937-3930, 800-334-1658; www.farmersdaughterhotel.com; 115 S Fairfax Ave; r $179-209; 🔀 🖳 🛜 🖳) Opposite the Original Farmers Market, Grove and CBS Studios, this perennial pleaser gets high marks for its sleek 'urban cowboy' look. Adventurous love birds should ask about the No Tell Room. Parking is $17.

Chateau Marmont (Map p79; ☎ 323-656-1010, 800-242-8328; www.chateaumarmont.com; 8221 W Sunset Blvd; r $345-785; 🔀 🖳 🛜 🖳) Its French-flavored indulgence may look dated, but this faux-chateau has long attracted A-listers – from Greta Garbo to Bono –

with its legendary discretion. The garden cottages are the most romantic, but not everyone is treated like a star. Parking is $28.

EATING
MALIBU
Reel Inn (Map p52; ☎ 310-456-8221; 18661 Pacific Coast Hwy; meals $10-32; ☼ lunch & dinner; Ⓟ 🤰) Across Pacific Coast Hwy from the ocean, this shambling shack with counter service and patio serves up fish and seafood for any budget and in many styles, including grilled, fried or Cajun. The coleslaw, potatoes and Cajun rice (included in most meals) have fans from Harley riders to beach bums and families.

Geoffrey's (Map p52; ☎ 310-457-1519; 27400 Pacific Coast Hwy; mains lunch $14-24, dinner $18-36; ☼ 11:30am-10pm Mon-Thu, 11:30am-11pm Fri, 10am-11pm Sat, 10am-10pm Sun) This posh classic has just the right mix of assets for the quintessential Malibu experience: the Pacific Ocean as a back yard, smartly executed Cal-Asian cuisine and a regular clutch of celebrity patrons. In short, it's the perfect date spot, especially at night when romance rules.

SANTA MONICA & VENICE
Omelette Parlor (Map p62; ☎ 310-399-7892; 2732 Main St, Santa Monica; mains $6-12; ☼ 6am-2:30pm Mon-Fri, 6am-4pm Sat & Sun; 🤰) An institution since when Main St was known as Dogtown, festooned with black-and-whites of old Santa Monica, a soundtrack of oldies and a leafy courtyard out back. Big-as-your-head omelettes and famous waffles for breakfast may last you to dinner.

Axe (Map p62; ☎ 310-664-9787; 1009 Abbot Kinney Blvd, Venice; mains lunch $6-12, dinner $18-26; ☼ lunch Wed-Fri, dinner Wed-Sun, brunch 9am-3pm Sat & Sun) An exercise in minimalist refinement, Axe (ah-*shay*) derives from a Yoruba word meaning 'go with the power of the deities,' presumably derived from the all-

organic, farm-fresh ingredients in inventive salads, fab 'flatbread and spreads' plate, or flat iron steak with chimichurri.

Real Food Daily (Map p62; ☎ 310-451-7544; 514 Santa Monica Blvd, Santa Monica; mains $8-17; ☼ 11:30am-10pm; Ⓥ) If you're tempted by tempeh (soybean cake) or seduced by *seitan* (wheat gluten), or even if you're not, RFD is worth checking out. A vegan place minus the hippie-commune trappings, plus food courtesy of celeb chef Ann Gentry.

DOWNTOWN LA
Empress Pavilion (Map p68; ☎ 213-617-9898; 3rd fl, Bamboo Plaza, 988 N Hill St; dim sum per plate $2-5, dinner $20-25; ☼ 9am-10pm; Ⓟ) This Hong Kong–style dim sum palace has seating for a small village. Dumplings, wontons, pot stickers, spring rolls, barbecued pork and other delicacies fly off the carts wheeled right to your table by a small army of servers.

Tiara Café (Map p68; ☎ 213-623-3663; 127 E 9th St; sandwiches $8-11, mains $14-16; ☼ 9am-3pm; Ⓥ) Pretty in pink beneath a high ceiling, celeb chef Fred Eric's Fashion District spot feeds designers, sales clerks and bargain hunters with healthy, organic fare: fresh, abundant salads, custom-made sandwiches and lovely, imaginative pizzettes. Check out the amazing collection of anime trinkets.

R-23 (Map p68; ☎ 213-687-7178; 923 E 2nd St; mains lunch $10-15, dinner $40-60; ☼ lunch Mon-Fri, dinner daily) Hidden in the gritty Arts District east of Little Tokyo, R-23 is a fantasy come true for serious sushi aficionados. Not even the bold art and bizarre Frank Gehry–designed corrugated cardboard chairs can distract from the exquisite, ultrafresh treats prepared by a team of sushi masters.

Chosun Galbee (off Map p68; ☎ 323-734-3330; 3300 Olympic Blvd, Koreatown; mains $12-24;

LOS ANGELES

BEVERLY HILLS, WEST HOLLYWOOD & MID-CITY

BEVERLY HILLS, WEST HOLLYWOOD & MID-CITY

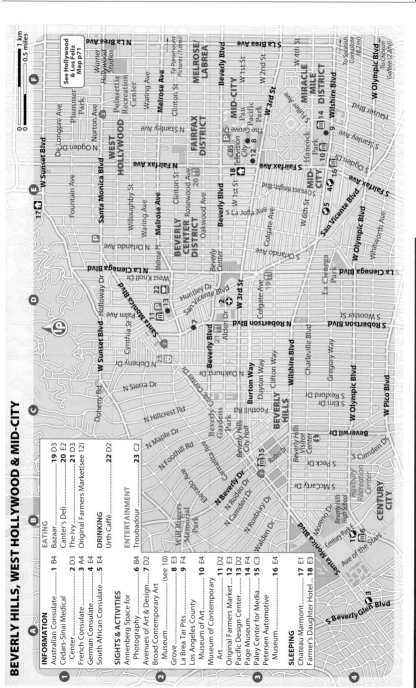

INFORMATION
Australian Consulate 1 B4
Cedars-Sinai Medical
Center 2 D3
French Consulate 3 A4
German Consulate 4 E4
South African Consulate 5 E4

SIGHTS & ACTIVITIES
Annenberg Space for
Photography 6 B4
Avenues of Art & Design....... 7 D2
Broad Contemporary Art
Museum .... (see 10)
Grove 8 E3
La Brea Tar Pits 9 F4
Los Angeles County
Museum of Art 10 E4
Museum of Contemporary
Art 11 D2
Original Farmers Market..... 12 E3
Pacific Design Center......... 13 D2
Page Museum 14 F4
Paley Center for Media 15 C3
Petersen Automotive
Museum 16 E4

SLEEPING
Chateau Marmont 17 E1
Farmer's Daughter Hotel 18 E3

EATING
Bazaar 19 D3
Canter's Deli 20 E2
The Ivy 21 D3
Original Farmers Market...(see 12)

DRINKING
Urth Caffé 22 D2

ENTERTAINMENT
Troubadour 23 C2

⊗ 11am-11pm) Great for Korean barbecue virgins as well as serious fanatics. Cook meat on a grill set into your table, preferably on the trendy bamboo-accented terrace. *Galbee* (short rib cubes), *bulgogi* (beef slices) and *dak bukgogi* (chicken) are marinated in tangy soy-sesame sauce. *Panchan* (side dishes, included in the price) are varied and excellent: marinated veggies, salads and *kimchi*, Korea's national dish of spicy pickled cabbage.

The stalls of the 1930s **Grand Central Market** (Map p68; ☎ 213-624-2378; 317 S Broadway, Downtown; ⊗ 9am-6pm) are atmospheric, historic and tasty. We love Maria's for Ensenada-style fish tacos. Also, browse **LA Live** (p66) for about a dozen restaurants from chichi Japanese (Katsuya by Starck) to rockin' fish (Rock'n Fish), Tiki tributes (Trader Vic's) and an all-American beer hall (Yard House).

HOLLYWOOD & LOS FELIZ
Waffle (Map p71; ☎ 323-465-6901; 6255 Sunset Blvd, Hollywood; most mains $9-12; ⊗ 6:30am-2:30am Sun-Thu, 6:30am-4:30am Fri & Sat) After a night out clubbing, do you really feel like filling yourself with garbage? Us too. But the Waffle's 21st-century diner food – cornmeal-jalapeño waffles with grilled chicken, carrot-cake waffles, mac 'n' cheese, heaping salads – is organic and locally sourced so it's (almost) good for you. Bonus: short but well-chosen wine list.

El Conquistador (off Map p71; ☎ 323-666-5136; 3701 W Sunset Blvd, Silver Lake; mains $10-17; ⊗ 11am-10pm Sun-Thu, 11am-11pm Fri & Sat) Halloween meets Margaritaville at this campy cantina that's a perfect launchpad for a night on the razzle. Cocktails are ginormous, so be sure to fill up on yummy nachos, quesadillas, enchiladas and other above-average classics.

Musso & Frank Grill (Map p71; ☎ 323-467-7788; 6667 Hollywood Blvd, Hollywood; mains $12-35; ⊗ 11am-11pm Tue-Sat) Hollywood history hangs thickly in the air at the boulevard's oldest eatery. Waiters balance platters of steaks, chops, grilled liver and other dishes harking back to the days when cholesterol wasn't part of our vocabulary. Service is smooth; so are the martinis.

RICHARD CUMMINS

Pier at Manhattan Beach (p70)

Grand Central Market (p80), Downtown LA

DAN HERRICK

WEST HOLLYWOOD & MID-CITY

Canter's Deli (Map p79; ☎ 323-651-2030; 419 N Fairfax Ave, Mid-City; dishes $7-16; ☻ 24hr) This institution, open since 1931, is the glue of this Jewish-meets-hipster neighborhood. Intimidated by the phone book-sized menu? Stick to the basics – matzo ball soup, pastrami or corned beef – and you'll be just fine. Service is as sassy as the pickles. The tiny Kibitz Room bar might be showing the game on TV or a rock band.

our pick Bazaar (Map p79; ☎ 310-246-5555; 465 S La Cienega Blvd, Mid-City; dishes $8-18; ☻ dinner nightly, brunch 11am-3pm Sat & Sun) In the SLS Hotel, be dazzled by over-the-top design by Philippe Starck and futuristic tapas by José Andrés: cotton candy foie gras, caprese salad with mozzarella balls that explode in your mouth, and mini-Philly cheesesteaks on 'air bread.' Cocktails and patisserie are similarly *outré*. Caution: those small plates add up.

The Ivy (Map p79; ☎ 310-274-8303; 113 N Robertson Blvd, West Hollywood; mains $20-38; ☻ 11:30am-11pm Mon-Fri, 11am-11pm Sat, 10am-11pm Sun) There always seems to be a paparazzi encampment in the heart of Robertson's fashion frenzy, where The Ivy's picket-fenced porch and rustic cottage are *the* power lunch spots. Chances of catching A-lister babes choke on a carrot stick or studio execs discussing sequels over the lobster omelette are excellent – if you're willing to put up with self-conscious servers and steep prices.

The **Original Farmers Market** (Map p79; 6333 W 3rd St; ☻ 9am-9pm Mon-Fri, 9am-8pm Sat, 10am-7pm Sun; P) is a great spot for a casual meal any time of day.

DRINKING
CAFES

Urth Caffé Santa Monica (Map p62; ☎ 310-314-7040; 2327 Main St); West Hollywood (Map p79; ☎ 310-659-0628; 8565 Melrose Ave) Everything costs $1 to $2 more than it should, but consider it the cost of seeing and being seen among hotties, producers and gawkers, over organic libations at these busy indoor-outdoor cafes. Pastries, salads and panini provide sustenance, and desserts can easily feed two normal people (or nine aspiring actresses).

Intelligentsia Venice Coffeebar (Map p62; ☎ 310-399-1233; 1331 Abbot Kinney Blvd, Venice) Twenty minutes to prepare a cup of joe? In this super-minimalist space, perfectionista baristas ensure that the water temperature is just right before hitting the coffee, and that the wait is just so before it meets your lips. Less time-intensive beverages are also available.

BARS
SANTA MONICA & VENICE

Chez Jay (Map p62; ☎ 310-395-1741; 1657 Ocean Ave, Santa Monica) Throw your peanut shells on the floor as the managers fill you in on some 50 years of intrigue at this bar-restaurant, steps from the Santa Monica Pier. Tales cover Hollywood romance, political machinations and general misbehavior.

On the Waterfront (Map p62; ☎ 310-392-0322; 205 Ocean Front Walk, Venice) Tall glasses of German beer and huge plates of Swiss snackables make for many a memorable afternoon watching the 'bladers, bikers and bohos on the Venice Boardwalk from this indoor-outdoor bar.

DOWNTOWN LA & HOLLYWOOD

Edison (Map p68; ☎ 213-613-0000; 108 W 2nd St, off Harlem Alley, Downtown; ☒ Wed-Sat) Metropolis meets Blade Runner at this industrial-chic basement boîte where you'll be sipping mojitos surrounded by turbines and other machinery back from its days as a boiler room. Don't worry, it's all tarted up nicely with cocoa leather couches, three cavernous bars and a dress code.

Velvet Margarita (Map p71; ☎ 323-469-2000; 1612 N Cahuenga Blvd, Hollywood) Sombreros, velvet Elvises, cheesy Mexican cult movie projections and margarita-swilling scenesters – it's Cabo San Lucas

meets Graceland at this palace of kitsch on the Cahuenga Corridor party drag.

ENTERTAINMENT

LA Weekly (www.laweekly.com) and the *LA Times* (theguide.latimes.com) have extensive entertainment listings. Snag tickets online, at the box office or through **Ticketmaster** (☎ 213-480-3232; www.ticketmaster.com). Half-price tickets to selected stage shows are available online through **Goldstar** (www.goldstar.com) and, for theater, **LAStageTIX** (www.theatrela.org) and **Plays 411** (www.plays411.com), and in person at the visitors centers in Hollywood and Downtown LA (p60).

CINEMAS

Angelenos are serious cinephiles, often remaining seated through the end credits. Seeing a flick at **Grauman's Chinese Theatre** (Map p71; ☎ 323-464-6266; 6925 Hollywood Blvd) is a thrill, and any gathering place worth visiting will also have a movie theater; there are 19 screens around Santa Monica's Third St Promenade alone. Here are some other unique venues. Book tickets through **Moviefone** (☎ from any LA area code 777-3456; www.moviefone.com).

American Cinematheque (☎ 323-466-3456; www.americancinematheque.com) Hollywood (Map p71; 6712 Hollywood Blvd); Santa Monica (Map p62; 1328 Montana Ave) Eclectic film fare from around the world.

ArcLight (Map p71; ☎ 323-464-4226; www.arclightcinemas.com; 6360 W Sunset Blvd, Hollywood) A cineaste's favorite, this ultra-modern multiplex features assigned seats, the latest technology and no commercials before films (only trailers).

LIVE MUSIC & DANCE CLUBS

Conga Room (Map p68; www.congaroom.com; LA Live, Downtown) LA's premier venue for Latin music – partly owned by J-Lo – is

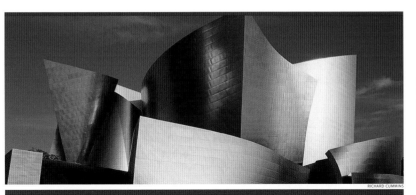

RICHARD CUMMINS

LOS ANGELES

ENTERTAINMENT

Frank Gehry's Walt Disney Concert Hall (p65)

↘ IF YOU LIKE...

If you like the class of the **Walt Disney Concert Hall** (p65) and the rock sounds of the **Troubadour** (p84), we think you'll like these other concert venues that combine an elegant space with kickin' music:

- **Hollywood Bowl** (Map p71; ☎ 323-850-2000; www.hollywoodbowl.com; 2301 N Highland Ave, Hollywood; tickets from $12) Since it opened in the 1920s, you haven't been able to throw a stick at the Grammys without hitting at least a dozen acts who've performed here, from Ella Fitzgerald to Itzhak Perlman and the Grateful Dead to Death Cab for Cutie. Bring a picnic and enjoy the overhead stars of this outdoor theater. Check the website for myriad public transportation options. While decent seats start around $40, the nosebleed section can be ridiculously cheap.

- **Greek Theatre** (Map p71; ☎ 323-665-5857; www.greektheatrela.com; 2700 N Vermont Ave, Griffith Park; tickets from $25) This 1929 open-air theater has been a favorite among concert-goers for generations. The theater has consistently been voted one of the top outdoor venues in the country for both its atmosphere and its great acoustics. With just 6000 seats, folks have been able to get intimate with the likes of Aretha Franklin, the White Stripes and the Russian National Ballet.

- **Ford Amphitheatre** (Map p71; ☎ 323-461-3673; www.fordamphitheatre.org; 2850 Cahuenga Blvd E, Hollywood; tickets from $5) Dance, jazz, Broadway performances, world music and big-name bands have made this small outdoor theater hugely popular. Bring your own blanket and food for a picnic against a forested backdrop. Parking is notoriously awful, so take the shuttle from the Universal City metro station instead.

- **Wiltern** (Map p52; ☎ 213-380-5005; www.livenation.com; 3790 Wilshire Blvd, Downtown LA; tickets from $20) One of the finest representations of art-deco architecture in all of California, the Wiltern shows off the best of LA and national talent. Almost destroyed in the 1970s to make way for a parking lot, the Los Angeles Conservancy saved the historic structure.

right across from the Nokia Theater. Look for sizzling nights courtesy of groups such as Ozomatli and Aterciopelados.

Troubadour (Map p79; ☎ 310-276-6168; www.troubadour.com; 9081 Santa Monica Blvd, West Hollywood) This legendary rock hall helped catapult the Eagles and Tom Waits to stardom and is still great for catching tomorrow's headliners. A beer-drinking crowd serious about its music keeps attitude to a minimum.

Zanzibar (Map p62; ☎ 310-451-2221; 1301 5th St, Santa Monica; ⊗ Wed-Sun) Electronica, Afrobeat and Latin spinmeisters work their turntable magic on throngs of hipsters at this boîte with sensuous African-themed decor. The wraparound bar is great for socializing, while comfy couches invite canoodling.

SHOPPING

Whether you're a penny-pincher or power shopper, LA bursts with opportunities to drop some cash.

Santa Monica has good boutique shopping on Montana Ave and Main St, while Venice's Abbot Kinney Blvd offers a spirited mix of art, fashion and new age. If money is no object, Beverly Hills beckons with international couture along Rodeo Drive. Fashionistas (and paparazzi) flock to **Robertson Blvd** (btwn N Beverly & W 3rd St) and **Melrose Ave** (btwn San Vicente & La Brea) in West Hollywood. Silver Lake has cool kitsch and collectibles, especially around **Sunset Junction** (Hollywood & Sunset Blvds), while bargain hunters haunt Downtown's Fashion District.

GETTING THERE & AWAY
AIR
LA's main gateway is **Los Angeles International Airport** (LAX; Map p52; ☎ 310-646-5252; www.lawa.org/lax), one of the world's five busiest. All major US carriers and dozens of international airlines fly here. About 22 miles southeast, **Long Beach Airport** (LGB; Map p52; ☎ 562-570-2600; www.longbeach.gov/airport) is much smaller and easier managed, served by Alaska, Delta, Jet Blue and US Airways. There are occasional fare wars to one air-

BRIAN CRUICKSHANK

Rodeo Drive, Beverly Hills

port or the other, though ground transit costs may cancel out any airfare savings.

BUS

The main **Greyhound bus terminal (Map p68; ☎ 213-629-8401, 800-231-2222; 1716 E 7th St)** is in an unsavory part of Downtown, so avoid arriving after dark. Some buses go directly to the **Hollywood bus terminal (Map p71; ☎ 323-466-6381; 1715 N Cahuenga Blvd).** Greyhound buses serve Santa Barbara ($18, three hours), San Francisco ($48, from 7½ hours), San Diego ($18, from two hours) and Anaheim for Disneyland ($10, 40 minutes).

CAR

The usual international car-rental agencies have branches throughout LA (see p392 for central reservation numbers). At LAX, if you don't have a prebooking, use courtesy phones in the arrival areas and catch free shuttles to the agencies' off-airport locations. Ecoconscious travelers can try Simply Hybrid (p393).

TRAIN

Amtrak trains roll into Downtown's historic **Union Station (Map p71; ☎ 800-872-7245; 800 N Alameda St)**. The *Pacific Surfliner* travels daily to San Diego ($34, three hours), Santa Barbara ($18, three hours) and San Luis Obispo ($38, 5½ hours).

GETTING AROUND
TO/FROM THE AIRPORT

At LAX airport, door-to-door shuttles operated by **Prime Time (☎ 800-473-3743; www.primetimeshuttle.com)** and **Super Shuttle (☎ 310-782-6600; www.supershuttle.com)** leave from the lower level of all terminals. Typical fares to Santa Monica, Hollywood or Downtown are $21, $26 and $16 respectively. **Disneyland Express (☎ 714-978-8855; www.grayline.com)**

travels at least hourly between LAX and Disneyland-area hotels (one way/round trip $22/32).

Curbside dispatchers will summon a taxi for you. There's a flat fare of $46.50 to Downtown LA, and metered fares average $30 to Santa Monica, $42 to Hollywood and up to $90 to Disneyland. There is a $2.50 surcharge for taxis departing LAX. See p86 for further information.

LAX Flyaway Buses (☎ 866-435-9529; www.lawa.org/flyaway) depart LAX terminals every 30 minutes from about 5am to midnight, nonstop to Westwood ($5, 30 minutes) and Union Station ($7, 45 minutes) in Downtown LA.

BICYCLE

Most buses are equipped with bike racks. Bikes are also allowed on Metro rail trains except during rush hours.

CAR & MOTORCYCLE

Parking at motels and cheaper hotels is usually free, while fancier ones charge anywhere from $8 to $30. Valet parking at restaurants, hotels and nightclubs is commonplace, with fees up to about $10, plus a small tip. Keep *plenty* of change in your car for meters. It goes without saying that you should try to avoid driving during rush hours.

PUBLIC TRANSPORTATION

LA's **Metro (☎ 800-266-6883; www.metro.net)** operates about 200 bus lines and six subway and light rail lines including:

Blue Line Downtown (7th St/Metro Center) to Long Beach.

Expo Line Downtown (7th St/Metro Center) to Culver City.

Green Line Norwalk to Redondo Beach.

Purple Line Downtown to Koreatown.

LOS ANGELES

GETTING AROUND

ACTUALLY, SOME PEOPLE *DO* WALK IN LA

'No one walks in LA,' the '80s band Missing Persons famously sang. That was then. Fed up with traffic, smog and high gas prices, the city that defined car culture is developing a foot culture. Angelenos are moving into more densely populated neighborhoods and walking, cycling and taking public transportation.

The turning point was the extension of the Metro Red Line subway in 2003, connecting Union Station in Downtown LA to the San Fernando Valley via Koreatown, Hollywood and Universal Studios. Stay near one of the arty stations and you may not need a car at all. Particularly convenient stations include Pershing Sq and 7th St/Metro Center in Downtown, and Hollywood/Highland in Hollywood. Unlimited-ride tickets ($5 per day) are a downright bargain, and given LA's legendary traffic it's often faster to travel below ground than above. Light-rail lines connect Downtown with Long Beach and a Culver City branch was due to open as we went to press.

The catch: going further afield. While eventual plans call for a 'Subway to the Sea,' for now you'll be busing it or driving yourself to Mid-City, Beverly Hills and Santa Monica. The easiest transfer is to the Rapid 720 bus (at Wilshire/Vermont station on the Red Line or Wilshire/Western on the Purple Line), which makes limited stops along Wilshire Blvd.

See Getting Around (p85) and visit www.metro.net.

Red Line Union Station to North Hollywood, via Downtown, Hollywood and Universal Studios.

Tickets cost $1.25 per boarding (get a transfer when boarding if needed). There are no free transfers between trains and buses, but 'TAP card' unlimited ride passes cost $5/17 per day/week. Bus drivers sell regular fares and same-day passes (exact fare required). Purchase train tickets at vending machines in stations. Trip planning help is available at ☎ 800-266-6883 or online at www.metro.net.

Local **DASH minibuses** (☎ your area code + 808-2273; www.ladottransit.com; $0.25) serve Downtown and Hollywood. Santa Monica-based **Big Blue Bus** (☎ 310-451-5444; www.bigbluebus.com; $0.75) serves much of western LA and LAX. Its Line 10 Freeway Express connects Santa Monica with Downtown LA ($1.75, one hour).

TAXI

Except for taxis lined up outside airports, train stations, bus stations and major hotels, it's best to phone for a cab. Fares are metered, $2.85 at flag fall plus $2.70 per mile. Taxis serving the airport accept credit cards, though sometimes grudgingly. Some recommended companies:
Checker (☎ 800-300-5007)
Independent (☎ 800-521-8294)
Yellow Cab (☎ 800-200-1085)

↘ SAN FRANCISCO

SAN FRANCISCO HIGHLIGHTS

1 GOLDEN GATE PARK

In 1865 the citizens of San Francisco submitted a petition for an ambitious park project. Since then wild schemes have unfolded in Golden Gate Park, including camel-riding, igloos, casinos and roller derbies. Luckily, its most enduring characteristic is a stretch of greenery so ruggedly romantic, an 1886 newspaper editorial cautioned that its park benches inspired 'excess hugging.' Windbreakers come in handy at the rugged western end of the park where quixotic bison run toward windmills.

⬊ OUR DON'T MISS LIST

❶ CALIFORNIA ACADEMY OF SCIENCES

Mad scientists would surely approve of the basement Eel Forest and the solar-paneled wildflower meadow on the roof. The Academy's (p102) tradition of weird science dates from 1853, with thousands of live animals and 46 scientists under one roof.

❷ MH DE YOUNG FINE ARTS MUSEUM

The sleek, copper-clad MH de Young Fine Arts Museum (p102) is oxidizing green to match the park. Its eclectic, globe-trotting collection is a standout, and includes Beat collage, international textiles and Oceanic art dating from the museum's 1894 origins.

❸ SAN FRANCISCO BOTANICAL GARDEN & STRYBING ARBORETUM

This botanical wonderland (p103) confounds all geography: South African cape grasses sway near the California redwood grove, not far from the Japanese Moon-Viewing Garden.

Clockwise from top: Conservatory of Flowers; Japanese Tea Garden; Pool of Enchantment, MH de Young Fine Arts Museum; Rooftop meadow, California Academy of Sciences

SAN FRANCISCO

SAN FRANCISCO HIGHLIGHTS

❹ JAPANESE TEA GARDEN

A signature attraction since 1894, this tiny garden (p103) erupts into cherry blossoms in spring and turns flaming red with maple leaves in fall. Inchworm-backed bridges, pagoda pavilions and miniature waterfalls offer photo-ops at every turn.

❺ CONSERVATORY OF FLOWERS

The prim and proper 1878 green-house (p103) has a definite flair for the exotic, from Amazonian water lilies to the fanged Dracula orchid and the occasional giant corpse flower, named for its unfortunate scent.

❶ California Academy of Sciences
❷ MH de Young Fine Arts Museum
❸ San Francisco Botanical Garden & Strybing Arboretum
❹ Japanese Tea Garden
❺ Conservatory of Flowers

↘ THINGS YOU NEED TO KNOW

Car-free weekends JFK Drive is closed from Stanyan St to 19th Ave on weekends and holidays **Free concerts** Check out Sharon Meadow or Polo Fields on weekends, especially in September and October **Transportation** Take the N Judah to 9th Ave or buses 71, 21 or 5 **For full Golden Gate Park details, see p102.**

SAN FRANCISCO HIGHLIGHTS

☞ EXPERIENCE CALIFORNIA CUISINE

Today the number one San Francisco tourist attraction is no longer the Golden Gate Bridge, but food, including the local, sustainable, seasonal bounty at Bay Area farmers markets (p120). San Francisco has more award-winning chefs per capita than any other US city, and enough exciting eateries to keep you in a perpetual swoon throughout your visit.

☞ CRUISE TO ALCATRAZ ISLAND

Housing infamous criminals like Al Capone, the lighthouse-topped bay island of Alcatraz (p100) later became the site of an American Indian occupation. Pace the stark prison via a self-guided audio tour, as inmates recount their stories of life on 'The Rock.' Named by Spanish explorers for its bird colonies ('alcatraz' means pelican in Spanish), it's still a sanctuary and breeding ground for seabirds.

SAN FRANCISCO

SAN FRANCISCO HIGHLIGHTS

4 ⟶ VINTAGE TRAINS & CABLE CARS

To see the city sights in old-fashioned style, board a historic F-line streetcar to cruise down Market St and skim along the Embarcadero piers. Feeling more adventurous? Nab a spot on a **cable car** (p119) running board and cling to the pole as it crests Nob Hill and plummets toward the bay.

5 ⟶ LINGER IN NORTH BEACH

Shrill, green parrots streak through the skies of **North Beach** (p108), a longtime Italian neighborhood with sidewalk cafes, scrumptious restaurants, scores of nightclubs and boozy watering holes, and one of the city's best bookstores. Score a scoop of gelato and loaf around the greens of Washington Square.

6 ⟶ MISSION DISTRICT

If the sun's to be found anywhere on a foggy San Francisco day, there's a good chance it's beaming in the palm-tree-dotted **Mission** (p108). Join a **mural tour** (p107) for an overview of expressive neighborhood art and then feast on the best burritos in town. At night, cross paths with mariachis for hire as you bar hop along Mission and Valencia Sts.

2 SABRINA DALBESIO; 3 LEE FOSTER; 4 SABRINA DALBESIO; 5 SABRINA DALBESIO; 6 SABRINA DALBESIO

2 Lunch at Greens (p111); 3 Alcatraz Island (p100); 4 San Francisco's distinctive cable cars; 5 City Lights bookstore (p94), North Beach; 6 Check out the Mission District's murals, including Joel Bergner's *Un Pasado Que Aún Vive*

SAN FRANCISCO'S BEST...

⤵ CHEAP THRILLS

- **Golden Gate Bridge** (p99) Ramble the city's iconic gateway.
- **Ferry Building Farmers Market** (p120) Sample fresh fruit and snacks.
- **TIX Bay Area** (p116) Half-price, same-day theater tickets.

⤵ PLACES FOR PEOPLE-WATCHING

- **Caffe Trieste** (p114) North Beach's most evocative cafe.
- **Café Flore** (p114) Sidewalk cafe where pretty boys gather.
- **Crissy Field** (p106) A nonstop parade of joggers, kite flyers and dog walkers.

⤵ KID MAGNETS

- **California Academy of Sciences** (p102) Attractions include a butterfly-filled Rainforest Dome, a walk-through aquarium and lots of exotic creepy crawlies.

- **Fisherman's Wharf** (p103) Blubbery sea lions push, shove and bark.
- **Yerba Buena Gardens** (p101) Take your pick from ice-skating, bowling, a carousel ride, a multimedia children's museum and a fantastic playground.
- **Exploratorium** (p104) A hands-on science museum.

⤵ FOGGY-DAY TREATS

- **Humphry Slocombe** (p113) A creamy scoop of 'Special Breakfast' (bourbon and cornflakes) will make the sun come out.
- **USS Pampanito** (p103) You won't notice gray weather aboard this restored WWII submarine.
- **Warming Hut** (p106) Curl up with a cappuccino and gaze at the Golden Gate Bridge.
- **Precita Eyes Mission Mural Tours** (p107) Vibrant murals are the perfect antidote to a monochrome day.

Left: Ferry Building Farmers Market (p120); Right: Tour the Embarcadero by Segway

THINGS YOU NEED TO KNOW

⬆ VITAL STATISTICS

- **Population** 7.5 million
- **Area** 49 sq miles
- **Area code** ☎415

⬆ NEIGHBORHOODS IN A NUTSHELL

- **The Embarcadero & Ferry Building** (p98) Destination farmers market and scenic esplanade.
- **Downtown, South of Market & Civic Center** (p100) Commercial center with hotels, museums and transit hubs.
- **Golden Gate Park** (p102) Expansive forest, gardens and top museums.
- **The Haight** (p108) Funky Victorian homes and youth-oriented shopping.
- **The Mission** (p108) A sunny enclave of Latinos and hipsters.
- **North Beach** (p108) Historically Italian and bohemian.
- **The Castro** (p108) Crossroads for the queer community.
- **Chinatown** (p108) Dense cityscape with restaurants and hidden alleyways.

⬆ ADVANCE PLANNING

- **Two months before** Buy tickets for Alcatraz Island (p100), especially if you plan to visit on a weekend.
- **One month before** Make dinner reservations for top restaurants.

⬆ RESOURCES

- **Bay Area Reporter** (www.ebar.com) and **Bay Times** (www.sfbaytimes.com) Free GLBT community papers.

- **Craig's List** (www.craigslist.org) SF's definitive community bulletin board.
- **San Francisco Chronicle** (www.sfgate.com) Northern California's largest daily.
- **San Francisco Visitors Information Center** (Map p96; ☎ 415-391-2000; www.onlyinsanfrancisco.com; lower level, Hallidie Plaza, cnr Market & Powell Sts; ⌚ 8:30am-5pm Mon-Fri, 9am-3pm Sat & Sun) Lots of city maps and information.
- **San Francisco's Bay Guardian website** (sfbg.com) Has events, local theater, art and more.

⬆ EMERGENCY NUMBERS

- **California Pacific Medical Center** (Map p95; ☎ 415-600-3333; www.cpmc.org; 2333 Buchanan St)

⬆ GETTING AROUND

- **Bus** (p119) MUNI buses provide extensive coverage of the city, but can be slow.
- **Cable car** (p119) A perennial favorite, but limited to a few lines in the northeast part of the city.
- **Taxi** (p120) Easy to hail downtown.
- **Train** (p119) BART trains run from the airport to downtown with a few stops in between, and MUNI streetcars radiate south and west from there.

⬆ BE FOREWARNED

- **Weather** Pack warm clothes: evenings (and daytimes) can be chilly any time of the year.

SAN FRANCISCO

DISCOVER SAN FRANCISCO

DISCOVER SAN FRANCISCO

Welcome to the bubble, America's most liberal city, where you can say what you like and act like a freak without anyone noticing.

'Eclectic' doesn't begin to describe a town where you can begin your day with a leisurely breakfast of *huevos rancheros* in the Mission sun, picnic on Italian *panini* among parrots and poets on North Beach stairway gardens, get goose bumps watching the fog billow over the Golden Gate Bridge from a nude beach, dine Downtown on cutting-edge cuisine inspired by California's cornucopia of produce, and end up partying at 5am with South of Market (SoMa) clubsters in a universal groove. So long, inhibitions; hello San Francisco.

Once you've ogled Victorians, ridden the cable cars and sailed to Alcatraz, explore the off-the-beaten-path neighborhoods to get a true sense of place. Don't underestimate poet George Sterling's 'cool, gray city of love': a couple of weeks here and you may start shopping for apartments.

ORIENTATION

San Francisco sits at the tip of a 30-mile-long peninsula and measures 7 miles by 7 miles. To the west lies the Pacific, to the east San Francisco Bay.

INFORMATION

BOOKSTORES

A Different Light Bookstore (Map p115; ☎ 415-431-0891; www.adlbooks.com; 489 Castro St; ⏰ 10am-11pm) Gay-specific titles.

ourpick City Lights (Map p105; ☎ 415-362-8193; www.citylights.com; 261 Columbus Ave; ⏰ 10am-midnight) A free-speech landmark bookseller and publisher; stocks literature and nonfiction, and is home to a legendary Beat poetry loft.

Fog City News (Map p96; ☎ 415-543-7400; www.fogcitynews.com; 455 Market St) Stellar selection of magazines, international periodicals and gourmet chocolate.

MONEY

Travelex (Map p96; ☎ 415-362-3453; 75 Geary St, Union Sq; ⏰ 9am-5pm Mon-Fri, 10am-6pm Sat, 10am-5pm Sun) Currency exchange;

there's another branch at SFO's International Terminal.

TOURIST INFORMATION

California Welcome Center (Map p105; ☎ 415-981-1280; www.visitcwc.com; 2 Pier 39; ⏰ 10am-5pm) Statewide information, brochures, maps and help with accommodations bookings (fees cost up to $5).

San Francisco Visitors Information Center (Map p96; ☎ 415-391-2000; www.onlyinsanfrancisco.com; lower level, Hallidie Plaza, cnr Market & Powell Sts; ⏰ 8:30am-5pm Mon-Fri, 9am-3pm Sat & Sun) Carries maps, guidebooks, brochures and accommodations information. Operates a 24-hour automated phone line with recorded information (☎ 415-391-2001).

DANGERS & ANNOYANCES

Keep your city smarts and wits about you, especially at night in SoMa, the Mission, Haight and all parks. Unless you know where you're going, avoid the Tenderloin, bordered by Polk St (west), Powell St (east), Market St (south) and O'Farrell St

SAN FRANCISCO

SAN FRANCISCO

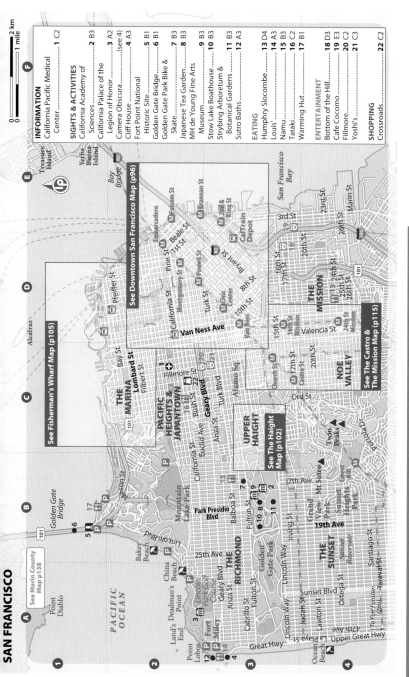

INFORMATION	
California Pacific Medical Center	1 C2
SIGHTS & ACTIVITIES	
California Academy of Sciences	2 B3
California Palace of the Legion of Honor	3 A2
Camera Obscura	(see 4)
Cliff House	4 A3
Fort Point National Historic Site	5 B1
Golden Gate Bridge	6 B1
Golden Gate Park Bike & Skate	7 B3
Japanese Tea Garden	8 B3
MH de Young Fine Arts Museum	9 B3
Stow Lake Boathouse	10 B3
Strybing Arboretum & Botanical Gardens	11 B3
Sutro Baths	12 A3
EATING	
Humphry Slocombe	13 D4
Louis'	14 A3
Namu	15 B3
Tataki	16 C2
Warming Hut	17 B1
ENTERTAINMENT	
Bottom of the Hill	18 D3
Cafe Cocomo	19 E3
Fillmore	20 C2
Yoshi's	21 C3
SHOPPING	
Crossroads	22 C2

DOWNTOWN SAN FRANCISCO

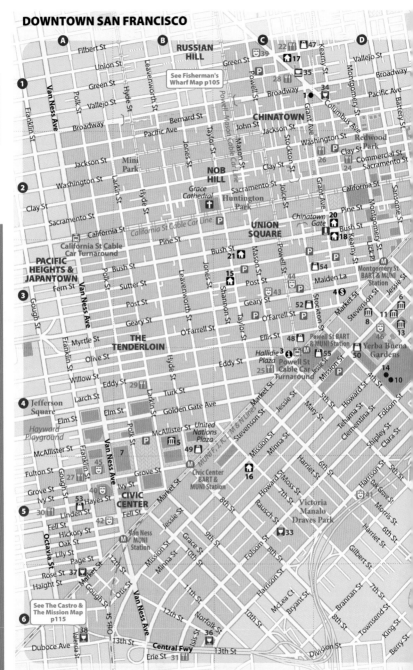

See Fisherman's Wharf Map p105

See The Castro & The Mission Map p115

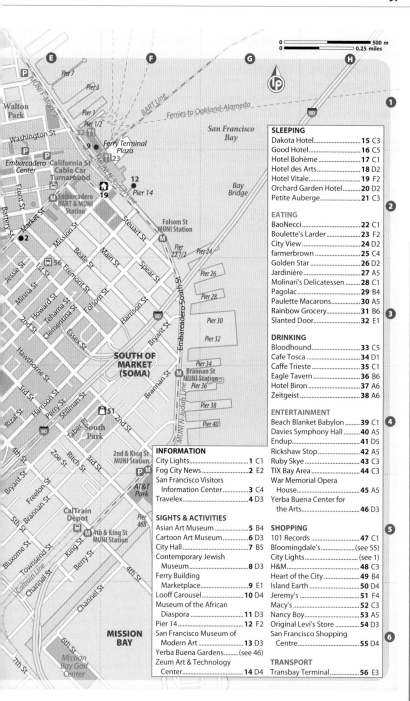

SAN FRANCISCO

DOWNTOWN SAN FRANCISCO

Walton Park

Pier 7
Pier 3

BART Line

Ferries to Oakland-Alameda

80

Pier 1
Pier 1/2
32

Washington St

Ferry Terminal Plaza

California St Cable Car Turnaround

Embarcadero Center

9

23

12

Pier 14

Bay Bridge

Front St

Embarcadero BART & MUNI Station

19

Battery St

Market St

Mission St

Steuart St

Folsom St MUNI Station

2

36

Beale St

Main St

Spear St

Pier 22 1/2

Pier 24

Jessie St

1st St

Minna St

Howard St

Tehama St

Clementina St

Folsom St

Harrison St

Pier 26

Pier 28

Pier 30

Pier 32

Essex St

Bryant St

Embarcadero South St

2nd St

Hawthorne St

Harrison St

3rd St

Rizal St

Perry St

Stillman St

SOUTH OF MARKET (SOMA)

Pier 34

Brannan St MUNI Station

Pier 36

Taber Pl

South Park

51

2nd St

Brannan St

Pier 38

Pier 40

80

4th St

Zoe St

Ritch St

3rd St

2nd & King St MUNI Station

Bryant St

Freelon St

AT&T Park

CalTrain Depot

4th & King St MUNI Station

Bluxome St

Townsend St

Caltrain Line

King St

Berry St

4th St

Pier 46B

Channel St

Channel St

6th St

MISSION BAY

Mission Bay Golf Center

7th St

INFORMATION
City Lights............................1 C1
Fog City News....................2 E2
San Francisco Visitors
   Information Center..........3 C4
Travelex..............................4 D3

SIGHTS & ACTIVITIES
Asian Art Museum..............5 B4
Cartoon Art Museum..........6 D3
City Hall.............................7 B5
Contemporary Jewish
   Museum..........................8 D3
Ferry Building
   Marketplace...................9 E1
Looff Carousel.................10 D4
Museum of the African
   Diaspora......................11 D3
Pier 14.............................12 F2
San Francisco Museum of
   Modern Art..................13 D3
Yerba Buena Gardens.........(see 46)
Zeum Art & Technology
   Center..........................14 D4

SLEEPING
Dakota Hotel.....................15 C3
Good Hotel.......................16 C5
Hotel Bohème...................17 C1
Hotel des Arts..................18 D2
Hotel Vitale.....................19 F2
Orchard Garden Hotel........20 D2
Petite Auberge.................21 C3

EATING
BaoNecci..........................22 C1
Boulette's Larder..............23 F2
City View.........................24 D2
farmerbrown.....................25 C4
Golden Star......................26 D2
Jardinière........................27 A5
Molinari's Delicatessen.......28 C1
Pagolac............................29 B4
Paulette Macarons............30 A5
Rainbow Grocery...............31 B6
Slanted Door.....................32 E1

DRINKING
Bloodhound......................33 C5
Cafe Tosca........................34 D1
Caffe Trieste.....................35 C1
Eagle Tavern.....................36 B6
Hotel Biron.......................37 A6
Zeitgeist..........................38 A6

ENTERTAINMENT
Beach Blanket Babylon.......39 C1
Davies Symphony Hall........40 A5
Endup..............................41 D5
Rickshaw Stop...................42 A5
Ruby Skye.........................43 C3
TIX Bay Area.....................44 C3
War Memorial Opera
   House............................45 A5
Yerba Buena Center for
   the Arts.........................46 D3

SHOPPING
101 Records......................47 C1
Bloomingdale's..................(see 55)
City Lights........................(see 1)
H&M................................48 C3
Heart of the City...............49 B4
Island Earth......................50 D4
Jeremy's...........................51 F4
Macy's..............................52 C3
Nancy Boy........................53 A5
Original Levi's Store...........54 D3
San Francisco Shopping
   Centre...........................55 D4

TRANSPORT
Transbay Terminal..............56 E3

(north). To cut through the Tenderloin, take Geary or Market Sts – still seedy, but tolerable. Avoid 6th St (aka Skid Row) between Market and Folsom Sts.

Expect to be asked for spare change often, but don't feel obliged – to address the causes of homelessness instead of the symptoms, consider a donation to a nonprofit organization such as the Haight Ashbury Food Program (Map p102; ☎ 415-566-0366; www.thefoodprogram.org; 1525 Waller St).

SIGHTS & ACTIVITIES

THE EMBARCADERO & FERRY BUILDING

Stroll or bike the eastern waterfront from SoMa to Fisherman's Wharf along wide-open sidewalks and take in picture-perfect views of Treasure Island and the Bay Bridge. At the foot of Market St, SF's historic 1898 transport hub now houses San Francisco's monument to slow food: the Ferry Building Marketplace (Map p96; ☎ 415-983-8000; www.ferrybuildingmarketplace.com; most shops 10am-6pm), which showcases gorgeous local, sustainable and regional foods by such culinary celebs as Cowgirl Creamery, Hog Island Oyster Co and Acme Bread, and farmers whose names you'll recognize on locavore restaurant menus. But the breakout star is the farmers market (see boxed text, p120), which wraps around the building. Sample the goods then stop for lunch at one of several acclaimed on-site restaurants. Ferries to Sausalito with the Golden Gate Ferry (☎ 415-455-2000; www.goldengate. org) and to Tiburon with the Blue & Gold

SAN FRANCISCO IN...

Ditch the car: bus fare and calf muscles let you see SF at its best.

One Day

Cruise to Alcatraz early in the day, then make your getaway in time for lunch at the chef's table at Boulette's Larder (p112). Witness the next breakthroughs in new media art at San Francisco Museum of Modern Art (SFMOMA; p100), then head over to the Asian Art Museum (p102), and let art transport you across centuries and oceans. Spirits are lifted by Michael Tilson Thomas conducting Beethoven down the block at Davies Symphony Hall (p116), and by cocktails around the corner at Jardinière (p112). End the night singing along to classic musicals at the Castro Theatre (p108) or being showered with glam-rock glitter at Café du Nord (p116).

Two Days

Take an eye-opening walking tour of Mission murals with Precita Eyes (p107), and fuel up at La Taquería (p110). Find pirate supplies and tall tales stocked at 826 Valencia (p117) on your way to the Haight for flashbacks at vintage clothing boutiques. From here, follow starry-eyed hippies to the Summer of Love site: Golden Gate Park (p102). Go global at MH de Young Fine Arts Museum (p102), then take a walk on the wild side in the Rainforest Dome of the California Academy of Sciences (p102). End your all-natural, cross-cultural San Francisco adventure with a fitting feast: Korean-inspired organic small plates at Namu (p112).

Fleet (☎ 415-705-8200; www.blueandgoldfleet. com) dock out the back.

For drop-dead vistas, take your goodies south to **Pier 14** (Map p96), a narrow pedestrian pier extending 600ft into the bay. Vintage streetcars run along the Embarcadero from Fisherman's Wharf to the Ferry Building, then up Market St to the Castro district.

GOLDEN GATE BRIDGE

Soaring symbol of the city and the Golden Gate National Recreation Area (GGNRA), the 1937 **Golden Gate Bridge** (Map p95; ☎ 415-921-5858; www.goldengatebridge.org; ⏱ pedestrian walkway 5am-9pm early Mar-Oct, to 6pm Nov-early Mar, bicycles 24hr; ♿) is a marvel of 20th-century engineering and a beauty besides. Those stunning looks take work:

at nearly 2 miles long and with a main span of 4200ft, the bridge gets touched up with about 10,000 gallons of 'international orange' paint annually.

Start your tour from the parking lot at the bridge's southern end (via Lincoln Blvd through the Presidio; or via Hwy 101 northbound to the 10mph hairpin exit marked 'Last SF Exit,' just before the toll plaza). There's a lookout here, along with a gift shop and a must-see cutaway of the 3ft-thick suspension cable. Follow the path to the bridge sidewalk. (If you're on a bicycle, follow signs to the appropriate westbound sidewalk.) Bring a jacket, even if it's sunny inland. MUNI buses 28 (from Golden Gate Park) and 29 (from the Marina) run to the toll plaza.

SAN FRANCISCO

SIGHTS & ACTIVITIES

CLOCKWISE FROM TOP ROBERTO GEROMETTA; LEE FOSTER; SABRINA DALBESIO; SABRINA DALBESIO

Clockwise from top left: Public art on display, Golden Gate Park (p102); Castro Theatre (p108); California Academy of Sciences (p102); exploring the city's murals (p107)

SAN FRANCISCO

SIGHTS & ACTIVITIES

JOHNNY HAGLUN

The Rock – a bird's-eye view of America's most notorious prison

⬎ ALCATRAZ ISLAND

America's most notorious prison from 1933 to 1963, 12-acre **Alcatraz Island** sits isolated by chilly waters and strong currents. Tour 'The Rock' by booking a ferry and tour with Alcatraz Cruises. On the self-guided audio tour of the cellblock, former guards and prisoners recall attempted prison breaks, visiting days and the library (no books with cursing, kissing or violence allowed). Native American leaders took over the island from 1969 to 1971 to protest US occupation of Native lands, and their standoff with the FBI is preserved in 'This Is Indian Land' water tower graffiti and an oral history centre. Reservations are essential, especially for popular night tours (adult/child 5-11yr $33/19.50): at peak summer periods, the parks service turns away 2000 people a day.

Things you need to know: Alcatraz Cruises; Map p105; ☎ 415-981-7625; www.alcatraz cruises.com; ferry & audio tour adult/child 5-11yr/family $26/16/79; ♿

If you drive across, stop at the first exit north of the bridge marked **Vista Point** for superb views of the city. Cars pay a $6 toll to return, except if you're carpooling with three or more people during weekday rush hours of 5am to 9am and 4pm to 6pm (there's no outbound toll).

DOWNTOWN, SOUTH OF MARKET & CIVIC CENTER
The commercial heart of Downtown SF, **Union Square** (Map p96), is ringed with hotels, department stores, designer boutiques and theaters.

SF's cultural cutting edge is South o' Market (SoMa) in the Yerba Buena Art District, anchored by **San Francisco Museum of Modern Art** (SFMOMA; Map p96; ☎ 415-357-4000; www.sfmoma.org; 15' 3rd St; adult/child under 12yr/student $15/free/9 ♡ 10am-5:45pm Fri-Tue, to 8:45pm Thu; ♿), designed by Mario Botta. Around a centra lightwell are massive mural installations an outstanding photography collection, a new rooftop sculpture garden and break through shows by new media maverick such as Matthew Barney, who debuted hi Vaseline-smeared videos here. Thursday evenings are half-price; the first Tuesday of the month is free.

Within a block are three other contemporary museums. The **Cartoon Art Museum** (Map p96; ☎ 415-227-8666; www.cartoonart.org; 655 Mission St; adult/child 6-12yr $6/2; ☺ 11am-5pm Tue-Sun; ♿) caters to fanboys and comix-chicas of all ages with original *Watchmen* covers, too-hot-to-print political cartoons and events with Oscar-winning, Oakland-based Pixar animators. On this same block is the always-poignant **Museum of the African Diaspora** (Map p96; ☎ 415-358-7200; www.moadsf.org; 685 Mission St; ☺ 11am-6pm Wed-Sat; ♿), tracing connections among African communities through art, storytelling and technology.

Architect Daniel Liebskind reshaped San Francisco's 1881 brick power plant with a blue steel extension into the Hebrew word *l'chaim* (to life) – a fitting home for the vibrant **Contemporary Jewish Museum** (Map p96; ☎ 415-655-7800; www.jmsf.org; 736 Mission St at 3rd; adult/senior & student/child under 18yr $10/free/8; ☺ 11am-5:30pm Fri-Tue, 1-8:30pm Thu; ♿), where

standout shows have included Chagall's theater backdrops and soundscapes based on the Hebrew alphabet by Lou Reed and Laurie Anderson.

Rest those weary museum legs by the Martin Luther King waterfall fountain in **Yerba Buena Gardens** (Map p96; ☎ 415-820-3550; www.yerbabuenagardens.com; ☺ 6am-10pm), or take the kids indoors for ice-skating, a bowling alley and the hand-carved 1906 **Looff carousel** (Map p96; cnr 4th & Howard Sts; tickets $2; ☺ 10am-6pm; ♿). Child prodigies prefer **Zeum Art & Technology Center** (Map p96; ☎ 415-822-3320; www.zeum.org; 221 4th St; adult/child 4-18yr $7/5; ☺ 11am-5pm Tue-Sun Jun-Aug, 1-5pm Wed-Fri & 11am-5pm Sat & Sun Sep-May; ♿) where they can play live-action video games, make claymation music videos and take CGI workshops with Silicon Valley innovators.

Up Market St in a perpetually 'transitional' (read sketchy) neighborhood, Civic Center is graced by the gilded beaux-arts **City Hall** (Map p96; ☎ 415-554-6139; cnr Van Ness Ave & Grove St; ☺ 8am-8pm Mon-Fri), modeled after St Peter's Basilica in Vatican

SAN FRANCISCO

SIGHTS & ACTIVITIES

SABRINA DALBESIO
Union Square, the heart of Downtown San Francisco

City. Wander in and see the grand rotunda, where anti-McCarthy protesters were hosed off the stairs in the first sit-in of the '60s and same-sex weddings were celebrated in 2004. Opposite City Hall, the Asian Art Museum (Map p96; ☎ 415-581-3500; www.asianart.org; cnr Larkin & McAllister Sts; adult/child/youth 13-17yr/student $12/free/7/8; ◷ 10am-5pm Tue-Wed & Fri-Sun, 10am-9pm Thu) transports you across Asia via an escalator in the Gae Aulenti-converted library, with exhibits ranging from ancient Persian miniatures to contemporary Chinese landscapes made entirely from toy dinosaurs.

GOLDEN GATE PARK

A mile-wide, 48-block stretch of the imagination, Golden Gate Park reaches nearly halfway across the peninsula. Pick up information on park features at McLaren Lodge (Map p102; ☎ 415-831-2700; www.parks.sfgov.org; park's eastern entrance, cnr Fell & Stanyan Sts; ◷ 8am-5pm Mon-Fri).

Architect Renzo Piano's 2008 landmark LEED-certified California Academy of Sciences (Map p95; ☎ 415-379-8000; www.calacademy.org; 55 Concourse Dr; weekday adult/child 7-11yr/youth 12-17yr $24.95/14.95/19.95, 3rd Wed of the month free, 6-10pm Thu over 21yr $12; ◷ 9:30am-5pm Mon-Sat, 11am-5pm Sun; ⦿) houses 38,000 weird and wonderful animals under a 'living roof' of California wildflowers. Kids squeal in the Eel Forest and butterfly-filled Rainforest Dome, but adults love NightLife, the Thursday-night open house with DJs, cocktails and penguins dozing off to a faux sunset. Across the music concourse is another showstopper: Herzog & de Meuron's sleek, copper-clad MH de Young Fine Arts Museum (Map p95; ☎ 415-750-3600; www.famsf.org/deyoung; adult/child over 13yr/senior $10/6/7, $2

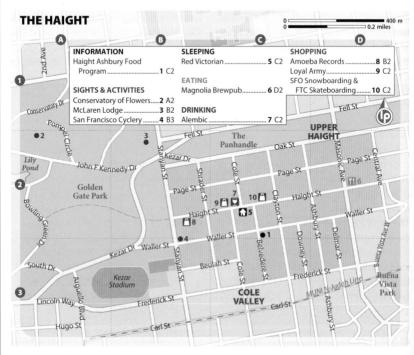

THE HAIGHT

0 ——————— 400 m
0 ——————— 0.2 miles

INFORMATION		SLEEPING		SHOPPING	
Haight Ashbury Food		Red Victorian.....................**5** C2		Amoeba Records.................**8** B2	
Program............................**1** C2				Loyal Army..........................**9** C2	
		EATING		SFO Snowboarding &	
SIGHTS & ACTIVITIES		Magnolia Brewpub..............**6** D2		FTC Skateboarding........**10** C2	
Conservatory of Flowers.....**2** A2					
McLaren Lodge....................**3** B2		DRINKING			
San Francisco Cyclery.........**4** B3		Alembic...............................**7** C2			

is oxidizing green to blend into the park. Inside are standout shows that celebrate inspired handiwork, from Andy Warhol's silkscreened pop-star portraits to Oceanic ceremonial masks.

The **Japanese Tea Garden** (Map p95; ☎ 415-752-1171; Hagiwara Tea Garden Dr; adult/child under 12yr $5/2; ✆ 9am-6pm Mar-Oct, 8:30am-5pm Nov-Feb) is stunning in spring when cherry trees and wisteria bloom, but its stone-studded Zen Garden, vintage footbridges and bonsai grove make it picturesque year-round. For $4, revive with *genmaicha* (green tea with roasted brown rice) and fortune cookies – invented in SF a century ago for the inauguration of this tea garden.

Plants thrive within the park's mild microclimates, and the 70-acre **San Francisco Botanical Garden & Strybing Arboretum** (Map p95; ☎ 415-661-1316; www.sfbotanicalgarden.org; Martin Luther King Dr; nonresident adult/family $7/15; ✆ 8am-4:30pm Mon-Fri, 10am-5pm Sat & Sun) includes species from around the world in its Garden of Fragrance, the California Collection of Native Plants and the Japanese Moon-Viewing Garden. Stop by the botany bookstore – a must for gardeners and naturalists – at the entrance for details on daily tours.

Carnivorous plants and outer-space orchids reveal a wild side to the upright 1879 Victorian **Conservatory of Flowers** (Map p102; ☎ 415-666-7001; www.conservatoryofflowers.org; adult/child 5-11yr/senior & youth 12-17yr $7/2/5; ✆ 9am-5pm Tue-Sun), flanked on the east side by the **Dahlia Garden**, where spiky hybrids contributed by SF's avid amateur horticulturalists are at their bodacious best in August. The 1960s beat goes on thanks to the drum circle at **Hippie Hill**, while strollers find a moment's peace in the contemplative valley of the **AIDS Memorial Grove**.

The park is packed with sporting facilities, including 7.5 miles of bicycle trails, countless miles of jogging trails, 12 miles of equestrian trails, an archery range, flycasting pools, a nine-hole golf course, lawn-bowling greens, four soccer fields, 21 tennis courts, and baseball and softball diamonds (conveniently backed by pagan altars, for prayers between innings). Rent rowboats and pedal boats from the **Stow Lake boathouse** (Map p95; ☎ 415-752-0347; per hr $13-17; ✆ 10am-4pm; ♿).

On Sunday, John F Kennedy Dr closes to traffic and hordes of in-line skaters, cyclists and street-hockey players fill the roadway. Lindyhoppers flip in the band shell on the Music Concourse, and old-school skaters bust synchronized moves at 6th Ave and Kennedy Dr.

Rent skates from **Golden Gate Park Bike & Skate** (Map p95; ☎ 415-668-1117; www.goldengateparkbikeandskate.com; 3038 Fulton St, cnr 6th Ave; skates per hr/day $5/20, in-line skates $6/24; ✆ daily, weather permitting); rent bikes from **San Francisco Cyclery** (Map p102; ☎ 415-379-3870; 672 Stanyan St; per 2/8hr $15/30; ✆ 10am-6pm Wed-Mon).

FISHERMAN'S WHARF

North of the Embarcadero, **Pier 39** marks the beginning of **Fisherman's Wharf** (Map p105), the epicenter of (bland) tourism and home of the city's fishing fleet. Not much of a working wharf any more, it better resembles a waterfront shopping mall. Locals are baffled that tourists are drawn there. But two cable-car lines end here, there are attractions for kids, and you can get fresh Dungeness crab from fish stands. Hamming it up off Pier 39's western end, a **sea-lion colony** barks, belly-flops and sets the SF standard for beach bumming.

Over six tours of duty, the WWII submarine **USS Pampanito** (Map p105;

☎ 415-775-1943; www.maritime.org/pamphome.htm; Pier 45; adult/child 6-12yr/senior/family $9/4/5/20; ☺ 9am-6pm Sun-Thu, 9am-8pm Fri & Sat mid-Oct-May, 9am-8pm Thu-Tue, 9am-6pm Wed Jun–mid-Oct) sunk six Japanese ships (including two carrying British and Australian POWs), battled three others, and survived to tell the tale. Take a self-guided tour of the beautifully restored, extra-tight quarters, booth-sized bathroom and ship-shape kitchen; pay $2 extra for the audio tour, with *Pampanito* servicemen describing tense days in underwater stealth mode.

On the docks you can guillotine a man for a quarter at the **Musée Mécanique** (Map p105; ☎ 415-346-2000; www.museemecaniquesf.com; Pier 45; admission free; ☺ 10am-7pm Mon-Fri, to 8pm Sat & Sun), where 19th-century arcade games such as the macabre French Execution compete for your spare change with Ms Pac-Man.

On fog-free days, rent a bicycle from **Blazing Saddles** (Map p105; ☎ 415-202-8888; www.blazingsaddles.com; from per hr/day $7/28; ☺ from 8am), ride over the Golden Gate Bridge and return via ferry from Sausalito.

There are branches at Pier 41, Pier 43 1/2 and 2715 Hyde St.

THE MARINA

West of Aquatic Park, a footpath traverses a wooded hill toward the Marina, a neighborhood of multimillion-dollar homes on seismically unstable ground. Stroll past the yacht harbor onto **Marina Green**, a six-block-long esplanade great for kite-flying, picnicking, skating and watching windsurfers and kiteboarders (who look like giant mosquitoes zipping up and down).

Bordering the Presidio, Bernard Maybeck's artificial Roman ruin of the **Palace of Fine Arts** (Map p105; Baker St at Bay St) was built for the 1915 Panama-Pacific Exposition, but has a timeless romantic look and a rotunda frieze with a recurring SF theme: 'Art Under Attack by Materialists, with Idealists Leaping to Her Rescue.'

Test the physics of skateboarding, learn the science of cuteness, and grope your way through the Tactile Dome to enlightenment at the **Exploratorium**

Palace of Fine Arts, built for the 1915 Panama-Pacific Exposition

RICHARD CUMMINS

FISHERMAN'S WHARF

INFORMATION

California Welcome Center	1	F2

SIGHTS & ACTIVITIES

Alcatraz Cruises	2	F3
Blazing Saddles (2715 Hyde St)	3	D3
Blazing Saddles (Pier 41)	4	E2
Blazing Saddles (Pier 43 1/2)	5	E2
Crissy Field	6	A3
Exploratorium	7	A3
Musée Mécanique	8	E2
Palace of Fine Arts	9	A3

INFORMATION

Presidio Visitors Center	10	A4
Yoda Statue	11	E2
	12	A4

SLEEPING

Hotel San Remo	13	E3

EATING

Crown & Crumpet	14	D3
Greens	15	C3
Kara's Cupcakes	16	B4
La Boulange	17	C4

ENTERTAINMENT

Teatro Zinzanni	18	F3

SHOPPING

Sports Basement	19	A3

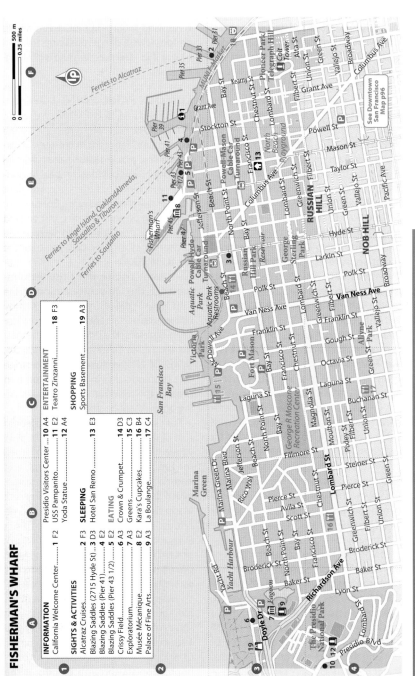

SAN FRANCISCO

FISHERMAN'S WHARF

(Map p105; ☎ 415-561-0360; www.explorato rium.edu; 3601 Lyon St; adult/child 4-12yr/student $14/9/11, Tactile Dome $17; ☺ 10am-5pm Tue-Sun; ⚹), SF's hands-on discovery museum. Reservations (☎ 415-561-0362) are strongly recommended for the Dome and children must be at least seven years old.

THE PRESIDIO & FORT POINT

Army sergeants would surely be scandalized by the frolicking in former army bases in the Presidio, founded in 1776 by Spanish explorers and now a 1480-acre National Parks Services (NPS) and GGNRA playground for rare shorebirds, kite-flyers and nudist lollygaggers. The generals might approve of one tenant however: George Lucas of *Star Wars* fame has his digital studio headquarters here; look for the Yoda statue (Map p105; 1 Letterman Dr). Get your bearings at the Presidio Visitors Center (Map p105; ☎ 415-561-4323; www.nps.gov/prsf; Officers' Club Bldg 50, Moraga Ave; ☺ 9am-5pm).

Along the bay, former military airstrip Crissy Field (Map p105; ☺ sunrise-sunset; ⚹) has been restored to a tidal marsh, with hiking and biking trails, picnic areas with barbecues and a grassy former airstrip for pooches and kite-flying. When the fog rolls in, the Warming Hut (Map p95; ☺ 9am-5pm) serves fairtrade coffee and organic pastries within walls insulated with old denim. Get knock-your-socks-off bridge views on the fishing pier opposite the Warming Hut – especially at night.

Directly under the southern span of the Golden Gate Bridge, the Fort Point National Historic Site (Map p95; ☎ 415-556-1693; www.nps.gov/fopo; ☺ 10am-5pm Fri-Sun) never actually used those guns in the 1861–65 Civil War, but made a killer backdrop for Alfred Hitchcock's *Vertigo*.

Along the ocean side of the peninsula, Baker Beach (Map p95; ☺ sunrise-sunset) features wind-sculpted pines, breathtaking bridge views, a dangerous undertow and a lot of skin – the northern end is clothing-optional.

LINCOLN PARK, POINT LOBOS, OCEAN BEACH & FORT FUNSTON

Golden Gate Park ends in blustery Ocean Beach (Map p95; ☺ sunrise-sunset; ⚹), too chilly for bikinis but ideal for beachcombing or watching pro surfers brave rip tides (casual swimmers beware). Bonfires are allowed in designated pits, but consult regulations first (online at www.parks conservancy.org) or call park police (☎ 415-561-5505).

At Point Lobos, the city's westernmost tip, the latest incarnation of the Cliff House (Map p95; ☎ 415-386-3330; www.cliffhouse.com) restaurant looks like a mausoleum. But along the cliff's edge is the mesmerizing 1946 Camera Obscura (Map p95; ☎ 415-750-0415; admission $2; ☺ 11am-sunset; ⚹), Leonardo da Vinci's invention that projects the view from outside the building onto a giant parabolic screen inside.

Follow the trail above the splendid ruin of the 1896 Sutro Baths (Map p95), where Victorian dandies once converged for bracing baths and workouts, and around Land's End (Map p95; ☺ sunrise-sunset; ⚹) for postcard-worthy views of Marin Headlands and the Golden Gate Bridge. The trail leads to the California Palace of the Legion of Honor (Map p95; ☎ 415-750-3600; www.thinker.org; 34th Ave at Clement St adult/senior/youth 13-17yr $10/6/7, $2 discount with MUNI ticket, 1st Tue of the month free; ☺ 9:30am-5.15pm Tue-Sun; ⚹), which mixes blockbuster exhibits of Fabergé eggs with shows of Max Klinger's obscure, macabre 19th-century *Waking Dream* etchings. Check out works on paper from post-impressionists through to pop at the

Achenbach Foundation for Graphic Arts, and the Rodin-rich sculpture garden donated by the Legion's benefactor, 'Big Alma' Spreckels, whose socialite career started as a nude sculptor's model. The museum is surrounded by an 18-hole **golf course** (☎ 415-750-4653, 415-221-9911).

One and a half miles south of Ocean Beach, watch hang gliders float above **Fort Funston** (off Map p95; ☼ sunrise-sunset; ♿) and hike along windswept cliffs to the beach below.

TOURS

Chinatown Alleyway Tours (☎ 415-984-1478; www.chinatownalleywaytours.org; adult/child 6-9yr/student 10-17yr $18/5/12; ☼ 11am-1pm Mon-Sat by appointment; ♿) Teens who grew up in the neighborhood lead two-hour tours through Chinatown's historic backstreets.

City Guides (☎ 415-557-4266; www.sfcityguides.org; ♿) Sponsored by the San Francisco Public Library, City Guides offers free walking tours led by savvy local historians. Tours include: Art Deco Marina, Gold Rush Downtown, Pacific Heights' Mansions. See the website for meeting times and locations.

Precita Eyes Mission Mural Tours (☎ 415-285-2287; www.precitaeyes.org; public tour adult $10-12, student/child under 12yr $2/5; ♿) Local artists lead two-hour tours on foot or bike, covering 60 to 70 murals within a six- to 10-block radius of mural-bedecked Balmy Alley. Tours depart 11am weekdays and 1:30pm weekends.

Victorian Home Walk (☎ 415-252-9485; www.victorianwalk.com; per person $25; ☼ 11am; ♿) Two-and-a-half-hour architectural walking tours ranging from Edwardian cottages to Queen Anne mansions, plus 'Painted Lady' Victorians with TV credits.

FESTIVALS & EVENTS

Chinese New Year Parade (☎ 415-986-1370; www.chineseparade.com) Chase the 200ft dragon (with toddler martial artists and frozen-smile runners-up for the Miss Chinatown title) through town in late January/early February.

Bay to Breakers (☎ 415-359-2800; www.baytobreakers.com) Thousands run costumed,

Surfer on Ocean Beach

ROBERTO GEROMETTA

SABRINA DALBESIO

Castro & 18th Sts, the Castro District

SLEEPING

⬎ IF YOU LIKE…

If you like touring the city's eclectic neighborhoods, we think you'll like exploring these historic and happening areas:

- **North Beach** Boutiques outnumber bohemians in the neighborhood where the Beat poets once howled, and tough stairway climbs lead to giddy vistas with wild parrots squawking overhead.
- **Chinatown** Stroll beneath the pagoda-style roofs and dragon lanterns of the shopping streets and listen for the clack of mah jong tiles on quiet alleyways.
- **The Castro** The heart of San Francisco's queer community, where you'll find scores of restaurants and bars as well as the ornate **Castro Theatre** (Map p115; ☎ 415-621-6120; 429 Castro St) arthouse cinema.
- **The Mission** Visit the oldest building in the city, tour colorful alley murals, devour a chunky burrito, and then kick back with the hipsters at one of its buzzing outdoor bars.
- **The Haight** The legendary intersection of Haight and Ashbury Sts was the place to be in the psychedelic '60s, now vintage boutiques comingle with head shops at this gateway to Golden Gate Park.

naked and/or clutching beer from Embarcadero to Ocean Beach on the third Sunday in May.

Carnaval (☎ 415-826-1401; www.carnavalsf.com) Brazilian, or just faking it with a wax and a tan? Shake your tail feathers in the Mission the last weekend of May.

SF Gay Pride Month (☎ 415-864-0831; www.sfpride.org) A day isn't enough to do SF proud: June begins with the Gay & Lesbian Film Festival, and goes out in style with Pink Saturday and the half-million-strong Pride parade, with trailing boas and bridal veils by the mile.

SLEEPING

Staying Downtown, by Union Sq, puts you near all public transportation. It's a neighborhood of high-rises, not Victorians. Watch your back in the Tenderloin (see p94). North Beach is exciting, but street parking is impossible – use hotel garages.

Rates in this section are published high-season prices; you can often do better. The San Francisco Visitors Information Center (p94) runs a **reservation line** (☎ 888-782-9673; www.onlyinsanfrancisco.com).

BUDGET

Hostelling International (HI; www.sfhostels. com) Has three locations in SF. Lombard St, in the Fisherman's Wharf area west of Van Ness Ave, is motel row – good when you show up without reservations.

Hotel San Remo (Map p105; ☎ 415-776-8688, 800-352-7366; www.sanremohotel.com; 2237 Mason St; r $75-99; 🖳 🛜) Long on Old West charm, the vintage 1906 San Remo has simple rooms with shared bathrooms. Cheapest rooms face the hallway; for air and light request one with a window.

Dakota Hotel (Map p96; ☎ 415-931-7475; 606 Post St at Taylor St; r $98-110; 🖳 🛜) Upgrade from hostel to hotel at this 1920s downtowner with clean, basic rooms with microwave, fridge and clawfoot bathtubs. Temperamental elevator.

MIDRANGE

Good Hotel (Map p96; ☎ 415-621-7001, 800-738-7477; www.jdvhotels.com; 112 7th St; r $109-169; 🔀 🛜 🐾) With a focus on green practices, Good Hotel is decorated with reclaimed and recycled fixtures. The candy-color paint jobs and low-slung platform beds make rooms look like the dorm you wish you'd had in college. Rooms on Mission St are loud; book in back. Some air-con rooms are available. Parking is free for hybrid vehicles (all others $20).

Hotel des Arts (Map p96; ☎ 415-956-3232, 800-956-4322; www.sfhoteldesarts.com; 447 Bush St; r with/without bathroom from $139/89; 🛜) Art freaks take note: every wall in specialty rooms at Hotel des Arts has been painted with jaw-dropping murals by up-and-coming underground street artists – it's like sleeping inside a painting. Standard rooms are less exciting, but clean and good value.

SAN FRANCISCO

SLEEPING

ANTHONY PIDGEON

The Red Victorian (p110) B&B, Haight St

Red Victorian (Map p102; ☎ 415-864-1978; www.redvic.net; 1665 Haight St; r incl breakfast with/without bathroom from $149/89; 🛜) The '60s live on at the tripped-out Red Vic. Individually decorated rooms pay tribute to peace, ecology and friendship. Only four have bathrooms; breakfast is in the organic cafe. Wi-fi in lobby.

Petite Auberge (Map p96; ☎ 415-928-6000, 800-365-3004; www.jdvhotels.com; 863 Bush St; r incl breakfast $169-219; 🛜) Like a country inn, this French-provincial charmer has cheerful rooms (some come with gas fireplaces). Rates include breakfast and a nightly wine-and-cheese hour, served fireside in the cozy salon.

Hotel Bohème (Map p96; ☎ 415-433-9111; www.hotelboheme.com; 444 Columbus Ave; r $174-194; 🛜) Like a love letter to the jazz era, the Bohème is decorated in moody color schemes – orange, black and sage-green – nodding to the late 1950s. Inverted Chinese umbrellas hang from the ceiling, and Beat-era photos decorate the walls. Rooms are smallish, and some front on noisy Columbus Ave, but the hotel sits smack in the middle of North Beach's vibrant street scene. For quiet, book rooms in back.

TOP END

Orchard Garden Hotel (Map p96; ☎ 415-399-9807, 888-717-2881; www.theorchardgardenhotel.com; 466 Bush St; r $179-249;) San Francisco's first all-green-practices hotel, opened in 2006, uses sustainably grown wood, recycled hypoallergenic fabrics and chemical-free cleaning products. The look is soothingly swank, with muted colors and deluxe touches such as fancy bedding and flat-screen TVs. Great location.

Hotel Vitale (Map p96; ☎ 415-278-3700, 888-890-8688; www.hotelvitale.com; 8 Mission St; r $239-339;) Mid-century modern meets contemporary chic at the coolly

minimalist Vitale, Downtown's sexiest hotel. Rooms are decorated in a soothing spa theme, and beds have silky-soft 450-thread-count sheets. Splurge on a bay-view room.

EATING
BUDGET

La Taquería (Map p115; ☎ 415-285-7117; 2889 Mission St at 25th; burritos $5-6.50; 🕙 11am-9pm Mon-Sat, to 8pm Sun;) No debatable tofu, saffron rice, spinach tortilla or mango salsa in these burritos and tacos: just classic tomatillo or mesquite salsa, marinated, grilled meats and flavorful beans inside a flour tortilla.

BaoNecci (Map p96; ☎ 415-989-1806; www.caffebaonecci.com; 516 Green St; sandwiches $6.50-8; 🕙 9am-5pm Tue-Sun;) Pull up a sidewalk chair in sunny North Beach for bold Southern Italian *panini* on house-baked ciabatta or focaccia. Taste buds sit up and pay attention to the Studente, a ham-and-cheese sandwich slathered with hot Calabrese red-pepper paste and green-olive spread.

Golden Star (Map p96; ☎ 415-398-1215; 11 Walter Lum Pl; dishes $7-9; 🕙 10am-9pm;) Elementary school cafeterias could outclass this Chinatown standby for atmosphere – but the Golden Star gets gold stars for *pho* (Vietnamese rice noodle soup). Five-spice chicken *pho* is rivaled only by *bun* (rice vermicelli) topped with thinly sliced grilled beef, imperial rolls, mint and ground peanuts.

Louis' (Map p95; ☎ 415-387-6330; 902 Pt Lobos Ave; dishes $7-10; 🕙 6:30am-4:30pm Mon-Fri, to 6pm Sat & Sun;) Try Louis' for decent burgers and Point Lobos views at half the price of nearby Cliff House. Hold out for a booth overlooking the splendid ruin of the Sutro Baths.

Pagolac (Map p96; ☎ 415-776-3234; 655 Larkin St; dishes $7-10; 🕙 10am-10pm Mon-Sat)

The sweet spot of 'Little Saigon' along gritty Larkin St, Pagolac has the richest *pho* and great char-grilled meats, with candlelit niches and smiles all around.

La Boulange (Map p105; ☎ 415-440-4450; www.baybread.com; 1909 Union St; lunch under $10; 7am-6pm;) Splurge at Union St boutiques and save on lunch: half a *tartine* (open-faced sandwich) with soup or salad and a fresh-baked macaroon for $10, plus Nutella and cornichons gratis at the condiment bar. Other locations: Hayes Valley (500 Hayes St at Octavia St) and Haight (1000 Cole St at Parnassus).

MIDRANGE

City View (Map p96; ☎ 415-398-2838; 662 Commercial St; small plates $3-5; 11am-2:30pm Mon-Fri, 10am-2:30pm Sat & Sun;) Hail carts piled to teetering with impeccable shrimp-and-leek dumplings and crisp Peking duck for decadent dim sum lunches at this sunny Chinatown restaurant. Three to four plates usually make a good meal.

Crown & Crumpet (Map p105; ☎ 415-771-4252; www.crownandcrumpet.com; 207 Ghirardelli Sq; tea & cake $8-12, 5-course tea service $32; 10am-6pm Mon-Thu, 9am-10pm Fri, 9am-9pm Sat, 9am-6pm Sun;) Girlfriends rehash hot dates over scones with strawberries and champagne, and dads and daughters clink teacups with crooked pinkies and eat finger sandwiches. Reservations recommended; large parties, request the corner table with Golden Gate Bridge views.

Greens (Map p105; ☎ 415-771-6222; www.greensrestaurant.com; Bldg A, Fort Mason; lunch $8-16, dinner $16-25; 8am-8pm Mon-Thu, 8am-5pm Fri & Sat, 9am-4pm Sun;) Inventive vegetarian cooking so savory, even hard-core meat eaters leave sated, and dazzled by Golden Gate Bridge views. On weekends, enjoy takeout black-bean chili with *crème fraîche* and pickled jalapeños at redwood-stump cafe tables or on sunny docks.

Magnolia Brewpub (Map p102; ☎ 415-864-7468; www.magnoliapub.com; 1398 Haight St; mains $8-19; noon-midnight Mon-Thu, noon-1am Fri, 10am-1am Sat, 10am-midnight Sun) A Haight staple named after a Grateful Dead song, serving organic salads, home-brew samplers and grass-fed Prather

ORIEN HARVEY

A nice place to chill – Caffe Trieste (p114)

Ranch burgers big enough for stoner appetites. Sit at chatty communal tables or shy-hippie booths.

our pick Namu (Map p95; ☎ 415-386-8332; www.namusf.com; 439 Balboa St; small plates $9-15; ⏰ 5-10:30pm Mon-Fri, 10am-3pm & 5:30-10:30pm Sat & Sun) SF's unfair culinary advantages are showcased in organic, Korean-inspired small plates of buttery *kampachi* with chili oil and *fleur de sel* (sea salt), tender spare ribs, and Niman Ranch Kobe beef with organic vegetables in a sizzling stone pot.

farmerbrown (Map p96; ☎ 415-409-3276; www.farmerbrownsf.com; 25 Mason St; mains $15-24; ⏰ 5-11pm Sun-Thu, 5pm-midnight Fri & Sat, bar open to 2am) Putting soul back into soul food with ribs that stick to yours, Tilamook cheddar grits, and coleslaw with a kick – all with ingredients sourced from local, organic and African American farmers. Downsides are harried service and a location on the wrong side of the block; upsides are shotgun-shack decor and $15 all-you-can-eat brunches with live music.

Boulette's Larder (Map p96; ☎ 415-399-1155; www.bouletteslarder.com; 1 Ferry Bldg; mains $15-28; ⏰ 9am-3pm Mon-Fri, noon-3pm Sat, 11am-3pm Sun) Dinner theater doesn't get better than Boulette's lunchtime communal table, strategically placed inside a working kitchen. Inspired by their truffled eggs and chili-dusted watermelon salads? Get spices and mixes to go at the pantry counter.

Delfina (Map p115; ☎ 415-552-4055; www.delfinasf.com; 3621 18th St; mains $18-26; ⏰ 5:30-10pm Mon-Thu, 5:30-11pm Fri & Sat, 5-10pm Sun) Simple, sensational, seasonal California fare: Sonoma duck with Barolo-roasted cherries, wild-nettle tagliatelle pasta, profiteroles with coffee gelato and candied almonds. Reserve ahead, or settle for Delfina Pizza next door.

TOP END

Reserve well ahead for all restaurants in this section.

Tataki (Map p95; ☎ 415-931-1182; www.tatakisushibar.com; 2815 California St; small plates $4-13; ⏰ lunch & dinner Mon-Fri, 5-11:30pm Sat, 5-9:30pm Sun) Pioneering sustainable sushi chefs Kin Lui and Raymond Ho rescue dinner and the oceans with sustainable delicacies: silky Arctic char drizzled with *yuzu* (Japanese citrus) and capers happily replaces at-risk wild salmon, and the Golden State Roll is a local hero, featuring spicy line-caught scallops, Pacific tuna, organic apple slivers and edible gold leaf.

Slanted Door (Map p96; ☎ 415-861-8032; www.slanteddoor.com; Ferry Bldg; lunch $9-18, dinner $15-28; ⏰ lunch 11am-2:30pm Mon-Sat, 11:30am-3pm Sun, dinner 5:30-10pm) James Beard Award–winning chef Charles Phan's Cal-Vietnamese landmark has looks and smarts, too: corner windows overlooking the bay and a menu blending Saigon street eats with NorCal ingredients, sourced locally and sustainably. Lunches are ideal for a leisurely pace, lower prices, and mesmerizing bridge-view vistas. When the place is booked, get Dungeness crab noodles from the Out the Door window, and enjoy them Bayside.

Jardinière (Map p96; ☎ 415-861-5555; www.jardiniere.com; 300 Grove St; mains $22-35; ⏰ 5-10:30pm Tue-Sat, to 10pm Sun & Mon) Iron Chef champ Traci Des Jardins has a way with organic vegetables, free-range meats and sustainable seafood, topping succulent octopus with crispy pork belly, and drizzling Sonoma lavender honey over squash blossoms bursting with molten sheep's cheese. Go Mondays, when $45 scores three courses with wine pairings, or hit the mood-lit lounge for an affordable bar menu with seasonal cocktails.

SABRINA DALBESIO

Slanted Door restaurant, Ferry Building

↘ IF YOU LIKE...

If you like the delicious sweet treats at Bi-Rite Market and Rainbow Grocery (see below), we think you'll like these indulgent dessert outposts:

■ Humphry Slocombe (Map p95; ☎ 415-550-6971; www.humphryslocombe.com; 2790 Harrison St; ☽ noon-9pm Tue-Sun; 🚼) The Mission's indie-rock ice cream may permanently spoil you for Top 40 flavors: once balsamic vinegar, caramel and olive oil have rocked your taste buds, cookie dough seems so obvious.

■ Kara's Cupcakes (Map p105; ☎ 415-563-2253; www.karascupcakes.com; 3249 Scott St; ☽ 10am-8pm Mon-Sat, to 6pm Sun; 🚼) Watch Proustian nostalgia wash over fully grown adults as they bite into retro-1970s carrot cake with cream-cheese frosting, or recall magician birthday parties over chocolate-marshmallow cupcakes.

■ Mission Pie (Map p115; ☎ 415-282-1500; www.missionpie.com; 2901 Mission St; ☽ 7am-9pm Mon-Thu, 7am-10pm Fri, 8am-10pm Sat, 9am-9pm Sun; 🚼) Like mom used to make, only better: from savory quiche to all-American apple pie, all purchases support a nonprofit sustainable farm where city kids learn about nutrition and cooking.

■ Paulette Macarons (Map p96; ☎ 415-864-2400; www.paulettemacarons.com; 437 Hayes St; ☽ 11am-7pm Tue-Sat, noon-6pm Sun & Mon; 🚼) Sorry, Oreo: the competition for the ultimate sandwich cookie is down to Paulette's Sicilian pistachio and passion fruit French macarons.

GROCERIES & QUICK EATS

Bi-Rite Market (Map p115; ☎ 415-241-9760; 3639 18th St) A showcase for local farmers, vintners, chocolatiers and cheese-makers. Take sandwiches to Dolores Park up the street, with organic ice cream across the street at Bi-Rite Creamery – trust us on the salted caramel.

Rainbow Grocery (Map p96; ☎ 415-863-0620; 1745 Folsom St; Ⓥ) A worker-owned cooperative, Rainbow offers no meat but a huge selection of natural foods, local organic veggies, Sonoma cheeses, breads, wines and organic skincare; this is the best spot to buy vitamins and supplements.

Molinari's Delicatessen (Map p96; ☎ 415-421-2337; 373 Columbus Ave) Plan a gourmet Italian picnic with salami, olives, bread and buffalo mozzarella from this famous delicatessen; head to Washington Sq Park to enjoy.

DRINKING
CAFES

Caffe Trieste (Map p96; ☎ 415-392-6739; 601 Vallejo St; 🛜) The West Coast's first espresso bar and former Beat hangout still has poetry graffiti in the bathroom. This is North Beach at its best, with Sinatra on the jukebox and monthly Saturday accordion shows.

Café Flore (Map p115; ☎ 415-621-8579; 2298 Market St; 🛜) Nicknamed the 'floor show' for its gorgeous parade of regulars, the Flore's outdoor patio is a cool scene on a sunny day. At night it's a mellow spot quiet enough for conversation. Good food too.

BARS

For pub crawls, hit the Mission (around 16th and Valencia Sts), North Beach, the Haight, and Polk St (north of Geary St).

Bloodhound (Map p96; ☎ 415-863-2840; 1145 Folsom St) Bloodhound feels vaguely Nordic, with white wood, antler chandeliers and fantastic art. Has top-shelf ingredients and a killer jukebox. Best on weeknights or before midnight on weekends.

Zeitgeist (Map p96; ☎ 415-255-7505; 199 Valencia St) *The* hangout for urban bikers – pedal- and motor-powered – has an enormous back patio with pot smoke lingering in the air. Heavy pours and good beers.

Hotel Biron (Map p96; ☎ 415-703-0403; 45 Rose St) Our favorite wine bar for an intimate tête-à-tête has a French-underground vibe

and great cheese plates; it gets impossibly crowded on weekends.

Cafe Tosca (Map p96; ☎ 415-986-9651; 242 Columbus Ave) A classic 1919 bar with old-world character, Tosca has a great jukebox with Rat Pack and Tin Pan Alley-American songbook classics. If you're stalking Sean Penn, start here.

Alembic (Map p102; ☎ 415-666-0822; 1725 Haight St) Haight St's spiffiest bar has an impressive array of whiskeys and mixology drinks, appealing to bon vivant 30-somethings who jam the tiny space nightly.

Elbo Room (Map p115; ☎ 415-552-7788; 647 Valencia St) Shoot pool downstairs with Mission-district scenesters or hear DJs and live bands upstairs. Dig the photo booth.

Toronado (Map p115; ☎ 415-863-2276; 547 Haight St) Beer mavens dig the 50-plus microbrews, with hundreds more in bottles.

ENTERTAINMENT

Pick up *SF Weekly* for listings; look online at **Nitevibe** (www.nitevibe.com), **SF Station** (www.sfstation.com) and **SF Gate** (www.sfgate.com); and strike up conversations with locals to gather tips.

CLUBS & LIVE MUSIC

Ruby Skye (Map p96; ☎ 415-693-0777; www.rubyskye.com; 420 Mason St; admission $10-25; ⏱ 9pm-late Fri & Sat, sometimes Thu & Sun) The city's premier-name nightclub hosts the who's who of the world's DJs on a state-of-the-art Funktion-One sound system. The very-mainstream crowd sometimes gets messy.

Fillmore (Map p95; ☎ 415-346-6000; www.thefillmore.com; 1805 Geary Blvd) Hendrix, Zeppelin, the Who – they all played the Fillmore. Its 1250 capacity means you're close to the stage. Dig the priceless collection in the upstairs poster-art gallery.

THE CASTRO & THE MISSION

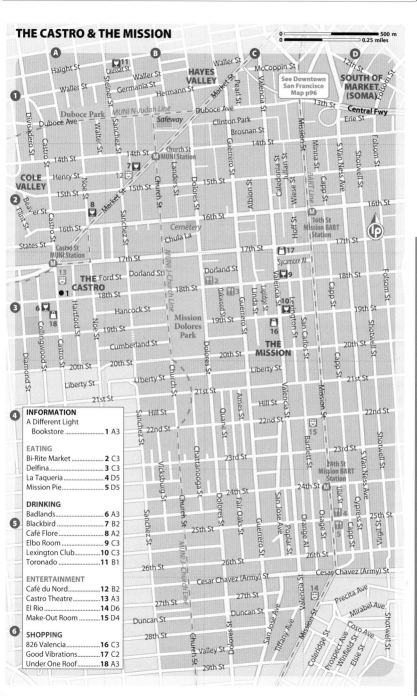

SAN FRANCISCO

THE CASTRO & THE MISSION

INFORMATION ⓸
A Different Light
  Bookstore **1** A3

EATING
Bi-Rite Market **2** C3
Delfina............................. **3** C3
La Taquería **4** D5
Mission Pie...................... **5** D5

DRINKING ⓹
Badlands.......................... **6** A3
Blackbird **7** B2
Café Flore **8** A2
Elbo Room **9** C3
Lexington Club............... **10** C3
Toronado **11** B1

ENTERTAINMENT
Café du Nord.................. **12** B2
Castro Theatre................ **13** A3
El Rio **14** D6
Make-Out Room **15** D4

SHOPPING ⓺
826 Valencia................... **16** C3
Good Vibrations.............. **17** C2
Under One Roof.............. **18** A3

Yoshi's (Map p95; ☎ 415-655-5600; www.yoshis.com; 1300 Fillmore St) San Francisco's definitive jazz club draws the world's top talent and occasionally hosts rare appearances; advance bookings recommended.

Bottom of the Hill (Map p95; ☎ 415-621-4455; www.bottomofthehill.com; 1233 17th St; ⏾ shows after 8:30pm Tue-Sat) On lower Potrero Hill, this indie-rock institution showcases happening local acts. Shoot pool in back and smoke on the outdoor patio.

Café du Nord (Map p115; ☎ 415-861-5016; www.cafedunord.com; 2170 Market St) The former speakeasy in the basement of the Swedish-American Hall rocks revelers with a cool changing lineup; check its calendar.

Cafe Cocomo (Map p95; ☎ 415-824-6910; www.cafecocomo.com; 650 Indiana St; ⏾ 7pm-midnight Mon, 6pm-midnight Thu, 6pm-2am Sat) Kick-ass salsa bands play Thursday and Saturday, and hundreds pack the dance floor. Monday there's no band, but those who come dance hard. Lessons precede parties.

Endup (Map p96; ☎ 415-646-0999; www.theendup.com; 401 6th St; ⏾ 10pm-4am Mon-Thu, 11pm Fri-11am Sat, 10pm Sat-10pm Sun) When you're grinding your teeth, desperate for a place to dance till noon on Saturday or Sunday, you've one choice. The crowd is tweaky, but the place is an institution.

THEATER
TIX Bay Area (Map p96; ☎ 415-433-7827; www.tixbayarea.org; Union Sq; ⏾ Tue-Sun) This free-standing kiosk on Powell St at Geary St sells half-price, day-of-performance tickets and full-price advance tickets. Cash only for same-day seats.

Beach Blanket Babylon (Map p96; ☎ 415-421-4222; www.beachblanketbabylon.com; 678 Green St; tickets $25-80) If you see only one show, make it hilarious Beach Blanket, where larger-than-life performers brilliantly spoof contemporary culture. And those hats – legendary!

Teatro Zinzanni (Map p105; ☎ 415-438-2668; http://zinzanni.org; Pier 29; tickets $145-195) A rotating cast of celebs star in Zinzanni's 19th-century, European-style circus – a sort of comedic Cirque du Soleil – with a surprisingly good five-course meal.

The world-renowned San Francisco Symphony performs in **Davies Symphony Hall** (Map p96; ☎ 415-864-6000; www.sfsymphony.org; cnr Grove St & Van Ness Ave). The beautiful **War Memorial Opera House** (Map p96; ☎ 415-864-3330; 301 Van Ness Ave) hosts the San Francisco Opera and the **San Francisco Ballet** (☎ 415-865-2000; www.sfballet.org). **Yerba Buena Center for the Arts** (Map p96; ☎ 415-978-2787; www.ybca.org; cnr Howard & 3rd Sts) hosts excellent contemporary performing arts.

SPORTS
San Francisco 49ers (☎ 415-656-4900; www.sf49ers.com; admission $25-100) The 49ers play NFL football at Candlestick Park, south of the city, but will likely move to Santa Clara in 2014.

San Francisco Giants (☎ 415-972-2000; www.sfgiants.com; admission $5-135; ♿) The Giants play Major League Baseball at AT&T Park.

SHOPPING
If you've forgotten underwear or a sweater, head to Union Sq, anchored by good-for-basics **Macy's** (Map p96; ☎ 415-397-3333; 170 O'Farrell St; ♿) and **Original Levi's Store** (Map p96; ☎ 415-501-0100; www.us.levi.com; 300 Post St), the flagship of SF's historic denim inventor.

Bloomingdale's (Map p96; ☎ 415-856-5300; 845 Market St) is the main attraction in the **San Francisco Shopping Centre** (Map p96; cnr **Market & 5th Sts**; ♿), but for cheap and chic it's hard to beat **H&M** (Map p96; ☎ 415-986-4215; 150 Powell St). Designers unload sample and runway-worn fashion at **Jeremy's** (Map p96; ☎ 415-882-4929; www. jeremys.com; 2 South Park Ave) for as much as 90% off.

For original fashion statements, get to Hayes St between Franklin and Laguna Sts in Hayes Valley (Map p96). Acquire that fogged-in SF glow with organic skincare 'tested on boyfriends, never animals' from local maker **Nancy Boy** (Map p96; ☎ 415-552-3802; www.nancyboy.com; 347 Hayes St). Chic boutiques and gift shops also line Union St, between Franklin and Fillmore Sts (Map p96).

Fashionistas shop the Pacific Heights boutiques along Fillmore St between Bush and Sacramento Sts and sell never-worn designer clothes and mint vintage at **Crossroads** (Map p95; ☎ 415-775-8885; www. crossroadstrading.com; 1901 Fillmore St; ☉ 11am-7pm Mon-Thu, 11am-8pm Fri & Sat, noon-7pm Sun). For vintage finery and T-shirts with cartoon California rolls bragging 'That's how we roll!' from **Loyal Army** (Map p102; ☎ 415-221-6200; www.loyalarmy.com; 1728 Haight St; ☉ 10am-8pm Mon-Sat, 11am-7pm Sun), hit Haight St.

Groove to your own beat at **Amoeba Records** (Map p102; ☎ 415-831-1200; 1855 Haight St; ☉ 10:30am-10pm Mon-Sat, 11am-9pm Sun), with SF's best selection of new and used CDs, or load up on vintage vinyl and guitars at **101 Records** (Map p96; ☎ 415-392-6369; 1414 Grant Ave; ☉ 10am-8pm Tue-Sat, noon-8pm Sun), the secret stash of Tom Waits, Carlos Santana and local DJs.

In the Mission, Valencia St between 16th and 24th Sts features locally designed clothing, Mexican folk art and pirate supplies at **826 Valencia** (Map p115; ☎ 415-642-5905; www.826valencia.org; 826 Valencia; ☉ noon-6pm), where sales of eye patches,

anti-scurvy lemondrops and McSweeney's publications fund youth writing workshops. For more feel-good shopping, Castro's volunteer-run **Under One Roof** (Map p115; ☎ 415-503-2300; www.under oneroof.org; 518a Castro St; ☉ 10am-9pm) sells gifts donated by local businesses, with 100% of proceeds donated to AIDS service organizations ($11 million to date). But to feel *really* good about your purchase, try **Good Vibrations** (Map p115; ☎ 415-522-5460; 603 Valencia St) for sex-positive adult toys – Margaret Cho's on the board, so you know they're not shy.

Sporty types can gear up before they split town near Golden Gate Bridge at **Sports Basement** (Map p105; ☎ 415-437-0100; www.sportsbasement.com; 610 Mason St; ☉ 9am-9pm Mon-Fri, 8am-8pm Sat & Sun),

SAN FRANCISCO

SHOPPING

SABRINA DALBESIO

101 Records, North Beach

GAY & LESBIAN SAN FRANCISCO

The mothership of gay culture, San Francisco is America's pinkest city, the easiest place in the US to be gay and where 'mos are accepted as part of mainstream society. (Remember, this is where gay marriage first became reality in the US.)

The intersection of 18th and Castro Sts is the heart of the gay scene, and there are bars a go-go, but most are predictably middlebrow. Dancing queens and slutty boys head South of Market (SoMa), the location of most thump-thump clubs and sex venues. Check Get Your Girl On (http://gogetyourgirlon.com) for concerts and parties; or plug into the A-gay scene on Betty's List (www.bettyslist.com). The *San Francisco Bay Times* (www.sfbaytimes.com) has good resources for transsexuals; the *Bay Area Reporter* (aka BAR; www.ebar.com) has gay news and listings.

BARS

The place on Sunday afternoons, the Eagle Tavern (Map p96; ☎ 415-626-0880; www.sfeagle.com; 398 12th St) serves all-you-can-drink beer ($10) from 3pm to 6pm. Wear leather and blend right in.

In the Castro, cologne-wearing 20-somethings (and gay-boy-loving straight girls) queue up to dance in the light of flickering videos at Badlands (Map p115; ☎ 415-626-9320; 4121 18th St) – if you're over 30, you'll feel old. A better bet for cocktails is see-and-be-seen Blackbird (Map p115; ☎ 415-503-0630; 2124 Market St); wear a tight T-shirt.

For *grlz,* the Mission-hipster spot is Lexington Club (Map p115; ☎ 415-863-2052; www.lexingtonclub.com; 3464 19th St), which has SF's best bathroom graffiti. Softball dykes go to off-the-beaten-path Wild Side West (☎ 415-647-3099; 424 Cortland St), but boys come to gab in the lush garden.

CLUBS

Juanita More (www.juanitamore.com) throws fierce parties attended by sexy boys (especially on Pride). Cockblock (www.cockblocksf.com), at the Rickshaw Stop (Map p96; ☎ 415-861-2011; www.rickshawstop.com; 155 Fell St), draws a happening gay-boy-and-girl crowd the second Saturday of the month. Fresh (http://freshsf.com), at Ruby Skye (p114), is the monthly circuit party. For gay salsa try Cafe Cocomo (p116) on the third Friday of the month.

Ladies: log on to Craigslist (www.craigslist.org) and click on women-seeking-women to search for monthly parties or post a query. Mango, from 3pm to 9pm the fourth Saturday of the month at El Rio (Map p115; ☎ 415-282-3325; www.elriosf.com; 3158 Mission St), is blazing hot. Hit the Lexington Club (see above) to inquire about roving-party Flourish – when dykes actually dress up. Hipster gals pack Stay Gold the last Wednesday of the month at the Make-Out Room (Map p115; ☎ 415-647-2888; www.makeoutroom.com; 3225 22nd St).

which sells every conceivable shoe and rents ski gear. Go for big air and big style from local maker **SFO Snowboarding & FTC Skateboarding** (Map p102; ☎ 415-626-1141; www.sfosnow.com; 1630 Haight St; ⏲ 11am-7pm).

GETTING THERE & AROUND

AIR
The Bay Area has three airports: **San Francisco International Airport** (SFO; ☎ 650-821-8211, 800-435-9736; www.flysfo.com), 15 miles south of the city via Hwy 101 or I-280; **Oakland International Airport** (OAK; ☎ 510-563-3300; www.flyoakland.com), 12 miles southeast, via the Bay Bridge and I-880; and **San Jose International Airport** (SJC; ☎ 408-277-4759; www.sjc.org), 45 miles south.

TO/FROM THE AIRPORTS
Take **Bay Area Rapid Transit** (BART; ☎ 415-989-2278; www.bart.gov) directly from SFO or OAK into Downtown San Francisco ($8.10, 30 minutes).

Taxis charge about $40 to $45 for a trip into the city, plus 15% gratuity.

Door-to-door shuttle vans leave the departures level outside terminals. Try **Lorrie's** (☎ 415-334-9000; www.gosfovan.com) and **Super Shuttle** (☎ 415-558-8500; www.supershuttle.com). Fares are about $15. Call ahead for city pick-ups.

Buses are cheapest. From SFO, take **SamTrans** (☎ 800-660-4287; www.samtrans.org) express-bus KX (adult $4.50, 30 minutes) or bus 292 ($1.75, 60 minutes); buses depart from the lower level.

For services from OAK, reserve 48 hours ahead with **Bayporter Express** (☎ 415-467-1800; www.bayporter.com; 1st passenger $32, each additional passenger $15).

To get from SJC to San Francisco, take the **Valley Transit Authority** (VTA; ☎ 408-321-2300; www.vta.org) bus 10, the Airport Flyer ($1.75), to the Santa Clara Caltrain Station and ride the train to San Francisco ($7.75).

BUS
Intercity buses operate from the **Transbay Terminal** (Map p97; 425 Mission St at 1st St). Take **AC Transit** (☎ 510-891-4700; www.actransit.org) to the East Bay, **Golden Gate Transit** (☎ 415-455-2000; www.goldengate.org) to Marin and Sonoma counties, and **SamTrans** (☎ 800-660-4287; www.samtrans.org) buses to points south.

Greyhound (☎ 415-495-1575, 800-231-2222; www.greyhound.com) operates nationwide buses; see p391 for more details about intra-California routes. Some typical one-way fares are: San Francisco to LA $39 to $50; SF to Santa Cruz $12 to $18; and SF to Arcata $42 to $56.

TRAIN
CalTrain (☎ 800-660-4287; www.caltrain.com; cnr 4th & Townsend Sts) operates commuter lines down the peninsula. MUNI's N-Judah streetcar line serves the station.

Amtrak (☎ 800-872-7245; www.amtrak.com) stops in Emeryville and Oakland, with connecting bus services to San Francisco's Ferry Building. Trains depart for Sacramento, Los Angeles and the east. For details about intra-California routes and fares, see p394.

CAR & MOTORCYCLE
Avoid driving; parking in SF is trying. When parallel parking on hills, back your wheels against the curb or face fines.

PUBLIC TRANSPORTATION
MUNI (☎ 415-673-6864; www.sfmuni.com) runs buses, streetcars and cable cars. Buses cost $2, cable cars $5 (or $10 all day). Transfers are valid for three trips within 90

SAN FRANCISCO

GETTING THERE & AROUND

SABRINA DALBESIO

Ferry Building Farmers Market

SAN FRANCISCO FARMERS MARKETS

Ferry Building (Map p96; www.cuesa.org; ⏰ 10am-2pm Tue & Thu, 8am-2pm Sat; ♿) California-grown produce, meat, seafood and eggs, plus local artisan cheeses, chocolates, olive oils and other gourmet foods. There's an excellent range of organics and sustainably harvested foods at moderate to premium prices.

Alemany (www.sfgov.org/site/alemany; 100 Alemany Blvd; ⏰ 6am-4pm Sat; ♿) Since 1945, this city-run market has been the place to go for local produce, with flowers, fish, eggs and food stalls for ready-to-eat foods. Expect bargain prices and a good range of organics and sustainably harvested foods.

Heart of the City (Map p96; UN Plaza; ⏰ 7am-4pm Wed, to 5pm Sun; ♿) Sell local produce, including an excellent selection of lesser-known varietals, plus prepared food stalls. Bargain prices, some organics.

Island Earth (Map p96; www.islandearthfarmersmarket.org; Yerba Buena Gardens entrance, lower level, Metreon; ⏰ 10am-7pm or 8pm) With local produce, food artisans and wine tasting. It's indoors and occasionally has a live DJ. Some organics, moderate prices.

minutes, except on cable cars. Buy multi-day passes at the Visitors Information Center or Union Sq TIX kiosk (p116). Children under four travel free; there's a discount for youths aged five to 17 years.

BART (☎ 415-989-2278; www.bart.gov) runs trains under Market and Mission Sts, linking San Francisco and the East Bay. Fares start at $1.75 (children under 4 years travel free).

TAXI
Taxi fares start at $3.10 for the first fifth of a mile and cost $0.45 per fifth of a mile thereafter. Be warned: taxis are almost impossible to find during the Friday evening rush. You can hail taxis on the street, or your hotel doorman will call one for you (for a tip).

HIGHLIGHTS

1 REDWOODS

The tallest living things on Earth, coast redwoods (Sequoia sempervirens) are found in a narrow, 450-mile-long strip along California's coast between Big Sur and southern Oregon. They can live for 2200 years, grow to 378ft tall and achieve a diameter of 22ft at the base, with bark up to 12in thick. Below the skyward canopies lie subtropical rainforests: primeval ferns, moss-covered decay, rooted fungi and psychedelic banana slugs.

↘ OUR DON'T MISS LIST

❶ MUIR WOODS NATIONAL MONUMENT

Don't have five hours to drive up the Northern California coast from San Francisco? Marin County's very own redwood grove (p144) is less than 30 minutes from the Golden Gate Bridge and is every bit as stunning as the Humboldt and Mendocino redwoods. Hint: leave the forest floor (and crowds) behind for the 3.4-mile-long Ocean View to Lost Trail, hiking about 1½ to two hours.

❷ REDWOOD NATIONAL PARK

Encompassing a vast area in the northern reaches of Humboldt County up to Del Norte County and the Oregon border is this most wild of redwood parklands. Although much of it is too remote for a visit, its most beautiful area – Lady Bird Johnson Grove – is in easy reach. Hike far enough back, however, and you might run into Ewoks (the planet of Endor was filmed here). See p168 for more.

Clockwise from top: Muir Woods National Monument (p144); Redwood Park (p165), Arcata; Humboldt Redwoods State Park (p156); Shrine Drive-through Tree (p159), Myers Flat, Avenue of the Giants

❸ AVENUE OF THE GIANTS

Skirting Hwy 101 just north of Garberville is the Avenue of the Giants (p156), a 32-mile-long scenic alternative through this park with several freeway connections. You don't even have to leave your car to experience the grandeur of the redwoods. In fact, you can drive through one in Myers Flat.

❹ PRAIRIE CREEK STATE PARK

Just past adorable Trinidad is the locals' favorite redwood park, Prairie Creek (p169), part of Redwood National Park. The must-see area is Fern Canyon, where its lush jungle conditions served as the perfect backdrop for *Jurassic Park II*. If that wasn't enough, throw in an elk preserve, windswept beach and 75 miles of hiking trails.

❺ ARCATA COMMUNITY FOREST

No need to retreat to a national park for banana slugs, jurassic ferns and giant redwoods – they're all here. The state's first city-owned parkland (p165) offers miles of trails for hikers and mountain bikers (and the occasional hippie living in a tree house or makeshift yurt).

❧ THINGS YOU NEED TO KNOW

Hiking safety Conditions can be treacherous – washed out hiking trails, rapidly rising tides, rushing rivers. Check in with a ranger first **Know before you go** It's true; your tongue really does go numb if you lick a banana slug

HIGHLIGHTS

2

⤡ MARIN HEADLANDS

Over the course of just one day, become a candy-striper for seals at the **Marine Mammal Center** (p140); watch majestic hawks and raptors glide the Marin coast at **Hawk Hill** (p137); bundle up for a stroll on black-sand **Rodeo Beach** (p140); and sleep it all off at the **HI Marin Headlands Hostel** (p140).

3

⤡ POINT REYES

Wander through town for a stroll, grab some cheese and picnic supplies at **Tomales Bay Foods & Cowgirl Creamery** (p145), and head out to the **Point Reyes National Seashore** (p146) to watch whales blow by in the late winter. Spend the afternoon **kayaking** (p147) in nearby Tomales Bay. Are you really only 1½ hours from San Francisco?

THE BAY AREA & NORTHERN CALIFORNIA

HIGHLIGHTS

4

◥ COASTAL HIGHWAY 1

Alfred Hitchcock meets Jane Austen on the Sonoma Coast (p149). State parks along rocky beaches, world-class dining and will-you-marry-me romantic inns add up to a one- or two-day Northern California coastal adventure. The beaches can be treacherous, though, for the most part, the birds are rather docile.

5

◥ FERNDALE

Is it possible to pinch an entire town on the cheek? Between the southern and northern redwood parks, Victorian Ferndale (p159) is so drippingly perfect that it's often used as a film location. One-of-a-kind shops, unique events and 'butterfat mansion' B&Bs make Ferndale a picturesque base from which to explore Humboldt County and the redwoods.

6

◥ MT SHASTA

Most folks who come to California stay within a few miles of the Pacific Ocean. But those willing to make the trek inland won't be disappointed by snow-covered Mt Shasta (p170). A sacred site for Native Americans for centuries (and, more recently, for new-agers), the stand-alone mountain is especially impressive because of its relative isolation.

2 JOHN ELK III; 3 LEE FOSTER; 4 ANDERS BLOMQVIST; 5 WITOLD SKRYPCZAK; 6 NICHOLAS PAVLOFF

2 Rodeo Beach (p140), Marin Headlands; 3 Kayaking at Tomales Bay, Point Reyes National Seashore (p146);
4 Sonoma Coast State Beach (p149); 5 'Butterfat mansions' in Ferndale (p159); 6 North face of Mt Shasta (p170)

BEST...

HIPPIE EXPERIENCES

- **Real Goods Solar Living Center** (p156) Minutes off Hwy 101 is the original sustainability store and solar-education center.
- **Green Gulch Farm & Zen Center** (p145) Day, weekend and long-term retreats and a guesthouse.
- **Kinetic Grand Championship** (p161) The three-day, 40-mile homemade-kinetic-contraption race where one rule is to travel with a teddy bear at all times.
- **CCAT House** (p165) A leading pioneer in the sustainable movement.

SHOPPING

- **Sausalito** (p140) Take the ferry to the Bay Area's fave vacation village.
- **Mendocino** (p152) One-of-a-kind shops line the downtown drag.
- **Ferndale** (p159) Handmade iron-works and a general store in a darling town.
- **Berkeley** (p130) Incense, books, college sweatshirts and water pipes.

PLACES TO TAKE KIDS

- **Bay Area Discovery Museum** (p141) Parents will enjoy the cove's view of the bay; preschoolers will love the hands-on exhibits.
- **Marine Mammal Center** (p140) Who doesn't love to watch cute baby seals get nursed to health?
- **Bodega Bay Cycles** (p148) Will rent kids bikes and direct you to a few easier rides.

OUTDOOR ADVENTURES

- **Salt Point State Park** (p151) Wild berries, rough-and-tumble coastline and animal species galore.
- **Lava Beds National Monument** (p174) Stark, moonlike landscapes, cave tours, and 10,000-year-old rock paintings and petroglyphs.
- **Mt Shasta** (p170) Worth the haul, if you're into that whole stunningly gorgeous mountain wilderness thing.

LEFT: JUDY BELLAH; RIGHT: JOHN ELK III

Left: Kinetic Grand Championship (p161), Arcata; Right: Waterfront houses, Sausalito (p140)

THINGS YOU NEED TO KNOW

⌲ VITAL STATISTICS

- Area codes ☎ North Coast 707; ☎ Berkeley 510; ☎ Marin 415; ☎ Shasta 530

⌲ LOCALITIES IN A NUTSHELL

- Sausalito and Tiburon (p140; p143) Houseboats, mansions, tourists, views.
- Sonoma Coast (p149) Only two to three hours from the Bay Area but the unmanicured landscape feels a world apart.
- Mendocino (p152) Sleep peacefully in your countryside B&B for a big day of beachcombing or window shopping for art.
- Arcata (p164) The first American city with a majority Green Party city council.

⌲ ADVANCE PLANNING

- Two months before Research outdoor activities and buy whatever gear you need.
- One month before Make your reservations at Chez Panisse (p134).
- Two weeks before Call ahead to reserve tours at the Marine Mammal Center (p140).

⌲ RESOURCES

- Redwood National and State Parks (www.nps.gov/redw) Official information.
- Muir Woods National Monument (www.nps.gov/muwo) Plan your visit in advance.
- Marin Headlands (www.parks conservancy.org) Info on Marin Headlands and Golden Gate National Parks.

⌲ GETTING AROUND

- Walking The best way to explore compact downtown areas.
- Ferry From San Francisco, the best way to visit Sausalito (p140) or Tiburon (p143).
- Bus Not convenient for the further reaches, but a great way to reach Muir Woods.
- Car Will allow you the most freedom to explore the redwoods and coast.

⌲ BE FOREWARNED

- Tidepools Read posted information or online guides to ensure you don't hurt the fragile ecosystem.
- Coast Many people have been killed, both on- and offshore. Watch your step while hiking, and keep an eye on riptides, sharks and storms.

THE BAY AREA & NORTHERN CALIFORNIA ITINERARIES

BAY AREA TOUR Three Days

One of the biggest mistakes folks make when visiting San Francisco is to stay in the city. Thirty minutes from downtown San Francisco and you can be in some of the most beautiful coastal areas in the state. First, head to the **(1) Marin Headlands** (p137), where you can frolic with hawks (p137) and recovering elephant seals (p140). Take a ferry to **(2) Sausalito** (p140) or **(3) Tiburon** (p143) on day two for lunch and art-gallery hopping. On your third day, take BART (p135) to the East Bay and **(4) Berkeley** (p130), where a trip up the Campanile on the UC Berkeley campus will give you a bird's-eye view of why you came to the Bay Area.

SEE THE REDWOODS Five Days

Don't let the distance scare you off; visiting the redwoods is an easy trip from the Bay Area in five days (or even less). To save time, take Hwy 101 instead of the coast. Stop first in **(1) Hopland** (p155) to take a crash course on sustainable technology at the Real Goods Solar Living Center (p156), then in **(2) Ukiah** (p156) for a peaceful lunch in the City of Ten Thousand Buddhas, before sleeping at the equally peaceful Benbow Inn. The next day you'll enter the **(3) Southern Redwood Coast** (p156) with a drive through Avenue of the Giants. You can spend an entire day hiking the area, but be sure to reach **(4) Ferndale** (p159) by nightfall to stay in one of the adorable town's 'butterfat mansion' B&Bs. Spend the next day in **(5) Arcata** (p164), a university town where the smell of biodiesel fuel and patchoulis hang in the air. The town's community forest (p165) is a quick stroll from downtown. At night, grab a salami, brie and apricot-jam pizza at Folie Douce (p166) and soak away your hike at the Finnish Country Sauna & Tubs (p165). Spend the rest of your time on the **(6) Northern Redwood Coast** (p168), hiking the moss-covered Fern Canyon (p169) or admiring the giant redwoods in Lady Bird Johnson Grove (p168).

ROMANTIC COAST One Week

Start your romantic journey up the coast in (1) Sausalito (p140) at the romantic Cavallo Point (p142) lodge, where you're likely to en-counter deer on your walk to one of the lectures in the deconsecrated chapel (the hotel is at the former Fort Baker military site). Head up the coast to (2) Muir Beach (p145) for a cozy lunch at The Pelican Inn English pub. Cross the county line into the Sonoma Coast, where you'll find the gorgeous (3) Salt Point State Park (p151) and the Kruse Rhododendron State Natural Reserve, where you'll be rewarded by

more than a bouquet of flowers; you'll be greeted by an entire forest filled with brilliantly pink rhododendron blossoms each May. Head to dinner in (4) Elk (p152) at La Petite Rive, a romantic, middle-of-nowhere destination restaurant. Spend the night in (5) Mendocino (p152) at one of their dozens and dozens of B&Bs.

DISCOVER THE BAY AREA & NORTHERN CALIFORNIA

Lift the lid on many left-of-center trends and you'll find the Bay Area & Northern California bubbling contentedly underneath. From organic cuisine to the first majority Green Party city council in the US, the northern third of California has a knack for pioneering change.

But Northern California is so much more than its politics. In the Bay Area, window-shopping in the ritzy seaside towns of Sausalito or Tiburon is just a bike ride or ferry across the San Francisco Bay. Nonconformist Berkeley serves up biodiesel refueling stations and one of the country's top-rated restaurants. The Coastal Hwy 1 towns from Bodega Bay to Mendocino marry romantic B&B weekends with stretches of isolated beaches and state parks. Keep going to reach Victorian Ferndale's strip of 'butterfat mansions' and shops, or tour hippie Arcata's sustainable technology house. Along the coast, you can hike below forested canopies, from Marin County's Muir Woods to just about anywhere along the Redwood Coast further north.

BERKELEY

pop 101,500

As the birthplace of the Free Speech and disability rights movements, and the home of the hallowed halls of the University of California, Berkeley is no bashful wallflower. A national hot spot of (mostly left-of-center) intellectual discourse and one of the most vocal activist populations in the country, this infamous college town has an interesting mix of graying progressives and idealistic undergrads. It's easy to stereotype 'Berserkeley' for some of its recycle-or-else PC crankiness, but the city is often on the forefront of environmental and political issues that eventually go mainstream.

INFORMATION

UC Berkeley Visitor Services Center (☎ 510-642-5215; www.berkeley.edu/visitors; 101 University Hall, 2200 University Ave) Campus maps and information are available. Free 90-minute campus tours are given at 10am Monday to Saturday and 1pm Sunday.

SIGHTS & ACTIVITIES

UNIVERSITY OF CALIFORNIA, BERKELEY

The Berkeley campus of the University of California (UCB, called 'Cal' by both students and locals) is the oldest university in the state. The decision to found the college was made in 1866, and the first students arrived in 1873. Today UCB has more than 30,000 students, more than 1000 professors and more Nobel laureates than you could point a particle accelerator at.

From Telegraph Ave, enter the campus via Sproul Plaza and Sather Gate, a center for people-watching, soapbox oration and pseudotribal drumming. Or you can enter from Center St and Oxford Lane, near the downtown BART station.

The **Campanile** (⏰ 10am-3.45pm Mon-Fri, to 4.45pm Sat, to 1:30pm & 3-4.45pm Sun), which is officially called Sather Tower, was modeled on St Mark's Basilica in Venice.

THE BAY AREA & NORTHERN CALIFORNIA

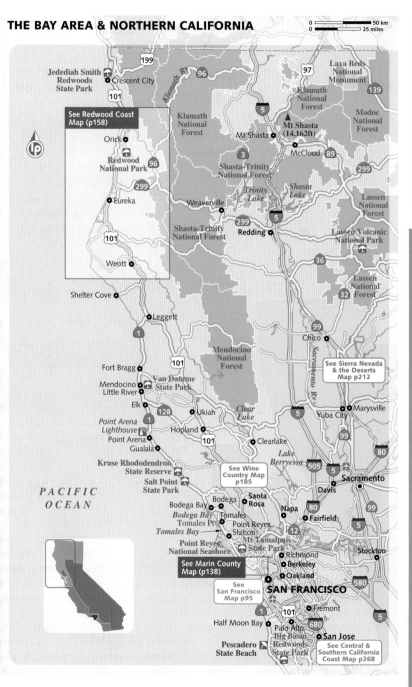

CENTRAL BERKELEY

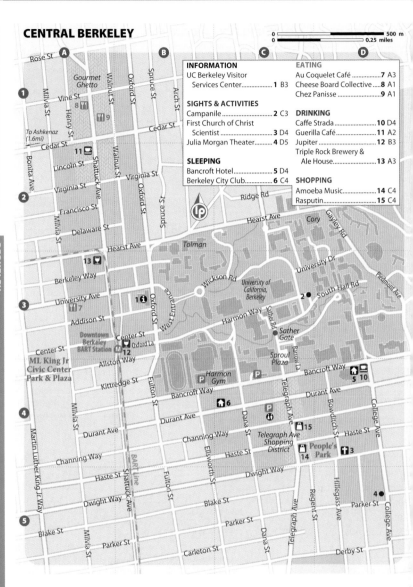

INFORMATION
UC Berkeley Visitor
Services Center.................. **1** B3

SIGHTS & ACTIVITIES
Campanile **2** C3
First Church of Christ
Scientist **3** D4
Julia Morgan Theater......... **4** D5

SLEEPING
Bancroft Hotel.................... **5** D4
Berkeley City Club.............. **6** C4

EATING
Au Coquelet Café **7** A3
Cheese Board Collective **8** A1
Chez Panisse **9** A1

DRINKING
Caffe Strada **10** D4
Guerilla Café **11** A2
Jupiter **12** B3
Triple Rock Brewery &
Ale House........................ **13** A3

SHOPPING
Amoeba Music.................... **14** C4
Rasputin............................ **15** C4

The 328ft spire offers fine views of the Bay Area, and at the top you can stare up into the carillon of 61 bells, ranging from the size of a cereal bowl to that of a Volkswagen. Recitals take place daily at 7:50am, noon and 6pm, with a longe piece performed at 2pm on Sunday.

SOUTH OF CAMPUS

Telegraph Avenue is undeniably the throbbing heart of studentville in Berkeley the sidewalks crowded with undergrads, postdocs and youthful shoppers squeezing their way past throngs of vendors, buskers and homeless people. Numerous cafes and budget food options cater to students, and most of them are very good.

On the park's southeast end stands Bernard Maybeck's impressive 1910 **First Church of Christ Scientist** (☎ 510-845-7199; 2619 Dwight Way; ✆ services Sun), which uses concrete and wood in its blend of arts-and-crafts, Asian and Gothic influences. Maybeck was a professor of architecture at UC Berkeley and designed San Francisco's Palace of Fine Arts, plus many landmark homes in the Berkeley Hills. Free tours happen the first Sunday of every month at 12:15pm.

To the southeast of the park is the beautifully understated, redwood-infused 1910 **Julia Morgan Theater** (☎ 510-845-8542; 2640 College Ave), a performance space (formerly a church) created by Bay Area architect Julia Morgan, who designed numerous Bay Area buildings and, most famously, the Hearst Castle (see p297).

NORTH BERKELEY

Not too far north of campus is a neighborhood filled with lovely garden-front homes, parks and an incredible concentration of some of the best restaurants in California. The popular **Gourmet Ghetto** stretches along Shattuck Ave north of University Ave for several blocks, anchored by Chez Panisse.

SLEEPING

our pick **Berkeley City Club** (☎ 510-848-7800; www.berkeleyhistorichotel.com; 2315 Durant Ave; r/ste incl breakfast from $145/235; 🖳 🛜) Designed by Julia Morgan, the architect of Hearst Castle, the 36 rooms in this 1929 historic landmark building were recently remodeled, and the entire premises

(which is also a private club) feels like a glorious time warp back to a more refined era. A full-time gardener tends the lush and serene Italianate courtyards, gardens and terraces, and the indoor pool is stunning. Elegant old-world rooms contain no TVs, and those with numbers ending in 4 and 8 have to-die-for views of the bay and the Golden Gate Bridge.

Bancroft Hotel (☎ 510-549-1000, 800-549-1002; www.bancrofthotel.com; 2680 Bancroft Way; r incl breakfast $149; 🛜) A gorgeous 1928 arts-and-crafts building that was originally a women's club, it's just across the street from campus and two blocks from Telegraph Ave. It has 22 comfortable, beautifully furnished rooms.

EATING

Jackpot! Telegraph Ave is packed with cafes, pizza counters and cheap restaurants, and Berkeley's Little India runs along the University Ave corridor. Many more restaurants can be found downtown along Shattuck Ave near the BART station.

Au Coquelet Café (☎ 510-845-0433; 2000 University Ave; mains $6-9; ✆ 6am-1am Mon-Fri, 7am-1am Sat & Sun) Open till late, Au Coquelet is a popular stop for postmovie meals or late-night studying (no wi-fi here, though). The front section serves coffee and cafe pastries, while the skylit and spacious back room does a big range of omelets, pastas, sandwiches, burgers and salads.

Cheese Board Collective (☎ 510-549-3183; 1504 & 1512 Shattuck Ave; pizza slice $2.55; ✆ 7am-1pm Mon, 7am-6pm Tue-Fri, 8.30-5pm Sat) Stop in to take stock of the more than 300 cheeses available at this worker-owned business and scoop up some fresh bread to make a picnic lunch. Or sit down for a slice of the fabulously crispy one-option-per-day veggie pizza just next door, where live music's often featured.

Chez Panisse (☎ **restaurant 510-548-5525, cafe 510-548-5049; 1517 Shattuck Ave; restaurant prix fixe excl alcohol $65-95, cafe mains $18-28;** **restaurant dinner Mon-Sat, cafe lunch & dinner Mon-Sat**) Foodies come to worship here at the church of Alice Waters, the inventor of California cuisine. The restaurant is as good and popular as it ever was, and despite its fame the place has retained a welcoming atmosphere. It's in a lovely arts-and-crafts house and you can choose to pull all the stops with a prix fixe meal downstairs, or go less expensive and a tad less formal in the cafe upstairs. Reserve weeks ahead.

DRINKING

our pick **Guerilla Café** (☎ **510-845-2233; 1620 Shattuck Ave**) Exuding a retro 1970s flavor, this small and sparkling cafe has a creative political vibe, with polka-dot tiles on the counter handmade by one of the artist-owners and order numbers spotlighting guerrillas and liberation revolutionaries. Organic and fair trade ingredients feature in the breakfasts and panini sandwiches, and locally roasted Blue Bottle coffee is served. Occasional film screenings pack the place, as do live music or DJ sessions on some weekend afternoons.

Caffe Strada (**2300 College Ave;**) A popular, student-saturated hangout with an inviting shaded patio and strong espressos. Try the signature white-chocolate mocha.

Jupiter (**2181 Shattuck Ave**) This downtown pub has loads of regional microbrews, a beer garden, good pizza and live bands most nights. Sit upstairs for a bird's-eye view of bustling Shattuck Ave.

Triple Rock Brewery & Ale House (**1920 Shattuck Ave**) Opened in 1986, Triple Rock was one of the country's first brewpubs. The house beers and pub grub are quite good, and the antique wooden bar and rooftop sun deck are delightful.

ENTERTAINMENT

Berkeley has plenty of intimate live-music venues. Cover charges range from $5 to $20, and a number of venues are all-ages or 18 and over.

RICK GERHARTER

Sproul Plaza, University of California, Berkeley (p130)

Ashkenaz (☎ 510-525-5054; 1317 San Pablo Ave; 👶) Ashkenaz is a 'music and dance community center' attracting activists, hippies and fans of folk, swing and world music who love to dance (lessons offered).

SHOPPING

Branching off the UC campus, Telegraph Ave caters mostly to students. It hawks a steady dose of urban hippie gear, handmade sidewalk-vendor jewelry and headshop paraphernalia. Audiophiles will swoon over the music stores.

Amoeba Music (☎ 510-549-1125; 2455 Telegraph Ave) If you're a music junkie you might plan on spending a few hours at the original Berkeley branch of Amoeba Music, packed with massive quantities of new and used CDs, DVDs, cassettes and records (yes, lots of vinyl).

Rasputin (☎ 800-350-8700; 2401 Telegraph Ave) Also on Telegraph Ave, Rasputin is another large store full of new and used music releases.

GETTING THERE & AWAY

BART

The easiest way to travel between San Francisco, Berkeley, Oakland and other East Bay points is on **BART** (☎ 510-465-2278, 511; www.bart.gov). Trains run approximately every 10 minutes from 4am to midnight on weekdays, with limited service from 6am on Saturday and from 8am on Sunday.

To get to Berkeley, catch a Richmond-bound train to one of three BART stations: Ashby (Adeline St and Ashby Ave), Downtown Berkeley (Shattuck Ave and Center St) or North Berkeley (Sacramento and Delaware Sts).

TRAIN

Though **Amtrak** (☎ 800-872-7245) does stop in Berkeley, the shelter (University Ave and 3rd St) is not staffed and direct connections are few. More convenient is the nearby **Emeryville Amtrak station** (☎ 510-450-1081; 5885 Horton St), a few miles south of the Berkeley stop.

To reach Emeryville station from downtown Berkeley, take BART to the MacArthur station and from there take AC Transit bus 57 or the free Emery Go Round bus (BART Shopper or Powell route) to the train station.

SOUTH TO PESCADERO

Hwy 1 hugs the coast from San Francisco to Pescadero, and makes for a perfect day trip. State beaches and parks run the length of the coast between Half Moon Bay and Santa Cruz; all charge $10 per car. The following are in north to south order. **San Gregorio**, 10 miles south of Half Moon Bay, is a driftwood-strewn beauty with a long, sandy strand. Families stick to the main beach, where kids can build forts from branches washed down the little stream that meets the sand. Note: the northern end is private, charges a fee, and is gay and nude.

For a flashback to the Old West, turn inland on Rte 84 from San Gregorio beach and go 1 mile to the **San Gregorio General Store** (☎ 650-726-0565; www.san gregoriostore.com; Stage Rd; ⏱ 9am-6pm). It's the classic cowboy emporium, catering to local farmers and ranchers who drink booze at the counter. Endure their stares to browse Western hats, flannel shirts, crockery and woodstoves. We most love coming on Saturdays and Sundays when bluegrass and folk musicians jam; call ahead for schedules.

Five miles south of Pescadero, the stately **Pigeon Point Lighthouse** rises 115ft – the tallest lighthouse on the

San Gregorio State Beach (p135)

ANN CECI

Pacific Coast. The tower is indefinitely closed because of damage sustained during a major storm in 2001, but you can wander the base and sit on the picket-fence-lined viewing deck to whale-watch, March to May. Down below there's a small beach with little tidepools; in springtime gorgeous wildflowers bloom. The former lightkeeper's quarters are a popular hostel (see below).

our pick Año Nuevo State Reserve (☎ 650-879-0227; www.parks.ca.gov; per car $10), 10 miles south of Pigeon Point, is the breeding ground of hundreds of elephant seals that took over abandoned Año Nuevo Island. You can view them as they fight for dominance and submission, December to March, during which time reservations are essential for the 2½-hour, 3-mile guided walking tour ($7).

South of Año Nuevo on the inland side, look for **Swanton Berry Farm** (☎ 831-469-8804; www.swantonberryfarm.com; Hwy 1, 2mi north of Davenport; ☉ self-pick 8am-6pm), where in spring and summer you can pick the Bay Area's best organic straw-

berries or pop into an old-fashioned unstaffed **farmstand** (☉ 8am-6pm spring, 8am-8pm summer) for flats of berries, berry pie, strawberry lemonade and hot chocolate – leave your money in the little box. Families gather at the picnic tables on the grassy lawns. This is old-school Northern California at its very best.

SLEEPING & EATING

Pigeon Point Lighthouse (☎ 650-879-0633; www.norcalhostels.org/pigeon; 210 Pigeon Point Rd, Pescadero; dm $23-25, s/d/tr from $53/61/84; ☉ reception 7:30am-10:30pm; ☐ ☎) The sound of the ocean lulls you to sleep at this former lightkeeper's house. There's also a blufftop ocean-view hot tub. Cyclists are never turned away.

Costanoa (☎ 650-879-1100, 877-262-7848; www.costanoa.com; 2001 Rossi Rd, Pescadero; tent cabins without bath $115-175, cabins without bath $185-195, lodge r with bath $210-270, tents & RVs $40-65; ☎ ☒) Four miles south of Pigeon Point, Costanoa is part ecolodge, part campground, tucked between three state parks. Great for outdoor enthusiasts, it feels like summer camp for former hippies turned moms and dads, with hiking on gorgeous, wide-open hillsides and weekend activities such as yoga and horseback riding. Accommodations range from comfy lodge rooms (with bath) to our favorite retreatlike modern duplex cabins (without bath), to tiny tent cabins with heated mattresses.

MARIN COUNTY

Majestic redwoods cling to coastal hillsides, while the thundering surf carves new shapes into the cliffs. Miles of verdant trails crisscross the Point Reyes National Seashore, Muir Woods and Mt Tamalpais National Park. Marinites get outdoors every chance they get. But if there's one thing other than their intense love of the outdoors that binds the residents of Marin County, it's their equally passionate appreciation of the good life. And they can afford it. Marin is the 11th-wealthiest county in America, and locals pride themselves on their laid-back lifestyle. Towns may look like idyllic rural hamlets, but shops cater to cosmopolitan tastes – pity the naive restaurateur who tries to make a go of it using non-organic ingredients.

MARIN HEADLANDS

Immediately northwest of the Golden Gate Bridge, the rugged natural beauty of the Marin Headlands stands in stark contrast to Downtown San Francisco's towers, visible across the bay. Once you're hiking atop the rolling hills, beyond earshot of cars, you'll hear only cawing birds, crashing surf and wind whooshing through tall grass. With winter's rains the hills turn vibrant green; in summer they dry up and turn golden brown. Plan to hike, picnic, walk or mountain bike; there's also limited camping.

SIGHTS & ACTIVITIES

Every fall, migratory birds and raptors – including hawks, falcons and eagles – congregate at Hawk Hill. Because open water doesn't support the thermals that the birds need to stay aloft, they use the headlands to gain altitude for the 2-mile crossing of the Golden Gate. Bring binoculars. Go 1.8 miles up Conzelman Rd, park along the road and walk up the west side

---

DETOUR: BIG BASIN REDWOODS STATE PARK

Big Basin (☎ 831-338-8860; www.bigbasin.org; 21600 Big Basin Way, Boulder Creek; day-use fee per car $10) became California's first state park in 1902, following heated battles between conservationists and loggers. Many old-growth redwoods in this 25-sq-mile park in the Santa Cruz Mountains have stood more than 1500 years. The hiking is exceptional – primordial forests fragrant with fir, cedar and bay; fern-lined waterfalls and high-mountain overlooks.

You can access the park from Hwy 1 at Waddell Creek Beach, but it's a 13-mile-long, steep climb (1000ft elevation gain) via the Skyline-to-the-Sea Trail. The main entrance is off Hwy 236, which connects with Hwy 9 about 15 miles north of Santa Cruz. The park has 146 family campsites (☎ 800-444-7275; www.reserveamerica.com; campsites $35) and 36 tent cabins (☎ 800-874-8368; www.bigbasintentcabins.com; cabins $65) with two double-bed platforms and wood-burning stoves.

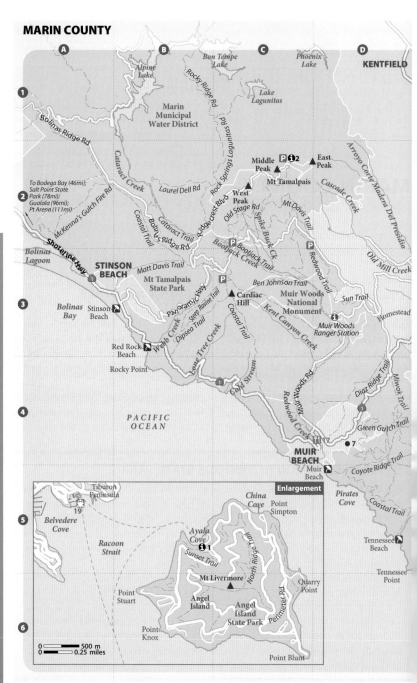

MARIN COUNTY

KENTFIELD

Alpine Lake

Bon Tempe Lake

Phoenix Lake

Rocky Ridge Rd

Marin Municipal Water District

Lake Lagunitas

Bolinas Ridge Rd

Cataract Creek

Rock Springs-Lagunitas Rd

Middle Peak

East Peak

Mt Tamalpais

Arroyo Corte Madera Del Presidio

West Peak

Laurel Dell Rd

Cascade Creek

To Bodega Bay (46mi);
Salt Point State
Park (78mi);
Gualala (96mi);
Pt Arena (111mi)

Ridgecrest Blvd

Old Stage Rd

Mt Davis Trail

Old Mill Creek

Coastal Trail

Cataract Trail

Bolinas Ridge Rd

McKenna's Gulch Fire Rd

Spike Buck Ck

Redwood Trail

Shoreline Hwy

Bolinas Lagoon

Bootjack Creek

Bootjack Trail

STINSON BEACH

Matt Davis Trail

Mt Tamalpais State Park

Ben Johnson Trail

Muir Woods National Monument

Sun Trail

Homestead

Bolinas Bay

Stinson Beach

Pan-Toll Hwy

Cardiac Hill

Kent Canyon Creek

Muir Woods Ranger Station

Red Rock Beach

Webb Creek

Steep Ravine Trail

Dipsea Trail

Coastal Trail

Lone Tree Creek

Rocky Point

Diaz Ridge Trail

Miwok Trail

PACIFIC OCEAN

Cold Stream

Redwood Creek

Muir Woods Rd

Green Gulch Trail

MUIR BEACH

Muir Beach

Coyote Ridge Trail

Pirates Cove

Coastal Trail

Enlargement

Tiburon Peninsula

China Cave

Point Simpton

Belvedere Cove

Ayala Cove

Racoon Strait

Sunset Trail

North Ridge Trail

Quarry Point

Tennessee Beach

Tennessee Point

Mt Livermore

Point Stuart

Angel Island

Angel Island State Park

Perimeter Rd

Point Knox

Point Blunt

0 — 500 m
0 — 0.25 miles

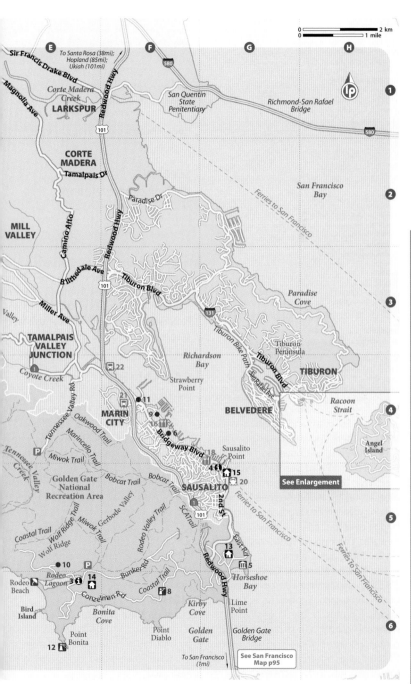

E

F

G

H

0   2 km
0   1 mile

Sir Francis Drake Blvd

To Santa Rosa (38mi);
Hopland (85mi);
Ukiah (101mi)

580

Magnolia Ave

Corte Madera
Creek

San Quentin
State
Penitentiary

Richmond-San Rafael
Bridge

580

LARKSPUR

Redwood Hwy

101

**CORTE
MADERA**

Tamalpais Dr

San Francisco
Bay

Paradise Dr

Ferries to San Francisco

**MILL
VALLEY**

Camino Alto

Redwood Hwy

Blithedale Ave

101

Tiburon Blvd

Paradise
Cove

Miller Ave

131

Valley

Tiburon Bike Path

Tiburon
Peninsula

Tiburon Blvd

**TAMALPAIS
VALLEY
JUNCTION**

Coyote Creek

1

22

Richardson
Bay

San Rafael Ave

TIBURON

Tennessee Valley Rd

Oakwood Trail

Strawberry
Point

BELVEDERE

Racoon
Strait

21

11

9

**MARIN
CITY**

16

6

Bridgeway Blvd

18

Sausalito
Point

Angel
Island

Tennessee
Creek

P

Marincello Trail

Miwok Trail

Bobcat Trail

Bobcat Trail

4

15

20

See Enlargement

**Golden Gate
National
Recreation Area**

Gerbode Valley

Rodeo Valley Trail

SAUSALITO

2nd St

101

Ferries to San Francisco

Coastal Trail

Wolf Ridge Trail

Miwok Trail

SCA Trail

Bunker Rd

East Rd

Ferries to San Francisco

Wolf Ridge

10

P

13

Redwood Hwy

Coastal Trail

Rodeo
Lagoon

3

14

Conzelman Rd

8

5

Rodeo
Beach

**Bird
Island**

**Bonita
Cove**

Point
Bonita

Point
Diablo

Kirby
Cove

Golden
Gate

Horseshoe
Bay

Lime
Point

Golden Gate
Bridge

12

To San Francisco
(1mi)

**See San Francisco
Map p95**

INFORMATION
Angel Island Visitors Center...**1** B5
East Peak Summit Visitors Center......................................**2** C2
Marin Headlands Visitors Center..**3** E6
Sausalito Visitors Center...**4** G5

SIGHTS & ACTIVITIES
Bay Area Discovery Museum..**5** G5
Bay Model Visitor Center..**6** F4
Green Gulch Farm & Zen Center...**7** D4
Hawk Hill..**8** F6
Heath Ceramics...**9** F4
Marine Mammal Center..**10** E5
Mike's Bikes...**11** F4
Plaza de Viña del Mar Park......................................(see 20)
Point Bonita Lighthouse...**12** E6
Sea Trek...(see 6)

SLEEPING
Cavallo Point..**13** G5
HI Marin Headlands Hostel..**14** E6
Hotel Sausalito...**15** G5
Lindisfarne Guest House...(see 7)
Pelican Inn...(see 17)
Waters Edge Hotel...(see 19)

EATING
Fish...**16** F4
Pelican Inn...**17** D4
Sam's Anchor Cafe...(see 19)
Sushi Ran..**18** G4

DRINKING
No Name Bar..(see 4)

TRANSPORT
Ferries to Angel Island & San Francisco......................**19** A5
Ferries to San Francisco..**20** G5
Muir Woods Shuttle (Marin County)..............................**21** F4
Muir Woods Shuttle (Mill Valley)....................................**22** F4

of the hill. For maps and details on which birds are there now, see www.ggro.org.

Near the end of Conzelman Rd is the still-operating Point Bonita Lighthouse (free tours at 12:30pm; 12:30-3:30pm Sat-Mon), a breathtaking half-mile walk from the parking area, ending at a suspension footbridge over the roiling surf (acrophobes beware). Looking west, the distant city skyline looks out of place.

The Marine Mammal Center (415-289-7325; www.tmmc.org; 4 Bunker Rd, admission free; 10am-4pm;), on the hill above Rodeo Lagoon, is the largest marine-mammal hospital in the world. In 2009 the center opened its all-green solar-powered hospital, with observation decks for visitors to get close to the recovering patients (mostly seals and sea lions) before they're released back into the wild. Spring brings oh-so-cute new pups – and the most visitors. Kids love the hands-on exhibits and see-through glass walls to the science labs and animal rooms.

At the end of Bunker Rd sits black-sand Rodeo Beach (ro-day-oh), protected from wind by cliffs.

SLEEPING

HI Marin Headlands Hostel (415-331-2777; www.norcalhostels.org/marin; Bldg 941, Fort Barry; dm/r $24/66; check-in 7:30am-11:30pm;) Set amid towering eucalyptus trees, this friendly, ecosensitive hostel has two parts: the main building (formerly a military infirmary), location of 76 dorm beds; and the cozier annex (formerly officers housing), location of most private rooms. Picture windows overlook the lush landscape. It has a good games room and offers easy access to hiking.

SAUSALITO

pop 7330

Sausalito is the first town you hit after crossing the Golden Gate. Perched above Richardson Bay, it's known for galleries, window-shopping and picture-postcard vistas of SF and Angel Island. And it's often sunny: the Headlands block the fog most days. However cute, though, Sausalito becomes a victim of its charm and beauty on summer weekends, when day-trippers jam the sidewalks, pricey shops and restaurants, and locals get stuck in heavy traffic.

SIGHTS

Plaza de Viña Del Mar Park, near the ferry terminal, has a fountain flanked by 14ft-tall elephant statues from the 1915 Panama–Pacific Exposition in San Francisco.

Until computers rendered obsolete the system at the **Bay Model Visitor Center** (☎ 415-332-3871; 2100 Bridgeway Blvd; suggested donation $3; ☼ 9am-4pm Tue-Fri, 10am-5pm Sat & Sun; ⚐), this enormous indoor 1.5-acre hydraulic model of the San Francisco Bay and delta helped scientists understand the effects of tides and currents on the land. A 24-hour period is represented in just 15 minutes. Look in the deepest water – under the Golden Gate Bridge – to grasp the force of tidal movement. This is a must-visit for geography buffs.

Famous **Heath Ceramics** (☎ 415-332-3732; www.heathceramics.com; 400 Gate Five Rd; ☼ 10am-5pm Sun-Wed, to 6pm Thu-Sat), founded by Edith Heath in the 1940s, crafts earthy tableware – and here it costs 30% off retail; free factory tours are offered weekends at 11am, Fridays at 12:30pm. Reservations requested.

Spread across a half-dozen former bunkers just under the Golden Gate Bridge, the **Bay Area Discovery Museum** (☎ 415-339-3900; www.baykidsmuseum.org; 557 McReynolds Rd; adult/child 1-17yr $8.50/7.50; ☼ 9am-4pm Tue-Fri, 10am-5pm Sat & Sun; ⚐) caters to the curious kindergarten set with hands-on science exhibits, musical instruments, festivals and camps.

ACTIVITIES

To get out on the bay, rent kayaks from **Sea Trek** (☎ 415-332-8494 weekdays, 415-332-4465 weekends; www.seatrekkayak.com; 85 Liberty Ship Way, Sausalito; s/d per hr $20/35; ☼ 9am-5pm), which also guides monthly summertime trips to Angel Island ($85).

Sausalito is also perfect for **cycling**. If you venture across the Golden Gate Bridge, note that cyclists generally use the western side, except on weekdays between 5am and 3:30pm when they must share the eastern side with pedestrians (who have the right of way). After 9pm, cyclists can still cross the bridge on the eastern side through a security gate. For more information on biking the Bay Area, contact the **San Francisco Bicycle Coalition** (☎ 415-431-2453; www.sfbike.org).

Mike's Bikes (☎ 415-332-3200; www.mikes bikes.com; 1 Gate Six Rd; 1/24hr $10/40), at the

ROBERTO GEROMETTA
Sea kayaking, Sausalito

northern end of Bridgeway Blvd near Hwy 101, rents road and mountain bikes. No reservations.

SLEEPING & EATING

Hotel Sausalito (☎ 415-332-4155; www.hotel sausalito.com; 16 El Portal; r $155-195, ste $265-285; ⌘ ☎) The guest rooms at this grand 1915 hotel are on the small side, but are decorated in soft golden and green hues, some with lovely stained-glass windows. Vouchers are provided for continental breakfast at the restaurant next door. Parking costs $12.

Cavallo Point (☎ 415-339-4700; www. cavallopoint.com; 601 Murray Circle; r from $275; ☎) Spread out over 45 acres of the Bay Area's most scenic park land, this brand-new buzz-worthy lodge flaunts a green focus, a full service spa and easy access to outdoor activities. Choose from richly renovated rooms in the landmark Fort Baker officers' quarters or more contemporary solar-powered accommodations with exquisite bay views (including a turret of the Golden Gate Bridge).

Sushi Ran (☎ 415-332-3620; www.sushiran. com; 107 Caledonia St; dishes $5-17; ☺ lunch Mon-Fri, dinner daily) One of the Bay Area's top sushi spots. A wine and sake bar ease the pain of long waits – and perhaps the bill.

Fish (☎ 415-331-3474; 350 Harbor Dr; mains $12-30; ☺ 11:30am-8:30pm; ☕) This kid-friendly dockside joint at the end of Harbor Rd hooks locals with sustainable, line-caught fish – some from their own boats – and down-home details like picnic-table seating and Mason-jar glasses. Sustainability has its price: the Saigon salmon sandwich will set you back $22 – but it's worth it. No credit cards.

DRINKING

No Name Bar (☎ 415-332-1392; 757 Bridgeway Blvd) Live bands play most nights at this old-school boho dive. During the daytime, feed the jukebox and kick back with a game of Pictionary. Cash only.

GETTING THERE & AWAY

We recommend taking a bike on the ferry from San Francisco to avoid awful week-

JUDY BELLAH

Serving up the catch of the day at Fish, Sausalito

end traffic. Driving to Sausalito from San Francisco, take the Alexander Ave exit (the first exit after the Golden Gate Bridge) and follow signs into Sausalito. There are five municipal parking lots in town – worth using as street-parking restrictions are strictly enforced.

Ferry is the ideal way to reach Sausalito. **Golden Gate Ferries** (☎ 415-923-2000; http://goldengateferry.org; one-way adult/child 6-18yr & senior $7.85/3.90) operate to and from the San Francisco Ferry Building nine times daily. **Blue & Gold Fleet** (☎ 415-773-1188; www.blueandgoldfleet.com; one-way adult/child 5-11yr $9.50/5.20) sails daily from San Francisco's Pier 41. Both take 30 minutes; bicycles are welcome on both services.

TIBURON

pop 8670

With a Lilliputian-sized Main St lined with clapboard buildings, Tiburon has retained more of the original wharf-rat vibe than its upper-crust neighbor to the west. Its name comes from the Spanish Punta de Tiburon (Shark Point). Take the ferry from San Francisco, browse the shops on Main St, grab a bite, and you've done Tiburon. The town is also the jumping-off point for nearby Angel Island.

SLEEPING & EATING

Waters Edge Hotel (☎ 415-789-5999; www.marinhotels.com/waters.html; 25 Main St; r $159-499; ⊠ ☎) This smart 23-unit hotel extends over the bay, and has a variety of room types and amenities. All rooms have crisp white bedspreads and balconies (limited views, except in suites); some have fireplaces. Those with wood ceilings are most atmospheric. There's complimentary in-room breakfast, and evening wine and cheese.

Sam's Anchor Cafe (☎ 415-435-4527; 27 Main St; dishes $10-25; ☻) Everyone wants an outdoor table but you can't reserve the bay-front patio at this way-popular seafood and burger shack – the town's oldest restaurant (look for the trapdoor that was used to spirit booze straight from ship to saloon). Good cioppino. Expect seagulls to alight tableside.

GETTING THERE & AWAY

Golden Gate Transit (☎ 415-923-2000; www.goldengatetransit.org) bus 10 travels daily from San Francisco (one-way adult/child 6-18yr & senior $3.95/1.95) and Sausalito (one-way $2/1) to Tiburon, via Mill Valley.

By car, on Hwy 101, look for the off-ramp for Tiburon Blvd, E Blithedale Ave and Hwy 131; driving east, it leads into town and intersects with Juanita Lane and Main St.

Blue & Gold Fleet (☎ 415-773-1188; www.blueandgoldfleet.com; one-way adult/child 5-11yr $9.50/5.25, bicycles free) sails daily from San Francisco's Pier 41 to Tiburon; ferries dock in front of Guaymas restaurant (5 Main St). From Tiburon, ferries connect to nearby Angel Island.

THE COAST

Unlike Marin's eastern side, the coast remains largely undeveloped. Craggy coves, rolling hills and sandy beaches extend northward from the Golden Gate, and the city feels a world away. A car gives you the most flexibility, but it's possible to take the bus to most of the destinations listed below (except Muir Beach). The **West Marin Stagecoach** (☎ 415-526-3239; www.marintransit.org; adult/child 6-18yr & senior $2/1) operates bus 61 daily from Marin City to Stinson Beach and Bolinas, via Panoramic Hwy and Mt Tam. Bus 68 operates daily from San Rafael to Point Reyes Station, via Sir Francis Drake Blvd. On Tuesday, Thursday and Saturday, bus 62 runs up the coast, from Stinson Beach to Point Reyes Station.

LEE FOSTER

Muir Woods National Monument

⬊ MUIR WOODS NATIONAL MONUMENT

Coastal redwoods are the Earth's tallest living things, and exist only on the California coast, from Santa Cruz to just over the Oregon border. Only 4% of the original forest remains, but you can explore a glorious old-growth stand at Muir Woods National Monument, 12 miles north of the Golden Gate Bridge. It gets crowded on weekends – come midweek if you can. Otherwise arrive early morning or late afternoon, when the tour buses have gone.

The 1-mile Main Trail Loop is easy, leading alongside Redwood Creek to 1000-year-old trees at Cathedral Grove; it returns via Bohemian Grove, where the park's tallest tree stands 254ft. The Dipsea Trail is a strenuous 2-mile hike to the top of aptly named Cardiac Hill, but it's possibly the most beautiful hike for views – a half-mile steep grade through lush, fern-fringed forest leads from the canyon to an exposed ridge, from which you can see Mt Tamalpais, the Pacific and San Francisco. Gorgeous. You can also trek to Stinson Beach if you're up for a longer stint.

The least stressful option – on you and the environment – is the Muir Woods Shuttle (☎ 415-923-2000; www.goldengatetransit.org; adult/child 6-18yr & senior $3/1) bus 66, which operates weekends and holidays, May to September, and runs about every 30 minutes from Marin City and Mill Valley, with limited service to the Sausalito ferry terminal. From Mill Valley, get the bus at Pohono St and Hwy 1; return trips from the woods drop passengers across the street at the Manzanita Park & Ride. Parking is free for shuttle users. From Marin City, pickup and drop-off is at Donahue St and Terners Dr, at the Gateway shopping center.

Things you need to know: ☎ 415-388-2595; www.nps.gov/muwo; adult/child under 16yr $5/free; ☀ 8am-sunset, call ahead

MUIR BEACH

The oh-so-English Tudor-style **Pelican Inn** (☎ 415-383-6000; www.pelicaninn.com; 10 Pacific Way; lunch $10-17, dinner $15-29) is Muir Beach's only commercial establishment. Its timbered restaurant and cozy pub are perfect for a pint and to warm up fireside on foggy days. The British fare is respectable, but nothing mind-blowing – it's the setting that's magical. Upstairs are seven luxe rooms (from $190), each individually decorated in Tudor style with cushy half-canopy beds.

About 2 miles north of the Hwy 1/Muir Woods Rd intersection, **Green Gulch Farm & Zen Center** (☎ 415-383-3134; www.sfzc.org/ggf; 1601 Shoreline Hwy) is a secluded Buddhist retreat above Muir Beach, with magnificent redwoods standing sentinel. Its Japanese-style **Lindisfarne Guest House** (r with shared bath $90-180) has 12 simple rooms surrounding a 30ft-tall atrium. Rates include buffet-style vegetarian meals.

STINSON BEACH

The premier beach along the Marin Coast draws big crowds on sunny weekends, when traffic through town grinds to a halt. The little bohemian village lacks sidewalks and locals amble around, often barefoot, without paying much mind to cars. Restaurants, inns, shops and bookstores line a short stretch of Hwy 1, but to bite into the local culture, drop by cafes, where you may hear jazz or spoken-word, sometimes simultaneously. Compared with other coastal towns, Stinson feels downright cosmopolitan – until the sun sets, that is.

About 3½ miles north of town on Hwy 1, climb the trails at **Audubon Canyon Ranch** (☎ 415-868-9244; www.egret.org; donations welcome; 10am-4pm Sat, Sun & holidays mid-Mar–mid-Jul;) to view great blue herons and snowy egrets feeding their newborn chicks in the treetops. The ranch supplies binoculars; from the hills you can watch these magnificent birds feed at low tide in the mudflats of **Bolinas Lagoon**.

POINT REYES STATION

An Old West patina clings to West Marin's small-town hub. Dominated by dairies and ranches, the region was invaded in the 1960s by artists, whose legacy remains in tie-dye shops and (ho-hum) galleries lining Main St. Plan to fuel up on gasoline and supplies.

A locavore's delight, **Osteria Stellina** (☎ 415-663-9988; 11285 Hwy 1; mains $13-20; 11:30am-2:30pm & 5-9pm Wed-Mon) is a cozy, heart-warming downtown bistro. Everything on the forward-thinking California menu is fresh, seasonal and often organic, from handmade *strozzapreti* (choke the priest) pasta to braised goat shoulder with herbed polenta. Don't skip the pastry chef's creamy and berry-licious desserts.

Tomales Bay Foods & Cowgirl Creamery (☎ 415-663-9335; 80 4th St; 10am-6pm Wed-Sun) stocks stellar picnic items. Cowgirl Creamery's famous organic, artisanal cheeses are made on the premises and run to about $20 a pound – splurge on the Mt Tam triple cream. Factory tours ($5; reservations recommended) are held at 11:30am on Friday. The attached Cowgirl Cantina serves a daily-changing menu of gourmet soups, sandwiches and salads.

Two miles south of Point Reyes Station in Olema, the **Bear Valley Inn** (☎ 415-663-1777; www.bearvinn.com; Sir Francis Drake Blvd & Bear Valley Rd; r $120-180, cottage $160-250;) has three snug B&B rooms inside a 1910 house, and a cottage that sleeps six. Breakfasts are organic and there's limitless nature at your doorstep. The owners knock off 15% if you cycle here – call for details on the 20-mile ride from the Larkspur ferry.

Twenty miles north of Point Reyes Station in tiny Marshall, Nick's Cove & Cottages (☎ 415-663-1033; http://nickscove.com; 23240 Hwy 1, Marshall; mains $14-30; 🕙 8am-9pm) is the area's only destination restaurant. Celeb chef Mark Franz runs the kitchen at this vintage 1930s roadhouse perched over Tomales Bay, with trophy heads mounted on knotty-pine walls and a roaring fireplace. Book a window table to bird-watch while you sup on impeccable seafood, grilled meats and local oysters – all sustainably farmed. Reservations essential. The adjoining cottages are expensive ($355 to $700), but oh-so romantic.

POINT REYES NATIONAL SEASHORE

On an entirely different tectonic plate from the mainland, the windswept peninsula of Point Reyes juts 10 miles out to sea and lures marine mammals, migratory birds and whale-watching tourists. In 1579 Sir Francis Drake landed here to repair his ship, the *Golden Hind*. In 1595 the *San Augustine* went down offshore, the first of scores of ships lost here; it was laden with luxury goods, including porcelain, and to this day bits of cargo wash up on shore. Even now, despite GPS systems, the dangerous waters and treacherous rocks still claim the occasional vessel, adding to the peninsula's mystique.

Point Reyes National Seashore, established by President Kennedy in 1963, includes 110 sq miles of pristine ocean beaches, wind-tousled ridgetops and diverse wildlife. With excellent hiking and camping, Point Reyes is one of the Bay Area's top day-trip excursions, and its surrounding villages make a romantic spot for a quick overnight stay. Bring warm clothing: even the sunniest days can quickly turn cold and foggy.

INFORMATION

The park headquarters, Bear Valley Visitor Center (☎ 415-464-5100; www.nps.

Point Reyes Lighthouse (p147)

EMILY RIDDELL

gov/pore; Bear Valley Rd, Olema; ☺ 9am-5pm Mon-Fri, 8am-5pm Sat & Sun) provides hiking maps, information and worthwhile exhibits.

SIGHTS & ACTIVITIES

ourpick Point Reyes Lighthouse (☎ 415-669-1534; ☺ 10am-4:30pm Thu-Mon) sits at the end of Sir Francis Drake Blvd atop a rocky promontory that gets buffeted by ferocious winds. It's one of the best spots for whale-watching along the coast (peak season happens January and March, with calving late April into May). The lighthouse sits 600ft below the headlands, down 308 steps, so that its light can shine below the fog that usually blankets the point. Be prepared for a steep downhill walk. The lens room and clockworks are open as conditions permit.

To explore the peninsula from the water, contact Point Reyes Outdoors (☎ 415-663-8192; www.pointreyesoutdoors.com; 11401 Hwy 1, Point Reyes Station; guided trips $85-110) or Blue Waters Kayaking (☎ 415-669-2600; www.bwkayak.com; guided trips $68-98, rentals $40-120), which has two locations, one in Inverness, the other in Marshall. The bird-watching at Tomales Bay is superb midwinter.

SLEEPING

Just off Limantour Rd, the rustic Point Reyes Hostel (☎ 415-663-8811; www.norcal hostels.org/reyes; off Limantour Rd; dm from $22; ☺ reception 7:30-10am & 4:30-9:30pm) lies in a secluded valley 2 miles from the ocean, and is surrounded by hiking trails. The one private room (from $64) is reserved for families traveling with a child under six.

NORTH COAST

Forget the sun-drenched vision of the Beach Boys' California – in lieu of bikinis and bright, sunny skies the North Coast has banks of spectral fog, towering redwoods and cliffs that drop into a menacing roar of surf. Forget the jammed freeways of Southern California; the northern stretch of the coast is traveled mostly on winding two-lane blacktop, where the biggest traffic problem is encountered behind a dawdling Winnebago. The further north you travel, the more dominant the landscape becomes, interrupted only by two-stoplight towns that are departure points for the wilds surrounding you.

Here, you don't have to go too far off-track to feel like you're in an overgrown set of *Land Of The Lost*. Sun dapples the forest floor beneath towering redwoods, lighting up bristly ferns and shaggy beds of moss. Sea lions and elephant seals laze upon crags jutting out of the Pacific, barking and braying; beneath them sea cucumbers, starfish and anemones cling to the rocks, despite the relentless surf. In winter, migrating whales breach offshore while eagles, falcons and vultures arc overhead.

Best of all, you're likely to have the place mostly to yourself. There's a libertarian spirit on the North Coast that only begrudgingly accepts interlopers, with weed farmers and hippies staking out territory next to logging companies; and though they don't get along, they cut each other a wide swath. Mostly though, this is a place to get lost, and in doing so, find the majesty of California's untamed coast.

COASTAL HIGHWAY 1

The snaking route that Hwy 1 takes along the North Coast is challengingly remote and *real:* white-knuckled drivers pass farms, fishing towns and hidden beaches, pausing on roadside pullouts where gusty cliffs overlook migrating whales. The drive takes four hours of daylight driving without stops. At night, and in the fog, it takes steely nerves and much longer.

BODEGA BAY
pop 1420

Bodega Bay is the first pearl in a string of sleepy fishing towns and the setting of Alfred Hitchcock's terrifying 1963 avian horror flick, *The Birds*. The skies are free from bloodthirsty gulls today, though you'd best keep an eye on the picnic. It's Bay Area weekenders who descend en masse on the bed and breakfasts and extraordinary state beaches.

SIGHTS & ACTIVITIES

Most views from the mainland are of the harbor, but the view of the ocean opens up at Bodega Head, 265ft above sea level, where windswept grassy hills drop into the churning surf. Among several easy hikes, the Bodega Head Trail around the point is the most rewarding. Look southward to spot Tomales Point, the northern tip of Point Reyes – which is geologically related to Bodega Head – and east across the harbor. On a clear day, the views are superb and it's an excellent place to scan the water for whales (seasonal). The wind promises to be fierce, so bring a kite from one of the shops lining Hwy 1. To reach Bodega Head, go west from Hwy 1 onto Eastshore Rd, then turn right at the stop sign onto Bay Flat Rd.

For an easy 8-mile ride to the headlands, get some wheels at Bodega Bay Cycles (☎ 707-875-2255; www.bodegabay cycles.com; 1580 Eastshore Rd; ⏲ 10am-6pm Mon & Wed-Sat, to 4pm Sun), a new bike shop that rents both adult and kids bikes. As an example, cruisers cost $9 per hour, $25 for a half-day. They also employ a full-time mechanic. Serious cyclists should inquire about exceptional rides in the area.

For high romance, arrange a horseback ride on the beach with Chanslor Riding Stables (☎ 707-875-3333; www.chanslor.com; 2660 Hwy 1; ⏲ 9am-5pm). Scenic group rides range from $30 to $70, though private tours can be arranged for a higher fee.

Make reservations for sportfishing charters and, from December to April,

JUDY BELLAH
Bodega Bay

popular whale-watching cruises. **Bodega Bay Sportfishing Center** (☎ 707-875-3344; www.bodegabaysportfishing.com; 1410b Bodega Bay Flat Rd), beside the Sandpiper Café, organizes full-day fishing trips ($75) and whale-watching excursions (adult/child $30/25). It also sells bait, tackle and fishing licenses, and can arrange harbor cruises. Outdoor activities are the major draw, but the renowned collection of modern Japanese prints and California works at the **Ren Brown Collection Gallery** (☎ 707-875-2922; www.renbrown.com; 1781 Hwy 1; ◐ 10am-5pm Wed-Sun) is a tranquil escape from the elements.

SLEEPING
Bodega Harbor Inn (☎ 707-875-3594; www. bodegaharborinn.com; 1345 Bodega Ave; r $80-155, cottages from $135; 🐾) Half-a-block inland from Hwy 1, surrounded by grassy lawns and furnished with both real and faux antiques, this modest blue-and-white shingled motel is the town's most economical option. Pets are allowed in some rooms for a fee of $15 plus security deposit of $50. Freestanding cottages have BBQs.

Chanslor Guest Ranch (☎ 707-875-2721; www.chanslorranch.com; 2660 Hwy 1; furnished tents & eco-cabins $100-175, r $265-340) A mile north of town, this working horse ranch has three rooms and options for upscale camping. Wildlife programs and guided horse tours make this one sweet place, with sweeping vistas across open grasslands to the sea.

EATING & DRINKING
Spud Point Crab Company (☎ 707-875-9472; 1860 Bay Flat Rd; dishes $4-10; ◐ 9am-5pm Thu-Tue; 🧒) In the classic tradition of dockside crab shacks, Spud Point makes sandwiches and salty-sweet crab cocktails served at picnic tables overlooking the marina. Take Bay Flat Rd to get here.

TOP FIVE COZY & CREATIVE EATS ON THE NORTH COAST

- **Terrapin Creek Café & Restaurant** Inventive California cuisine that explodes with freshness (see below)
- **Franny's Cup & Saucer** Baked goods to die for and elegant summer brunches (p150)
- **Cafe Beaujolais** Mendocino's top dining room serves a local, organic and sustainable menu (p154)
- **La Petite Rive** Tiny and intimate, this is the North Coast's most romantic dining experience (p152)
- **3 Foods Cafe** A menu executed with enough waggish character to suit perfectly an eclectic college crowd (p166)

Terrapin Creek Café & Restaurant (☎ 707-875-2700; www.terrapincreekcafe.com; 1580 Eastshore Dr; mains $18-30; ◐ lunch Thu-Sun, dinner 4:30-9pm Thu-Sun) Occupying the site of the much-beloved (now-defunct) Seaweed Café, this has quickly emerged as Bodega Bay's most exciting restaurant. Run by a husband-and-wife team, the elegant little cafe espouses the Slow Food movement and serves local dishes sourced from the surrounding area. Even modest comfort-food offerings such as the pulled pork sandwich are artfully executed, though the Dungeness crab salad is fresh, briny and perfect. Jazz and warm light complete the atmosphere.

SONOMA COAST STATE BEACH
Stretching for 19 miles from Bodega Head to north of Jenner, the **Sonoma Coast State Beach** (☎ 707-875-3483) is actually a series of excellent beaches, a place to

explore foggy coves, take in crumbling, rocky headlands, and picnic. However inviting the water seems, though, these are *not* swimming beaches. The surf is treacherous, with rip currents and unpredictable sneaker waves and it's often unsafe to wade. Never turn your back on the ocean, stay above the high-tide line and keep an eye on kids.

Heading north along the coast, notable beaches include Miwok Beach; 2-mile-long Salmon Creek Beach; sandy Portuguese and Schoolhouse Beaches; Shell Beach for tidepooling and beachcombing; and, our favorite, the scenic Goat Rock (Mile 19.15) with its yawning colony of harbor-seals who lounge at the mouth of the Russian River. Volunteers protect the seals and educate tourists during pupping season, between March and August. To stretch the legs a bit, take the Kortum Trail, a well-marked 5-mile trip that's stunning.

GUALALA

St Orres Inn (☎ 707-884-3303, dining room 707-884-3335; www.saintorres.com; 36601 Hwy 1; B&B $90-130, cottages $120-350) is renowned for its trippy, redwood, Russian-inspired architecture – and rightly so. There's no place quite like this hotel, an eye-popping structure with dramatic rough-hewn timbers and copper domes. On the property's 90 acres, hand-built cottages range from rustic to luxurious. If you can swing it, eat at the inn's dining room (mains $40), open for dinner only, which serves California cuisine in one of the coast's most romantic rooms. The nightly specials are exhaustive and delicious.

Bones Roadhouse (☎ 707-884-1188; 39350 S Hwy 1; mains $10-20; 🕑 11:30am-9pm Sun-Thu, to 10pm Fri & Sat), with its bawdy bric-a-brac on the wall, savory smoked meats and a pulled pork sandwich designed

for the Harley drivers, serves Gualala's best lunch. On weekends, they may even have a codgerly blues outfit growling out 'Mustang Sally.'

our pick Mar Vista Cottages (☎ 707-884-3522, 877-855-3522; www.marvistamendocino.com; 35101 S Hwy 1; 1-bedroom cottages $140-205, 2-bedroom cottages $200-230; 🛜 🐾 🐕) is our favorite escape on the entire California coast. All 12 brightly painted, 1930s fishing cottages have been retrofitted with elegant simplicity: beds with feather-light duvets, polished hardwood floors, comfy reading chairs, wood-burning stoves and full kitchens. Chickens peck around the 9-acre grounds laying fresh eggs for breakfast. Guests may indulge in seasonal herbs and veggies from the open garden. Across the road there's a hidden beach. If you're looking for a retro-cozy hideaway cottage, look no further.

POINT ARENA
pop 460

Thirty minutes north of Gualala, tiny downtown Point Arena looks like Main Street USA, but the centerpiece of the former fishing village is a windswept point crowned by the 1908 Point Arena Lighthouse (☎ 707-882-2777; www.pointarenalighthouse.com; 🕑 10am-3:30pm; 🐕). Just 2 miles north of town, it's the only lighthouse in California you can ascend. Check in at the museum, then climb the 145 steps to the top and see the Fresnel lens and the jaw-dropping view which includes a bird's-eye glimpse of the San Andreas Fault (adult/child $7.50/1). You can also rent one of the former Coast Guard homes (☎ 877-725-4448; homes $125-225) next to the lighthouse. They look like tract houses and are simply furnished, but offer unreal views.

Franny's Cup & Saucer (☎ 707-882-2500; www.frannyscupandsaucer.com; 213 Main

MSZ/IMAGEBROKER

Tafoni (honeycombed-sandstone formations) at Salt Point State Park

THE BAY AREA & NORTHERN CALIFORNIA

NORTH COAST

◺ SALT POINT STATE PARK

If you stop at only one park along the Sonoma Coast, make it 6000-acre Salt Point State Park, where sandstone cliffs drop dramatically into the kelp-strewn sea, and hiking trails crisscross windswept prairies and wooded hills, connecting pygmy forests and coastal coves rich with tidepools. The 6-mile-wide park is bisected by the San Andreas Fault – the rock on the east side is vastly different from that on the west. Check out the eerily beautiful *tafoni,* honeycombed-sandstone formations, near Gerstle Cove.

For views of the pristine coastline, walk to the platform overlooking Sentinel Rock; it's just a short stroll from the Fisk Mill Cove parking lot at the park's north end. Just south, Stump Beach has picnic areas with fire pits and beach access. Further south, seals laze at Gerstle Cove Marine Reserve, one of California's first underwater parks. Tread lightly around tidepools and don't lift the rocks: even a glimpse of sunlight can kill some critters. Kids can check out an 'Adventure Pack' from the Gerstle Cove entrance station or the tiny visitors center and use it to ID animals and plants in tidepools.

If it's springtime, you *must* see Kruse Rhododendron State Reserve. Growing abundantly in the forest's filtered light, magnificent pink rhododendrons reach heights of more than 30ft, making them the tallest species in the world; turn east from Hwy 1 onto Kruse Ranch Rd and follow the signs.

Two campgrounds, Woodside and Gerstle Cove (☎ 800-444-7275; www.reserve america.com; campsites $35), both signposted off Hwy 1, have campsites with cold water. Inland Woodside is well protected by Monterey pines. Gerstle Cove's trees burned over a decade ago and have only grown halfway back, giving the gnarled, blackened trunks a ghostly look when the fog twirls between the branches.

Things you need to know: ☎ 707-847-3221; entry per car $8; ⌚ visitors center weekend afternoons when volunteer staff is available

St; ⊙ 8am-4pm Wed-Sat) The cutest patisserie on this stretch of coast is run by Franny and her mother, Barbara (a veteran of Chez Panisse). The fresh berry tarts and rich chocolaty desserts seem too beautiful to eat, until you take the first bite and immediately order another. Between April and June, try to reserve ahead for their Sunday garden brunch (seatings at 10am and 1:30pm, $25).

ELK
pop 210

Thirty minutes north of Point Arena, itty-bitty Elk is famous for its stunning clifftop views of 'sea stacks,' towering rock formations jutting out of the water. There is *nothing* to do after dinner, so bring a book – and sleeping pills if you're a night owl. And you can forget about the cell phone, too; reception here is nonexistent.

ourpick La Petite Rive (☎ 707-937-4945; www.lapetiterive.com; 7750 Hwy 1; 5-course prix fixe $24-35; ⊙ dinner Wed-Mon), a warmly romantic, French dining room in Little River (15 miles north of Elk) with misty ocean views, has become the talk of the North Coast. From the first exhilarating moment of the amuse-bouche, through the following four courses of elegant, seasonal fare, this is the best food on the coast, north of San Francisco. It's also *tiny*. There are seven tables and two seatings – at 5:30pm and 8pm only – so reservations are crucial. Robert Redford drove more than two hours for the tomato soup, waited in the parking lot and was turned away. Seriously.

MENDOCINO
pop 820

Mendocino is the North Coast's salt-washed gem, with B&Bs surrounded by rose gardens, white picket fences and New England–style redwood water towers leading out to a gorgeous headland. Here, visitors walk along the headland among berry bramble and wildflowers, where cypress trees stand guard over dizzying cliffs. Nature's power is evident everywhere; from driftwood-littered fields and cave tunnels to the raging surf.

Mendocino, bathed in early morning sunlight

STEPHEN SAKS

The town itself is full of cute shops – no chains – and has earned the nickname 'Spendocino,' for its upscale goods.

INFORMATION

Ford House Visitors Center & Museum (☎ 707-937-5397; www.gomendo.com; 735 Main St; donation requested $2; 11am-4pm) Maps, books, information and exhibits including a scale model of 1890 Mendocino. There's also hot cider, picnic tables and restrooms.

SIGHTS

Point Cabrillo Lighthouse (☎ 707-937-0816; www.pointcabrillo.org; Point Cabrillo Dr; 11am-4pm Sat & Sun Jan & Feb, daily Mar-Oct, Fri-Mon Nov & Dec;) Restored in 1909, this lighthouse stands on a 300-acre wildlife preserve north of town, between Russian Gulch and Caspar Beach. Admission is free. The head lighthouse keeper's home is now a B&B (see below right). Guided walks of the preserve leave at 11am on Sundays from May to September.

ACTIVITIES

Catch a Canoe & Bicycles, Too! (☎ 707-937-0273, 800-331-8884; www.stanfordinn.com; cnr Comptche-Ukiah Rd & Hwy 1; 9am-5pm;), situated on the bank of the Big River, is a friendly shop that rents bikes, kayaks and special outrigger canoes ($28 for three hours) for self-guided trips up the 8-mile Big River tidal estuary, the longest undeveloped estuary in Northern California. Without highways or buildings, it's exceedingly peaceful to float or roll past forests, frolicking otters or historic logging structures.

Literally and philosophically distant from the frou-frou places in town, the **Old Mill Farm School of Country Living** (☎ 707-937-0244, 707-937-3047; www.oldmillfarm.org; cabins $95) is a working or-

ganic farm powered by biodiesel. It offers a chance to shear sheep or harvest grapes. The farm is about 30 minutes from Mendocino: take Little Lake Rd east out of town for 6 miles. After the pavement ends, the road forks. Bear left on Rd 408 and continue for another 3 miles, looking for signs. Check the website for info on farm events and workshops.

SLEEPING

Sea Gull Inn (☎ 707-937-5204, 888-937-5204; www.seagullbb.com; 44960 Albion St; r incl breakfast $75-165, cottages $185) With a lovely garden and morning delivery of the organic breakfast, this centrally located small inn is one of the best deals in town. The cottage has a TV and a refrigerator.

John Dougherty House (☎ 707-937-5266, 800-486-2104; www.jdhouse.com; 571 Ukiah St; r $150-275) Decked out in a spiffy-looking blue-and-white nautical theme that would do any sailor boy proud, rooms at this elegant, uncluttered B&B have more contemporary style than others in town. Some have fireplaces and ocean views. Top choice for gay travelers, but all welcome.

Lighthouse Inn at Point Cabrillo (☎ 707-937-6124, 866-937-6124; www.mendocino lighthouse.pointcabrillo.org; Point Cabrillo Dr; r $177-272) On 300 acres, in the shadow of Point Cabrillo Lighthouse, the lighthouse keeper's house and several cottages have been turned into B&B rooms, with atmospheric details such as redwood paneling. At night, the light from the brilliant Fresnel lens sweeps overhead, making it a fabulous spot for a nighttime stroll. Rates include a private night tour of the lighthouse and a five-course breakfast.

EATING

Lu's Kitchen (☎ 707-937-4939; 45013 Ukiah St; dishes $7-10; 11:30am-5:30pm;) Lu serves

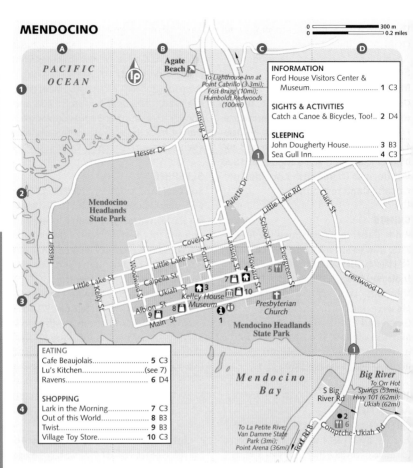

MENDOCINO

0 _____ 300 m
0 _____ 0.2 miles

PACIFIC
OCEAN

Agate
Beach

To Lighthouse Inn at
Point Cabrillo (3.3mi);
Fort Bragg (10mi);
Humboldt Redwoods
(100mi)

Hesser Dr

Mendocino
Headlands
State Park

Palette Dr

Little Lake Rd

Clark St

Crestwood Dr

Hesser Dr

Covelo St

School St

Howard St

Evergreen St

Little Lake St

Ford St

Lansing St

Woodward St

Little Lake St

Calpella St

Kelly St

Ukiah St

Albion St

Main St

Kelley House
Museum

Presbyterian
Church

Mendocino Headlands
State Park

INFORMATION
Ford House Visitors Center &
   Museum.............................. 1 C3

SIGHTS & ACTIVITIES
Catch a Canoe & Bicycles, Too!.. 2 D4

SLEEPING
John Dougherty House.............. 3 B3
Sea Gull Inn............................. 4 C3

Mendocino
Bay

Big River
To Orr Hot
Springs (53mi);
Hwy 101 (62mi);
Ukiah (62mi)

S Big
River Rd

Comptche-Ukiah Rd

To La Petite Rive;
Van Damme State
Park (3mi);
Point Arena (36mi)

EATING
Cafe Beaujolais........................ 5 C3
Lu's Kitchen.........................(see 7)
Ravens.................................... 6 D4

SHOPPING
Lark in the Morning................. 7 C3
Out of this World.................... 8 B3
Twist....................................... 9 B3
Village Toy Store.................... 10 C3

fab organic-veggie burritos and colorful salads out of this tiny shack. On warm days, the picture is completed by the outdoor seating in the adjacent garden lot, which buzzes with lazy bumblebees.

Ravens (☎ 707-937-5615; www.stanfordinn. com; Stanford Inn, Comptche-Ukiah Rd; breakfast $8-15, dishes $20-28; ⊙ breakfast 8-10:30am Mon-Sat, to 12:15pm Sun, dinner 5:30-8pm; Ⓥ) Who knew vegetarian food could be so good? Omnivores may forswear meat after dining here, where the haute-contemporary menu features everything from pizza to sea-palm strudel. Produce comes from

the inn's own organic gardens, where you can stroll after dinner. The breakfasts are Mendocino's best, and the view looks over rolling hills to the sea beyond.

Cafe Beaujolais (☎ 707-937-5614; www. cafebeaujolais.com; 961 Ukiah St; lunches $9-16, mains $24-36; ⊙ lunch Wed-Sun, dinner daily) Mendocino's iconic, beloved country-Cal-French restaurant occupies an 1896 house that's been restyled into a monochromatic urban-chic dining room, perfect for holding hands by candlelight. The refined and inspired cooking draws diners from San Francisco, who make this the centerpiece of their trip. Bring your credit card; you'll need it.

SHOPPING

Mendocino is all about local art, and the galleries around town can be surprisingly affordable sources of one-of-a-kind gifts.

Lark in the Morning (☎ 707-937-5275; 45011 Ukiah St) In addition to a stock of fine acoustic guitars and banjos, the walls of this fantastic shop are lined with handmade and rare instruments from around the world – everything from hammer dulcimers and Celtic harps to African marimbas.

Out of this World (☎ 707-937-3335; 451000 Main St) Bird-watchers, astronomy buffs and science geeks: head directly to this telescope, binocular and science-toy shop.

Twist (☎ 707-937-1717; 45140 Main St) Twist stocks ecofriendly, natural-fiber clothing and trippy hand-blown 'tobacco-smoking accessories' (dude: that means bongs).

Village Toy Store (☎ 707-937-4633; 10450 Lansing St) Get a kite to fly on Bodega head or browse the old-world selection of wooden toys and games that you won't find in the chains – and hardly anything requires batteries!

INLAND HIGHWAY 101

To get into the most remote and wild parts of the North Coast on the quick, eschew winding Hwy 1 for inland Hwy 101, which runs north from San Francisco as a freeway, then as a two- or four-lane highway north of Sonoma County, occasionally pausing under the traffic lights of small towns.

HOPLAND

pop 2230

One hundred miles north of San Francisco, little Hopland is a quaint gateway to Mendocino County's Wine Country, with worthy tasting rooms. Spend an hour getting lost in (and eating your way through) the **Fetzer Vineyards Organic Gardens** (☎ 800-846-8637; www.fetzer.com; 13601 Eastside Rd; ☼ 9am-5pm), possibly the most gorgeous meandering gardens in Northern

Vichy Hot Springs Resort (p156), Ukiah

GARY CRABBE/ALAMY

California, attached to a winery that sets a high standard for sustainable wine growing; from Hwy 101, turn east onto Hwy 175 and drive one mile.

The progressive, futuristic 12-acre campus of **Real Goods Solar Living Center** (☎ 707-744-2100; www.solarliving.org; 13771 S Hwy 101; ⏱ 10am-7pm; ♿) greets visitors at the south end of town. There's no charge but the suggested donation is from $1 to $5.

If you're spending the night in town, your only choice is a good one: the 1890 **Hopland Inn** (☎ 707-744-1890, 800-266-1891; www.hoplandinn.com; 13401 S Hwy 101; r $110-140; ⌨). Enjoy bevvies from the full bar downstairs in their cozy, wood-paneled library. For no-frills American fare in burly portions, hit the **Bluebird Café** (☎ 707-744-1633; 13340 S Hwy 101; breakfast & lunch $5-10, dinner $10-15; ⏱ 7am-2pm Mon-Thu, 8am-8pm Fri-Sun; ♿).

UKIAH

The warm springs at the **Vichy Hot Springs Resort** (☎ 707-462-9515; www.vichysprings.com; 2605 Vichy Springs Rd; RV campsites $20, lodge s/d $135/195, creekside r $195/245, cottages from $280; ⌨ ⚓) are the only naturally carbonated mineral baths in North America; two-hour day-use costs $30, all day runs to $38. There's a communal kitchen. Unlike Orr, it also requires swimwear (you might be thankful).

If you can't imagine soaking with a suit on, **Orr Hot Springs** (☎ 707-462-6277; hot water@pacific.net; campsites $45-50, dm $55-65, s $100-125, d $135-155, cottages $185-215; ⏱ 10am-10pm), the cousin to Vichy, is *the* place for back-to-the-land hipsters and backpackers who like to get naked. Rates include access to the communal redwood hot tub, private porcelain tubs, outdoor tile-and-rock heated pools, the sauna, spring-fed rock-bottom swimming pool,

steam, massage and magical gardens. There's also a communal kitchen. Day-use costs $25; reservations are required.

City of Ten Thousand Buddhas (☎ 707-462-0939; www.cttbusa.org; 2001 Talmage Rd; ⏱ 8am-6pm) is a sprawling 488-acre Chinese-Buddhist community on the grounds of a former state psychiatric hospital, three miles east of Ukiah, via Talmage Rd. Don't miss the temple hall (which really does have 10,000 Buddhas!) or lunch in the vegetarian **restaurant** (4951 Bodhi Way; dishes $6-9; ⏱ 11am-3pm Mon, Wed & Thu, to 6pm Fri-Sun; Ⓥ).

SOUTHERN REDWOOD COAST

There's some real magic in the loamy soil and misty air 'beyond the redwood curtain'; it yields the tallest trees and most potent herb on the planet. North of Fort Bragg, Bay Area weekenders and antique-stuffed B&Bs give way to lumber wars, pot farmers and an army of carved bears. The 'growing' culture here is intense and the huge profit it brings to the region has evident cultural side effects – an omnipresent population of transients who work the harvests, a chilling respect for 'No Trespassing' signs and a political culture that is an uneasy balance between gun-toting libertarians, ultraleft progressives and typical college-town chaos. Nevertheless, the reason to visit is to soak in the magnificent landscape, which runs through a number of pristine, ancient redwood forests.

HUMBOLDT REDWOODS STATE PARK & AVENUE OF THE GIANTS

Of all of California's redwood parks, **Humboldt Redwoods State Park** (☎ 707-946-2409) packs the biggest punch, if only because it's easily accessible by car. The park covers 53,000 acres – 17,000 of which are old-growth – and protects some of the world's most magnificent trees, including 74 of the 100 tallest.

If you're anywhere near the area, exit Hwy 101 at the **Avenue of the Giants** to travel through the park. The incredible 32 miles of two-lane blacktop is parallel to Hwy 101, under the canopy of the world's tallest trees. All perspective gets lost in the shadow of these stately trunks; suddenly the other cars on the road seem like toys. If you have the inclination, the route is perfect for cycling, with smooth pavement and moderate elevation changes. A string of small towns line the drive, with chances to get deli food, gas up and shop for redwood carved knickknacks. Driving the Avenue instead of Hwy 101 adds only 15 minutes to your northbound travel time.

South of Weott, a volunteer-staffed **visitors center** (☎ 707-946-2263; 🕒 9am-5pm summer, 10am-4pm winter; ♿) has picnic areas, a small **museum** littered with cool taxidermy, exhibits and seasonal kids programs. The pièce de résistance is the historic 1917 'Travel Log,' a full-sized RV made from the trunk of a carved-out redwood.

Primeval **Rockefeller Forest**, 4.5 miles west of the Avenue via Mattole Rd, appears as it did a century ago. It's the world's largest contiguous old-growth redwood forest and contains about 20% of all such remaining trees. In **Founders Grove**, north of the visitors center, the **Dyerville Giant** was knocked over in 1991 by another falling tree. A walk along its gargantuan 370ft length, with its humongous trunk towering above, helps you appreciate how huge these ancient trees are.

ACTIVITIES

The park has more than 100 miles of trails for hiking, mountain biking and horseback riding. Trails are muddy and may be brush-covered until mid-June, when seasonal river bridges go up. Easy walks include short nature trails in Founders Grove and Rockefeller Forest and the **Drury-Chaney Loop Trail**. The **Bull Creek Flats Trail** is the only trail that loops through the heart of the contiguous

Avenue of the Giants, Humboldt Redwoods State Park

MARK NEWMAN

REDWOOD COAST

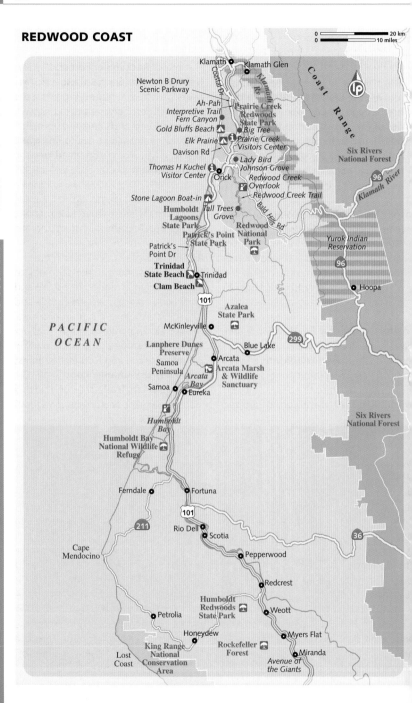

0   20 km
0   10 miles

Klamath
Klamath Glen

Coast Dr

Newton B Drury
Scenic Parkway

Coast Range

Ah-Pah
Interpretive Trail
Fern Canyon
Gold Bluffs Beach
Elk Prairie
Davison Rd
Thomas H Kuchel
Visitor Center
Orick

Prairie Creek
Redwoods
State Park
Big Tree
Prairie Creek
Visitors Center

Six Rivers
National Forest

96

Klamath River

Lady Bird
Johnson Grove
Redwood Creek
Overlook
Redwood Creek Trail

Stone Lagoon Boat-in
Humboldt
Lagoons
State Park
Tall Trees
Grove

Patrick's Point
State Park

Patrick's
Point Dr

Bald Hills Rd

Redwood
National
Park

Yurok Indian
Reservation

96

Trinidad
State Beach
Clam Beach

Trinidad

Hoopa

101

Azalea
State Park

PACIFIC
OCEAN

McKinleyville

Lanphere Dunes
Preserve

Blue Lake

Samoa
Peninsula

Arcata
Arcata Marsh
& Wildlife
Sanctuary

299

Samoa

Arcata
Bay

Eureka

Humboldt
Bay

Six Rivers
National Forest

Humboldt Bay
National Wildlife
Refuge

Ferndale

Fortuna

101

211

Rio Dell
Scotia

36

Cape
Mendocino

Pepperwood

Redcrest

Humboldt
Redwoods
State Park

Petrolia

Weott

Honeydew

King Range
National
Conservation
Area

Rockefeller
Forest

Myers Flat

Miranda

Lost
Coast

Avenue of
the Giants

➤ DRIVE-THROUGH REDWOODS

What better way to bond with a redwood than driving through its belly? Three carved-out (but alive!) redwoods await along Hwy 101.

Chandelier Drive-Through Tree Fold in your mirrors and inch forward, then cool off in the uberkitschy gift shop in Leggett.

Shrine Drive-Through Tree Look up to the sky as you roll through, on the Avenue of the Giants in Myers Flat. The least impressive of the three.

Tour Through Tree Squeeze through then check out the emu off exit 769 in Klamath.

old-growth forest – and it's moderately easy. Schedule half a day and plan to swim in the creek (summer only). The most challenging is the **Grasshopper Peak Trail**, south of the visitors center, which climbs to the 3379ft fire lookout.

SLEEPING & EATING

Miranda Gardens Resort (☎ 707-943-3011; www.mirandagardens.com; 6766 Ave of the Giants, Miranda; cottages $105-185, with kitchen $165-265; 🏊) One of the best resorts in the area and family friendly. The cozy, slightly rustic cottages have redwood paneling; some have fireplaces. They're a tad musty – as is everything under the redwoods – but the bathrooms are clean and there's a pool. Across the street there's a family restaurant.

ourpick Vacation House in the Redwoods (☎ 707-722-4330; www.floodplain produce.com; 31117 Ave of the Giants, Pepperwood; house $135) This is a lovely one-bedroom cottage surrounded by a sunny flower farm. It sleeps up to five. A hammock, deck and hot tub sweeten the deal.

Eternal Treehouse Café (☎ 707-722-4247; 2650 Ave of the Giants, Redcrest; 🕐 8:30am-6:30pm; 🚼) With stick-to-your-ribs biscuits and gravy, and dinner staples, this is an old-school stop along the Avenue that's good for families. The 'Hungry Logger' breakfast ($8) is not to be trifled with.

A monument to 1920s rustic elegance, **Benbow Inn** (☎ 707-923-2124, 800-355-3301; www.benbowinn.com; 445 Lake Benbow Dr, Benbow; r $135-489, cottages $395; 🐾 🍸) is a national historic landmark and the Redwood Empire's first luxury resort. Hollywood's elite once frolicked in the Tudor-style resort's lobby, where you can play chess by the crackling fire and enjoy complimentary afternoon tea and evening hors d'oeuvres. Rooms are appointed with antique furniture, a decanter of sherry and a basket of paperbacks. The window-lined dining room (breakfast and lunch $10 to $15, dinner mains $22 to $32) serves good Euro-Cal cuisine and Sunday brunch. There's an adjoining golf course and tidy RV park.

FERNDALE
pop 1400

The North Coast's most charming town is stuffed with impeccable Victorian buildings – known locally as 'butterfat mansions' because of the dairy wealth that built them. There are so many, in fact, that the entire place is a state and federal historical landmark. Dairy farmers built the town in the 19th century and it's still run by the 'milk mafia': you're not a local till you've lived here 40 years. A stroll down Main St offers galleries, old-world emporiums and soda fountains. Although Ferndale relies on tourism, it has avoided becoming a tourist trap, and has no chain stores.

Victorian-style architecture, Main St, Ferndale

WITOLD SKRYPCZA

Though a lovely place to spend a summer night, it's as dead as a doornail in winter.

SIGHTS & ACTIVITIES

The 'butterfat' palaces that you'll want to check out should start with the Gingerbread Mansion (400 Berding St), an 1898 Queen Anne–Eastlake and the town's most photographed building. Shaw House (703 Main St) was the first permanent structure in town and houses the first post office. The 1866, 32-room Fern Cottage (☎ 707-786-4835; www.ferncottage. org; Centerville Rd; adult/child/student/senior $5/free/2.50/4; ☺ 10am-4pm Wed-Sun Jul-Sep), west of town, was originally a Carpenter Gothic that grew as the family did. Only one family ever lived here, so nothing got thrown away and it's all been preserved. Call ahead for winter hours.

Ferndale has two museums that are very different in style. Though little ones might get a bit antsy from the pile of artifacts, slightly cheesy installations and working seismograph at the Ferndale Museum (☎ 707-786-4466; www.

ferndale-museum.org; cnr Shaw & 3rd Sts; donation requested; ☺ 11am-4pm Wed-Sat, 1-4pm Sun), the museum's light-up diorama style dollhouses spark the imagination. Quite a contrast is the Kinetic Sculpture Museum (www.kineticgrandchampionship.com; 580 Main St; ☺ 10am-5pm Mon-Sat, noon-4pm Sun; ♿), housing fanciful, astounding kinetic sculptures used in the town's annual Kinetic Grand Championship (see the boxed text, right). This place is a real trip and admission is free.

Half a mile from downtown via Bluff St, tramp through fields of wildflowers, along ponds, redwood and eucalyptus trees at 110-acre Russ Park. The cemetery, also on Bluff St, is worth exploring. Five miles down Centerville Rd, Centerville Beach is one of the few off-leash dog beaches in Humboldt County.

FESTIVALS & EVENTS

Kinetic Grand Championship (www. kineticgrandchampionship.com) The famous race is held during the Memorial Day weekend.

Humboldt County Fair (www.humboldt countyfair.org) In mid-August; horse racing is the big event. This is an unexceptionally good county fair.

SLEEPING

Hotel Ivanhoe (☎ 707-786-9000; www. ivanhoe-hotel.com; 315 Main St; r $95-145) Ferndale's oldest hostelry opened in 1875 and retains its Old West style for excellent value. The 2nd-floor porch overlooking downtown is perfect for morning coffee.

Shaw House (☎ 707-786-9958, 800-557-7429; www.shawhouse.com; 703 Main St; r $120-175, ste $200-260; 🛜 🐾) California's oldest B&B and Ferndale's first home, this storybook place is perched atop a grassy hill behind a white picket fence. The three parlors are lovely, as are the original details. Book a full breakfast or cheaper continental breakfast in advance. Pets allowed in some rooms for $35 per night.

Gingerbread Mansion Inn (☎ 707-786-4000, 800-952-4136; www.gingerbread-mansion. com; 400 Berding St; r $160-400; 🛜) Ferndale's iconic B&B drips with gingerbread trim.

The 11 exquisitely detailed rooms are decked out with high-end 1890s Victorian furnishings. Rates include high-tea service, evening wine and a three-course breakfast. No kids under 12.

EATING

Curley's Grill (☎ 707-786-9696; 400 Ocean Ave; dishes $8-21; 🕙 11:30am-9pm Sun-Thu, to 10pm Fri & Sat) Spare yourself the trip to Eureka by ordering from a Cal-American, comfort-food menu, served on bright Fiestaware and big oak tables. It can be a bit inconsistent, but when you hit it right, it's spot-on. The bar? Never misses.

Hotel Ivanhoe (☎ 707-786-9000; 315 Main St; mains $14-30; 🕙 dinner Wed-Sun) Chicken marsala is the specialty at this Victorian dinner-house and pub, but when it's available, lamb is the standout. There's prime rib on Friday and Saturday (and sometimes Sunday), and on Tuesday there's great beef stroganoff made with the weekend's leftover prime rib. There's a small-portions menu ($10 to $14), also available at the bar. Top choice for dinner.

CRAZY CONTRAPTIONS

The **Kinetic Grand Championship** (formerly the Kinetic Sculpture Race) was born in 1969 when Ferndale artist Hobart Brown decided to spruce up his son's tricycle to make it more interesting, creating a wobbly, five-wheeled red 'penta-cycle.' Initially, five odd contraptions raced down Main St on Mother's Day, and a 10ft turtle sculpture won. The race was expanded in the early '70s and has now blossomed into a three-day, amphibious event with contraptions competing over 38 miles from Arcata to Ferndale. Held over Memorial Day weekend (late May), the race attracts thousands of spectators and usually at least a few dozen entrants (one year there were 99). Cities around the world have followed in Ferndale's footsteps, with far-flung places such as Perth, Australia, now holding their own kinetic races.

A few of the race rules are as bizarre as the entrants, including 'It is legal to get assistance from the natural power of water, wind, sun, gravity and friendly extraterrestrials (if introduced to the judges prior to the race).'

ENTERTAINMENT

Ferndale Repertory Theatre (☎ 707-786-5483; www.ferndale-rep.org; 447 Main St) This theater produces worthwhile shows and musicals year-round.

SHOPPING

Ferndale's main drag is great for window-shopping and unique gifts.

Golden Gait Mercantile (☎ 707-786-4891; 421 Main St) The shelves of this old-fashioned store are filled with yesteryear's goods, as well as fun bric-a-brac and tasty jams.

Blacksmith Shop & Gallery (☎ 707-786-4216; www.ferndaleblacksmith.com; 455 & 491 Main St) From wrought-iron art to hand-forged furniture, this is the largest collection of contemporary blacksmithing in America. Of all Ferndale's shops, this one's not to be missed.

Hobart Gallery (☎ 707-786-9259; 393 Main St) The steel, brass and copper works of the late Hobart Brown, father of kinetic racing, are stunning. It's a cozy space to shop or browse.

EUREKA
pop 26,100

One hour north of Garberville, on the edge of the giant Humboldt Bay, lies Eureka, the largest bay north of San Francisco. With strip-mall sprawl surrounding a lovely historic downtown, it wears its role as the county seat a bit clumsily. Make for Old Town, a small district with colorful Victorian buildings, good shopping and a revitalized waterfront. For night life, head to Eureka's trippy sister up the road, Arcata.

SIGHTS

The free *Eureka Visitors Map,* available at tourist offices, details architectural and historical walking tours and drives. Old Town, along 2nd and 3rd Sts, from C St

to M St, was once Eureka's down-and-out area, but has been refurbished into an inviting pedestrian district of galleries, shops, cafes and restaurants. The F Street Plaza and Boardwalk run along the waterfront at the foot of F St.

The most famous of Eureka's Victorians is the **Carson Mansion** (134 M St), the ornate 1880s home of lumber baron William Carson, designed by Samuel and Joseph Newsom, notable 19th-century architects. It took 100 men a full year to build. Today, it's a private club. The pink house opposite, the **Wedding Mansion** (202 M St), is an 1884 Queen Anne Victorian by the same architects, built as a wedding gift for Carson's son.

Who says they don't build 'em like that anymore? **Carter House** (cnr 3rd & L Sts) was built in the 1980s by bon vivant Mark Carter, using 19th-century blueprints he'd found in an antique store. He's a local celeb; you can meet him at the Hotel Carter, across the street.

SLEEPING

Carter House Inns (☎ 707-444-8062, 800-404-1390; www.carterhouse.com; r $100-285, ste $350-450, cottages $595) Stay in one of three sumptuously decorated houses: a single-level 1900 house, a honeymoon-hideaway cottage or a replica of an 1880s San Francisco mansion. Unlike elsewhere, you won't see the innkeeper unless you want to. Guests can have an in-room breakfast or eat at the adjacent hotel's elegant restaurant.

Abigail's Elegant Victorian Mansion (☎ 707-444-3144; www.eureka-california.com; 1406 C St; r incl breakfast $125-190; ☎) Outclassing the frilly faux Victorian fuss of most B&Bs, this National Historic Landmark is practically a Victorian museum, stuffed with carefully selected period pieces. The sugar-sweet innkeepers dote on everyone, and offer a trip around town in a 1920s ride.

Hotel Carter (☎ 877-443-7583; www.carter house.com; 301 L St; r $165-225, ste $275-350; 🛜 🐾) This standard-bearing luxury North Coast inn was recently constructed in period style – a Victorian lookalike without drafty windows. Stylish without being fussy, rooms have top-quality linens, unfinished pine antiques and modern amenities; suites have in-room whirlpools and marble fireplaces. Rates include made-to-order breakfast, plus evening wine and hors d'oeuvres.

EATING & DRINKING

Hurricane Kate's (☎ 707-444-1405; www.hur ricanekates.com; 511 2nd St; mains lunch $9-14, dinner $16-26; 🕐 11:30am-2pm & 5-9pm Tue-Sat) The favorite spot of local bon vivants, Kate's open kitchen pumps out pretty good, eclectic, tapas-style dishes ($10 to $14) and roast meats, but the wood-fired pizzas are the standout option. Full bar.

Restaurant 301 (☎ 707-444-8062; www. carterhouse.com; 301 L St; breakfast $11, dinner $20-34; 🕐 breakfast & dinner) Eureka's top table, romantic and sophisticated 301 serves a contemporary California menu, using produce from its organic gardens (tours available). Mains are pricey, but the four-course prix-fixe menu ($45) is a good deal.

Lost Coast Brewery (☎ 707-445-4480; 617 4th St; 🕐 11am-midnight; 🛜) A great North Coast brewery. The Downtown Brown and Great White are both delicious and there's pub grub – fries, wings and good burgers (mains $6 to $14) – all day.

GETTING THERE & AROUND

Horizon Air (☎ 800-547-9308; horizonair. alaskaair.com) and **United Express** (☎ 800-241-6522; www.united.com) serve **Arcata/ Eureka Airport** (ACV; ☎ 707-839-5401; http:// co.humboldt.ca.us/aviation), 20 miles north. Horizon is a better option if you're flying from LA (3½ hours, flights every day except Thursday) and United is better from the Bay Area (two hours), though neither is cheap; prices start at around $500 for the short flights.

JOHN ELK III

Eureka's famous Carson Mansion

ARCATA

pop 16,500

There's no place in California quite like Arcata, the North Coast's most progressive town, set around a tidy central square that fills with an agreeable mix of college students, campers, the slightly disheveled and tourists. Sure, it occasionally reeks of patchouli and its politics may lean toward the far left (in April 2003 the City Council did not simply vote to condemn the USA Patriot Act, it outlawed voluntary compliance with it), but its earnest embrace of sustainability has long harbored some of the most progressive civic action in America. Here, garbage trucks run on biodiesel, recycling gets picked up by tandem bicycle, wastewater gets filtered clean in marshlands and almost every street has a bike lane.

ORIENTATION & INFORMATION

Streets run on a grid, with numbered streets traveling east to west and lettered streets north to south. G and H Sts run north and south (respectively) to

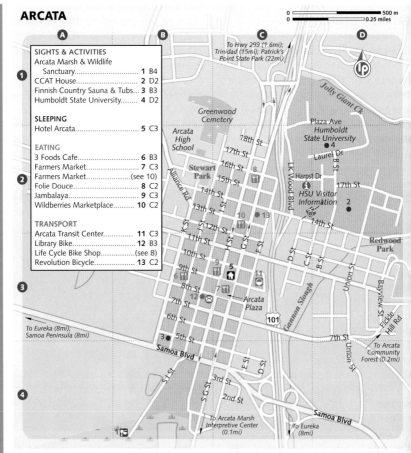

ARCATA

0   500 m
0   0.25 miles

SIGHTS & ACTIVITIES
Arcata Marsh & Wildlife
    Sanctuary............................. **1** B4
CCAT House............................. **2** D2
Finnish Country Sauna & Tubs... **3** B3
Humboldt State University........ **4** D2

SLEEPING
Hotel Arcata............................. **5** C3

EATING
3 Foods Cafe............................. **6** B3
Farmers Market......................... **7** C3
Farmers Market....................(see 10)
Folie Douce............................... **8** C2
Jambalaya................................. **9** C3
Wildberries Marketplace.......... **10** C2

TRANSPORT
Arcata Transit Center.............. **11** C3
Library Bike.............................. **12** B3
Life Cycle Bike Shop...............(see 8)
Revolution Bicycle.................. **13** C2

To Hwy 299 (1.6mi);
Trinidad (15mi); Patrick's
Point State Park (22mi)

Greenwood Cemetery

Plaza Ave
Humboldt
State University
● 4

Arcata
High
School

18th St
17th St
16th St
Stewart
Park
15th St
14th St
13th St
12th St
11th St
10th St
9th St
8th St
7th St
6th St

Laurel Dr
Harpst Dr
HSU Visitor
Information
17th St
14th St

Redwood
Park

Arcata
Plaza

101

To Eureka (8mi);
Samoa Peninsula (8mi)

3 ● 5th St
Samoa Blvd

Cannon Slough

7th St

To Arcata
Community
Forest (0.2mi)

Union St

Bayview St
Fickle
Hill Rd

3rd St
2nd St

To Arcata Marsh
Interpretive Center
(0.1mi)

To Eureka
(8mi)

Samoa Blvd

WITOLD SKRYPCZAK
Cafe dining on Arcata Plaza, Arcata

Humboldt State University and Hwy 101. The plaza is bordered by G and H and 8th and 9th Sts. Eureka is 5 miles, or 10 minutes, south on Hwy 101. Or, take Samoa Blvd to Hwy 255 for a scenic route around Arcata Bay.

Arcata Eye (www.arcataeye.com) Free newspaper listing local events; the 'Police Log' column is hysterical.

SIGHTS

Humboldt State University (HSU; ☎ 707-826-3011; www.humboldt.edu) is on the northeastern side of town. The Campus Center for Appropriate Technology (CCAT) is a world leader in sustainable technologies; on Fridays at 2pm you can take a self-guided tour of the **CCAT House** (☎ 707-826-3551; Buck House, HSU; 🕑 9am-5pm Mon-Fri; ♿), a converted residence that uses only 4% of the energy of a comparably sized dwelling.

Arcata Marsh & Wildlife Sanctuary, on the shores of Humboldt Bay, has 5 miles of walking trails and outstanding bird-watching – and it doubles as the city's (nearly) odor-free wastewater treatment facility. Friends of Arcata Marsh guide tours on Saturdays at 2pm from the **Arcata Marsh Interpretive Center** (☎ 707-826-2359; www.arcatamarshfriends.org; 600 South G St; 🕑 9am-5pm Tue-Sun, 1-5pm Mon; ♿). The **Redwood Region Audubon Society** (☎ 707-826-7031; www.rras.org) offers guided walks of the marsh on Saturdays at 8:30am, rain or shine, from the parking lot at I St's south end. These are free, but donations are welcome.

At the east end of 11th and 14th Sts, **Redwood Park** has beautiful redwoods and picnic areas. Adjoining the park is the **Arcata Community Forest**, a 575-acre old-growth forest crisscrossed by 10 miles of trails, with dirt paths and paved roads good for hikers and mountain bikers.

ACTIVITIES

Finnish Country Sauna & Tubs (☎ 707-822-2228; cnr 5th & J Sts; 🕑 noon-10pm Sun-Thu, to 12:30am Fri & Sat) is a nirvana for sore hikers. You can sip chai by the fireside or in meditative gardens, and rent a private open-air redwood hot tub ($9 per half hour) or sweat in a sauna. Reserve ahead, especially on weekends.

FESTIVALS & EVENTS

Arcata's most famous event is the Kinetic Grand Championship (www.kineticgrand championship.com), held on Memorial Day weekend (late May). People on self-propelled contraptions travel the 38 miles from Arcata to Ferndale (see the boxed text, p161).

SLEEPING & EATING

Hotel Arcata (☎ 707-826-0217, 800-344-1221; www.hotelarcata.com; 708 9th St; r $90-105, ste $111-156) The renovated 1915 Hotel Arcata anchors the plaza. The small rooms are nice enough, but the best reason to roost here is to spy on the hippies, nerds, skaters, stoners, hikers, rednecks and retirees that populate the square.

Jambalaya (☎ 707-822-4766; 915 H St; lunch $7-9, dinner $15-20; ☺ lunch Mon-Fri, dinner daily) Probably the most vibrant dining option in town, Jambalaya serves a mishmash of Caribbean-influenced dishes – at lunch Cuban sandwiches, at dinner wild salmon and (of course) jambalaya. The menu also rules, with fresh fruit cocktails and a great beer selection. As if this wasn't fun enough, they also host Arcata's best live music scene.

3 Foods Cafe (☎ 707-822-9474; 835 J St; brunch $8-14, dinner $10-30; ☺ 5:30am-10pm Tue-Thu, to 11pm Fri & Sat, to 9pm Sun) This newcomer fits perfectly into the Arcata dining scene: whimsical, creative, worldly dishes (think Korean beef in a spicy chili sauce) at moderate prices (a prix fixe is sometimes available for $20 and the 'Times Are Tough Tuesday' menu features all-you-can-eat pasta for a measly $5). The lavender-infused cocktails start things off on the right foot. For a $1 fee, you can get your attending wait staff to do a silly walk.

Folie Douce (☎ 707-822-1042; 1551 G St; dinner $23-32; ☺ 5:30-9pm Tue-Thu, to 10pm Fri & Sat) Folie Douce presents a short but inventive menu of seasonally inspired bistro cooking, from Asian to Mediterranean, with an emphasis on local organics.

JUDY BELLAH

Participants in the Kinetic Grand Championship, Arcata

LEE FOSTER

Whitewater rafting on the Trinity River

ꙮ IF YOU LIKE...

If you made it this far to see the redwoods, we think you'll also like the following:

- **Patrick's Point State Park** Five miles north of adorable Trinidad (about 15 minutes north of Arcata) is this tiny park. Bouldering around the stark rock formations while watching passing whales is a favorite pastime here, as is visiting **Sumêg**, a village built by the local Yurok tribespeople to educate their youth and visitors about Yurok culture and history.

- **Trinidad Head** In Trinidad proper, look for the giant, proud promontory sticking into the treacherous Pacific Ocean. The head is sacred ground to the Yurok, and a network of trails and an otter-populated pier make it an excellent outing. Heading out of town (back toward the Trinidad lighthouse) is the incomparable **Katy's Smokehouse & Fishmarket** (☎ 707-677-0151; www.katyssmokehouse.com; 740 Edwards St, Trinidad; ꙮ 9am-6pm), which uses line-caught local seafood to make delectable chemical-free smoked and canned fish. Follow the signs to the left.

- **Jedediah Smith State Park** Eleven miles northeast of dreary Crescent City (in itself an hour past Arcata, almost to the Oregon border) is this state park, where bald eagles and Ewoks flit about an impossibly tall canopy of old-growth redwoods. Well, technically, Ewoks don't actually live here. Or, they haven't since the 1980s when George Lucas shot the Endor scenes here.

- **Trinity Alps** If you're coming across Hwy 299 from Redding, you'll be driving through the Trinity Alps, a wilderness area as beautiful as it is overlooked. Catch your breath in this peaceful spot, and then have it taken away while rafting the Trinity River with **Bigfoot Rafting** (☎ 530-629-2263, 800-722-2223; www.bigfootrafting.com; half-day guided trips from $79, rafts & kayaks from $32). Keep an eye out for the Sasquatch himself; he's been spotted so many times around here, there's an annual festival in his honor (August).

Wood-fired pizzas ($12 to $18) are a specialty. Reservations are essential.

There are fantastic **farmers markets** (☎ 707-441-9999; Arcata Plaza ⏰ 9am-2pm Sat Apr-Nov; outside Wildberries ⏰ 3:30-6:30pm Tue Jun-Oct), and **Wildberries Marketplace** (☎ 707-822-0095; 747 13th St; ⏰ 7am-11pm) is Arcata's best grocery, with natural foods, a good deli, bakery and juice bar.

GETTING AROUND

Only in Arcata: borrow a bike from **Library Bike** (☎ 707-822-1122; www.arcata.com/green bikes; 865 8th St) for a $20 deposit, which gets refunded when you return the bike – up to six months later! They're beaters, but they ride. **Revolution Bicycle** (☎ 707-822-2562; 1360 G St) and **Life Cycle Bike Shop** (☎ 707-822-7755; 1593 G St; ⏰ Mon-Sat) rent, service and sell bicycles.

NORTHERN REDWOOD COAST

Congratulations, traveler, you've reached the middle of nowhere, or at least the top of the middle of nowhere. Here, the trees are so large that the tiny towns along the road seem even smaller. The scenery is pure drama: cliffs and rocks, native lore, legendary salmon runs, mammoth trees, redneck towns and RVing retirees. It's certainly the *weirdest* part of the California coast.

REDWOOD NATIONAL PARK

Sure, if you've explored southern areas of the California coast, you may *think* that you've experienced the majesty of the redwoods, but this is the big show: the world's tallest living trees will stagger the mind, predating the Roman Empire by more than 500 years and standing as an imposing reminder of nature's pure grandeur. In the summer of 2006, researchers found a trio of trees here that were bigger than any they'd ever measured before; the biggest one, Hyperion, is nearly 40 stories tall.

SIGHTS & ACTIVITIES

Just north of the visitors center, turn east onto Bald Hills Rd, then it's 2 miles to **Lady Bird Johnson Grove**, one of the park's most beautiful groves, accessible via a gentle 1-mile loop trail. Follow signs. Continue another 5 miles up Bald Hills Rd to **Redwood Creek Overlook**. On the top of the ridgeline at 2100ft elevation, you'll see over the trees and the entire watershed – provided it's not foggy. Past the overlook lies the gated turn-off for **Tall Trees Grove**, the home to some of the world's tallest trees. Rangers issue only 50 vehicle permits per day, but they rarely run out. Pick one up, along with the gate-lock combination, from the Thomas H Kuchel Visitor Center (Map p158) or park headquarters in Crescent City. Allow four hours for the round-trip, which includes a 6-mile drive down a rough dirt road (speed limit 15mph) and a steep 1.3-mile one-way hike, which descends 800ft to the grove.

The 4.5-mile **Dolason Prairie Trail** drops 2400ft in elevation, passing through various ecological zones, from open grasslands high above the trees into the lush forest below. The trailhead is 11 miles up Bald Hills Rd from Hwy 101; catch a shuttle car at Tall Trees Grove and spare yourself the uphill return.

The 2.7-mile **Emerald Ridge Trail** originates 600ft from the Tall Trees trailhead and drops to Redwood Creek, crisscrossing the stream and gravel bars (bring appropriate footwear and attempt this trail in summer only, when the water is low). Instead of following trail markers downstream, make an *upstream* detour for swimming holes, stunning scenery and total solitude.

PRAIRIE CREEK REDWOODS STATE PARK

Famous for virgin redwood forests and unspoiled coastline, this 14,000-acre section of Redwood National and State Parks has 70 miles of hiking trails and spectacular scenic drives. Pick up information and sit by the fire at Prairie Creek Visitors Center (☎ 707-465-7354; per car $8; ◷ 9am-5pm Mar-Oct, 10am-4pm Nov-Feb; ♿), which has the best bookstore of all the redwood parks' visitor centers – including park headquarters. Kids love the taxidermy dioramas and their push-button, light-up displays. Outside, Roosevelt elk roam grassy flats.

SIGHTS & ACTIVITIES

Newton B Drury Scenic Parkway parallels Hwy 101 and is a worthy 8-mile detour through untouched ancient redwoods. Numerous trails branch off from roadside pullouts to allow visitors to wander agape under the canopies.

There are 28 mountain-biking and hiking trails through the park, from simple to strenuous. If you're tight on time or have mobility impairments, stop at Big Tree, an easy 100yd walk from the parking lot. Several other short nature trails start near the visitors center, including the Revelation Trail, Five-Minute Trail, Elk Prairie Trail and Nature Trail. If you only have a few hours, try the 3.5-mile South Fork-Rhododendron-Brown Creek Loop, particularly if it's spring when rhododendrons and wildflowers bloom. The best all-day option is the 11.5-mile Coastal Trail, though you'll want to approach from the Brown Creek to South Fork direction to spare a grueling incline. Another option for the conservation-minded wanderer is the Ah-Pah Interpretive Trail at the park's north end, where you can stroll a recently reforested logging road.

The Coastal Drive follows Davison Rd to access Gold Bluffs and Fern Canyon. Go west 3 miles north of Orick and doubleback north over corrugated gravel for 3½ miles over the coastal hills, where you'll find the often-unstaffed fee station (per vehicle $6). Up the coast is the lovely Gold Bluffs Beach Campground, where you can picnic or camp. One mile ahead, hike through Fern Canyon, where 60ft fern-covered sheer-rock walls can be seen from Steven Spielberg's *Jurassic Park 2: The Lost World*. This is one of the most photographed spots on the North Coast – damp and lush, all emerald green – and *totally* worth getting your toes wet to see.

WITOLD SKRYPCZAK

Avalanche Gulch, Mt Shasta (p170)

THE BAY AREA & NORTHERN CALIFORNIA

NORTH COAST

◥ LOCAL VIEW ON LAVA BEDS

When asked which is her favorite cave or lava tube, National Park Service ranger Kristin 'Kale' Bowling responds 'whichever I'm in at the time.' Bowling is effusive in her descriptions of all of the varieties of caves: freezing, with skylights, with ferns, with glow-in-the-dark mineral deposits…the list goes on and on. And she's equally enthusiastic when describing the 14 species of bats found at Lava Beds National Monument (p174). She's careful, though, to caution new cavers to check in with the visitors center before exploring: she wants no damage to the caver or to the fragile geological and biological resources in the park.

SLEEPING & EATING

Welcome to the great outdoors: without any motels or cabins, the option here is to pitch a tent in the campgrounds at the southern end of the park. Look for rentals in nearby Eureka (p162).

Elk Prairie Campground (☎ reservations 800-444-7275; www.reserveamerica.com; campsites $35) Elk roam this popular campground, where you can sleep under redwoods or at the prairie's edge. The camp has hot showers and some hike-in sites. There's also a shallow creek to splash in. Sites 1 to 7 and 69 to 76 are on grassy prairies and get full sun; sites 8 to 68 are wooded. To camp in a mixed redwood forest, book sites 20 to 27.

Gold Bluffs Beach Campground (campsites $35) This campground sits between 100ft cliffs and wide-open ocean, but there are some windbreaks and solar-heated showers. Look for sites up the cliff under the trees. There are 29 first-come, first-served sites, with enough basic amenities to satisfy a family; you can't make reservations.

MT SHASTA & AROUND

One hypnotic glimpse of Mt Shasta and you'll find it hard to stay away. Hike, mountain-bike, whitewater raft, ski or snowshoe: take your pick as you explore the peak and surrounding Shasta-Trinity National Forest.

Northeast of Mt Shasta, a long drive and a world away, is remote, eerily beautiful Lava Beds National Monument, a blistered badland of petrified fire.

MT SHASTA

'When I first caught sight of it I was 50 miles away and afoot, alone and weary. Yet all my blood turned to wine, and I have not been weary since,' wrote naturalist John Muir in 1874. Mt Shasta's beauty is intoxicating, and the closer you get to it the headier you begin to feel. Dominating the landscape, the mountain is visible for more than 100 miles from many parts of northern California and southern Oregon. Though not California's highest peak (at 14,162ft it ranks fifth), Mt Shasta is especially magnificent because it rises alone on the horizon, unrivaled by other mountains.

The mountain and surrounding Shasta-Trinity National Forest (www.fs.fed.us/r5/shastatrinity) are crisscrossed by trails and dotted with alpine lakes. It's easy to spend days or weeks camping, hiking, river rafting, skiing, mountain-biking and boating.

VISITING THE MOUNTAIN

You can drive almost the whole way up the mountain via the Everitt Memorial Hwy (Hwy A10) and see exquisite views at any time of year. Simply head east on

Lake St from downtown Mt Shasta City, then turn left onto Washington Dr and keep going. **Bunny Flat** (6860ft), which has a trailhead for Horse Camp and the Avalanche Gulch summit route, is a busy place with parking spaces, information signboards and a toilet. The section of highway beyond Bunny Flat is only open from about mid-June to October, depending on snows. This road leads to **Lower Panther Meadow**, where trails connect the campground to a Wintu sacred spring, in the upper meadows near the **Old Ski Bowl** (7800ft) parking area. Shortly thereafter is the highlight of the drive, **Everitt Vista Point** (7900ft), where a short interpretive walk from the parking lot leads to a stone-walled outcropping affording exceptional views of Lassen Peak to the south, the Mt Eddy and Marble Mountains to the west and the whole Strawberry Valley below.

MT SHASTA BOARD & SKI PARK

On the south slope of Mt Shasta, off Hwy 89 heading toward McCloud, this winter skiing and snowboarding **sports park** (☎ snow reports 530-926-8686; www.skipark.com; lift tickets adult/child Mon-Thu $29/15, Fri-Sun $39/20; ☺ 9am-9pm Wed-Sat, 9am-4pm Sun-Tue winter, 10am-4pm Wed, Thu & Sun, 10am-9pm Fri & Sat late Jun-early Sep) opens depending on snowfall. The park has a 1390ft vertical drop, more than two dozen alpine runs and 18 miles of cross-country trails. Rentals, instruction and weekly specials are available. It's Northern California's largest night-skiing operation.

In summer, the park offers scenic chairlift rides, paragliding flights, a 24ft climbing tower and Frisbee golf. Mountain-bikers take the chairlift up and come whooshing back down.

MT SHASTA CITY & MCCLOUD

SLEEPING

Stoney Brook Inn (☎ 530-964-2300, 800-369-6118; www.stoneybrookinn.com; 309 W Colombero Dr, McCloud; s/d without bath $53/79, with bath $65/94, ste with kitchen $99-156) Smack dab in the middle of town, under a stand of pines, this alternative B&B also

JOHN ELK III

The peak of Mt Shasta makes for a stunning backdrop for the town of McCloud

THE BAY AREA & NORTHERN CALIFORNIA

NORTH COAST

KRISTIN PILJAY

Hiking the Lost Coast

↘ IF YOU LIKE...

If you like the isolated beauty of Lava Beds National Monument (p174), then we think you'll like these other natural areas:

- **Mt Tamalpais** It's rare to find a remote location in the Bay Area, but Mt Tamalpais has trails that remain comparatively uncrowded, especially during the week (and especially in comparison to Muir Woods).

- **Van Damme State Park** Five minutes south of Mendocino, this gorgeous 1831-acre park draws divers, beachcombers and kayakers to its easy-access beach and pygmy forest, where the acidic soil has created a bonsai forest under a foot tall. To access nearby sea caves, contact Lost Coast Kayaking (☎ 707-937-2434; www.lostcoastkayaking.com; tours from $50).

- **Lost Coast** You know you've found one of the most seriously isolated spots in California when you're on the Lost Coast. The North Coast's superlative backpacking destination is a rugged, mystifying stretch of coast where narrow dirt trails ascend rugged coastal peaks and volcanic beaches of black sand, ethereal mist hovers above the roaring surf and majestic Roosevelt elk graze the forests. Wildflowers bloom from April through May and gray whales migrate from December through April. The warmest, driest months are June through August, but days are foggy.

- **Lassen Volcanic National Park** The dramatic crags, volcanic formations and alpine lakes of Lassen Volcanic National Park remain surprisingly under-touristed and pristine when you consider that they are only a few hours from the Bay Area. Snowed in through most of winter, the park blossoms in late spring. In a fuming display, the terrain is marked by roiling hot springs, steamy mud pots, noxious sulfur vents, fumaroles, lava flows, cinder cones, craters and crater lakes.

sponsors group retreats. Creature comforts include an outdoor hot tub, a sauna, a Native American sweat lodge, and massage (by appointment). Downstairs rooms are nicest. Vegetarian breakfast available.

ourpick McCloud B&B Hotel (☎ 530-964-2822, 800-964-2823; www.mccloudhotel. com; 408 Main St, McCloud; r incl breakfast $100-235; ❄) This regal, block-long, butter-yellow, grand hotel opposite the depot first opened in 1916. The elegant historic landmark has been lovingly restored to a luxurious standard, and the included breakfast is taken very seriously. One room is accessible for travelers with disabilities.

ShasTao (☎ 530-926-4154; www.shastao. com; 3609 N Old Stage Rd, Mt Shasta City; s/d incl breakfast $115/175; ▣ 🛜) A pair of very mellow, affable philosophy professors runs this wooded, peaceful retreat. You won't find your granny's wallpaper here…or her library: they've got bookshelves stacked with titles from aestheticism to Zen. They also loan bikes and snowshoes

to guests. Vegetarian/vegan breakfast included.

ourpick Shasta MountInn Retreat & Spa (☎ 530-926-1810; www.shastamountinn. com; 203 Birch St, Mt Shasta City; r without/with fireplace $125/175; ▣) Antique on the outside, this Victorian farmhouse is all relaxed minimalism inside. Each airy room has a designer mattress and exquisite views of the luminous mountain. Enjoy the expansive garden, wraparound deck and outdoor sauna.

EATING

Trinity Café (☎ 530-926-6200; 622 N Mt Shasta Blvd, Mt Shasta City; mains $17-27; 🕑 dinner Tue-Sat) Trinity has long rivaled any big-city 'haute' spot. The owners, who hail from Napa, infuse the bistro with a Wine Country feel, not to mention an extensive, excellent wine selection. The organic menu ranges from delectable, perfectly cooked steaks to creamy-on-the-inside, crispy-on-the-outside polenta. The warm, mellow mood makes for an overall delicious experience.

MAX PAOLI & RUTH EASTHAM

Bubbling mud pots, Lassen Volcanic National Park

Fumarole steam vents, Lassen Volcanic National Park (p172)

WITOLD SKRYPCZAK

LAVA BEDS NATIONAL MONUMENT

Off Hwy 139, immediately south of Tule Lake National Wildlife Refuge, Lava Beds National Monument (☎ 530-667-8100; www.nps.gov/labe; 7-day entry per vehicle/hiker/biker $10/5/5) is a truly remarkable 72-sq-mile landscape of volcanic features – lava flows, craters, cinder cones, spatter cones, shield volcanoes and amazing lava tubes.

Lava tubes are formed when hot, spreading lava cools and hardens on the surfaces exposed to the cold air. The lava inside is thus insulated and stays molten, flowing away to leave an empty tube of solidified lava. Nearly 400 such tubular caves have been found in the monument, and many more are expected to be discovered. About two dozen or so are currently open for exploration by visitors.

On the south side of the park, the visitors center (☎ 530-667-2282, ext 230; ⏲ 8am-6pm summer, 8:30am-5pm rest of year) has free maps, activity books for kids, and information about the monument and its volcanic features and history.

Rangers loan flashlights, rent helmets and kneepads for cave exploration, and lead summer interpretive programs, including campfire talks and guided cave walks. To explore the caves, it's essential you use a high-powered flashlight, wear good shoes and long sleeves (lava is sharp), and not go exploring alone.

The weathered Modoc petroglyphs at the base of a high cliff at the far northeastern end of the monument, called Petroglyph Point, are thousands of years old. At the visitors center, be sure to take the leaflet explaining the origin of the petroglyphs and their probable meaning. Look for the hundreds of nests in holes high up in the cliff face, which provide shelter for birds that sojourn at the wildlife refuges nearby.

Indian Well Campground (tent & RV sites $10), near the visitors center at the south end of the park, has water and flush toilets, but no showers. A couple of motels are on Hwy 139 in the nearby town of Tulelake.

↘ WINE COUNTRY

WINE COUNTRY HIGHLIGHTS

1 WINE TASTING

Before heading out to swirl, sniff and swish, familiarize yourself with the varietals in the region. Near the coast, nighttime fog blankets the vineyards, which is good for pinot noir and chardonnay. Alexander, Sonoma and much of Dry Creek Valley (as well as Napa Valley) are fog-protected, so they're good for cabernet sauvignon, sauvignon blanc and merlot. Head to Napa for cabernet. Zinfandel, syrah and viognier grow in both regions, warm and cool.

OUR DON'T MISS LIST

❶ ALL ABOARD!

Spend three hours in luxury as you're whisked from Napa to St Helena on the vintage Pullman cars of the **Napa Valley Wine Train** (p185). Dine on a gourmet multicourse lunch or dinner with wine pairings as you click-clack through the towns and vineyards of Yountville, Oakville and Rutherford, stopping for a tasting along the way. For a twist, try a special full moon tour or a murder mystery dinner excursion.

❷ CULINARY INSTITUTE OF AMERICA

A must-see for foodies, the **CIA** (p192) will boggle your mind with tasty options beyond its celebrated Wine Spectator Greystone Restaurant. Not only does it offer cooking demonstrations, but also wine flight lessons, olive oil tastings, multiday boot camps and chocolate sampling. Home chefs should budget time to ogle the more than 1000 cookbook titles at its shop.

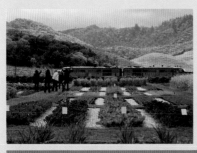

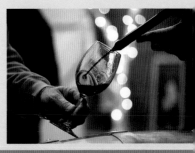

Clockwise from top: Cabernet grape harvest, Oakville, Napa Valley; Rosé is one of the local varieties; Taste wine direct from the barrel in the Alexander Valley (p205); Napa Valley Wine Train (p185)

CLOCKWISE FROM TOP: JERRY ALEXANDER; JERRY ALEXANDER; JERRY ALEXANDER; JERRY ALEXANDER

❸ 'CRUSH' TIME

Fall harvest takes place in September, along with sunny weather, colorful leaves and the smell of crushed grapes. It's a busy time for winemakers, but during this month, there are special barrel tastings, behind-the-scenes tours and other events you won't get the rest of the year.

❹ TAKING WINE HOME

If a tasting fee seems steep, note that many wineries will deduct it from the cost of a wine purchase. And if you're flying out of Santa Rosa airport, note that passengers can check a case of up to a dozen bottles without paying an extra luggage charge.

❺ NORCAL SPECIALTIES

Don't even think about leaving before you try a chardonnay (remember this is the one that beat the French in 1976; 'steely' chardonnays aged in steel tanks are the latest rage); rosé (ranging from watermelon-ripe pinks to sultry and smoky); pinot noir (hints of rose petals, redcurrant, and 'forest-floor' flavors such as moss and black truffles); zinfandel (juicy blackberry and hints of dark chocolate or black pepper); and cabernet sauvignon (Napa's specialty).

⬎ THINGS YOU NEED TO KNOW

Best time to visit Spring and fall, though lodging prices skyrocket for the fall 'crush' **Transportation** Traffic can be heavy on summer weekends **Restaurants** Make reservations for top tables **Day-tripping tip** Picnicking mostly prohibited in Napa Valley wineries but allowed throughout Sonoma County

WINE COUNTRY HIGHLIGHTS

2

◥ NAPA VALLEY WINE

Believe the hype – the wines of Napa Valley (p186) merit their reputation among the world's finest. If you love deep red wines with complex noses and luxurious finishes, Napa Valley will make you swoon. Stretching along a single gorgeous valley, its 200 side-by-side wineries are easy to visit. Don't miss the family-owned boutique houses because it can be difficult to find many of these wines elsewhere.

3

◥ LOUNGE ALONG THE RUSSIAN RIVER

A longtime summertime weekend destination for Northern Californians, the Russian River (p202) entices visitors who want to canoe, wander country lanes, taste wine, hike redwood forests and live at a lazy pace. So claim a comfy river-side spot, feel the balmy sunshine and make sure you get in the water and splash at least once an hour.

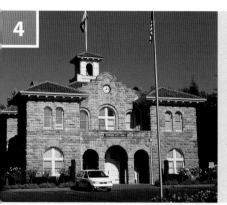

4

↘ HISTORIC SONOMA

Stroll around Sonoma Plaza and Sonoma State Historic Park (p200) for vestiges of the 1846 revolution against Mexico, when some American settlers, tanked up on liquid courage, declared independence in the town of Sonoma. Tour the military barracks, now a museum, as well as the Mission San Francisco Solano de Sonoma.

5

↘ JACK LONDON STATE HISTORIC PARK

Pay homage to one of the area's literary lions, the author and namesake of Jack London State Historic Park (p203). You can visit London's writing cottage and residence as well as his grave site, then kick up some dust as you explore hiking trails set in the undulating oak-dotted woodlands of his former farm.

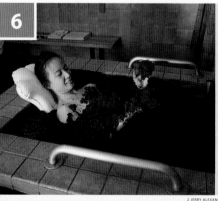

6

↘ CALISTOGA SPAS

Soak your stress away in decadent hot springs and paint your body in warm mud until it radiates. At the spas of low-key Calistoga (p194), there's scant attitude, just ample opportunity for blissful relaxation. Stay for a few days and choose from a full menu of steam baths, clay-mud (fango) baths, herbal wraps or a couples massage.

2 JERRY ALEXANDER; 3 JERRY ALEXANDER; 4 GLENN VAN DER KNIJFF; 5 JERRY ALEXANDER; 6 JERRY ALEXANDER

2 Wine-tasting, Napa Valley (p186); 3 Canoeing along the Russian River (p202); 4 Sonoma City Hall, Sonoma Plaza (p200); 5 Jack London State Historic Park (p203); 6 Mud bath, Calistoga (p194)

WINE COUNTRY'S BEST...

CAR-FREE TRANSPORTATION

- **Ballooning** (p188) Soar above the rolling hills and vineyard valleys.
- **Cycling** (p185) Explore quiet roads and wine-taste using your own pedal power.
- **Ferry** Cruise in via Vallejo (www.blueandgoldfleet.com/ferry) from San Francisco.
- **Wine Train** (p185) Coast the countryside in a vintage Pullman dining car.
- **Hiking** Hike the volcanic cone of Mt St Helena at Robert Louis Stevenson State Park (p196).

PLACES FOR KIDS

- **Safari West** (p197) Take an expedition through a free-roaming exotic animal reserve.
- **Old Faithful Geyser** (p196) Hourly water jets to the sky, plus a fun petting zoo.

- **Indian Springs Resort** (p195) An old-school resort with a toasty spring-fed swimming pool and outdoor games.

WINERY PICNIC SPOTS

- **Casa Nuestra** (p189) Relax beneath weeping willows.
- **Gundlach-Bundschu** (p197) One of Sonoma Valley's oldest and most lovely estate vineyards.
- **Preston Vineyards** (p189) Spread out under a shady walnut tree.

ROMANTIC RESTAURANTS & INNS

- **MacArthur Place** (p201) Spa suites have double-sized bathtubs and private outdoor hot tubs.
- **Poetry Inn** (p191) Private balconies, wood-burning fireplaces and indoor-outdoor showers.
- **Martini House** (p192) A grand main dining room and a dreamy, sun-dappled garden.

LEFT: JERRY ALEXANDER; RIGHT: JERRY ALEXANDER

Left: Giraffes at Safari West (p197); Right: Hot-air ballooning (p188) over the Napa Valley

THINGS YOU NEED TO KNOW

⇗ VITAL STATISTICS

- Population 600,000
- Area 2365 sq miles
- Area code ☎ 707
- Best time to visit Spring and fall

⇗ TOWNS IN A NUTSHELL

- Napa (p188) A happening city of arts and food.
- Yountville (p191) Napa Valley dining mecca.
- St Helena (p192) Chichi town with historic center.
- Calistoga (p194) Unpretentious Napa Valley spa town.
- Sonoma (p199) Historic buildings and old-fashioned charm.
- Guerneville (p205) Queer-friendly resort town on the Russian River.
- Santa Rosa (p207) Wine Country's biggest city.
- Healdsburg (p208) Sonoma Valley foodie destination.

⇗ ADVANCE PLANNING

- Two months before Try to book a table at French Laundry (p192).
- From several weeks to a few days before Make tasting appointments at wineries that require them.

⇗ RESOURCES

- Healdsburg (www.healdsburg.org) Chamber of Commerce & Visitors Bureau.
- Napa Valley (www.napavalley.org) Napa Valley Conference & Visitors Bureau.

- Press Democrat (www.pressdemocrat. com) Daily regional newspaper, based in Santa Rosa.
- Russian River (www.russianriver.com) Russian River Chamber of Commerce & Visitor Center.
- Sonoma Valley (www.sonomavalley. com) Site of the Sonoma Valley Visitors Bureau.

⇗ EMERGENCY NUMBERS

- Santa Rosa Memorial Hospital (☎ 707-935-5000; 347 Andrieux St)

⇗ GETTING AROUND

- Air Horizon Air has regional services to the Sonoma County Airport (www.sonomacountyairport.org) in Santa Rosa.
- Bike Visit wineries via quiet back roads.
- Car Needed for extensive winery-hopping, unless you stay in major hub towns such as Napa or Sonoma, or book a limousine.

⇗ BE FOREWARNED

- Traffic Expect heavy traffic on summer weekends.
- Don't drink and drive The curvy roads are dangerous, and police monitor traffic, especially on Napa's Hwy 29.

WINE COUNTRY

THINGS YOU NEED TO KNOW

WINE COUNTRY

WINE COUNTRY ITINERARIES

WINE COUNTRY ITINERARIES

ROOTED IN HISTORY Three Days

Laid out by Mexican General Vallejo in 1834, the plaza in **(1) Sonoma** (p199) contains mission-revival buildings dating from the local revolution, and remains the heart of a lively downtown lined with hotels, restaurants and shops. Inspect the town's mission chapel and a military barracks that's now a period museum. Then trace the lives of two of the region's best-known authors, visiting **(2) Robert Louis Stevenson State Park** (p196) in Napa Valley, where the writer honeymooned (and the intrepid can summit the peak of Mt St Helena), and a museum of his memorabilia in **(3) St Helena** (p192). In Sonoma Valley, **(4) Jack London State Historic Park** (p203) contains the final resting spot for the creator of *The Call of the Wild*. Lastly, swing through the city of **(5) Santa Rosa** (p207) to pay homage to the world's most beloved beagle at the Charles M Schulz Museum.

HOT MUD & COOL WATER Five Days

Base yourself in the classic Napa Valley resort town of **(1) Calistoga** (p194) for a bit of pampering and stress reduction. Book a full day of spa treatments, complete with paint-on mud and massage, and spend another day lazing around a hot-springs-fed swimming pool. Then broaden your horizons past your navel and venture out to explore the area's geothermal activity. Volcanic ash and mud from nearby Mt St Helena embalmed a stand of redwood trees a few million years ago, and you can see the rock-solid results at the **(2) Petrified Forest** (p196), between Calistoga and Santa Rosa. Then off to Napa Valley's **(3) Old Faithful Geyser** (p196), which shoots 60ft to 100ft into the sky a bit short of every hour, and where you can let the kids go wild in a petting zoo as you await the next scheduled eruption. On your final day, divert west to **(4) Guerneville** (p205) for a refreshing canoe trip down the Russian River and a saunter under the cloud-blocking canopy of a redwood forest.

FLIGHTS OF FANCY One Week

Let's not mince words: you deserve this. Prepare your taste buds for the epicurean ambrosia to come with a wine-tasting class at the Culinary Institute of America in **(1) St Helena** (p192), and spruce up last season's wardrobe with a few items from the town's many boutiques. In the morning, depart from **(2) Napa** (p188) for a white-tablecloth excursion aboard the Napa Valley Wine Train, and for your evening meal, partake of the pinnacle of local French cuisine as you dine in gourmet-thick **(3) Yountville** (p191). Not merely content to see the landscape by rail, have a champagne breakfast and toast the day as you take to the sky by hot-air balloon, and arrive by limousine for an

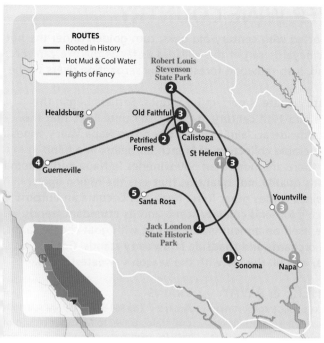

afternoon tour of Napa Valley wineries. Make certain to include (4) Calistoga (p194), where a moat surrounds the eye-poppingly opulent and faithfully reproduced 12th-century Italian castle that houses the Castello di Amoroso winery. Take a tour to the brick catacombs and a fully equipped period torture chamber. In Calistoga, schedule two dedicated spa days to recuperate from the troubling sights you've seen. Round out your trip with a final wine tasting hurrah through the Dry Creek Valley near (5) Healdsburg (p208), and a meal in this gastronomic capital of Sonoma County.

WINE COUNTRY

DISCOVER WINE COUNTRY

DISCOVER WINE COUNTRY

Rolling hills, dotted with century-old oaks, turn golden under the hot summer sun. Vineyards carpet the hillsides as far as the eye can see. Where they end, lush redwood forests follow serpentine rivers to the sea.

The temperate climate is perfect for grapes. Settlers began the tradition in the mid-19th century, but it wasn't until 1976 that the region won worldwide acclaim in Paris, when two Napa Valley wines outscored a venerable collection of French Bordeaux in a blind tasting. Today there are more than 500 wineries in Napa and Sonoma Counties. But it's quality, not quantity, that sets the region apart.

With great wines comes great food. Napa has become an outpost of San Francisco's top-end culinary scene and its attendant trends. Sonoma prides itself on agricultural diversity, with goat-cheese farms, pick-your-own orchards and roadside strawberry stands. Get lost on the back roads, and fill the car with the season's sweetest fruits.

GETTING THERE & AWAY

From San Francisco, public transportation gets you to the valleys, but it's insufficient for vineyard-hopping. For public-transit information, dial ☎ 511 from Bay Area telephones, or get information online at http://transit.511.org.

BUS

Golden Gate Transit (☎ 415-455-2000; www.goldengate.org) operates buses from San Francisco to Petaluma ($8.40) and to Santa Rosa ($9.25); catch them at 1st and Mission Sts, across from the Transbay Terminal in San Francisco.

Greyhound (☎ 800-231-2222; www.greyhound.com) operates from San Francisco to Santa Rosa ($18 to $26) and Vallejo ($14 to $20); transfer for local buses.

Napa Valley Vine (☎ 800-696-6443, 707-251-2800; www.nctpa.net) operates bus 10 from the Vallejo ferry terminal and Vallejo Transit bus station, through Napa to Calistoga ($2.90); it also runs free trolleys in Napa.

TRAINS

Amtrak (☎ 800-872-7245; www.amtrak.com) trains travel to Martinez (south of Vallejo), with connecting buses to Napa (45 minutes), Santa Rosa (1¼ hours) and Healdsburg (1¾ hours).

BART trains (☎ 415-989-2278; www.bart.gov) run from San Francisco to El Cerrito (30 minutes). Transfer to **Vallejo Transit** (☎ 707-648-4666; www.vallejotransit.com) for Vallejo (30 minutes), then take Napa Valley Vine buses to Napa and Calistoga.

GETTING AROUND
BICYCLE

Touring Wine Country by bicycle is unforgettable. Stick to the back roads. We most love pastoral West Dry Creek Rd, northwest of Healdsburg in Sonoma County. Through Sonoma Valley, take Arnold Dr instead of Hwy 12; through Napa Valley take the Silverado Trail instead of Hwy 29.

Cycling between wineries isn't demanding – the valleys are mostly flat – but crossing between Napa and Sonoma Valleys is intense, particularly via steep

WINE COUNTRY

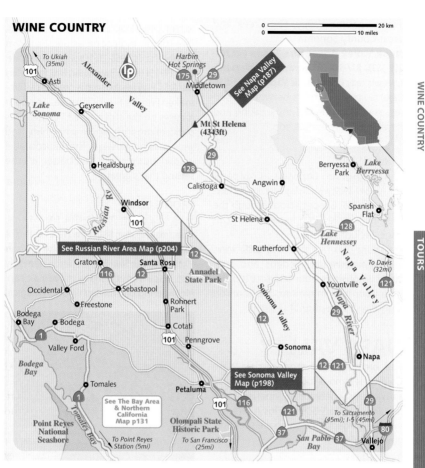

0   20 km
0   10 miles

Oakville Grade and Trinity Rd (between Oakville and Glen Ellen).

PUBLIC TRANSPORTATION

Sonoma County Transit (☎ 707-576-7433, 800-345-7433; www.sctransit.com) operates buses from Santa Rosa to Petaluma (70 minutes), Sonoma (1¼ hours) and western Sonoma County, including the Russian River Valley towns (30 minutes).

TRAIN

A cushy, if touristy, way to see Wine Country, the **Napa Valley Wine Train** (☎ 707-253-2111, 800-427-4124; www.winetrain. com; incl lunch $50-124, incl dinner $99-129) offers three-hour daily trips in vintage Pullman dining cars, from Napa to St Helena and back. Trains depart from McKinstry St near 1st St.

TOURS
BICYCLE

Guided tours start around $120 per day including bikes, tastings and lunch. Daily rentals cost $25 to $40; make reservations. **Good Time Touring** (☎ 707-938-0453, 888-525-0453; www.goodtimetouring.com)

Tours Sonoma Valley, Dry Creek and West County Sonoma.

Napa Valley Adventure Tours (☎707-259-1833, 877-548-6877; www.napavalleyadventuretours.com; Oxbow Public Market, 610 1st St, Napa) Guides bike tours between wineries, as well as off-road trips, hiking and kayaking. Daily rentals, too.

LIMOUSINE

Flying Horse Carriage Company (☎707-849-8989; www.flyinghorse.org; 4hr tours per person $145) Clippety-clop through the Alexander Valley in a horse-drawn carriage. Includes a picnic.

Magnum Tours (☎707-753-0088; www.magnumwinetours.com) Sedans and specialty limousines from $65 to $100 per hour (four-hour minimum, five hours on Saturdays). Exceptional service.

NAPA VALLEY

The birthplace of modern-day Wine Country is famous for its regal cabernets, sauvignons, châteaulike wineries and a fabulous culinary scene. Plus it remains visually gorgeous – if you have the time, you should come.

NAPA VALLEY WINERIES

Cab is king in Napa. No varietal captures imaginations like the fruit of the cabernet-sauvignon vine – Bordeaux is the French equivalent – and no wine fetches a higher price.

Many of the valley's 230 wineries are small, and because of strict county-zoning laws, some cannot legally receive drop-in visitors; unless you've come strictly to buy, not taste, you'll have to call first. This is *not* the case with all wineries. Unless otherwise stated, they do not require appointments.

RUBICON ESTATE

The former Inglenook estate, **Rubicon Estate** (☎707-968-1161; www.rubiconestate.com; 1991 St Helena Hwy, Rutherford; mandatory tour $25; ⏰ by appointment) is owned by filmmaker Francis Ford Coppola. The tour focuses on the striking 1887 château, its parklike grounds, and a small film- and wine-making museum. The Rubicon label is solid, but you can find better; it's the setting that's great.

FROG'S LEAP

Frog's Leap (☎707-963-4704, 800-959-4704; www.frogsleap.com; 8815 Conn Creek Rd; tours & tastings $20, ⏰ tastings 10am-4pm Mon-Sat, tours 10:30am-2:30pm Mon-Fri; ⚹) If you see only one Napa winery, make it Frog's Leap. Meandering paths wind through magical

Rubicon Estate winery

NAPA VALLEY

WINE COUNTRY

NAPA VALLEY

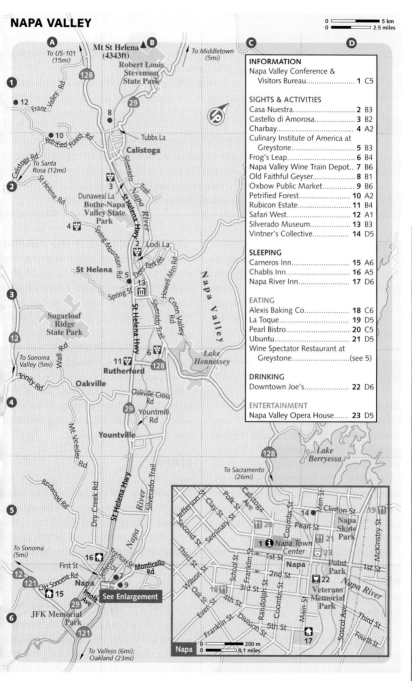

0 — 5 km
0 — 2.5 miles

INFORMATION
Napa Valley Conference &
Visitors Bureau 1 C5

SIGHTS & ACTIVITIES
Casa Nuestra 2 B3
Castello di Amorosa 3 B2
Charbay 4 A2
Culinary Institute of America at
Greystone 5 B3
Frog's Leap 6 B4
Napa Valley Wine Train Depot.. 7 B6
Old Faithful Geyser 8 B1
Oxbow Public Market 9 B6
Petrified Forest 10 A2
Rubicon Estate 11 B4
Safari West 12 A1
Silverado Museum 13 B3
Vintner's Collective 14 D5

SLEEPING
Carneros Inn 15 A6
Chablis Inn 16 A5
Napa River Inn 17 D6

EATING
Alexis Baking Co. 18 C6
La Toque 19 D5
Pearl Bistro 20 C5
Ubuntu 21 D5
Wine Spectator Restaurant at
Greystone .... (see 5)

DRINKING
Downtown Joe's 22 D6

ENTERTAINMENT
Napa Valley Opera House 23 D5

WINE COUNTRY

FLYING & BALLOONING

Wine Country is stunning from the air – a multihued tapestry of undulating hills, deep valleys and rambling vineyards.

The **Vintage Aircraft Company** (Map p198; ☎ 707-938-2444; www.vintageaircraft. com; 23982 Arnold Dr) flies over Sonoma in a vintage biplane with an awesome pilot who'll do loop-de-loops on request (add $50). Twenty-minute tours cost $175/270 for one/two adults.

Napa Valley's signature hot-air balloon flights leave early, around 6am or 7am, when the air is coolest; they usually include a champagne breakfast on landing. Adults pay about $200 to $250, and kids $130 to $150. Call **Balloons above the Valley** (☎ 707-253-2222, 800-464-6824; www.balloonrides.com) or **Napa Valley Balloons** (☎ 707-944-0228, 800-253-2224; www.napavalleyballoons.com), both in Yountville.

NAPA VALLEY

gardens and fruit-bearing orchards – pick peaches in July – surrounding an 1884 barn and farmstead with cats and chickens. But more than anything, it's the vibe that's wonderful: casual and down-to-earth, with a major emphasis on *fun*. Sauvignon blanc is its best-known wine, but the merlot merits attention. There's also a dry, restrained cabernet – a style atypical in Napa. All are organically grown.

CHARBAY

Most know **Charbay** (☎ 707-963-9327; www. charbay.com; 4001 Spring Mountain Rd, St Helena; tastings $20; ☺ by appointment) for its top-shelf flavored vodkas and spirits, made by a master 12th-generation Serbian distiller. Alas, by law you can't sample the spirits, but you can taste excitingly crisp aperitif wines, including a brandy-infused chardonnay, a lip-smacking sangria-like rosé and excellent ports. Charbay is old Napa: the winery is a farm and a garage with plastic chairs and tables, a giant alembic still in the driveway and a yappy dog to greet you.

CASTELLO DI AMOROSA

Castello (☎ 707-967-6272; www.castellodi amorosa.com; 4045 N St Helena Hwy, Calistoga;

tastings $16, tours $31-41; ☺) For over-the-top grandeur, this place wins hands-down. It took 14 years to build this perfectly replicated 12th-century Italian castle, complete with moat, hand-cut stone walls, ceiling frescoes by Italian artisans, Roman-style cross-vault brick catacombs and a torture chamber with period equipment. You can taste without an appointment, but you'd be crazy to miss the tour. Oh, the wine? Some very respectable Italian varietals, including a velvety Tuscan blend, and a merlot blend that goes great with pizza.

NAPA

pop 75,000

The valley's workaday hub was once a nothing-special city of storefronts, Victorian cottages and riverfront warehouses, but booming real-estate values caused an influx of new money that transformed Napa into a happening city of arts and food.

ORIENTATION & INFORMATION

Napa Valley Conference & Visitors Bureau (☎ 707-226-7459; www.napavalley.org; 1310 Napa Town Center; ☺ 9am-5pm) The biggest information center is in a mall between 1st and Pearl Sts, two blocks west of Main St. Pick up the free *Inside Napa Valley,* with its almost-comprehensive winery guide. Staff will make same-day reservations, but not advance.

SIGHTS & ACTIVITIES

The **Oxbow Public Market** (☎ 707-226-6529; www.oxbowpublicmarket.com; 610 1st St; admission free; ☼ 9am-7pm Mon-Sat, to 8pm Tue, 10am-5pm Sun; 🚹), opened in 2008, showcases all

Wine-tasting at Porter Creek

JERRY ALEXANDER

WINE COUNTRY

NAPA VALLEY

⚓ IF YOU LIKE...

If you like the organic and sustainable practices at Frog's Leap (p186), we think you'll like these other wineries:

- **Preston Vineyards** (☎ 707-433-3327; www.prestonvineyards.com; 9282 W Dry Creek Rd, Healdsburg; tastings $5) An organic family farm, its signature is citrusy sauvignon blanc, though Lou Preston is also known for his bread.

- **Porter Creek** (☎ 707-433-6321; www.portercreekvineyards.com; 8735 Westside Rd, Healdsburg; tastings free) The tasting bar is a former bowling-alley lane plunked atop two barrels inside a vintage-1920s garage. The grapes are organically grown and equipment runs on biodiesel; high-acid, food-friendly pinot noir and chardonnay are the specialties.

- **Michel-Schlumberger** (☎ 800-447-3060; www.michelschlumberger.com; 4155 Wine Creek Rd, Healdsburg; tours $20-30, tastings $10; ☼ tastings 11am-5pm, tours by appointment) A leader in organic farming, it makes superb Bordeaux-style wines – cabernet sauvignon, chardonnay and syrah – all in French oak, a rarity in California. A 'green tour' focuses on local ecology and sustainable winemaking, and culminates with a hilltop tasting.

- **Casa Nuestra** (☎ 707-963-5783, 866-844-9463; www.casanuestra.com; 3451 Silverado Trail, St Helena; tastings $10; ☼ by appointment; 🚹) An old-school, 1970s-vintage, mom-and-pop outfit, it produces unusual blends, interesting varietals and 100% cabernet franc. Vineyards are all organic and the buildings are solar-powered.

WINE COUNTRY

NAPA VALLEY

Dining hall at Castello di Amorosa winery (p188)

EMILY RIDDELL

things culinary – from produce stalls to kitchen stores to fantastic edibles.

At supercool **Vintner's Collective** (☎ 707-255-7150; www.vintnerscollective.com; 1245 Main St; tastings $25; 🕙 11am-6pm), sample tiny-scale-production high-end wines from 18 wineries too small to have their own tasting rooms.

SLEEPING

Chablis Inn (☎ 707-257-1944; 800-443-3490; www.chablisinn.com; 3360 Solano Ave; r Mon-Fri $89-109, Sat & Sun $139-159; ⛶ 🛜 🅿 ♿) This well-kept two-story motel is good value and has a hot tub.

Napa River Inn (☎ 707-251-8500, 877-251-8500; www.napariverinn.com; 500 Main St; r Mon-Fri $180-309, Sat & Sun $180-394; ⛶ 🛜) On the river in the historic 1884 Hatt Building, this inn has upper-midrange rooms with extras such as triple-sheeted beds, quality fabrics and bathrobes; for $25, get a doggie bed, cookies and chardonnay biscuits.

our pick **Carneros Inn** (☎ 707-299-4900, 888-400-9000; www.thecarnerosinn.com; 4048 Sonoma Hwy; r Mon-Fri $395-590, Sat & Sun $650-795; ⛶ 🛜 🅿 ♿) The pinnacle of chic for the under-50s, Carneros Inn's snappy design aesthetic and retro small-town-agricultural theme shatters the predictable Wine Country mold. The semidetached, corrugated-metal units look like itinerant housing, but inside are cherry-wood floors, ultrasuede headboards, bright white duvets, leather club chairs, wood-burning fireplaces, heated-tile bathroom floors, giant soaking tubs and indoor-outdoor showers. Splurge on a vineyard-view room.

EATING

Alexis Baking Co (☎ 707-258-1827; www.alexisbakingcompany.com; 1517 3rd St; dishes $7-11; 🕙 breakfast & lunch; 🅅 ♿) Our fave spot for scrambles, granola, focaccia-bread sandwiches, big cups of joe and boxed lunches to go.

Pearl Bistro (☎ 707-224-9161; www.therestaurantpearl.com; 1339 Pearl St; mains $15-19; 🕙 Tue-Sat) Meet locals at this dog-friendly bistro with red-painted concrete floors, pinewood tables and open-rafter ceilings. The winning, down-to-earth cooking includes double-cut pork chops, chicken verde with polenta, steak tacos and the specialty, oysters.

La Toque (☎ 707-257-5157; www.latoque.om; 1314 McKinstry St; 3-/4-/5-course menu 48/74/90; ☽ dinner) Napa's unsung hero of Gallic cooking, chef Ken Frank, exquisitely crafts haute-contemporary French cuisine, and is a master with foie gras and truffles. The artistry is mirrored in the wine director's accompanying selections. Service is refreshingly unpretentious. La Toque isn't for everyone, but if you're a foodie this might be your trip's best meal. Men: wear a jacket. Reservations essential.

DRINKING & ENTERTAINMENT

Downtown Joe's (☎ 707-258-2337; 902 Main t at 2nd St; ☈) Live music plays Thursday to Sunday, and TV sports show nightly at this often-packed microbrewery-restaurant.

Napa Valley Opera House (☎ 707-226-7372; www.nvoh.org; 1030 Main St) This restored vintage-1880s opera house stages straight plays, comedy and live musicians such as Ravi Shankar.

YOUNTVILLE

pop 2900

Say *yawnt*-ville. This once quiet town, 9 miles north of Napa, gets overrun with tourists most afternoons, but outstanding restaurants justify fighting traffic. If you're not into food, consider skipping it.

SLEEPING

Napa Valley Railway Inn (☎ 707-944-2000; www.napavalleyrailwayinn.com; 6523 Washington St; r $125-260; ⚊ ♿) Sleep in a converted railroad car, part of two short trains parked at a central platform. They've little privacy, but are moderately priced. Kids love 'em.

Poetry Inn (☎ 707-944-0646; www.poetryinn.com; 6380 Silverado Trail; r incl breakfast $500-1500; ⚊ ☈ ⚊) There's no better view of the Napa Valley than from this understatedly chic, five-room inn, located high on the valley wall east of Yountville. The rooms are decorated in arts-and-crafts-inspired style, and feature private balconies, wood-burning fireplaces, 1000-thread-count sheets and enormous baths with indoor-outdoor showers.

WINE COUNTRY

NAPA VALLEY

JERRY ALEXANDER

Thomas Keller's French patisserie, Bouchon Bakery, is located next to Bouchon bistro (p192) in Yountville

EATING

Make reservations for the following.

Bistro Jeanty (☎ 707-944-0103; www.bistrojeanty.com; 6510 Washington St; mains $17-29) A bistro is classically defined as serving comfort food to weary travelers, and that's exactly what French-born chef-owner Philippe Jeanty does, with great cassoulet, coq au vin, steak-*frites,* braised pork with lentils, and scrumptious tomato soup.

Bouchon (☎ 707-944-8037; www.bouchonbistro.com; 6534 Washington St; mains $17-36) At celeb chef Thomas Keller's French brasserie, everything from food to decor is so authentic, from zinc bar to white-aproned waiters, you'd swear you were in Paris – even the Bermuda-shorts-clad Americans look out of place. On the menu: giant platters of oysters, onion soup, roasted chicken, leg of lamb, trout with almonds, runny cheeses and profiteroles for dessert, all impeccably prepared.

French Laundry (☎ 707-944-2380; www.frenchlaundry.com; 6640 Washington St; prix fixe incl service charge $250; dinner, lunch Fri-Sun) The pinnacle of California dining, Thomas Keller's French Laundry is epic, a high-wattage culinary experience on par with the world's best. Book two months ahead at 10am sharp. Avoid booking before 7pm; first-service seating moves faster than the second – sometimes too fast.

ST HELENA

pop 5900

You'll know you're arriving when traffic halts. St Helena (say ha-*lee*-na) is the Rodeo Drive of Napa, with fancy boutiques lining Main St (Hwy 29). The historic downtown is good for a stroll, with great window-shopping, but parking is next-to-impossible summer weekends.

The **Chamber of Commerce** (☎ 707-963-4456, 800-799-6456; www.sthelena.com; Suite A, 1010 Main St; 10am-5pm Mon-Fri) has information and lodging assistance.

SIGHTS & ACTIVITIES

Silverado Museum (☎ 707-963-3757; www.silveradomuseum.org; 1490 Library Lane; admission free; noon-4pm Tue-Sat) contains a fascinating collection of Robert Louis Stevenson memorabilia. In 1880 the author – then sick, penniless and unknown – stayed in an abandoned bunkhouse at the old Silverado Mine with his wife, Fanny Osbourne. His novel *The Silverado Squatters* is based on his time there.

The **Culinary Institute of America at Greystone** (CIA; ☎ 707-967-2320; www.ciachef.edu/california; 2555 Main St; cooking demonstration $15; demonstrations 10:30am & 1:30pm), a continuing-education campus for food and wine professionals, occupies the Christian Brothers' 1889 château and offers public cooking demonstrations on Saturday and Sunday.

SLEEPING

Hotel St Helena (☎ 707-963-4388; www.hotelsthelena.net; 1309 Main St; r with bath $145-275, without bath $105-195;) Decorated with period furnishings, this 1881 hotel sits right downtown. Rooms are tiny but a bargain, especially those with shared bathrooms.

El Bonita Motel (☎ 707-963-3216, 800-541-3284; www.elbonita.com; 195 Main St; r $145-269;) Book in advance to secure a room at this sought-after motel, with up-to-date rooms (quietest are in back), attractive grounds, a hot tub and a sauna.

EATING

Martini House (☎ 707-963-2233; www.martinihouse.com; 1245 Spring St; lunch mains $17-28, dinner mains $17-32; lunch Fri-Sun, dinner daily) One of Wine Country's most handsome dining rooms, Martini House occupies a 1923 California arts-and-crafts-style house, with food as fine as the room is gorgeous. Celeb chef-owner Todd Humphries is a master with mushrooms; consider ordering his signature tasting menu ($56).

JERRY ALEXANDER

A peek into the kitchen at French Laundry (p192), Yountville

↘ IF YOU LIKE...

If you like the culinary delights of French Laundry (p192), we think you'll like these other excellent restaurants:

- Farmhouse Inn (☎ 707-887-3300; www.farmhouseinn.com; 7871 River Rd, Forestville; mains $35-40; ☽ dinner Thu-Mon) One of Wine Country's best, the Farmhouse changes its seasonal Euro-Cal menu daily, using locally raised, organic ingredients such as Sonoma lamb, wild salmon and rabbit.

- Madrona Manor (☎ 707-433-4231, 800-258-4003; www.madronamanor.com; 1001 Westside Rd, Healdsburg; prix fixe $73-91; ☽ dinner Wed-Sun) You'd be hard-pressed to find a lovelier place to pop the question than on the mansion's garden-view veranda, while supping on sophisticated Euro-Cal cooking.

- Ubuntu (☎ 707-251-5656; www.ubuntunapa.com; 1140 Main St, Napa; mains $12-20; ☽ dinner daily, lunch Sat & Sun; Ⓥ) A splurge-worthy vegetarian option on par with Napa's top tables.

- Terra (☎ 707-963-8931; www.terrarestaurant.com; 1345 Railroad Ave, St Helena; mains $20-36; ☽ dinner Wed-Mon) Inside an 1884 stone building, Terra wows diners with its seamlessly blended Japanese, French and Italian culinary styles. The signature is a stellar broiled, sake-marinated black cod and shrimp dumplings in shiso broth.

- Café La Haye (☎ 707-935-5994; www.cafelahaye.com; 140 E Napa St, Sonoma; mains $17-25; ☽ dinner Tue-Sat) One of Sonoma's top tables for earthy New American cooking, made with produce sourced from within 60 miles. The tiny room is cheek-by-jowl and service borders on perfunctory, but the clean simplicity and flavor-packed cooking make it foodies' first choice.

WINE COUNTRY

NAPA VALLEY

Wine Spectator Restaurant at Greystone (☎ 707-967-1010; www.ciachef.edu; 2555 Main St; mains $17-34) Inside the renowned Culinary Institute of America, head directly to the gorgeous patio bar for cocktails or garden-view lunch, or sit inside and watch the chefs in the open kitchen. The menu is pure California, with a broad selection of local wines and microbrews.

Market (☎ 707-963-3799; www.marketsthelena.com; 1347 Main St; mains $19-29; ⊙ 11am-9pm Mon-Thu, 11:30am-10pm Fri & Sat, 9am-9pm Sun) We love the big portions of simple, fresh American cooking at Market. Maximizing the season's best produce, the chef creates enormous, inventive salads and soul-satisfying mains such as buttermilk fried chicken. The stone-walled dining room dates to the 19th century, as does the ornate back bar, where cocktails are muddled to order.

SHOPPING

Diva Perfumes (☎ 707-963-4057; 1309 Main St) If you can't get to Paris, get hard-to-find perfumes here.

Woodhouse Chocolates (☎ 800-966-3468; 1367 Main St) Woodhouse looks more like Tiffany & Co than a candy shop, and the chocolates are priced accordingly: $84 per pound.

CALISTOGA
pop 5200

The least gentrified town in Napa Valley feels refreshingly simple, with an old-fashioned main street lined with shops, not boutiques, and a diverse mix of characters wandering the sidewalks.

Calistoga is synonymous with the mineral water bearing its name, bottled here since 1924. Its springs and geysers have earned it the nickname the 'hot springs of the West.' Plan to visit one of the town's spas, where you can indulge in the local specialty: a hot-mud bath, made of the volcanic ash from nearby volcanic Mt St Helena.

ORIENTATION & INFORMATION
Chamber of Commerce & Visitors Center (☎ 707-942-6333, 866-306-5588;

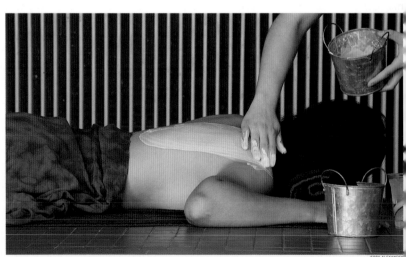

JERRY ALEXANDER

Calistoga is famous for its mud baths and hot-spring spas

www.calistogachamber.com; 1133 Washington
St; ⏰ 9am-5pm)

SIGHTS & ACTIVITIES

Calistoga is famous for **hot-spring spas**
and **mud-bath emporiums**, where you're
buried in hot mud and emerge feeling
supple, detoxified and enlivened. The
mud is made with volcanic ash and peat;
the higher the ash content, the better the
bath.

Packages take 60 to 90 minutes and
cost $75 to $85. You start semisubmerged
in hot mud, then soak in hot mineral
water. A steam bath and blanket-wrap
follow. The treatment can be extended
with a massage, increasing the cost to
$120 or more.

The following spas in downtown
Calistoga offer one-day packages. Some
also offer discounted spa-and-lodging
packages.

Calistoga Spa Hot Springs (☎ 707-942-
6269, 866-822-5772; www.calistogaspa.com; 1006
Washington St; ⏰ appointments 8:30am-4:30pm
Tue-Thu, to 9pm Fri-Mon; ♿) offers traditional
mud baths and massage at a motel complex. There are two huge swimming
pools, where kids can play while you soak
(pool passes cost $25 during the week;
free with spa appointment Saturday and
Sunday).

our pick **Indian Springs** (☎ 707-942-4913;
www.indianspringscalistoga.com; 1712 Lincoln Ave;
⏰ 9am-8pm) is the longest continually operating spa. This original Calistoga resort
has concrete mud tubs and mines its own
ash. Treatments include use of the huge,
hot-spring-fed pool. Great cucumber
body lotion.

Mount View Spa (☎ 707-942-6877, 800-
816-6877; www.mountviewhotel.com; 1457 Lincoln
Ave; ⏰ 9am-7pm) Traditional, full-service,
12-room spa good for those who prefer
painted-on mud to submersion.

SLEEPING

**Dr Wilkinson's Motel & Hideaway
Cottages** (☎ 707-942-4102; www.drwilkinson.
com; 1507 Lincoln Ave; r $149-299, housekeeping
cottages from $164; ♿ 🌐 🏊 ♿) This good-
value vintage-1950s motel has well-kept
rooms facing a courtyard. There's no hot
tub, but there are three pools (one indoors) – and, of course, mud baths. Doc
Wilkinson's rents housekeeping units at
its sister property, Hideaway Cottages.

Indian Springs Resort (☎ 707-942-4913;
www.indianspringscalistoga.com; 1712 Lincoln Ave;
motel r $225-290, studios $195-280, 1-bedroom
bungalows $225-355, 2-bedroom bungalows $495-
595; ♿ 🌐 🏊 ♿) The definitive Calistoga
resort, Indian Springs has bungalows
facing a central lawn with palm trees,
shuffleboard, bocce, hammocks and
Weber grills – not unlike an old-school
Florida resort. Some bungalows sleep six.
There are also top-end motel-style rooms.
All have great beds.

EATING & DRINKING

All Seasons Bistro (☎ 707-942-9111; www.
allseasonsnapavalley.net; 1400 Lincoln Ave; lunch
mains $10-15, dinner mains $18-22; ⏰ lunch &
dinner Tue-Sun) The dining room looks like
a white-tablecloth soda fountain, but All
Seasons makes some of the best food in
town, from simple steak-*frites* to composed dishes such as cornmeal-crusted
scallops with summer succotash, all using
sustainably grown ingredients. Great wine
list.

Solbar (☎ 707-226-0850; www.solbarnv.
com; 755 Silverado Trail; lunch $15-19, dinner $19-
36) At last Calistoga has a dining room
on par with down-valley restaurants.
The look is spare, with concrete floors,
exposed-wood tables and soaring ceilings. Flavors are clean and bright, maxi-
mizing the use of seasonal produce. Each
dish is elegantly composed on the plate,

WINE COUNTRY

NAPA VALLEY

JERRY ALEXANDER

A giant rests in the Petrified Forest

with a strong interplay of sweet, salt and acid, as in the wine-braised short ribs with pungent gremolata and creamy risotto.

SHOPPING

Wine Garage (☎ 707-942-5332; www.wine garage.net; 1020 Foothill Blvd) Every bottle costs less than $25 at this cool wine store, formerly a service station.

Calistoga Pottery (☎ 707-942-0216; www.calistogapottery.com; 1001 Foothill Blvd) Winemakers aren't the only artisans in Napa. Watch a potter throw vases, bowls and plates, all for sale.

AROUND CALISTOGA

OLD FAITHFUL GEYSER

Calistoga's mini version of Yellowstone's Old Faithful shoots boiling water 60ft to 100ft into the air, every 45 minutes. The vibe is pure roadside Americana, with folksy hand-painted interpretive exhibits, picnicking and a little petting zoo.

The **geyser** (☎ 707-942-6463; www.oldfaith fulgeyser.com; 1299 Tubbs Lane; adult/child under 6yr/child 6-12yr/senior $10/free/3/7; ☼ 9am-6pm summer, to 5pm winter; ♿) is 2 miles north of town, off Silverado Trail. Look for discount coupons around town.

PETRIFIED FOREST

Three million years ago, a volcanic eruption at nearby Mt St Helens blew down a stand of redwoods between Calistoga and Santa Rosa. The trees fell in the same direction, away from the blast, and were covered in ash and mud. Over the millennia, the mighty giants' trunks turned to stone; gradually the overlay eroded, exposing them. The first stumps were discovered in 1870. A monument marks Robert Louis Stevenson's 1880 visit.

The **petrified forest** (☎ 707-942-6667; www.petrifiedforest.org; 4100 Petrified Forest Rd; adult/child/senior $10/5/9; ☼ 9am-7pm summer, to 5pm winter) is 5 miles northwest of town off Hwy 128. Check online for 15%-off coupons.

ROBERT LOUIS STEVENSON STATE PARK

The long-extinct volcanic cone of Mt St Helena marks the valley's end, 8 miles north of Calistoga. The undeveloped **state park** (☎ 707-942-4575; www.parks.ca.gov; admission free) on Hwy 29 often gets snow in winter.

It's a strenuous 5-mile climb to the peak's 4343ft summit, but what a view – 200 miles on a clear winter's day. Check conditions before setting out. Also consider 2.2-mile one-way Table Rock Trail (go south from the summit parking area) for drop-dead valley views.

The park includes the site of the Silverado Mine where Stevenson and his wife honeymooned in 1880.

SAFARI WEST

Safari West (☎ 707-579-2551, 800-616-2695; www.safariwest.com; 3115 Porter Creek Rd; adult/child $68/30;) covers 400 acres and protects zebras, cheetahs and other exotic animals, which mostly roam free. See them on a guided three-hour safari in open-sided jeeps; reservations required. You'll also walk thorough an aviary and a lemur condo. The reservations-only cafe serves lunch and dinner. If you're feeling adventurous, stay overnight in nifty canvas-sided **tent cabins** (incl breakfast $200-295), right in the preserve.

SONOMA VALLEY

We have a soft spot for Sonoma's folksy ways. Unlike in fancy-pants Napa, nobody cares if you drive a clunker and vote Green. Locals call it 'Slow-noma.' Anchoring the bucolic 17-mile-long Sonoma Valley, the town of Sonoma makes a great jumping-off point for exploring Wine Country – it's only an hour from San Francisco – and has a marvelous sense of place, with storied 19th-century historical sights surrounding the state's largest town square. If you've more than a day, explore Sonoma's quiet, rustic side along the Russian River Valley (p202) and work your way to the sea.

SONOMA VALLEY WINERIES

Rolling grass-covered hills rise from 17-by-7-mile-long Sonoma Valley. Its 72 wineries get less attention than Napa's, but many are equally good. If you love zinfandel and syrah, you're in for a treat.

GUNDLACH-BUNDSCHU

One of Sonoma Valley's oldest and prettiest wineries, **Gundlach-Bundschu** (☎ 707-938-5277; www.gunbun.com; 2000 Denmark St; tastings

NAPA OR SONOMA?

Napa and Sonoma valleys run parallel, a few miles apart, separated by the narrow, imposing Mayacamas Mountains. The two couldn't be more different. It's easy to mock aggressively sophisticated Napa, its monuments to ego, trophy homes and trophy wives, $1000-a-night inns, $30+ tastings and wine-snob visitors, but Napa makes some of the world's best wines. Constrained by its geography, it stretches along a single valley, so it's easy to visit. Drawbacks are high prices and heavy traffic, but there are 200 nearly side-by-side wineries. And the valley is gorgeous.

Sonoma County is much more down-to-earth and politically left leaning. You'll see lots more rusted-out pick-ups. Though becoming gentrified, Sonoma lacks Napa's chic factor, and locals like it that way.

WINE COUNTRY

SONOMA VALLEY

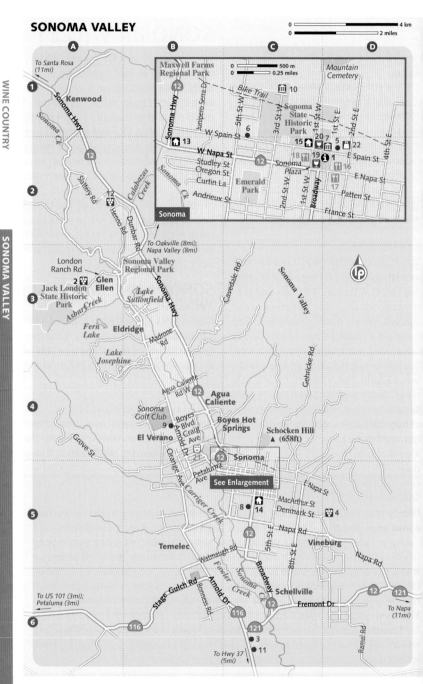

SONOMA VALLEY

0 — 4 km
0 — 2 miles

A   **B**   **C**   **D**

To Santa Rosa (11mi)

Kenwood

Sonoma Hwy

Sonoma Ck

12

Slattery Rd

Calabazas Creek

Henno Rd

Dunbar Rd

12

Sonoma Ck

Sonoma (Enlargement)

Maxwell Farms Regional Park

0 — 500 m
0 — 0.25 miles

12

Junipero Serra Dr

Bike Trail

Mountain Cemetery

10

5th St W

3rd St W

2nd St W

1st St W

1st St E

2nd St E

4th St E

Sonoma State Historic Park

W Spain St   6

15   7   5   22

18   19   1   E Spain St

Sonoma Plaza   16

W Napa St   **12**

Studley St
Oregon St
Curtin La

Emerald Park

Andrieux St

E Napa St

17

Patten St

2nd St W

1st St W

Broadway

France St

Sonoma

13

To Oakville (8mi);
Napa Valley (8mi)

Sonoma Valley Regional Park

London Ranch Rd

2   Glen Ellen

Jack London State Historic Park

Ashbury Creek

Lake Suttonfield

Sonoma Hwy

Fern Lake

Eldridge

Madrone Rd

Lake Josephine

Cavedale Rd

Sonoma Valley

Gehricke Rd

Agua Caliente Rd W

12   Agua Caliente

Sonoma Golf Club

Boyes Blvd   9

Boyes Hot Springs

Schocken Hill
▲ (658ft)

El Verano

Arnold Dr

Craig Ave

Grove St

Orange Ave

12   Sonoma

Petaluma Ave

Carriger Creek

See Enlargement

E Napa St

MacArthur St

8   14   Denmark St   4

Napa Rd   Vineburg

Napa Rd

12

5th St E

8th St E

Temelec

Watmaugh Rd

Fowler Creek

Sonoma Ck

Broadway

Schellville

12   **121**

Fremont Dr

To Napa (11mi)

121

To US 101 (3mi);
Petaluma (3mi)

Stage Gulch Rd

Arnold Dr

Bonness Rd

116

116

121   3

11

To Hwy 37 (5mi)

Ramal Rd

INFORMATION
Sonoma Valley Visitors Bureau.............................**1** D2

SIGHTS & ACTIVITIES
Bear Flag Monument...(see 1)
Benziger..**2** A3
City Hall..(see 1)
Cornerstone Gardens...**3** C6
Gundlach-Bundschu...**4** D5
Mission San Francisco Solano de Sonoma.............**5** D2
Ramekins Sonoma Valley Culinary School............**6** C1
Sonoma Barracks...**7** D2
Sonoma Valley Cyclery...**8** C5
Spa at Sonoma Mission Inn...................................**9** B4
Vallejo Home...**10** C1
Vintage Aircraft Company...................................**11** C6
Wellington..**12** A2

SLEEPING
El Pueblo Inn...**13** B2
MacArthur Place...**14** C5
Sonoma Hotel..**15** C2

EATING
Café La Haye..**16** D2
Della Santina's...**17** D2
girl & the fig..(see 15)
Harvest Moon Café...**18** C2

DRINKING
Steiner's..**19** C2
Swiss Hotel..**20** C2

ENTERTAINMENT
Little Switzerland..**21** B4

SHOPPING
Vella Cheese Co..**22** D2

$5-10) was founded in 1858 by Bavarian immigrant Jacob Gundlach. Rieslings and gewürztraminers are the signatures, but 'Gun-Bun' was the first in America to produce 100% merlot. Tours of the 2000-barrel cave ($20) are available Friday to Sunday. Situated up a winding road, it's a good bike-to winery, with picnicking, hiking and a small lake.

BENZIGER

If you're new to wine, make **Benziger** (☎ 707-935-3000, 888-490-2739; www.benziger. com; 1883 London Ranch Rd, Glen Ellen; tastings $10-15; 🚻) your first stop for Sonoma's best crash course in winemaking. The worthwhile, nonreservable tour ($15) includes an open-air tram ride through biodynamic vineyards and a four-wine

tasting. Little ones love the peacocks. The large-production wine's OK (head for the reserves); the tour's the thing.

WELLINGTON

Known for port (including a white) and meaty reds, **Wellington** (☎ 707-939-0708, 800-816-9463; www.wellingtonvineyards.com; 11600 Dunbar Rd, Glen Ellen; tastings $5) makes great zinfandel, one from vines planted in 1892 – wow, what color! The noir de noir is a cult favorite.

SONOMA & AROUND

pop 9900

Fancy boutiques may be replacing hardware stores, but Sonoma still retains an old-fashioned charm, thanks to the plaza – California's largest town square – and its surrounding historic buildings.

Sonoma has a rich history. In 1846 it was the site of a second American revolution, this time against Mexico, when General Mariano Guadalupe Vallejo deported all foreigners from California, prompting outraged American frontiersmen to occupy the Sonoma presidio (military post) and declare independence. They dubbed California the Bear Flag Republic after the battle flag they'd fashioned.

The republic was short-lived. The Mexican American War broke out a month later, and California was annexed by the US. The revolt gave California its flag, which remains emblazoned with the words 'California Republic' beneath a muscular brown bear. Vallejo was initially imprisoned, but ultimately returned to Sonoma and played a major role in the region's development.

ORIENTATION & INFORMATION
Sonoma Valley Visitors Bureau (☎ 707-996-1090, 866-996-1090; www.sonomavalley.com; 453 1st St E; 🕑 9am-5pm Mon-Sat, 10am-5pm Sun)

WINE COUNTRY

SONOMA VALLEY

WINE COUNTRY

SONOMA VALLEY

Arranges accommodations; has a good walking-tour pamphlet and information on events.

SIGHTS
SONOMA PLAZA & AROUND
Smack in the plaza's center, the mission-revival-style **City Hall** (1906–08) has identical facades on four sides, reportedly because plaza businesses all demanded City Hall face their direction. At the plaza's northeast corner, the **Bear Flag Monument** marks Sonoma's moment of revolutionary glory.

SONOMA STATE HISTORIC PARK
The mission, Sonoma Barracks and Vallejo Home are part of **Sonoma State Historic Park** (☎ 707-938-9560; www.parks.ca.gov; adult/child under 17yr $3/2; ☯ 10am-5pm Fri-Wed).

The **Mission San Francisco Solano de Sonoma** (E Spain St), at the plaza's northeast corner, was built in 1823, in part to forestall the Russian coastal colony at Fort Ross from moving inland. The mission was the 21st and final California mission and the only one built during the Mexican period (the rest were founded by the Spanish). It marks the northernmost point on El Camino Real. Five of the mission's original rooms remain. The not-to-be-missed chapel dates from 1841.

The adobe **Sonoma Barracks** (E Spain St) were built by Vallejo between 1836 and 1840 to house Mexican troops. The barracks later became American military quarters. Now a museum, the barracks houses displays on life during the Mexican and American periods.

A half-mile northwest, the **Vallejo Home**, otherwise known as Lachryma Montis (Latin for 'Tears of the Mountain'), was built in 1851–52 for General Vallejo. It's named for the spring on the property; the Vallejo family later made a handy income piping water to town. A bike path leads to the house from downtown.

CORNERSTONE GARDENS
There's nothing traditional about **Cornerstone Gardens** (☎ 707-933-3010; www.cornerstonegardens.com; 23570 Hwy 121;

JUDY BELLAH

Ring-tailed lemurs, Safari West (p197)

admission free; 🕙 10am-4pm), which showcases the work of 25 renowned avant-garde landscape designers. We especially love Pamela Burton's 'Earth Walk,' which descends into the ground; and McCrory and Raiche's 'Rise,' which exaggerates space.

ACTIVITIES

Many local inns provide bicycles, or you can rent one from **Sonoma Valley Cyclery** (☎ 707-935-3377; www.sonomacyclery.com; 20091 Broadway; 🕙 10am-6pm Mon-Sat, to 4pm Sun) for $6 per hour, $25 per day.

Few Wine Country spas compare with glitzy **Spa at Sonoma Mission Inn** (☎ 707-938-9000, 877-289-7354; www.fairmont.com/sonoma; 100 Boyes Blvd). Book two treatments and get free access to the Romanesque bathhouse.

COURSES

Ramekins Sonoma Valley Culinary School (☎ 707-933-0450; www.ramekins.com; 450 W Spain St) offers demonstrations and hands-on classes for home chefs. Ask about winemaker dinners.

SLEEPING

El Pueblo Inn (☎ 707-996-3651, 800-900-8844; www.elpuebloinn.com; 896 W Napa St; r $169-299; ❄ 🖵 🛜 🐾 🕭) One mile west of downtown, family-owned El Pueblo has surprisingly cushy rooms with great beds. The big lawns and the heated pool are perfect for kids; moms like the small spa.

Sonoma Hotel (☎ 707-996-2996, 800-468-6016; www.sonomahotel.com; 110 W Spain St; r $175-200; ❄ 🛜) This spiffy vintage-1880s hotel is decked with Spanish-colonial and American-country-crafts furnishings. There's no elevator.

MacArthur Place (☎ 707-938-2929, 800-722-1866; www.macarthurplace.com; 29 E MacArthur St; r from $350, ste from $450; ❄ 🖵 🛜 🐾) Built on the grounds of a former estate, with gorgeous 150-year-old plantings, splurge-worthy MacArthur is Sonoma's top inn, with sumptuous rooms in a historic house and outlying cottages. Spa suites have double-sized bathtubs and private gardens with outdoor hot tubs – perfect for a kiss-and-make-up weekend.

EATING

girl & the fig (☎ 707-938-3634; www.thegirlandthefig.com; 110 W Spain St; lunch mains $10-15, dinner mains $17-23) For a festive evening, book a garden table at this soulful French-provincial bistro, known for its hearty cooking and party atmosphere. We love the small plates (from $10 to $14), especially the steamed mussels with matchstick fries, and duck confit with lentils. The weekday three-course prix-fixe menu costs $32; add $8 for wine. Stellar cheeses. Reservations essential.

Della Santina's (☎ 707-935-0576; www.dellasantinas.com; 135 E Napa St; mains $11-18) The waiters have been at Della Santina's forever, and its 'specials' never change (*penne con funghili* and veal parmigiana), but the food is consistent ($12 plates of pasta pesto, $15 rotisserie chickens) and the brick courtyard is charming, especially on warm evenings. Try the *delizia* for dessert.

Harvest Moon Café (☎ 707-933-8160; www.harvestmooncafesonoma.com; 487 1st St W; mains $18-25; 🕙 10am-2pm & 5:30-9pm Wed-Mon) Inside an 1836 adobe, this casual bistro uses local ingredients in its changing menu, with dishes such as duck risotto with Bellwether Farms ricotta. Lovely back patio.

DRINKING

Steiner's (☎ 707-996-3812; 456 1st St W) Open since 1927, Steiner's is Sonoma's oldest bar. It's crowded on Sunday afternoons with cyclists and motorcyclists. We dig the taxidermy mountain lions.

Swiss Hotel (☎ 707-938-2884; 18 W Spain St) Locals and tourists crowd side-by-side at the 1909 Swiss Hotel for afternoon cocktails. There's OK food, but the bar's the thing.

ENTERTAINMENT

Little Switzerland (☎ 707-938-9990; www.lilswiss.com; 19080 Riverside; Fri-Sun;) Long before Sonoma became 'Wine Country,' locals drank at this old-fashioned beer garden. Live bands play Latin music Friday evenings; jazz, swing or zydeco on Saturdays; and – the great tradition – polka on Sunday afternoons, when you can bring the family. It sometimes serves barbecue; call ahead.

SHOPPING

Vella Cheese Co (☎ 707-928-3232; 315 2nd St E) Known for its dry-jack cheeses (made here since the 1930s), Vella also makes good mezzo secco with cocoa-powder-dusted rind. Staff will vacuum-pack for shipping.

RUSSIAN RIVER AREA

Lesser-known west Sonoma County was formerly famous for its apple farms and vacation cottages. Lately vineyards are replacing the orchards, and the Russian River has now taken its place among California's important wine appellations for superb pinot noir.

'The River,' as locals call it, has long been a summertime weekend destination for Northern Californians, who come to canoe, wander country lanes, taste wine, hike redwood forests and live at a lazy pace. In winter the river floods and nobody's here.

RUSSIAN RIVER AREA WINERIES

RUSSIAN RIVER VALLEY

Nighttime coastal fog drifts up the Russian River Valley, then clears around midday. Pinot noir does beautifully here, as does chardonnay, which also grows in hotter regions but prefers the longer 'hang time' of cooler climes.

JERRY ALEXANDER

An invitation to sample the wine selection, Bella Vineyards (p204)

JERRY ALEXANDER

Traversing the trails of Jack London State Historic Park

🪶 JACK LONDON STATE HISTORIC PARK

Napa has Robert Louis Stevenson, but Sonoma's got Jack London. The 1400-acre Jack London State Historic Park traces the last years of the author's life.

Changing his occupation from Oakland fisherman to Alaska gold prospector to Pacific yachtsman – and novelist on the side – London (1876–1916) ultimately took up farming. He bought Beauty Ranch in 1905 and moved there in 1910. With his second wife, Charmian, he lived and wrote in a small cottage while his mansion, Wolf House, was under construction. On the eve of its completion in 1913, it burned down. This disaster devastated London, and although he toyed with rebuilding, he died before construction got underway. The widow Charmian built the House of Happy Walls, which has been preserved as a museum. It's a half-mile walk from there to the remains of Wolf House, passing London's grave along the way. Other paths wind around the farm to the cottage where he lived and worked. Miles of trails (some of which are open to mountain bikes) weave through oak-dotted woodlands, between 600ft and 2300ft in elevation.

Things you need to know: ☎ 707-938-5216; www.parks.ca.gov; off Hwy 12, Glen Ellen; parking $8; ⏱ 10am-5pm

HARTFORD FAMILY WINERY

Surprisingly upscale Hartford Family (☎ 707-887-8030; www.hartfordwines.com; 8075 Martinelli Rd, Forestville; tastings $5-15) sits in a pastoral valley surrounded by redwood-forested hills on one of the area's prettiest back roads. It specializes in single-vineyard pinot (eight kinds), chardonnay and zinfandel, some from old-vine fruit.

J WINERY

Swanky J (☎ 707-431-3646; www.jwine.com; 11447 Old Redwood Hwy, Healdsburg; tastings $20) makes crisp sparkling wines – one of Wine Country's best – a terrific pinot noir and a lesser-known pinot gris.

DRY CREEK VALLEY

Hemmed in by 2000ft-high mountains, Dry Creek Valley is relatively warm, ideal for sauvignon blanc, zinfandel and (in spots) cabernet sauvignon. It's west of Hwy 101, between Healdsburg and Lake Sonoma. Parallel-running West Dry Creek Rd is an undulating country lane with no center stripe – one of Sonoma's great back roads, ideal for biking.

BELLA VINEYARDS

Atop the valley's north end, always-fun **Bella** (☎ 707-473-9171, 866-572-3552; www. bellawinery.com; 9711 W Dry Creek Rd; tastings $5-10) has caves built into the hillside. The estate-grown grapes include 110-year-old vines from the Alexander Valley. The focus is on big reds – zin and syrah – but there's terrific rosé, an ideal barbecue wine, and late-harvest zin that goes fabulously with brownies. The wonderful vibe and dynamic staff make Bella special.

UNTI VINEYARDS

Inside a fluorescent-lit, windowless garage, **Unti** (☎ 707-433-5590; www.untivineyards.com; 4202 Dry Creek Rd; ⏱ by appointment) makes estate-grown reds, including a

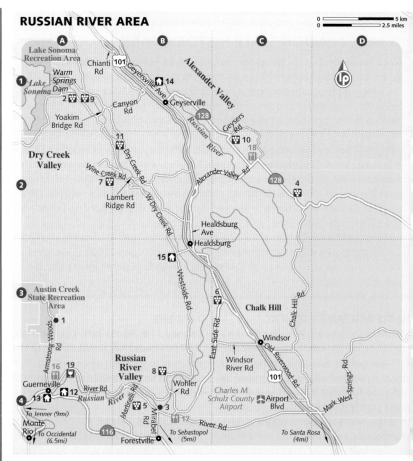

RUSSIAN RIVER AREA

Châteauneuf-du-Pape-style granache, a powerful and compelling syrah, and a 100% sangiovese, favored by oenophiles. If you love wine, don't miss Unti.

ALEXANDER VALLEY

Bucolic Alexander Valley flanks the Mayacamas Mountains immediately west of Napa, with postcard-perfect vistas and wide-open vineyards. Summers are hot, perfect for cabernet sauvignon, merlot and warm-weather chardonnay, but there's also fine sauvignon blanc and zinfandel. For events info, including First Weekend happenings, visit www.alexandervalley.org.

STRYKER SONOMA

Wow! What a view from the hilltop concrete-and-glass tasting room at **Stryker Sonoma** (☎ **707-433-1944; www.strykersonoma.com; 5110 Hwy 128, Geyserville; tastings $10**). Plan to picnic. The standouts are fruit-forward zinfandel and sangiovese, which you can't buy anywhere else.

SIGHTS & ACTIVITIES		
Armstrong Woods State Reserve	1	A3
Bella Vineyards	2	A1
Burke's Canoe Trips	3	B4
Hanna	4	C2
Hartford Family Winery	5	B4
J Winery	6	C3
Michel-Schlumberger	7	A2
Porter Creek	8	B4
Preston Vineyards	9	A1
Stryker Sonoma	10	C2
Unti Vineyards	11	B2
SLEEPING		
Applewood Inn	12	A4
Creekside Inn & Resort	13	A4
Geyserville Inn	14	B1
Madrona Manor	15	B3
EATING		
Applewood Inn Restaurant	(see 12)	
Coffee Bazaar	16	A4
Farmhouse Inn	17	B4
Jimtown Store	18	C2
Madrona Manor	(see 15)	
DRINKING		
Stumptown Brewery	19	A4

JERRY ALEXANDER

Wine barrels at Stryker Sonoma

HANNA

Abutting oak-studded hills, **Hanna** (☎ **707-431-4310, 800-854-3987; www.hannawinery.com; 9280 Hwy 128, Healdsburg; tastings $5-10; 🕑 10am-4pm**) resembles a Tuscan-style train depot. At the bar, look out for estate-grown merlot and cabernet, as well as big-fruit zins and syrah. There's an appointment-only sit-down tasting of reserve wine, cheese and charcuterie available for $15. There are stellar views and good picnicking.

GUERNEVILLE

Pop 5570

The Russian River's biggest vacation-resort town, Guerneville gets packed on summer weekends with party-hardy gay boys, sun-worshipping lesbians and

WINE COUNTRY

RUSSIAN RIVER AREA

long-haired beer-drinking Harley riders, earning it the nickname 'Groin-ville.' The gay scene has died back since the unfortunate closure of Fife's, the world's first gay resort, but fun-seeking crowds still come to canoe, hike redwoods and hammer cocktails poolside.

ORIENTATION & INFORMATION

Russian River Chamber of Commerce & Visitor Center (☎ 707-869-9000, 877-644-9001; www.russianriver.com; 16209 1st St, Guerneville; ☺ 10am-5pm Mon-Sat, to 4pm Sun)

SIGHTS & ACTIVITIES

A magnificent redwood forest 2 miles north of Guerneville, the 805-acre

---

Armstrong Redwoods State Reserve (☎ 707-869-2015; www.parks.ca.gov; 17000 Armstrong Woods Rd; day use per vehicle $8) was set aside by a 19th-century lumber magnate. Walk or cycle in for free; pay only to drive in. Short interpretive trails lead into magical forests, with miles of backcountry trails and campgrounds.

Look for sandy beaches and swimming holes along the river. There's year-round fishing. Outfitters operate mid-May to early October, after which winter rains dangerously swell the river.

You can't beat **Burke's Canoe Trips** (☎ 707-887-1222; www.burkescanoetrips.com; 8600 River Rd, cnr Mirabel Rd, Forestville; ☺ Memorial Day-Sep; ♿) for a day on the river. Self-guided canoe trips cost $60 per canoe and include shuttles back to your car. Camping in the riverside redwood grove costs $10 per person.

SLEEPING

Creekside Inn & Resort (☎ 707-869-3623, 800-776-6586; www.creeksideinn.com; 16180 Neeley Rd; B&B r $98-175, cottages $125-270, ste $198; ⛐ 🛜 🐾) Across the river from downtown, quiet and secluded-feeling Creekside has well-tended cottages with kitchens (some with fireplaces), and homey B&B rooms in the main house. Creekside is enviro-conscious: new 'green cottages' were built with solar panels. There's a hot tub and a pool beneath redwoods. Some air-con.

Applewood Inn (☎ 707-869-9093, 800-555-8509; www.applewoodinn.com; 13555 Hwy 116; r $195-345; ⛐ 🛜 🐾) A former estate on a wooded hilltop, the Applewood has marvelous arts-and-crafts-era detail, with dark wood and heavy furniture. Rooms sport hot tubs, couples' showers and top-end linens; some have fireplaces and air-con.

⟫ A WINE COUNTRY PRIMER

When people talk about Sonoma, they're referring to the *whole* county, which unlike Napa is huge. It extends all the way from the coast, up the Russian River Valley, into Sonoma Valley and eastward to Napa Valley; in the south it stretches from San Pablo Bay (an extension of San Francisco Bay) to Healdsburg in the north. It's essential to break Sonoma down by district.

West County refers to everything west of Hwy 101 and includes the **Russian River Valley** and the coast. **Sonoma Valley** stretches north-south along Hwy 12. In northern Sonoma County, **Alexander Valley** lies east of Healdsburg, and **Dry Creek Valley** lies north of Healdsburg. In the south, **Carneros** straddles the Sonoma-Napa border, north of San Pablo Bay.

Charles M Schulz Museum (p208), Santa Rosa
JERRY ALEXANDER

EATING

Coffee Bazaar (☎ 707-869-9706; 14045 Armstrong Woods Rd; dishes $3-9; ⏰ 6am-8pm; 📶) This happenin' hangout serves salads, sandwiches and pastries. It's attached to a bookstore.

Applewood Inn Restaurant (☎ 707-869-9093, 800-555-8509; www.applewoodinn.com; 13555 Hwy 116; mains $28-37; ⏰ dinner Tue-Sun) It's cozy by the fire in the treetop-level dining room at Guerneville's best resort. The bold Euro-Cal cooking maximizes seasonal produce, with dishes such as rack of lamb with minted *chimichurri* (garlic-parsley vinaigrette), and a roast chicken with bacon, corn, cabbage, lentils and mash. Make reservations.

DRINKING

Stumptown Brewery (☎ 707-869-0705; 15045 River Rd, Guerneville) Guerneville's best straight bar is gay-friendly and has a foot-stompin' jukebox, a pool table, a riverside beer garden (great for smokers) and nine tap beers (three made on-site).

Kaya Organic Espresso (☎ 707-869-2230; 16626 Main St, Guerneville; ⏰ 6am-2pm Mon-Fri, 7am-2pm Sat & Sun) Hippie kids strum guitars at this all-organic coffee shack.

SANTA ROSA

pop 154,200

Wine Country's biggest city is known for traffic and suburban sprawl. It lacks small-town charm, but has reasonably priced accommodations and easy access to Sonoma County and Valley.

SIGHTS & ACTIVITIES
LUTHER BURBANK HOME & GARDENS

Pioneering horticulturist Luther Burbank (1849–1926) developed many hybrid plant species at his 19th-century Greek-revival home, at Santa Rosa and Sonoma Aves. The extensive **gardens** (☎ 707-524-5445; www.lutherburbank.org; admission free; ⏰ 8am-dusk) are lovely. The house and adjacent **Carriage Museum** (guided tour adult/child $7/free, free self-guided cell-phone audio tour;

WINE COUNTRY

RUSSIAN RIVER AREA

Armstrong Redwoods State Reserve, Guerneville (p206)
JERRY ALEXANDER

⏱ 10am-3:30pm Tue-Sun Apr-Oct) have displays on Burbank's life and work.

CHARLES M SCHULZ MUSEUM

Charles Schulz, creator of *Peanuts* cartoons, was a long-term Santa Rosa resident. Born in 1922, he published his first drawing in 1937, introduced the world to Snoopy and Charlie Brown in 1950, and produced Peanuts cartoons until just before his death in 2000.

At the **museum** (☎ 707-579-4452; www.schulzmuseum.org; 2301 Hardies Lane; adult/child & senior $10/5; ⏱ 11am-5pm Mon-Fri, 10am-5pm Sat & Sun, closed Tue Sep-May), a glass wall overlooks a courtyard with a Snoopy labyrinth. Exhibits include *Peanuts*-related art and Schulz's actual studio.

HEALDSBURG

pop 10,960

Once a sleepy agriculture town best known for its Future Farmers of America parade, Healdsburg has emerged as northern Sonoma County's hot new destination. Foodie-scenester restaurants and cafes, wine-tasting rooms and chic boutiques line Healdsburg Plaza, the town's sun-dappled central square (bordered by Healdsburg Ave and Center, Matheson and Plaza Sts). Healdsburg is a must-visit, if only to stroll the pretty tree-lined streets, sample locavore cooking and soak up the NorCal-now flavor.

INFORMATION

Healdsburg Chamber of Commerce & Visitors Bureau (☎ 707-433-6935, 800-648-9922; www.healdsburg.org; 217 Healdsburg Ave; ⏱ 9am-5pm Mon-Fri, to 3pm Sat, 10am-2pm Sun) Has winery maps and information on hot-air ballooning, golf, tennis, spas and nearby farms (get the *Farm Trails* brochure); 24-hour walk-up booth.

SIGHTS

East of the plaza, **Healdsburg Museum** (☎ 707-431-3325; www.healdsburgmuseum.org; 221 Matheson St; donation requested; ⏱ 11am-4pm Wed-Sun) is worth a visit for a glimpse of Healdsburg's past. Exhibits include Native American basketry and compelling installations on northern Sonoma County history. Pick up a historic-homes walking-tour pamphlet.

ACTIVITIES

River's Edge Kayak & Canoe Trips (☎ 707-433-7247; www.riversedgekayakandcanoe.com; 13840 Healdsburg Ave) rents canoes and kayaks ($65/$85 per half/full day) from April to September, including transportation. Call about guided trips.

Getaway Adventures (☎ 707-763-3040, 800-499-2453; www.getawayadventures.com) guides spectacular morning vineyard cycling in Alexander Valley, followed by lunch and optional canoeing on Russian River (from $150 to $175).

Relish Culinary School (☎ 707-431-9999, 877-759-1004; www.relishculinary.com) teaches courses for home chefs and operates out of local kitchens.

SLEEPING

Geyserville Inn (☎ 707-857-4343, 877-857-4343; www.geyservilleinn.com; 21714 Geyserville Ave, Geyserville; r $149-299; 🔀 🛜 💻) Eight miles north of Healdsburg, this immaculately kept top-end motel is surrounded by vineyards. It has unexpectedly smart furnishings, such as overstuffed side chairs and fluffy feather pillows. Be sure to request a remodeled room.

Madrona Manor (☎ 707-433-4231, 800-258-4003; www.madronamanor.com; 1001 Westside Rd; r & ste $280-485; 🔀 🛜 💻) The first choice for lovers of country inns and stately manor homes, the regal 1881 Madrona Manor exudes Victorian elegance. Surrounded by 8 acres of woods and gardens, the hilltop mansion is decked out with many original furnishings. There are also rooms in a carriage house, a cottage and a former schoolhouse. A mile west of Hwy 101, it's convenient to Westside Rd's wineries.

EATING

Healdsburg is the gastronomic capital of Sonoma County – the hardest decision may be where to eat. Reservations are essential.

Jimtown Store (☎ 707-433-1212; www.jimtown.com; 6706 Hwy 128; sandwiches under

Dining options in Healdsburg include Cyrus (p210)

JERRY ALEXANDER

WINE COUNTRY

RUSSIAN RIVER AREA

Bear Republic Brewing Company, Healdsburg

JERRY ALEXANDER

$10) If you're heading to Alexander Valley, don't miss Jimtown – one of our favorite stopovers – famous for its picnic supplies and sandwiches made using housemade flavor-packed spreads (eg artichoke, olive and caper; fig and olive).

Barndiva (☎ 707-431-0100; www.barn diva.com; 231 Center St; lunch mains $12-18, dinner mains $23-28; ☽ noon-11pm Wed-Sun) Barndiva's cavernous dining room and giant bar have an austerely sexy lounge vibe. The nontraditional menu is 'flavor profiled,' with food to fit your mood: from light to spicy to comfort cooking. Despite the aggressive style, there's substance behind the New American cooking, all made with sustainably farmed ingredients. On Sunday there's brunch in the garden.

Cyrus (☎ 707-433-3311; www.cyrusrestau rant.com; 29 North St; lunch & dinner prix fixe $102-130; ☽ dinner Thu-Mon, lunch Sat) Napa's venerable French Laundry (p192) has stiff competition in swanky Cyrus, an ultrachic dining room in the great tradition of the French country auberge. The emphasis is on luxury foods – foie gras, caviar, lobster – expertly prepared with a French sensibility and flavored with global spices, as in the signature Thai-marinated lobster. From the caviar cart to the cheese course, Cyrus is one meal to remember.

DRINKING

Flying Goat Coffee (☎ 707-433-3599; www. flyinggoatcoffee.com; 324 Center St; ☽ 7am-7pm) See ya later, Starbucks. Flying Goat is what coffee should be – fair-trade and locally roasted. This is where to meet locals.

Bear Republic Brewing Company (☎ 707-433-2337; 345 Healdsburg Ave; ☽ 11:30am-9:30pm Sun-Thu, to 10pm Fri & Sat) Bear Republic features handcrafted award-winning ales and a (so-so) pub-style menu.

SIERRA NEVADA & THE DESERTS

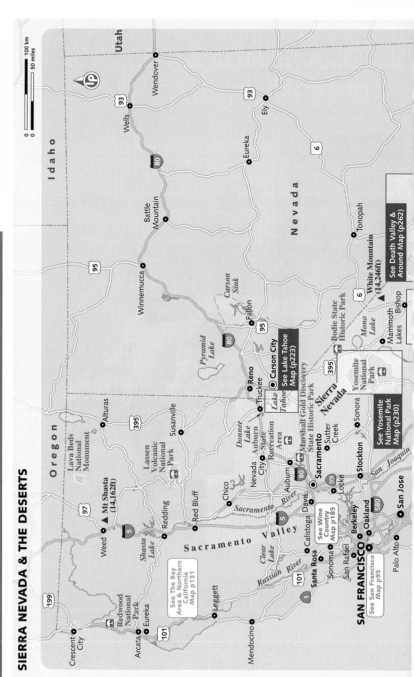

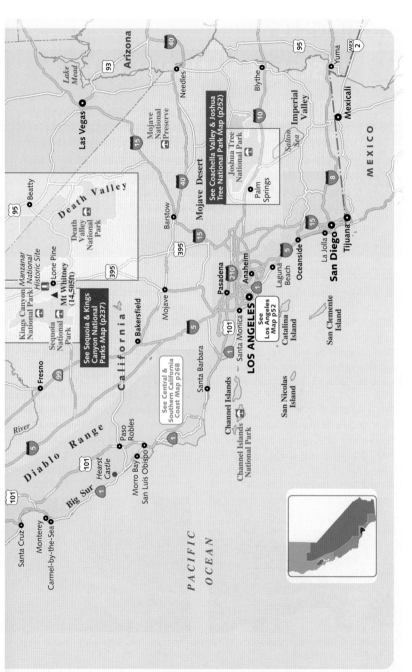

SIERRA NEVADA & THE DESERTS

HIGHLIGHTS

HIGHLIGHTS

1 YOSEMITE NATIONAL PARK

Yosemite has a way with humans. Its beauty – which can be utterly overwhelming – inspired writers and artists such as John Muir and Ansel Adams to produce some of their finest work. It's one of those rare places that touches you and makes you want to slow down but hurry back. Though Yosemite Valley can be a crush of humanity in July and August, there are still scores of untrammeled trails to be claimed even in the height of summer.

⌐ OUR DON'T MISS LIST

❶ YOSEMITE VALLEY
In May and June, Yosemite Valley (p231) thunders with the sound of rampaging ice melt from Yosemite Falls. Don raingear or get drenched while approaching Bridalveil Fall, where a rainbow hovers below clouds of spray.

❷ GLACIER POINT
Over 3000ft above the valley floor, a huge array of superstar sights unfold from Glacier Point (p231). You'll find the entire eastern Yosemite Valley spread out before you, from Half Dome

to Yosemite Falls, as well as the distant peaks that ring Tuolumne Meadows. Half Dome looms ahead, and beneath you, the Merced River snakes through green meadows and groves of trees.

❸ MARIPOSA GROVE
With their massive stature and multi-millennium maturity, the chunky high-rise sequoias of Mariposa Grove (p232) will make you feel rather insignificant. The largest grove of giant sequoias in the park, it has approximately

Clockwise from top: Nevada Fall, Liberty Cap and Half Dome (p231); California Tunnel Tree, Mariposa Grove (p232); Glacier Point (p231)

500 mature trees towering over 250 acres, many right by the parking lot.

❹ HETCH HETCHY

In little-visited **Hetch Hetchy** (p233), soaring waterfalls, granite domes and sheer cliffs rival its more glamorous counterpart in Yosemite Valley. Inspect the massive O'Shaughnessy Dam, tip-toe through a damp rock tunnel and make your way to the viewing bridge at impressive Wapama Falls.

❺ LYELL CANYON

Hike the **Lyell Canyon** section of the John Muir Trail to trace the serpentine Lyell Fork of the Tuolumne River. The path stays mostly flat, so daydream away through this subalpine meadow buffeted by tree-covered granite peaks.

❶ Yosemite Valley   ❹ Hetch Hetchy
❷ Glacier Point   ❺ Lyell Canyon
❸ Mariposa Grove

0 ▭▭▭▭▭ 20 km
0 ▭▭▭▭▭ 10 miles

Yosemite National Park

Tioga Pass
Tuolumne Meadows ❺
❹
❶ Yosemite Valley
❷
Bridalveil Fall
Sierra National Forest
❸
Fish Camp

⤴ THINGS YOU NEED TO KNOW

Best photo ops Valley View and Tunnel View **Top survival tip** For the bears' survival, store food according to park rules **Peak waterfall viewing** May through June **Best travel tip** Park and use the free Valley Shuttle **Top planning tip** Make camping reservations five months in advance

HIGHLIGHTS

2

↘ PLAYTIME IN LAKE TAHOE

Seen from the summit of a powdery white mountain or from a kayak streaming through placid waters, the peak-ringed idyll of **Lake Tahoe** (p222) rejuvenates and inspires. The largest alpine lake in North America, 'Big Blue' is a year-round outdoor playground that beckons you to experience it on foot, bike or skis, or by boat or car.

3

↘ SIZZLE IN DEATH VALLEY

Top off the radiator and grab a chilled drink before entering the aptly named inferno of **Death Valley** (p261). Bring an egg to fry on the pavement and watch the mercury burst the thermometer as you reach the lowest elevation point in the Western Hemisphere. But it's all not all scorched earth and parched devil tongues – the spring wildflower show is a vibrant response to the area's meager rain.

4

↘ JOSHUA TREE NATIONAL PARK

Ramble through a boulder-strewn landscape of Joshua trees, prickly cholla cacti and palm tree oases in the stark and mystical high desert of Joshua Tree (p256). Time your visit for the spring wildflower bonanza, or just come for the world-class rock climbing and bouldering and the chance to hear the coyotes' eerie nighttime cries.

5

↘ HUNT FOR GOLD

So what if it's been over 160 years, maybe there's still a fortune to be discovered near the Marshall Gold Discovery State Historic Park (p248). Visit the epicenter of the Gold Rush days, when prospectors swarmed here to make their fortunes, and try your own luck panning for gold.

6

↘ RAFT THE AMERICAN RIVER

Steel yourself for a face full of spray as you run the churning gorges of the American River (p248). Adrenaline-seekers can top up with a bracing dose of springtime white water, while lazy day paddlers can drift along and float with the current of more mellow waters.

2 FEARGUS COONEY; 3 KRISTIN PILJAY; 4 RICHARD CUMMINS; 5 RICHARD CUMMINS; 6 LEE FOSTER

2 Emerald Bay (p226), Lake Tahoe; 3 Death Valley National Park (p261); 4 Joshua Tree National Park (p256); 5 Marshall Gold Discovery State Historic Park (p248); 6 White-water rafting on the American River (p248)

BEST...

⬎ TIME WARPS

- **Vikingsholm Castle** (p226) A 1920s Scandinavian-style mansion on the bay.
- **Bodie State Historic Park** (p241) A well-preserved high-desert ghost town.
- **Laws Railroad Museum** (p246) A train depot and re-created town from the 1880s.
- **Sutter's Fort State Historic Park** (p249) Sacramento's first white settlement.

⬎ PLACES TO GET HIGH

- **Mt Whitney** (p247) The highest point in the continental US.
- **Palm Springs Aerial Tramway** (p250) Ascend from desert to cool pine forest.
- **Telescope Peak** (p265) A snow-capped mountain in Death Valley.
- **Half Dome** (p231) Climb the near-vertical cables to this iconic summit.

⬎ FLORA & FAUNA

- **Anza-Borrego Desert State Park** (p258) The desert explodes into a wildflower wonderland after the winter rains.
- **Mariposa Grove** (p232) Towering redwoods in Yosemite National Park.
- **Giant Forest** (p239) The largest living trees on Earth, in Sequoia National Park.
- **Stream Profile Chamber** (p225) Lets you explore underwater wild-life in South Lake Tahoe.

⬎ SCENIC DRIVES

- **Hwy 395** (p241) Be wowed by snowy Eastern Sierra mountain views.
- **Alabama Hills** (p247) Burnt-orange hills at the base of the Sierras.
- **Kings Canyon Scenic Byway** (p238) A jaw-dropping descent into deep rock canyon.
- **Artists Drive** (p263) Death Valley's picturesque loop of brilliant hills.

LEFT: JOHN ELK III; RIGHT: WITOLD SKRYPCZA

Left: Palm Springs Aerial Tramway (p250); Right: Giant Forest (p239), Sequoia National Park

THINGS YOU NEED TO KNOW

⬊ VITAL STATISTICS

- **Best time to go** Winter for deserts and snow sports, summer for Eastern Sierra, and year-round for everywhere else
- **Highest point** Mt Whitney (14,505ft)
- **Lowest point** Death Valley (-282ft)
- **Area of Sierra Nevada** over 25,000 sq miles

⬊ LOCALITIES IN A NUTSHELL

- **Lake Tahoe** (p222) Year-round outdoor recreation destination.
- **Yosemite National Park** (p229) California's top park.
- **Sequoia & Kings Canyon National Parks** (p236) Home of giant sequoias.
- **Eastern Sierra** (p241) The state's high-altitude backbone.
- **Gold Country** (p247) Home of the state's capital and its Gold Rush history sites.
- **The Deserts** (p250) Southern region encompassing Death Valley and Palm Springs.

⬊ ADVANCE PLANNING

- **Five months before** Reserve a campsite in Yosemite (p229).
- **One week before** Buy ski lift tickets online for discounts at Mammoth Mountain (p244) and Heavenly (p222).

⬊ RESOURCES

- **Desert Sun** (www.mydesert.com) News and information for the Palm Springs area.
- **Sacramento Bee** (www.sacbee.com) Sacramento daily paper.
- **Sierra Web** (www.thesierraweb.com) Comprehensive Eastern Sierra visitor information.
- **Sierra Wave** (www.ksrw.sierrawave.net) Eastern Sierra news.

⬊ GETTING AROUND

- **Air** Larger airports in Sacramento, Palm Springs and Reno, Nevada; limited service to Fresno and Mammoth Lakes.
- **Train** Amtrak runs from the Bay Area to Sacramento and Lake Tahoe, with connections to Yosemite. Route via Palm Springs to eastern US.
- **Car** The best way to explore off-the-beaten-track destinations.
- **Bus** Good local and regional transportation options.

⬊ BE FOREWARNED

- **Road closures** Hwy 120 (across Yosemite) shuts down from about November through May, and heavy snow sometimes closes Hwy 89 near Emerald Bay at Lake Tahoe.
- **Desert heat** Summertime temperatures are brutal and can be deadly.

SIERRA NEVADA & THE DESERTS ITINERARIES

TAHOE OUTDOOR GETAWAY Three Days

Spend the weekend in mountain-ringed Lake Tahoe, stopping by serene **(1) Donner Lake** (p227) to learn something about the area's pioneer, immigrant and railroad history. Afterwards, play in plain sight of 'Big Blue,' shredding the wintertime slopes at one of the many ski and snowboard resorts near the north-shore settlement of **(2) Tahoe City** (p226). Then jaunt south to **(3) Emerald Bay** (p226) for spectacular lake and island vistas, and a hike to a secluded 1920s mansion. Continue on to **(4) South Lake Tahoe** (p224), where you can survey the vast lake by paddlewheel cruise and then ascend the panoramic Heavenly gondola to straddle the California–Nevada border. In warm weather, save time to venture west toward Sacramento for a half day of rough and tumble whitewater river rafting at the **(5) Auburn State Recreation Area** (p248).

DESERT WINTER WONDERLAND Five Days

Balmy winter temperatures and a diverse mix of palm tree oases and snowy mountains create an intoxicating backdrop in **(1) Palm Springs** (p250). Toss in some stunning modern architecture, an exhilarating mountain cable car and scores of luxurious spas, and you may not care to leave after two days. But tear yourself away to catch the brief yet incredible wildflower bloom in massive **(2) Anza-Borrego Desert State Park** (p258), home to bighorn sheep and wind caves etched in sandstone outcroppings. Then swing past the deserted and fish-fragrant Salton Sea to explore the cacti and Joshua-tree-dotted high desert of **(3) Joshua Tree National Park** (p256). The otherworldly and boulder-strewn terrain makes it a favorite training ground for climbers, and an excellent place to stretch your legs on a desert hike. **(4) Mojave National Preserve** (p260) is your final destination, with towering cinder cones, fascinating wildlife such as desert tortoises and sorrowful coyotes, and a multicultural and natural history museum housed in a restored 1920s railway depot.

HIGH PEAKS & HIGHER TEMPERATURES One Week

Start off seven days of natural extremes and marvels in (1) Yosemite National Park (p229), gazing at daredevil waterfalls and ageless monoliths crowded into the crown jewel of Yosemite Valley. Spend two days pinching yourself before driving northeast to the stream-crossed high country of Tuolumne Meadows. East of the park sits the divine apparition of tufa formations poking out of saline (2) Mono Lake (p242). Drive south to spend the night and eat well in cosmopolitan

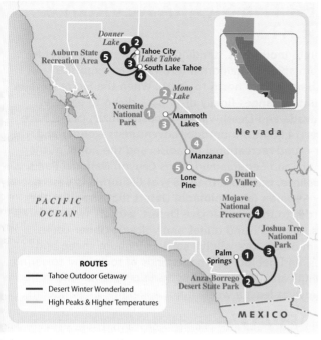

3) Mammoth Lakes (p244) and to see the curious rock columns of Devils Postpile. Ask the locals about where to find the best natural hot springs nearby, then continue driving south, touring the WWII-era concentration camp of **(4) Manzanar** (p246), a desolate former settlement shadowed by looming Mt Williamson. Further south in the town of **(5) Lone Pine** (p246), turn west to explore the golden movie-star mounds of the Alabama Hills and reach the terminus for the hike to Mt Whitney, the highest peak in the lower 48. South of Lone Pine, detour east to wilt in the dry heat of **(6) Death Valley** (p261), the lowest – and often the hottest – point in North America.

DISCOVER THE SIERRA NEVADA & THE DESERTS

With fierce granite mountains standing watch over high-altitude lakes, the eastern spine of California throws up an exquisite topographical barrier from north to south. When the Sierra Nevada and White Mountain ranges finally drop back down to earth at the basin of Nevada and Death Valley, almost a dozen peaks have topped out over 14,000ft. An outdoor adventurer's wonderland, the region's a year-round recreational paradise, and the home of the majestic Yosemite and Sequoia and Kings Canyon National Parks.

It's hard to believe, but more than 25% of California is desert, from the lower Sonoran (aka Colorado) Desert that straddles the US–Mexico border to the vast Mojave Desert, with its twisted forests of Joshua trees, 'singing' sand dunes and volcanic cinder cones. Hidden fan-palm oases, rare wildlife such as bighorn sheep and desert tortoises, and geological wonderlands of rocks and towering mountain summits are all protected by various national and state parks that deserve at least a week, if not a lifetime, of wandering.

SIERRA NEVADA

LAKE TAHOE

Shimmering softly in myriad shades of blue and green, Lake Tahoe, which straddles the California–Nevada state line, is one of the most beautiful lakes in the USA and also its second deepest with an average depth of 1000ft. The largest alpine lake in North America, at 6225ft it is one of the highest lakes in the country; driving around the lakeshore's 72 miles would give you quite a workout behind the wheel, but also reward you with spellbinding scenery.

TAHOE SKI AREAS

Northstar-at-Tahoe (**☎ 530-562-1010, 800-466-6784; www.northstarattahoe.com; Hwy 267; adult/child/teen $84/32/74; 8:30am-4pm**) An easy 6 miles south of I-80, this hugely popular resort has great intermediate terrain, although advanced and expert skiers can look for challenges on the back of the mountain.

Squaw Valley USA (**☎ 530-583-6985, 800-403-0206; www.squaw.com; off Hwy 89; adult/child/teen $83/10/61; 9am-9pm Mon-Fri, 8:30am-9pm Sat & Sun**) Few ski hounds can resist the siren call of this mega-sized, world-class see-and-be-seen resort that hosted the 1960 Winter Olympic Games. Hardcore skiers thrill to white-knuckle cornices, chutes and bowls, while beginners can practice their turns in a separate area on the upper mountain.

Heavenly (**☎ 775-586-7000, 800-432-8365; www.skiheavenly.com; cnr Wildwood & Saddle; adult/child $82/45; 9am-4pm Mon-Fri, 8:30am-4pm Sat & Sun**) The mother of all Tahoe mountains boasts the most acreage, the longest run and the biggest vertical drop in the western USA. Follow the sun by skiing on the Nevada side in the morning and moving to the California side in the afternoon. Views of the lake and the high desert are heavenly indeed.

LAKE TAHOE

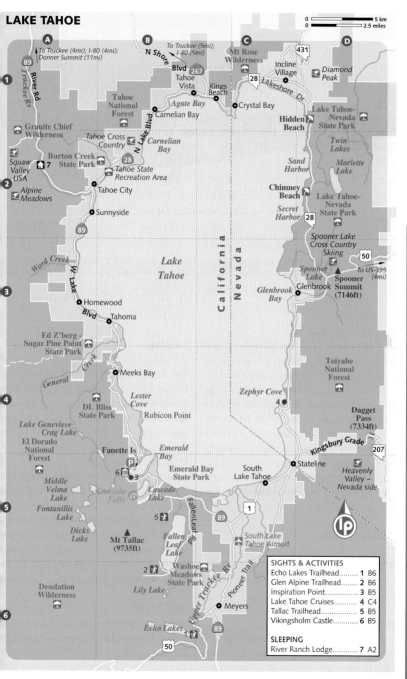

SIERRA NEVADA & THE DESERTS

LAKE TAHOE

SIGHTS & ACTIVITIES	
Echo Lakes Trailhead	**1** B6
Glen Alpine Trailhead	**2** B6
Inspiration Point	**3** B5
Lake Tahoe Cruises	**4** C4
Tallac Trailhead	**5** B5
Vikingsholm Castle	**6** B5
SLEEPING	
River Ranch Lodge	**7** A2

LEE FOS

Skiing at Heavenly (p222), Lake Tahoe

SOUTH LAKE TAHOE & STATELINE

pop 27,700 / elev 6254ft

The most developed section around the lake, South Lake Tahoe is a commercial strip bordering the lake and framed by picture-perfect snowy mountains. At the foot of the world-class Heavenly resort and bustling with casinos across the Nevada border in Stateline, this southern area boasts the most tourist infrastructure, drawing visitors looking for lots of lodging and restaurant options, easy access to wintertime mountain runs and 24-hour gambling.

ORIENTATION

Casinos are located in Stateline, which is officially a separate city. All addresses are in South Lake Tahoe unless otherwise noted.

INFORMATION

Lake Tahoe Visitors Authority (☎ 800-288-2463; www.bluelaketahoe.com); Stateline (☎ 775-588-5900; 169 Hwy 50; ☼ 9am-5pm);

South Lake Tahoe (☎ 530-541-5255; 306 Lake Tahoe Blvd; ☼ 9am-5pm)

SIGHTS

CASINOS

The siren song of blackjack and slot machines lures the masses across the stateline to Nevada. It's no Vegas, but there are plenty of ways to help you part with your paycheck.

HEAVENLY GONDOLA

Soar to the top of the world as you ride this **gondola** (Heavenly Village; adult/child/teen/senior $32/20/26/26; ☼ 9am-4pm Mon-Fri 8:30am-4pm Sat & Sun winter), which sweeps you from Heavenly Village some 2.4 miles up the mountain in 12 minutes for panoramic views of the entire Tahoe Basin, the Desolation Wilderness and Carson Valley.

ACTIVITIES

Three major trailheads provide easy access to the evocatively named Desolation Wilderness: **Echo Lakes** (south of town; Map p223); **Glen Alpine** (near Lily Lake south of Fallen Leaf Lake; Map p223); and Tallac (near the northwestern end of Fallen Leaf Lake; Map p223).

SOUTH LAKE TAHOE FOR CHILDREN
A submerged glass structure in a teeming creek, the Stream Profile Chamber at the Taylor Creek Visitors Center (☎ 530-543-2674; Hwy 89; ☺ 8am-5:30pm mid-Jun–Sep, to 4:30pm Oct) lets you check out what plants and fish live below the waterline. The best time to visit is in October during the Kokanee salmon run, when the brilliant red beauties arrive to spawn.

TOURS
Two paddle wheelers operated by Lake Tahoe Cruises (☎ 775-589-4906, 800-238-2463; www.zephyrcove.com) ply the 'Big Blue' year-round with a variety of food and sightseeing cruises, including a narrated two-hour trip to Emerald Bay (p226). The *Tahoe Queen* (adult/child $46/15) leaves from the Ski Run Marina, right in South Lake Tahoe, while the MS *Dixie II* (adult/child $39/15) is based at the Zephyr Cove Resort & Marina.

SLEEPING
Camp Richardson Resort (☎ 530-541-1801, 800-544-1801; www.camprichardson.com; 1900 Jameson Beach Rd; tent sites from $35, RV sites with partial/full hookups from $40/45, r $105-145, cabins $113-355; ☺ camping May–mid-Oct) A world removed from the downtown strip-mall aesthetic, this sprawling resort is a busy place with lodging options ranging from camping (213 tent-only lakeside and forest sites and a separate area for 110 RVs) to beachside hotel rooms.

Deerfield Lodge at Heavenly (☎ 530-544-3337, 888-757-3337; www.tahoedeerfieldlodge.com; 1200 Ski Run Blvd; r/ste incl breakfast $179/259; 🖳 🛜) A small boutique hotel close to Heavenly's California Lodge, all

12 rooms here have a patio or balcony facing out over the green courtyard, kitchenettes, and amusing coat racks crafted from skis and snowboards.

EATING
Ernie's Coffee Shop (☎ 530-541-2161; 1207 Hwy 50; mains $7-10; ☺ 6am-2pm) A sun-filled local institution, it dishes out filling four-egg omelets, hearty biscuits with gravy and bottomless cups of locally roasted coffee. Toddlers can happily munch the ears off the Mickey Mouse pancake.

Café Fiore (☎ 530-541-2908; 1169 Ski Run Blvd; mains $18-33; ☺ dinner) Upscale Italian without pretension, this tiny eatery pairs delectable pasta, seafood and meats with an award-winning 300-vintage wine list. Locals and visitors swoon over its rack of lamb, homemade white-chocolate ice cream and near-perfect garlic bread. With only seven tables (13 in summer), reservations are essential.

DRINKING & ENTERTAINMENT
Brewery at Lake Tahoe (☎ 530-544-2739; 3542 Lake Tahoe Blvd) A crazy-popular brewpub pumping its signature Bad Ass Ale into grateful patrons; its restaurant has dynamite barbecue and awesome crab cakes to boot.

blu (☎ 775-586-2000; MontBleu casino, 15 Hwy 50, Stateline) With booths and beds stocked with furry pillows, this Top 40 and techno dance club draws a young party crowd that enjoys getting an in-house body painting.

GETTING THERE & AROUND
South Lake Tahoe's two main transportation hubs are the South Y Transit Center, just south of the 'Y,' and the Stateline Transit Center in Heavenly Village. Amtrak Thruway buses to Sacramento stop at both locations daily ($34, 2½ hours), but

can only be boarded in conjunction with a train ticket.

WESTERN SHORE

Hwy 89 sinuously wends past gorgeous state parks with swimming beaches, easy trails, pine-shaded campgrounds and fanciful historic mansions. Several trailheads access the rugged splendor of the Desolation Wilderness.

EMERALD BAY STATE PARK

Sheer granite cliffs and a jagged shoreline hem in glacier-carved **Emerald Bay** (☎ 530-541-6498; www.parks.ca.gov; day-use fee $7; ☽ late May-Sep), a teardrop cove that will get you digging for your camera. Its most captivating aspect is the water, which changes from cloverleaf green to light jade depending on the angle of the sun.

SIGHTS

There are plenty of pullouts along Hwy 89, including one at **Inspiration Point**. Just to the south of here, the road shoulder evaporates on both sides of a steep drop-off, revealing a perfect panoramic view of Emerald Bay to the north and Cascade Lake to the south.

The mesmerizing blue-green waters frame the impeccably placed **Fannette Island**. This uninhabited granite speck, the only island in Lake Tahoe, holds the vandalized remains of a tiny 1920s house formerly used as a 'tea house' for heiress Lora Knight, who would occasionally motorboat guests to the island from **Vikingsholm Castle** (tours adult/child $5/3; ☽ 10am-4pm late May-Sep), her Scandinavian-style mansion on the bay. Completed in 1929, it has trippy design elements aplenty, including sod-covered roofs that sprout wildflowers in late spring.

TAHOE CITY

pop 1760 / elev 6240ft

The north shore's commercial hub, Tahoe City straddles the junction of Hwys 89 and 28 and is handy for grabbing food supplies and renting less expensive snow gear.

Winter sunrise at Emerald Bay, Lake Tahoe

WITOLD SKRYPCZA

SLEEPING

Pepper Tree Inn (☎ 530-583-3711, 800-624-8590; www.peppertreetahoe.com; 645 N Lake Blvd; r Mon-Fri $112-157, Sat & Sun $152-197; 🖳 🛜) The tallest building in town – you can't miss this somberly painted establishment with bird's-eye lake views. Comfortable modern rooms have microwave, fridge and coffeemaker, with top-floor rooms most in demand.

River Ranch Lodge (☎ 530-583-4264, 866-991-9912; www.riverranchlodge.com; Hwy 89 at Alpine Meadows Rd; r incl breakfast $135-195) Drift off to dreamland as the Truckee River tumbles below your window at this delightful inn. Rooms bulge with character and feature either elegant antiques or classy lodgepole-pine furniture; upstairs rooms have splendid balconies.

EATING

Rosie's Cafe (☎ 530-583-8504; 571 N Lake Blvd; breakfast & lunch $8-14, dinner $14-20; ⏱ 7am-9pm) Decorated with shiny bikes, antique skis and lots of pointy antlers, this quirky place serves breakfast until 2:30pm.

River Ranch Lodge (☎ 530-583-4264; Hwy 89 at Alpine Meadows Rd; lunch $11-14, dinner $20-32) This riverside place is a popular stop, drawing rafters and bikers to its patio for festive summer barbecue lunches. Dinner is a meat-heavy gourmet affair, with rotating standouts like filet mignon and roasted duck.

GETTING THERE & AROUND

With the sauciest damn acronym and very reliable service, **Tahoe Area Rapid Transit** (TART; ☎ 530-550-1212, 800-736-6365; www.laketahoetransit.com) operates buses along the northern shore as far as Incline Village, south along the western shore to Sugar Pine Point State Park (June through September only) and to Truckee via Hwy 89.

TRUCKEE & DONNER LAKE

pop 15,700 / elev 5840ft

Cradled by mountains and the Tahoe National Forest, Truckee is a thriving town steeped in Old West history. It was put on the map by the railroad, grew rich on logging and ice harvesting, and even had its brush with Hollywood during the 1924 filming of Charlie Chaplin's *The Gold Rush*. Today tourism fills much of the city's coffers, thanks to a well-preserved historic downtown and its proximity to Lake Tahoe and world-class ski resorts.

INFORMATION

Visitors center (☎ 530-587-8808; www.truckee.com; 10065 Donner Pass Rd; internet access per 15min $3; ⏱ 9am-6pm) Inside the Amtrak train depot; free walking tour maps.

SIGHTS

DONNER LAKE

In the 19th century, tens of thousands of people migrated west along the Overland Trail with dreams of a better life in California. Among them was the ill-fated Donner Party. By the time the party reached the eastern foot of the Sierra Nevada, near present-day Reno, morale and food supplies had run dangerously low. To restore energies and provisions, they decided to rest for a week.

But an exceptionally fierce winter came early, quickly rendering Donner Pass impassable and forcing the pioneers to build basic shelter near Donner Lake. Snow fell for weeks, reaching a depth of 22ft.

By the time the first rescue party arrived at Donner Lake in late February, the trapped pioneers were still surviving – barely – on boiled ox hides. But when the second rescue party made it through in March, evidence of cannibalism was everywhere. Journals and reports tell of 'half-crazed people living in absolute filth, with naked, half-eaten bodies strewn about the cabins.'

On the lake's eastern end, **Donner Memorial State Park** (☎ 530-582-7892; www.parks.ca.gov; vehicle fee $8) occupies one of three sites where the Donner Party got trapped. The vehicle fee includes admission to the excellent **Emigrant Trail Museum** (☎ 530-582-7892; ☀ 9am-4pm), which has exhibits and a 25-minute film re-enacting the Donner Party's horrific plight, and which is slated for a major revamping soon. A short trail leads to a memorial at one family's cabin site.

SLEEPING

Clair Tappaan Lodge (☎ 530-426-3632, 800-679-6775; www.sierraclub.org/outings/lodges/ctl; 19940 Donner Pass Rd; dm members/nonmembers Easter-late Nov $50/55, Dec-Easter from $55/60; ♿) About a mile west of Sugar Bowl, this cozy Sierra Club-owned rustic mountain lodge puts you near major ski resorts and has space for 140 people in dorms and family rooms. Rates include

family-style meals, but you're expected to do small chores and bring your own sleeping bag, towel and swimsuit (for the hot tub!).

Cedar House Sport Hotel (☎ 530-582-5655; www.cedarhousesporthotel.com; 10918 Brockway Rd; r incl breakfast Mon-Fri/Sat & Sun from $170/200; ☏) A new, environmentally conscious, contemporary boutique hotel aimed at getting folks out into nature, it boasts countertops made from recycled paper, 'rain chains' that redistribute water from the green roof garden to land-scaped areas, low-flow plumbing and in-room recycling, but doesn't skimp on good robes, pillow-top mattresses and a hot tub.

EATING & DRINKING

Moody's (☎ 530-587-8688; 10007 Bridge St; mains lunch $12-15, dinner $18-34) With its so-phisticated supper-club looks and live jazz (Thursday to Saturday), this gour-met restaurant in the Truckee Hotel oozes surprisingly urbane flair. Only the freshest

LEE FOSTER

Northstar (p222), Lake Tahoe

organic ingredients make it into the perfectly pitched concoctions.

Fifty Fifty Brewing Co. (☎ 530-587-2337; 11197 Brockway Rd) Inhale the aroma of toasting grains at this brand-new brewpub near Hwy 267. Try the popular Donner Party Porter with some upscale pub grub or just a huge plate of nachos.

GETTING THERE & AROUND
Greyhound buses stop at the train depot, as do Amtrak Thruway buses and the daily *California Zephyr* train to Emeryville/San Francisco ($43, 6½ to seven hours), Reno ($14, 1½ hours) and Sacramento ($40, 4½ hours).

YOSEMITE
The jaw-dropping head-turner of America's national parks, Yosemite (yo-*sem*-ih-tee) garners the devotion of all who enter. From the waterfall-striped granite walls buttressing emerald green Yosemite Valley to the skyscraping giant sequoias catapulting into the air at Mariposa Grove, you feel a sense of awe and reverence that so much natural beauty exists in one place.

HISTORY
The Ahwahneechee, a group of Miwok and Paiute peoples, lived in the Yosemite area for 4000 years before a group of pioneers, most likely led by legendary explorer Joseph Rutherford Walker, came through in 1833. During the Gold Rush era, conflict between the miners and native tribes escalated to the point where a military expedition (the Mariposa Battalion) was dispatched in 1851 to punish the Ahwahneechee, eventually forcing the capitulation of Chief Tenaya and his tribe later that year.

In 1864 President Abraham Lincoln signed the Yosemite Grant, which eventually ceded Yosemite Valley and the Mariposa Grove of Giant Sequoias to California as a state park. This landmark decision paved the way for a national park system, of which Yosemite became a part in 1890 thanks to efforts led by pioneering conservationist John Muir.

ORIENTATION
There are four main entrances: South Entrance (Hwy 41), Arch Rock (Hwy 140), Big Oak Flat (Hwy 120 W) and Tioga Pass (Hwy 120 E). Hwy 120 traverses the park as Tioga Rd, connecting Yosemite Valley with the Eastern Sierra.

Gas up year-round at Wawona and Crane Flat inside the park or at El Portal on Hwy 140 just outside its boundaries. In summer, gas is also sold at Tuolumne Meadows.

INFORMATION
Yosemite's entrance fee is $20 per vehicle or $10 for those on bicycle or foot and is valid for seven consecutive days.

For recorded park information, campground availability and road and weather conditions, call ☎ 209-372-0200.

INTERNET RESOURCES
Yosemite National Park (www.nps.gov/yose) Official Yosemite National Park Service site, with the most comprehensive and current information.

TOURIST INFORMATION
Extended summer hours may apply.
Yosemite Valley Visitors Center (Map p232; ☎ 209-372-0299; Yosemite Village; ☼ 9am-5pm) The main office, with exhibits and free film screenings of *Spirit of Yosemite*.
Yosemite Wilderness Center (Map p232; ☎ 209-372-0745; Yosemite Village; ☼ 7:30am-5pm May-Sep) Wilderness permits, maps and backcountry advice.

YOSEMITE NATIONAL PARK

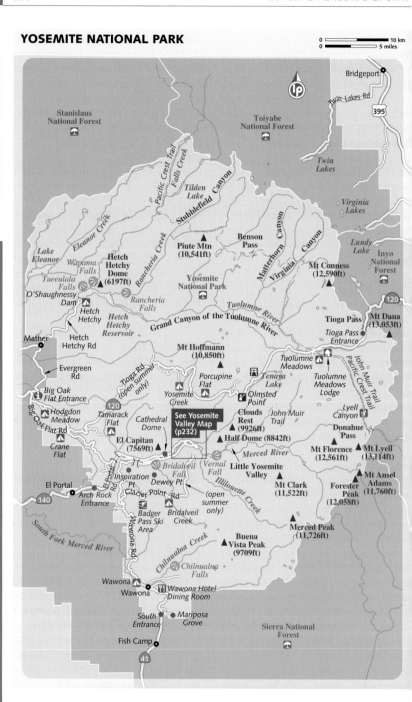

0   10 km
0   5 miles

Bridgeport

Twin Lakes Rd

395

Stanislaus
National Forest

Toiyabe
National Forest

Twin
Lakes

Pacific Crest Trail

Falls Creek

Tilden
Lake

Stubblefield Canyon

Rancheria Creek

Virginia
Lakes

Lake
Eleanor

Eleanor Creek

Wapama
Falls

Hetch
Hetchy
Dome
(6197ft)

Piute Mtn
(10,541ft)

Benson
Pass

Matterhorn Canyon

Virginia Canyon

Lundy
Lake

Inyo
National
Forest

Tueeulala
Falls

O'Shaughnessy
Dam

Hetch
Hetchy

Hetch
Hetchy
Reservoir

Rancheria
Falls

Yosemite
National Park

Tuolumne River

Mt Conness
(12,590ft)

120

Mt Dana
(13,053ft)

Grand Canyon of the Tuolumne River

Tioga Pass

Tioga Pass
Entrance

Mather

Hetch
Hetchy Rd

Mt Hoffmann
(10,850ft)

Tuolumne
Meadows

John Muir Trail
Pacific Crest Trail

Evergreen
Rd

Tioga Rd
(open summer
only)

Porcupine
Flat

Tenaya
Lake

Tuolumne
Meadows
Lodge

Big Oak
Flat Entrance

Yosemite
Creek

Olmsted
Point

Lyell
Canyon

Big Oak Flat Rd

Hodgdon
Meadow

Tamarack
Flat

120

Cathedral
Dome

See Yosemite
Valley Map
(p232)

Clouds
Rest
(9926ft)

John Muir
Trail

Donahue
Pass

Crane
Flat

El Capitan
(7569ft)

Half Dome (8842ft)

Mt Florence
(12,561ft)

Mt Lyell
(13,114ft)

El Portal Rd

Bridalveil
Fall

Vernal
Fall

Merced River

Little Yosemite
Valley

Mt Ansel
Adams
(11,760ft)

El Portal

Inspiration
Pt

Dewey Pt

Glacier Point

Bridalveil
Creek

Illouette Creek

Mt Clark
(11,522ft)

Forester
Peak
(12,058ft)

140

Arch Rock
Entrance

Badger
Pass Ski
Area

(open
summer
only)

Merced Peak
(11,726ft)

Wawona Rd

South Fork Merced River

Chilnualna Creek

Buena
Vista Peak
(9709ft)

Chilnualna
Falls

Wawona

Wawona

Wawona Hotel
Dining Room

South
Entrance

Mariposa
Grove

Sierra National
Forest

Fish Camp

41

DANGERS & ANNOYANCES
Yosemite is prime black bear habitat. Mosquitoes can be pesky in summer, so bug spray's not a bad idea.

SIGHTS
YOSEMITE VALLEY
The park's crown jewel, spectacular, meadow-carpeted Yosemite Valley stretches 7 miles long, bisected by the rippling Merced River and hemmed in by some of the most majestic chunks of granite nature has wrought anywhere on earth. The most famous are, of course, the monumental 7569ft **El Capitan** (El Cap; Map p230), one of the world's largest monoliths and a magnet for rock climbers, and 8842ft **Half Dome** (Map p230), the park's spiritual centerpiece, whose rounded granite pate forms an unmistakable silhouette. You'll have great views of both from **Valley View** (off Map p232) on the valley floor, but for the classic photo op head up Hwy 41 to **Tunnel View** (off Map p232), which boasts a new viewing area.

Yosemite's waterfalls mesmerize even the most jaded traveler, especially when the spring runoff turns them into thunderous cataracts. Most are reduced to a mere trickle by late summer. **Yosemite Falls** (Map p232) is considered the tallest in North America, dropping 2425ft in three tiers. No less impressive are nearby **Bridalveil Fall** (Map p230) and others scattered throughout the valley.

Any aspiring Ansel Adamses should lug their camera gear along the 1-mile paved trail to **Mirror Lake** (off Map p232) early or late in the day to catch the ever-shifting reflection of Half Dome in the still waters. The lake all but dries up by late summer.

South of here, where the Merced River courses around two small islands, lies **Happy Isles**, a popular area for picnics, swimming and strolls. It also marks the start of the John Muir Trail and Mist Trail to several waterfalls and Half Dome. The **Happy Isles Nature Center** (Map p232; admission free; ☽ May-Sep) keeps kids' attention with cool interactive exhibits.

Places of cultural interest in the valley include the **Yosemite Museum** (Map p232; ☎ 209-372-0200; admission free; ☽ 9am-5pm, closed for lunch), which has Miwok and Paiute artifacts, including woven baskets, beaded buckskin dresses and dance capes made from feathers. There's also an **art gallery** (Map p232) and, behind the museum, a reconstructed **Indian village** (Map p232), c 1870.

GLACIER POINT
A lofty 3200ft above the valley floor, 7214ft Glacier Point (Map p232) presents one of the park's most eye-popping vistas and practically puts you at eye level with Half Dome. To the left of Half Dome lies U-shaped, glacially carved Tenaya Canyon, while below you'll see Vernal and Nevada Falls. Glacier Point is about an hour's drive from Yosemite Valley via Glacier Point Rd, off Hwy 41. Along the road, hiking trails lead to other spectacular viewpoints, such as **Dewey Point** (Map p230) and **Sentinel Dome** (Map p232).

TIOGA ROAD & TUOLUMNE MEADOWS
Tioga Road (Hwy 120 E), the only road to traverse the park, travels through 56 miles of superb high country at elevations ranging from 6200ft at Crane Flat to 9945ft at Tioga Pass. Heavy snowfall keeps it closed from about November until May. Beautiful views await after many a bend in the road, the most impressive being **Olmsted Point** (Map p230), where you can gawp all the way down Tenaya Canyon to the backside of Half Dome. Above the canyon's east side

SIERRA NEVADA & THE DESERTS

SIERRA NEVADA

YOSEMITE VALLEY

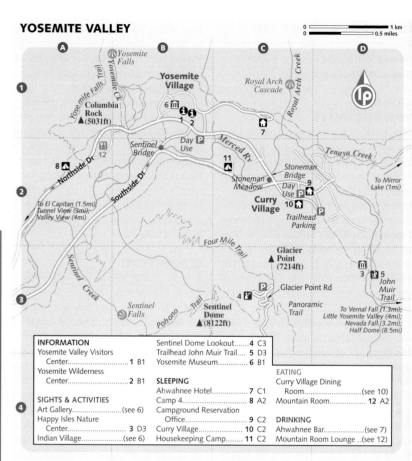

INFORMATION
Yosemite Valley Visitors
  Center............................**1** B1
Yosemite Wilderness
  Center............................**2** B1

SIGHTS & ACTIVITIES
Art Gallery......................(see 6)
Happy Isles Nature
  Center............................**3** D3
Indian Village..................(see 6)

Sentinel Dome Lookout.......**4** C3
Trailhead John Muir Trail....**5** D3
Yosemite Museum..............**6** B1

SLEEPING
Ahwahnee Hotel................**7** C1
Camp 4.............................**8** A2
Campground Reservation
  Office.............................**9** C2
Curry Village....................**10** C2
Housekeeping Camp........**11** C2

EATING
Curry Village Dining
  Room..........................(see 10)
Mountain Room.................**12** A2

DRINKING
Ahwahnee Bar..................(see 7)
Mountain Room Lounge ..(see 12)

looms the aptly named, 9926ft **Clouds Rest** (Map p230). Continuing east on Tioga Rd soon drops you at **Tenaya Lake** (Map p230), a placid blue basin framed by pines and granite cliffs.

Beyond here, about 55 miles from Yosemite Valley, 8600ft **Tuolumne Meadows** (Map p230) is the largest subalpine meadow in the Sierra. It provides a dazzling contrast to the valley, with its lush open fields, clear blue lakes, ragged granite peaks and domes, and cooler temperatures.

WAWONA

Wawona, about 27 miles south of Yosemite Valley, is the park's historical center, but the main lure is really the **Mariposa Grove of Giant Sequoias** (Map p230), the biggest and most impressive cluster of big trees in Yosemite. The star of the show – and what everyone comes to see – is the **Grizzly Giant**, a behemoth that sprang to life some 2700 years ago – about the time the ancient Greeks held the first Olympic Games. Also nearby is the walk-through **California Tunnel Tree**, which continues to survive despite having its heart hacked out in 1895.

HETCH HETCHY

In the park's northwestern corner, Hetch Hetchy (which is Miwok for 'place of tall grass') gets the least amount of traffic yet sports waterfalls and granite cliffs that rival its famous counterparts in Yosemite Valley. The main difference is that Hetch Hetchy Valley is now filled with water, following a long political and environmental battle in the early 20th century.

The 8-mile long Hetch Hetchy Reservoir, its placid surface reflecting clouds and cliffs, stretches behind **O'Shaughnessy Dam** (Map p230), site of a parking lot and trailheads. An easy 5.4-mile (round-trip) trail leads to the spectacular **Tueeulala** (*twee*-lala) and **Wapama Falls** (Map p230), which each plummet more than 1000ft over fractured granite walls on the north shore of the reservoir.

ACTIVITIES
HIKING

Over 800 miles of hiking trails tempt trekkers of all abilities. Take an easy half-mile stroll on the valley floor; venture out

all day on a quest for viewpoints, waterfalls and lakes or go wilderness camping in the remote outer reaches of the backcountry.

Some of the park's most popular hikes start right in Yosemite Valley, including the most famous of all, to the top of **Half Dome** (Map p230; 17-mile round-trip). It follows a section of the **John Muir Trail** and is strenuous, difficult and best tackled in two days with an overnight in Little Yosemite Valley. Reaching the top can only be done after rangers have installed fixed cables. Depending on snow conditions, this may occur as early as late May or as late as July, and the cables usually come down in mid-October. When the cables are up, advance **permits** (www.nps.gov/yose/planyourvisit/hdpermits.htm) are currently required Friday through Sunday and on holidays to prevent human logjams.

The less ambitious or physically fit will still have a ball following the same trail as far as **Vernal Fall** (2.6-mile round-trip), the top of **Nevada Fall** (6.5-mile round-trip) or

EMILY RIDDELL

Yosemite Falls (p231), Yosemite National Park

idyllic **Little Yosemite Valley** (Map p230; 8-mile round-trip).

ROCK CLIMBING

With its sheer spires, polished domes and soaring monoliths, Yosemite is rock-climbing nirvana. The main climbing season runs from April to October. Most climbers, including some legendary stars, stay at Camp 4 near El Cap, especially in spring and fall.

RAFTING

From around late May to July, floating the **Merced River** from Stoneman Meadow, near Curry Village, to Sentinel Bridge is a leisurely way to soak up Yosemite Valley views. Six-person **raft rentals** (☎ 209-372-8319; per adult/child $26/16) for the 3-mile trip are available at Curry Village and include equipment and a shuttle ride back to the rental kiosk.

WINTER SPORTS

The white coat of winter opens up a different set of things to do, as the valley becomes a quiet, frosty world of snow-draped evergreens, ice-coated lakes and vivid vistas of gleaming white mountains sparkling against blue skies. Most of the action converges on the family-friendly **Badger Pass Ski Area** (Map p230; ☎ 209-372-8430; www.yosemitepark.com/BadgerPass.aspx; lift ticket adult/child $42/20), one of California's oldest ski resorts, the gentle slopes of which are perfect for families and beginning skiers and snowboarders.

TOURS

First-timers often appreciate the two-hour **Valley Floor Tour** (per adult/child $25/13; ☯ year-round), which covers the valley highlights. For other tour options stop at the tour and activity desks at Yosemite Lodge, Curry Village or Yosemite Village, call ☎ 209-372-1240 or check www.yosemitepark.com.

SLEEPING

All noncamping reservations within the park are handled by **DNC Parks & Resorts** (☎ 801-559-5000; www.yosemitepark.com) and

Merced River, Yosemite National Park
RICHARD I'ANSON

can be made up to 366 days in advance; they are absolutely critical from May to early September.

BUDGET
Competition for campsites is fierce from May to September, when arriving without a reservation and hoping for the best is tantamount to getting someone to lug your Barcalounger up Half Dome. Even first-come, first-served campgrounds tend to fill by noon, especially on weekends and around holidays. **Reservations** (☎ 518-885-3639, 877-444-6777; www.recreation. gov) are accepted up to five months in advance, beginning the 15th of each month.

Housekeeping Camp (Map p232; Yosemite Valley; units $90-92; ☼ Apr-Oct) This cluster of 266 cabins, each walled in by concrete on three sides and lidded by a canvas roof, is crammed and noisy, but the setting along the Merced River has its merits.

MIDRANGE & TOP END
Curry Village (Map p232; Yosemite Valley; canvas cabins $93-132, cabins with/without bath $141/102, r from $179; 🐾) Founded in 1899 as a summer camp, Curry has hundreds of units squished tightly together beneath towering evergreens. The canvas cabins are basically glorified tents, so for more comfort, quiet and privacy get one of the cozy wood cabins, which have bedspreads, drapes and vintage posters.

Tuolumne Meadows Lodge (Map p230; Tioga Rd; tent cabins $208; ☼ mid-Jun–mid-Sep) In the high country, about 55 miles from the valley, this option attracts hikers to its 69 canvas tent cabins with four beds, a wood-burning stove and candles (no electricity).

Ahwahnee Hotel (Map p232; Yosemite Valley; r from $449; 🐾 💻 🐾 🛜) The crème de la crème of Yosemite's lodging, this sumptuous historic property dazzles with soaring ceilings, Turkish kilims lining the hallways and atmospheric lounges with mammoth stone fireplaces. It's the gold standard for upscale lodges, though if you're not blessed with bullion, you can still soak up the ambience during afternoon tea, a drink in the bar or a gourmet meal.

EATING
Curry Village Dining Pavilion (Map p232; Curry Village; breakfast $12, dinner $16; ☼ Apr-Nov) Although the cafeteria-style setting has all the charm of a train station waiting room, the all-you-can-eat breakfast and dinner buffets are great for families, gluttons and the undecided.

Wawona Hotel Dining Room (Map p230; ☎ 209-375-1425; Wawona Hotel; breakfast buffet $15, lunch mains $10-15, dinner mains $17-35; ☼ mid-Mar–Nov & Dec holidays) Beautiful sequoia-painted lamps light this old-fashioned white-tablecloth dining room, and the Victorian detail makes it an enchanting place to have an upscale (though somewhat overpriced) meal. 'Tasteful, casual attire' is the rule for dinner dress, and there's a barbecue on the lawn every Saturday during summer.

Mountain Room (Map p232; ☎ 209-372-1274; Yosemite Lodge; mains $15-40; ☼ dinner year-round) With a killer view of Yosemite Falls, the window tables at this casual and elegant contemporary steakhouse are a hot commodity. The chefs at the lodge whip up some of the best meals in the park, with flat-iron steak and locally caught mountain trout wooing diners under a rotating display of nature photographs.

DRINKING
Mountain Room Lounge (Map p232; Yosemite Lodge, Yosemite Valley) Catch up on the latest sports news while knocking

back draft brews at this large bar that buzzes in wintertime.

Ahwahnee Bar (Map p232; Ahwahnee Hotel, Yosemite Valley) The perfect way to experience the Ahwahnee without dipping too deep into your pockets; settle in for a drink at this cozy bar, complete with pianist.

GETTING THERE & AWAY

Yosemite is one of the few national parks that can be reached by public transportation relatively easily. Greyhound buses and Amtrak trains serve Merced west of the park, where they are met by buses operated by **Yosemite Area Regional Transportation System** (YARTS; ☎ 209-388-9589, 877-989-2787; www.yarts.com). Buses travel to Yosemite Valley along Hwy 140 several times daily year-round, stopping along the way. In summer, another Yarts route runs from Mammoth Lakes (p244) along Hwy 120 East via the Tioga Pass.

GETTING AROUND
BICYCLE

Bicycling is an ideal way to take in Yosemite Valley. You can rent a wide-handled cruiser (per hour/day $9.50/25.50) or a bike with an attached child trailer (per hour/day $16/50.50) at the Yosemite Lodge at the Falls or Curry Village.

CAR

Roadside signs with red bears mark the many spots where bears have been killed by motorists, so think before you hit the accelerator. Glacier Point and Tioga Rds are closed in winter. Call ☎ 800-427-7623 for road and weather conditions.

PUBLIC TRANSPORTATION

The free, air-conditioned Yosemite Valley Shuttle Bus is a comfortable and comparatively efficient way of traveling around

the park. Buses operate year-round at frequent intervals and stop at 21 numbered locations, including parking lots, campgrounds, trailheads and lodges.

SEQUOIA & KINGS CANYON

The twin parks of Sequoia and Kings Canyon dazzle with superlatives, though they're often overshadowed by Yosemite, their smaller neighbor to the north. With towering forests of giant sequoias containing some of the largest trees in the world, and the mighty Kings River careening through the depths of Kings Canyon, one of the deepest chasms in the country, the parks are lesser-visited jewels where it's easier to find quiet and solitude.

The two parks, although distinct, are operated as one unit with a single admission (valid for seven consecutive days) of $20 per carload or $10 for individuals arriving on bicycle or foot. For 24-hour recorded information, call ☎ 559-565-3341 or visit www.nps.gov/seki, the parks' comprehensive website.

KINGS CANYON NATIONAL PARK

With a dramatic cleft deeper than the Grand Canyon, Kings Canyon offers true adventure to those who crave seemingly endless trails, rushing streams and gargantuan rock formations. The camping, backcountry exploring and climbing here are all superb, with opportunities for surveying giant sequoias, gushing waterfalls, an exquisite cavern and a scenic driving road.

INFORMATION

Cedar Grove Visitor Center (☎ 559-565-3793; ⏰ 9am-5pm late May-Sep) For tourist information.

Grant Grove Visitor Center (☎ 559-565-4307; ⏰ 8am-8pm mid-Jun-Sep, 9am-4:30pm

SEQUOIA & KINGS CANYON NATIONAL PARKS

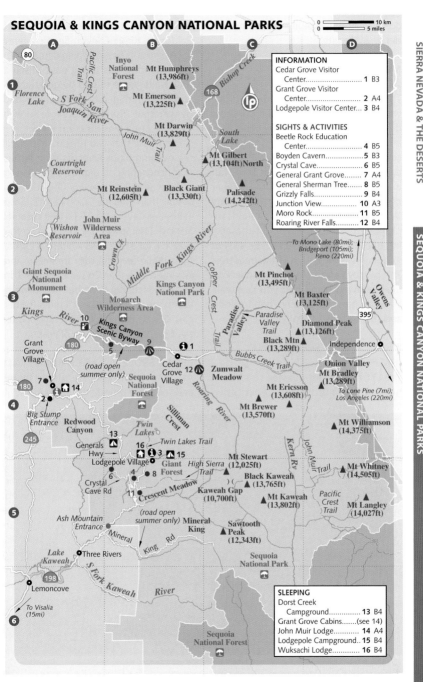

SIERRA NEVADA & THE DESERTS

SEQUOIA & KINGS CANYON NATIONAL PARKS

INFORMATION
Cedar Grove Visitor
Center.......................... 1 B3
Grant Grove Visitor
Center.......................... 2 A4
Lodgepole Visitor Center... 3 B4

SIGHTS & ACTIVITIES
Beetle Rock Education
Center........................... 4 B5
Boyden Cavern.................5 B3
Crystal Cave.....................6 B5
General Grant Grove.......... 7 A4
General Sherman Tree....... 8 B5
Grizzly Falls..................... 9 B4
Junction View................. 10 A3
Moro Rock..................... 11 B5
Roaring River Falls.......... 12 B4

SLEEPING
Dorst Creek
Campground............... 13 B4
Grant Grove Cabins.......(see 14)
John Muir Lodge............ 14 A4
Lodgepole Campground.. 15 B4
Wuksachi Lodge............. 16 B4

SIERRA NEVADA & THE DESERTS

SIERRA NEVADA

Oct–mid-Jun) Has exhibits, maps and wilderness permits.

SIGHTS & ACTIVITIES
GENERAL GRANT GROVE
The magnificence of this sequoia grove was recognized in 1890 when Congress designated it General Grant National Park, and in 1940 it became part of the newly created Kings Canyon National Park. The paved half-mile **General Grant Tree Trail** is an interpretive walk that visits a number of mature sequoias, including the 27-story **General Grant Tree**. This giant holds triple honors as the world's third-largest living tree, a memorial to US soldiers killed in war and as the nation's Christmas tree. The nearby **Fallen Monarch**, a massive, fire-hollowed trunk that you can walk through, has been a cabin, hotel, saloon and stables for US Cavalry horses.

KINGS CANYON SCENIC BYWAY (HIGHWAY 180)
The 31-mile roller-coaster road connecting Grant Grove and Cedar Grove ranks among the most dazzling in all of California. Kings Canyon Scenic Byway soon begins its jaw-dropping descent into the canyon, serpentining past chiseled rock walls, some tinged by green moss and red iron minerals, others decorated by waterfalls. Turnouts provide superb views, especially at **Junction View**.

Eventually the road runs parallel with the gushing Kings River, its thunderous roar ricocheting off granite cliffs soaring as high as 8000ft, making Kings Canyon deeper than even the Grand Canyon. Stop at **Boyden Cavern** (☎ 559-338-0959; adult/child $13/8; ☼ 10am-5pm Jun-Sep, 11am-4pm Apr-May & Oct-Nov) for a tour of its whimsical formations. While beautiful, they are smaller and less impressive than Crystal Cave (p240) in Sequoia National Park, but no advance tickets are required. About 5 miles further east, **Grizzly Falls** can be torrential or drizzly, depending on the time of year.

CEDAR GROVE VILLAGE & ROADS END
At Cedar Grove Village a simple lodge and snack bar provide the last outpost of

JOHN MOCK

Suspension bridge over Woods Creek, Kings Canyon National Park

civilization before the rugged grandeur of the backcountry. Pretty spots around here include Roaring River Falls, where water whips down a sculpted rock channel before tumbling into a churning pool, and the 1.5-mile Zumwalt Meadow Loop, an easy nature trail around a verdant green meadow bordered by river and granite canyon.

SLEEPING

Grant Grove Cabins (☎ 559-335-5500, 866-522-6966; www.sequoia-kingscanyon.com; Grant Grove Village; tent cabins $62-77, cabins with private bath $129-140, without bath $77-92) Set amid colossal sugar pines, 50-odd cabins range from the decrepit tent-top shacks in 'Tent City' to the rustic yet comfortable heated duplexes (a few of which are wheelchair-accessible) with electricity and private bathrooms.

John Muir Lodge (☎ 559-335-5500, 866-522-6966; www.sequoia-kingscanyon.com; Grant Grove Village; r $172-186) An atmospheric wooden building lined with historic old black-and-white photographs, this newer hotel is a comfortable place to lay your head and still feel like you're in the forest.

EATING

Grant Grove Restaurant (☎ 559-335-5500; breakfast & lunch $7-10, dinner $14-20; ☀ year-round; ♿) More of a diner than a restaurant. Most visitors eat here, and there can be a wait at times. There's breakfast, lunch sandwiches and filling all-American dinners.

GETTING THERE & AROUND

The road to Cedar Grove Village is only open from around April or May until the first snowfall.

SEQUOIA NATIONAL PARK

Picture unzipping your tent flap and crawling out into a 'front yard' of trees as high as a 20-story building and as old as the Bible. Brew some coffee as you plan your day in this extraordinary park with its soul-sustaining forests and gigantic peaks soaring above 12,000ft.

INFORMATION

Lodgepole Visitor Center (☎ 559-565-4436; ☀ 7am-6pm late May-Aug, 7am-5pm Sep, 8am-4:30pm Oct, closed Nov–mid-May) Maps, information, exhibits, Crystal Cave tickets and wilderness permits (7am to 11am and noon to 3:30pm).

SIGHTS & ACTIVITIES
GIANT FOREST

Named by John Muir in 1875, this area is the top destination in the parks; it's about 2 miles south of Lodgepole Village. By volume the largest living tree on earth, the massive General Sherman Tree rockets 275ft to the sky. Pay your respects via a short descent from the Wolverton Rd parking lot, or join the Congress Trail, a paved 2-mile pathway that takes in General Sherman and other notable named trees, including the Washington Tree, the world's second biggest, and the see-through Telescope Tree.

Bugs, bones and artificial animal scat are just some of the cool things children get to play with at the Beetle Rock Education Center (☎ 559-565-4480; admission free; ☀ 10am-4pm summer; ♿). A bright and cheerful cabin with activity stations galore, here inquisitive kiddos can scan bugs with digital microscopes, touch a taxidermied bobcat, put on a puppet show and paint ecology posters. Tents are set up for inside play, and binoculars lure youngsters out back for spotting animals.

Open in the warmer months, Crescent Meadow Rd heads east from the museum for 3 miles to Crescent Meadow, a relaxing picnic spot, especially in spring when it's ablaze with wildflowers. The road also passes **Moro Rock**, a landmark granite dome whose top can be reached via a quarter-mile carved staircase for breathtaking views of the Great Western Divide, a chain of mountains running north to south through the center of Sequoia National Park.

SLEEPING & EATING

ALONG GENERALS HIGHWAY

Dorst Creek (☎ 877-444-6777; www.recreation.gov; tent & RV sites $20; ☾ late May-early Sep) Big and busy campground with 204 sites and flush toilets; quieter back sites are tent-only.

Wuksachi Lodge (☎ 559-565-4070, 866-807-3598; www.visitsequoia.com; r May-Sep $194-257, Oct-Apr $102-231; ☾ year-round; ☎) Six miles north of Giant Forest, the modern Wuksachi is the most upscale lodging and dining option in the parks. Spacious rooms, all with TV and telephone, come in three sizes and are in three buildings a short walk from the main lodge; a restaurant is open for all meals (dinner mains $20 to $30).

Watchtower Deli & Snack Bar (Lodgepole Village; meals $5-10; ☾ deli 11am-6pm,

Stalactites inside Crystal Cave
HOWARD STAPLETON/ALAMY

➘ CRYSTAL CAVE

Discovered in 1918 by two fishermen, Crystal Cave was carved by an underground river and has formations estimated to be 10,000 years old. Stalactites hang like daggers from the ceiling, and milky-white marble formations take the shape of ethereal curtains, domes, columns and shields. The 45-minute tour covers a half-mile of chambers.

Tickets are sold *only* at the Lodgepole and Foothills visitors centers, *not* at the cave. Allow about one hour to get to the cave entrance, which is a half-mile walk from the parking lot at the end of a twisty 7-mile road; the turnoff is about 3 miles south of the Giant Forest. Bring a sweater or light jacket, as it's a huddle-for-warmth 48°F (9°C) inside.

Things you need to know: ☎ 559-565-3759; www.sequoiahistory.org; Crystal Cave Rd; adult/child/senior $13/6.50/12; ☾ tours 11am-4pm mid-May–Oct

Remnants of the past at Bodie State Historic Park

STEPHEN SAKS

snack bar 8am-7:45pm) The snack bar serves less expensive fast-food breakfasts, burgers, pizza and hot dogs, while the deli doles out healthier, prepared fare such as deli salads and focaccia sandwiches.

EASTERN SIERRA

Cloud-dappled hills and sun-streaked mountaintops dabbed with snow typify the landscape of the Eastern Sierra, where slashing peaks – many over 14,000ft – rush abruptly upward from the arid expanses of the Great Basin and Mojave deserts. Pine forests, lush meadows, ice-blue lakes, simmering hot springs and glacier-gouged canyons are only some of the fabulous beauty you'll find in this region.

The Eastern Sierra Scenic Byway, officially known as Hwy 395, runs the entire length of the range. Turnoffs dead-ending at the foot of the mountains deliver you to pristine wilderness and countless trails, including the famous Pacific Crest Trail, John Muir Trail and main Mt Whitney Trail.

GETTING THERE & AROUND

The Eastern Sierra is easiest to explore under your own steam, although it is possible to access the area by buses operated by **Eastern Sierra Transit Authority** (☎ 800-922-1930; www.easternsierratransit authority.com).

BODIE STATE HISTORIC PARK

For a time warp back to the Gold Rush era, swing by **Bodie** (☎ 760-647-6445; www.parks. ca.gov; Hwy 270; adult/child $5/3; 8am-6pm Jun-Aug, 10am-3pm Sep-May), one of the West's most authentic and best-preserved ghost towns. Gold was first discovered here in 1859, and within 20 years the place grew from a rough mining camp to an even rougher boomtown, with a population of 10,000 and a reputation for unbridled lawlessness. The hills disgorged some $35 million worth of gold and silver in the 1870s and '80s, but when production plummeted, so did the population, and eventually the town was abandoned to the elements.

About 200 weather-beaten buildings still sit frozen in time in this cold, barren and windswept valley. The former Miners' Union Hall now houses a **museum** and **visitors center** (8am-7pm daily Jun-Aug, variable hours Sep-Oct & May).

Bodie is about 13 miles east of Hwy 395 via Rte 270; the last 3 miles are unpaved. Although the park is open year-round, the road is usually closed in winter and early spring, so you'd have to don snowshoes or cross-country skis to get there.

MONO LAKE

North America's second-oldest lake is a quiet and mysterious expanse of deep blue water whose glassy surface reflects jagged Sierra peaks, young volcanic cones and the unearthly tufa (too-fah) towers that make Mono Lake so distinctive. Jutting from the water like drip sand castles, the tufas form when calcium bubbles up from subterranean springs and combines with the carbonate in the alkaline lake waters.

The brackish water teems with buzzing alkali flies and brine shrimp, both considered delicacies by dozens of migratory bird species that return here year after year. So do about 85% of the state's nesting population of California gulls, which take over the lake's volcanic islands from April to August.

INFORMATION

Mono Basin Scenic Area Visitors Center (760-647-3044; Hwy 395, usually 8am-5pm mid-Apr–late Nov) Half a mile north of Lee Vining. Maps, interpretive displays, wilderness permits, bear-canister rentals ($5 minimum), bookstore and a 20-minute movie about Mono Lake.

SIGHTS & ACTIVITIES

Tufa spires ring the lake, but the biggest grove is the **South Tufa Reserve** (760-

647-6331; adult/child $3/free), on the south rim with a mile-long interpretive trail. Ask about ranger-led tours at the visitors center. To get to the reserve, head south of Lee Vining on Hwy 395 for 6 miles, then east on Hwy 120 for 5 miles to the dirt road leading to a parking lot.

The best place for swimming is at **Navy Beach**, just east of the reserve. Navy Beach is also the best place to put in canoes or kayaks. From late June to early September, the Mono Lake Committee operates one-hour **canoe tours** (760-647-6595; www.monolake.org/visit/canoe; tours $22; 8am, 9:30am & 11am Sat & Sun) around the tufas. Half-day kayak tours along the shore or out to Paoha Island are also offered by **Caldera Kayaks** (760-934-1691; www.calderakayak.com; tours $75, kayaks $40; mid-May–mid-Oct). Both places require reservations.

Rising above the south shore, **Panum Crater** is the youngest (about 640 years old), smallest and most accessible of the craters that string south toward Mammoth Mountain.

SLEEPING & EATING

El Mono Motel (760-647-6310; www.elmonomotel.com; 51 Hwy 395, Lee Vining; r $65-95; May-Oct;) Grab a board game or soak up some mountain sunshine in this friendly, flower-ringed place, attached to an excellent cafe. In operation since 1927 and often booked solid, each of its 11 simple rooms is unique, decorated with vibrant and colorful art and fabrics.

Tioga Pass Resort (www.tiogapassresort.com; Hwy 120; summer r $115 & cabins $185-228, winter dm/cabin incl all meals per person from $110/145) Founded in 1914 and located 2 miles east of Tioga Pass, it attracts a fiercely loyal clientele to its basic and cozy cabins beside Lee Vining Creek. The thimble-size cafe (mains $8 to $18) serves excellent fare

DOUGLAS STEAKLEY

Lakeside stretch of the June Lake Loop

⬎ IF YOU LIKE...

If you like **Mono Lake** (p242) and **Lake Tahoe** (p222) we think you'll be dazzled by these other high-altitude lakes:

- **Twin Lakes** West of Bridgeport, eager anglers line the shoreline of this gorgeous duo of basins cradled by the fittingly named Sawtooth Ridge. The area's famous for its fishing; other activities include mountain-biking and hiking in the Hoover Wilderness and on into the eastern, lake-riddled reaches of Yosemite National Park.
- **Lundy Lake** Northwest of Mono Lake, Lundy Lake is a picturesque spot, especially in spring when wildflowers carpet the canyon along Mill Creek, or in fall when it is brightened by colorful foliage.
- **June Lake Loop** Under the shadow of massive Carson Peak (10,909ft), this 14-mile loop meanders through a picture-perfect horseshoe canyon past the relaxed resort town of June Lake and four sparkling, fish-rich lakes named Grant, Silver, Gull and June. Catch the loop (Hwy 158) a few miles south of Lee Vining.
- **Convict Lake** Southeast of Mammoth Lakes, Convict Lake is one of the area's prettiest, with emerald water embraced by massive peaks. Skirting the water, a gentle trail passes through aspen and cottonwood trees. A trailhead on the southeastern shore gives access to Genevieve, Edith, Dorothy and Mildred Lakes, in the John Muir Wilderness.

all day long at a few tables and a broken horseshoe counter, with a house pastry chef concocting dozens of freshly baked desserts daily. Reserve lodging via email.

Whoa Nellie Deli (☎ 760-647-1088; near junction of Hwys 120 & 395, Lee Vining; mains $13-19; ⏲ 7am-9pm mid-May–Oct) Great food in a gas station? Come on… No, really, you gotta try this amazing kitchen, where chef Matt 'Tioga' Toomey feeds delicious fish tacos, wild-buffalo meatloaf and other tasty morsels to locals and clued-in passersby.

MAMMOTH LAKES

pop 7400 / elev 7800ft

A small mountain resort town endowed with larger-than-life scenery – active outdoorsy folks worship at the base of its dizzying 11,053ft Mammoth Mountain. Everlasting powder clings to these slopes, and when the snow finally fades, the area's an outdoor wonderland of mountain-bike trails, excellent fishing, endless alpine hiking and blissful hidden spots for hot-spring soaking. The Eastern Sierra's commercial hub and a four-season resort, outdoorsy Mammoth is backed by a ridgeline of jutting peaks, ringed by clusters of crystalline alpine lakes and enshrouded by the dense Inyo National Forest.

INFORMATION

The **Mammoth Lakes Visitors Bureau** (☎ 760-934-2712, 888-466-2666; www.visitmammoth.com; 🕑 8am-5pm) and the **Mammoth Lakes Ranger Station** (☎ 760-924-5500; www.fs.fed.us/r5/inyo; 🕑 8am-5pm) share a building on the north side of Hwy 203.

ACTIVITIES

SKIING & SNOWBOARDING

Mammoth Mountain Ski Area (☎ information 760-934-0745, 800-626-6684, 24hr snow report 888-766-9778; www.mammothmountain.com; lift tickets adult/senior & child $92/46) is still a true skiers' and snowboarders' dream resort, where playing hard and having fun are more important than anything else. Sunny skies, reliable snow (the season generally runs from November to June) and over 3500 acres of fantastic tree-line and open-bowl skiing prove to be a potent cocktail.

HIKING

Mammoth Lakes rubs up against the Ansel Adams Wilderness and the John Muir Wilderness, both laced with fabulous trails leading to shimmering lakes, rugged peaks and hidden canyons. Major trailheads leave from the Mammoth Lakes Basin, Reds Meadow and Agnew Meadows; the latter two are accessible only by shuttle (see p246). Shadow Lake is a stunning 7-mile day hike from Agnew Meadows.

MOUNTAIN-BIKING

Come summer, **Mammoth Mountain** (☎ 760-934-0706; day pass adult/child $42/21; 🕑 9am-5:30pm) morphs into a massive mountain bike park with more than 80 miles of well-kept single-track trails. Several other trails traverse the surrounding forest.

SLEEPING

Davison Street Guest House (☎ 760-924-2188, reservations 858-755-8648; www.mammoth-guest.com; 19 Davison St; dm $28-49, r $59-110) An A-frame hostel on a quiet residential street. You can whip up entire meals in the stocked kitchen and enjoy mountain views from the living room with fireplace or sun deck.

Tamarack Lodge & Resort (☎ 760-934-2442, 800-626-6684; www.tamaracklodge.com; Lakes Loop Rd, Twin Lakes; lodge r $89-129, cabins $179-600; 🛜) A charming year-round resort on the shore of Lower Twin Lake. In business since 1924, the cozy lodge includes a fireplace, bar, excellent restaurant, 11 rustic rooms and 34 cabins. The cabins range from very simple to simply deluxe, and come with full kitchen, telephone, private bath, porch and wood-burning stove.

EATING & DRINKING

Petra's Bistro & Wine Bar (☎ 760-934-3500; 6080 Minaret Rd; mains $14-32; 🕑 dinner Tue-Sun) Settle in here for seasonal California cuisine and wines recommended by the three staff sommeliers. In wintertime, the best seats in the house are the cozy fireside couches. Start the evening with a cheese course and choose from 28 wines available by the glass or 240 vintages by the bottle.

Lakefront Restaurant (☎ 760-934-3534; Lakes Loop Rd, Twin Lakes; mains $23-32; 🕑 lunch summer, dinner year-round, closed Tue & Wed in fall & spring) For a splurge, the Tamarack Lodge has an intimate and romantic dining room overlooking Twin Lakes. The chef crafts French-California specialties like elk medallions au poivre and heirloom tomatoes with Basque cheese, and the staff are superbly friendly.

Mammoth Brewing Company (☎ 760-934-2555; cnr Minaret Rd & Main St; 🕑 5-9pm summer, 4-9pm winter) Upstairs at Whiskey Creek; it's a popular and noisy hangout with a pool table and large-screen TVs, with the decibels rising during the early-evening happy hour. It serves beers brewed on-site as well as fancy pub grub.

GETTING THERE & AWAY
Once-daily round-trip bus service between Mammoth and Yosemite Valley (one way $15, four hours) is run by **Yarts** (☎ 209-388-9589, 877-989-2787; www.yarts.com) on Saturdays and Sundays in June and September, and daily from July through August.

To the horror of some and the delight of others, daily flights from Los Angeles (and seasonal winter service from San Jose) to Mammoth's updated airport (called Mammoth Yosemite) began in 2008 on **Horizon Air** (www.alaskaair.com).

AROUND MAMMOTH LAKES
REDS MEADOW
One of the beautiful and varied landscapes near Mammoth is the Reds Meadow valley, west of Mammoth Mountain. Drive on Hwy 203 as far as **Minaret Vista** for eye-popping views (best at sunset) of the Ritter Range, the serrated Minarets and the remote reaches of Yosemite National Park.

To minimize impact, the road is closed to private vehicles beyond here unless you are camping, have lodge reservations

Horseback riding around Duck Lake, Mammoth Lakes

LEE FOSTER

or are disabled. An access fee (per adult/ child $7/4, maximum $20 per car) is good for three days, and pays your passage for unlimited rides on the mandatory shuttle bus.

The most fascinating attraction here is the surreal volcanic formation of **Devils Postpile National Monument**. The 60ft curtains of near-vertical, six-sided basalt columns formed when rivers of molten lava slowed, cooled and cracked with perplexing symmetry. This honeycomb design is best appreciated from atop the columns, reached by a short trail. The columns are an easy, half-mile hike from the **Devil's Postpile Ranger Station** (☎ 760-934-2289; www.nps.gov/depo; 🕑 9am-5pm).

The Reds Meadow Rd is accessible only from about June until September, weather permitting.

MANZANAR NATIONAL HISTORIC SITE

A stark wooden guard tower alerts drivers to one of the darkest chapters in US history, which unfolded on a barren and windy sweep of land some 5 miles south of Independence. Little remains of the infamous war internment camp, a dusty square mile where more than 10,000 people of Japanese ancestry were corralled during WWII following the attack on Pearl Harbor. The camp's lone remaining building, the former high school auditorium, houses a superb **interpretive center** (☎ 760-878-2194; www.nps.gov/manz; admission free; 🕑 9am-4:30pm Nov-Mar, to 5:30pm Apr-Oct).

Watch the 20-minute documentary, then explore the thought-provoking exhibits that chronicle the stories of the families who languished here yet built a vibrant community. Afterwards, take a self-guided 3.2-mile driving tour around the grounds, which takes you past vestiges of buildings and gardens as well as the haunting camp cemetery.

LONE PINE

pop 1700 / elev 3700ft

A tiny town, Lone Pine is the gateway to big things, most notably Mt Whitney (14,505ft), the loftiest peak in the contiguous USA, and Hollywood. In the 1920s cinematographers discovered that the nearby Alabama Hills were a picture-perfect movie set for Westerns, and stars from Gary Cooper to Gregory Peck could often be spotted swaggering about town.

ORIENTATION & INFORMATION

Eastern Sierra InterAgency Visitor Center (☎ 760-876-6222; www.fs.fed.us/r5/inyo; 🕑 8am-5pm, extended summer hrs) USFS information central for the Sierra, Death Valley and Mt Whitney; about 1.5 miles south of town at the junction of Hwys 395 and 136.

⤡ LAWS RAILROAD MUSEUM

Railroad and Old West aficionados should make the 6-mile detour north on Hwy 6 to the **Laws Railroad Museum** (☎ 760-873-5950; www.lawsmuseum.org; requested donation $5; 🕑 10am-4pm; 👶). It re-creates the village of Laws, an important stop on the route of the *Slim Princess*, a narrow-gauge train that hauled freight and passengers across the Owens Valley for nearly 80 years. The original 1883 train depot is here, as are a post office, a schoolhouse and other rickety old buildings.

JOHN ELK III

Japanese memorial, Manzanar National Historic Site

SIERRA NEVADA & THE DESERTS

GOLD COUNTRY

SIGHTS & ACTIVITIES

MT WHITNEY

West of Lone Pine, the jagged incisors of the Sierra surge skyward in all their raw and fierce glory. Cradled by scores of smaller pinnacles, Mt Whitney is a bit hard to pick out from Hwy 395, so for the best views take a drive along Whitney Portal Rd, through the Alabama Hills. As you get a fix on this majestic megalith, remember that the country's lowest point is only 80 miles (as the crow flies) east of here: Badwater (p263) in Death Valley.

ALABAMA HILLS

Located on Whitney Portal Rd, the warm colors and rounded contours of the Alabama Hills stand in contrast to the jagged snowy Sierras just behind. The setting for countless ride-'em-out movies and the popular *Lone Ranger* TV series, the stunning orange rock formations are a beautiful place to experience sunrise or sunset. A number of graceful rock arches are within easy hiking distance of the roads.

SLEEPING & EATING

Dow Hotel & Dow Villa Motel (☎ 760-876-5521, 800-824-9317; www.dowvillamotel.com; 310 S Main St; hotel r with/without bath $68/52, motel r $99-147; ☒ ☜) John Wayne and Errol Flynn are among the stars who have stayed at this venerable hotel. Built in 1922, the place has been restored but retains much of its rustic charm. The rooms in the newer motel section are more comfortable and bright, but also more generic.

Seasons (☎ 760-876-8927; 206 N Main St; mains $16-39; ☺ dinner daily Apr-Oct, Tue-Sun Nov-Mar) Sautéed trout, roasted duck, filet mignon and plates of carb-replenishing pasta will revitalize your appetite, and nice-and-naughty desserts will leave you purring.

GOLD COUNTRY

Gold Country is where California was born. These hills were technically still Mexico when James Marshall caught a glimpse of a curiously shiny rock at John Sutter's Mill, starting the uproar that became California. The stampede of 300,000 '49ers who rushed these hills jump-started the new state's economy, but they got only a fraction of the gold before the catastrophic environmental impacts caused a halt to the mining. The scars have healed beautifully though, leaving hills covered in pine, oak and a string of historic towns – some restored to lacy Victorian elegance, others wilting in the high heat.

AUBURN STATE RECREATION AREA

The deep gorges of this popular **park** (☎ 530-885-4527; www.parks.ca.gov, day use fee for some areas $10) were cut by the rushing waters of the North and Middle Forks of the **American River**, which converge below a bridge on Hwy 49, about 4 miles south of Auburn. In the early spring, when waters are high, they're immensely popular for whitewater rafting, as the rivers offer a range of difficulty levels.

MARSHALL GOLD DISCOVERY STATE HISTORIC PARK

Compared to the stampede of gun-toting, hill-blasting, hell-raising settlers that populate tall tales along Hwy 49, the **Marshall Gold Discovery State Historic Park** (☎ 530-622-3470; Hwy 49, Coloma; admission per car $8; ☼ 8am-sunset) is a place of bucolic tranquillity, with two tragic heroes in John Sutter and James Marshall. Sutter, who had a fort in Sacramento, partnered with Marshall to build a sawmill on a swift stretch of the American River in 1847. It was Marshall who discovered gold here on January 24, 1848, and though the men tried to keep their findings secret, it eventually brought a chaotic rush of prospectors from around the world.

The pastoral park is quietly befitting of this legacy, with a grassy area bordered on the east by the river. Follow a simple dirt path to the place along the bank where Marshall found gold and started the revolutionary birth of the Golden State.

SACRAMENTO

pop 460,000 / elev 17ft

Square in the middle of the sweltering valley, Sacramento's downtown is couched by the confluence of two cool rivers – the American and the Sacramento – and its streets are shushed by the leaves of huge oaks.

INFORMATION

Convention & Visitors Bureau (☎ 800-292-2334; www.discovergold.org; 1608 I St; ☼ 8am-5pm Mon-Fri) Local information, including event and bus schedules.

SIGHTS
CALIFORNIA STATE CAPITOL

The **California State Capitol** (☎ 916-324-0333; cnr 10th & L Sts; ☼ 9am-5pm) is Sacramento's most recognizable structure. Built in the late 19th century, it underwent major reconstruction in the 1970s, and its marble halls offer a cool place for a stroll.

OLD SACRAMENTO

At Old Sac's north end is the excellent **California State Railroad Museum** (☎ 916-445-6645; www.csrmf.org; cnr 2nd & I Sts; adult/child $9/4; ☼ 10am-5pm), the largest of its kind in the US. It has an impressive collection of railcars, locomotives, toy models and memorabilia, and fully outfitted Pullman sleeper and vintage diner cars to induce a joyful palsy in railroad enthusiasts. Tickets include entrance to the restored **Central Pacific Passenger Depot**, across the plaza from the museum entrance. On weekends from April to September, you can board a steam-powered passenger train from the depot (adult/child $9/4) for a 40-minute jaunt along the riverfront.

SUTTER'S FORT STATE HISTORIC PARK

Sutter's Fort State Historic Park (☎ 916-445-4422; www.parks.ca.gov; cnr 27th & L Sts; adult/child $5/3; ⏱ 10am-5pm), originally built by John Sutter, was once the only trace of white settlement for hundreds of miles – hard to tell by the housing developments that surround the park today. California history buffs should carve out a couple hours to stroll within its walls, where original furniture, equipment and a working ironsmith are straight out of the 1850s.

SLEEPING & EATING

Delta King (☎ 916-444-5464, 800-825-5464; www.deltaking.com; 100 Front St; r $101-230; 🅿 🛜) If you stay near Old Town, you can't beat the experience of sleeping aboard the *Delta King*, a docked 1927 paddle wheeler that lights up like a Christmas tree at night.

La Bonne Soupe Cafe (☎ 916-492-9506; 920 8th St; $8-10; ⏱ lunch Mon-Fri) Chef Daniel Pont assembles his divine sandwiches with such loving, affectionate care that the line of downtown lunchers snakes out the door. If you do have time, consider yourself lucky and ponder: smoky duck breast or apples and brie? Braised pork or smoked salmon? And the creamy soups made from scratch prove the restaurant's name is a painful understatement.

Mulvaney's Building & Loan (☎ 916-441-6022; 1215 19th St; mains $20-40; ⏱ lunch Tue-Fri, dinner Tue-Sat) With an obsessive flourish for seasonality, the menu here changes every single day. Patrick Mulvaney flutters between the kitchen and the dining room, offering delicate pasta dishes and buttery braised meats.

GETTING THERE & AWAY

Amtrak Station (cnr 5th & I Sts) is between downtown and Old Sac.

RICHARD CUMMINS

Historic Old Sacramento

THE DESERTS

For early Western explorers such as conquistador Juan Bautista de Anza and frontier trailblazer Jedediah Smith, the desert was just a barrier to the California coast. Treasure-seeking miners also came and went, establishing now ghostly towns that died as the minerals played out, leaving their skeletons and stories scattered in the sand.

PALM SPRINGS & COACHELLA VALLEY

In the 1950s and '60s, Palm Springs, some 100 miles east of LA, was the swinging getaway of Sinatra, Elvis and dozens of other stars, partying the night away in midcentury-modern estate homes. In today's PS, elderly denizens mix amicably with younger hipsters and an active gay and lesbian community. Around here, you can hike palm-oasis canyons or snowshoe high into the mountains (or both in the same day), hunt down midcentury modern architecture, sample a date milkshake, tour a windmill or straddle a fault line.

INFORMATION

Palm Springs Official Visitors Center (Map p252; ☎ 760-778-8418, 800-347-7746; www.visitpalmsprings.com; 2901 N Palm Canyon Dr; 🕘 9am-5pm) North of downtown, the city's main visitor center books hotels, offers specialty tourism guides (mobility-impaired, gay and lesbian, architecture etc) and sells maps.

SIGHTS

PALM SPRINGS AERIAL TRAMWAY

A highlight of any Palm Springs getaway, this revolving **cable car** (Map p252; ☎ 760-325-1391, 888-515-8726; www.pstramway.com; 1 Tramway Rd; round-trip adult/child $23.25/16.25; 🕘 departures 10am-8pm Mon-Fri, 8am-8pm Sat &

Sun, last tram back down 9:45pm Sun-Thu & 10:30pm Fri & Sat; 🔧) climbs nearly 6000 vertical feet through five different vegetation zones from the Sonoran desert floor into the San Jacinto Mountains, in less than 15 minutes. It's 30°F to 40°F (17°C to 22°C) cooler as you step out into pine forests at the top, so bring warm clothing – the 2.5-mile ascent is said to be the temperature equivalent of driving from Mexico to Canada.

INDIAN CANYONS

Streams flowing from the San Jacinto Mountains sustain a rich variety of plants in oases around Palm Springs. Home to Native American communities for hundreds of years and now part of the Agua Caliente Indian Reservation, these **canyons** (Map p252; ☎ 760-323-6018; www.indian-canyons.com; adult/child $8/4, incl 90min guided hike $11/6; 🕘 8am-5pm daily Oct-Jun, 8am-5pm Fri-Sun Jul-Sep) are a delight to hike, shaded by fan palms and surrounded by towering cliffs.

From downtown Palm Springs, head south on Palm Canyon Dr (continue straight when the main road turns east) for about 2 miles to the reservation entrance. Trail posts at the entrance to each canyon have maps and hiking info.

ACTIVITIES
GOLF

Golf is huge here, with more than 100 public, semiprivate, private and resort golf courses in the Coachella Valley (greens fees from $155). Some efforts are being made to reduce the million gallons of water per day used to irrigate the courses, but even so, it's far from ecofriendly in the desert. **Stand By Golf** (☎ 760-321-2665; www.standbygolf.com) books tee times for discounted same-day or next-day play at a few dozen courses around the valley.

HIKING, SKIING & SNOWSHOEING

For hiking in summer, and snowshoeing and cross-country skiing in winter, ride the **Palm Springs Aerial Tramway** (see opposite) up to Mt San Jacinto State Park. For desert hikes near downtown Palm Springs, check out **Indian Canyons** (see opposite) and **Tahquitz Canyon** (Map p254).

SPAS

Palm Springs and 'Down Valley' towns have dozens of sumptuous spas. Wherever you go, make reservations first.

East Canyon (Map p254; ☎ 760-320-1928, 877-324-6835; www.eastcanyonps.com; 288 E Camino Monte Vista) Palm Springs' only exclusively gay spa.

Spa Resort Casino (Map p254; ☎ 760-778-1772, 888-999-1995; www.sparesortcasino.com; 401 E Amado Rd) Try a 'taking of the waters' course through the valley's original hot springs.

FESTIVALS & EVENTS

Modernism Week (www.modernismweek. com) In mid-February, a modernism art show, lectures, screenings and architecture tours revolve around the Palm Springs Art Museum (Map p254).

Coachella Valley Music & Arts Festival (www.coachella.com; 3-day ticket $269) In late April, Indio's Empire Polo Club hosts one of the hottest music festivals of its kind, with acts ranging from hip indie no-names to Björk, Beck and Prince.

SLEEPING

Del Marcos Hotel (Map p254; ☎ 760-325-6902, 800-676-1214; www.delmarcoshotel.com; 225 W Baristo Rd; r $99-388; ❄ 🐾 🛜) After suffering years of bad remodels, this 1947 gem finally looks like it should. Groovy tunes in the lobby usher you to a saltwater pool and ineffably chic rooms named for local architectural luminaries. Breakfast isn't provided, but you're right downtown.

our pick **Orbit In** (Map p254; ☎ 760-323-3585, 877-996-7248; www.orbitin.com; 562 W Arenas Rd; d incl breakfast $149-259; ❄ 💻 🐾 🛜) Swing back into the 1950s

Anza-Borrego Desert State Park (p258)

WITOLD SKRYPCZAK

COACHELLA VALLEY & JOSHUA TREE NATIONAL PARK

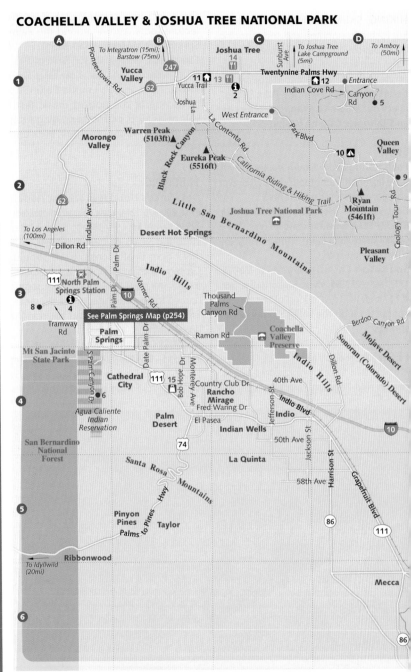

A **B** **C** **D**

1

To Integratron (15mi);
Barstow (75mi)

Pioneertown Rd

247

Yucca
Valley

62

Joshua Tree

Sunburst Ave

To Joshua Tree
Lake Campground
(5mi)

To Amboy
(50mi)

14

Twentynine Palms Hwy

11 13

Yucca Trail

2

Indian Cove Rd

12

Entrance

Canyon
Rd

5

Joshua

West Entrance

La Contenta Rd

Warren Peak
(5103ft)

Black Rock Canyon

Eureka Peak
(5516ft)

California Riding & Hiking Trail

Park Blvd

10

Queen
Valley

9

Morongo
Valley

2

62

Indian Ave

Little San Bernardino Mountains

Joshua Tree National Park

Ryan
Mountain
(5461ft)

Geology Tour Rd

Pleasant
Valley

To Los Angeles
(100mi)

Desert Hot Springs

Dillon Rd

Palm Dr

Indio Hills

3

111

North Palm
Springs Station

8

4

Tramway
Rd

Varner Rd

Palm Dr

10

Date Palm Dr

See Palm Springs Map (p254)

Palm
Springs

Thousand
Palms
Canyon Rd

Ramon Rd

Coachella
Valley
Preserve

Berdoo Canyon Rd

Indio Hills

Sonoran (Colorado) Desert

Mojave Desert

Mt San Jacinto
State Park

S Palm Canyon Dr

Cathedral
City

111

6

Bob Hope Dr

Monterey Ave

15

Country Club Dr

Rancho
Mirage

Fred Waring Dr

40th Ave

Jefferson St

Indio Blvd

Indio

Dillon Rd

10

4

Agua Caliente
Indian
Reservation

Palm
Desert

El Pasea

Indian Wells

50th Ave

Jackson St

San Bernardino
National
Forest

Santa Rosa Mountains

74

La Quinta

58th Ave

Harrison St

Grapefruit Blvd

5

Pinyon
Pines

Palms to Pines Hwy

Taylor

86

111

Ribbonwood

To Idyllwild
(20mi)

6

Mecca

86

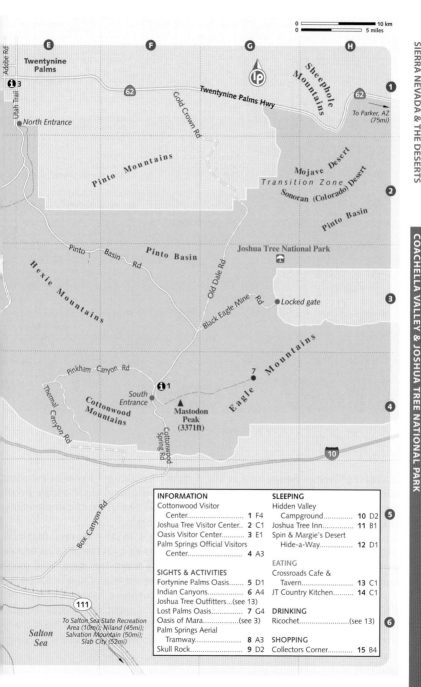

SIERRA NEVADA & THE DESERTS

COACHELLA VALLEY & JOSHUA TREE NATIONAL PARK

INFORMATION		
Cottonwood Visitor		
Center...........................	1	F4
Joshua Tree Visitor Center..	2	C1
Oasis Visitor Center...........	3	E1
Palm Springs Official Visitors		
Center...........................	4	A3

SIGHTS & ACTIVITIES		
Fortynine Palms Oasis.......	5	D1
Indian Canyons.................	6	A4
Joshua Tree Outfitters...(see 13)		
Lost Palms Oasis...............	7	G4
Oasis of Mara................(see 3)		
Palm Springs Aerial		
Tramway.....................	8	A3
Skull Rock........................	9	D2

SLEEPING		
Hidden Valley		
Campground..............	10	D2
Joshua Tree Inn...............	11	B1
Spin & Margie's Desert		
Hide-a-Way...............	12	D1

EATING		
Crossroads Cafe &		
Tavern.......................	13	C1
JT Country Kitchen..........	14	C1

DRINKING		
Ricochet.......................(see 13)		

SHOPPING		
Collectors Corner............	15	B4

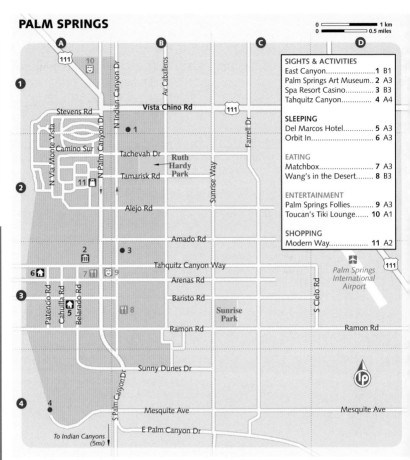

PALM SPRINGS

SIGHTS & ACTIVITIES	
East Canyon.......................**1** B1	
Palm Springs Art Museum..**2** A3	
Spa Resort Casino.............**3** B3	
Tahquitz Canyon.............**4** A4	
SLEEPING	
Del Marcos Hotel.............**5** A3	
Orbit In...........................**6** A3	
EATING	
Matchbox........................**7** A3	
Wang's in the Desert.......**8** B3	
ENTERTAINMENT	
Palm Springs Follies...........**9** A3	
Toucan's Tiki Lounge......**10** A1	
SHOPPING	
Modern Way.................**11** A2	

during the 'Orbitini' happy hour at this fabulously retro property, with high-end midcentury modern furniture (Eames, Noguchi et al) around a quiet pool with a Jacuzzi and firepit. Throwback touches include LP record players (juxtaposed with plasma-screen TVs) and retro beach-cruiser bikes to borrow.

EATING & DRINKING

Matchbox (Map p254; ☎ 760-778-6000; 2nd level, 155 S Palm Canyon Dr; mains $13-26; ☻ 5-11pm Sun-Thu, to 1am Fri & Sat) A winner, with gourmet wood-oven-fired pizzas made

from fresh dough, a plaza-view patio and martini-and-cigar happy hours California bistro classics can sometime be hit-or-miss.

Wang's in the Desert (Map p254 ☎ 760-325-9264; 424 S Indian Canyon Dr; main $12-21; ☻ dinner) The menu may sound like standard-issue Chinese fusion, ye the atmosphere is anything but. Thi mood-lit outpost, with indoor koi pond and giant cocktails, is a darling of the in crowd. Come early or make reservations Kiss, kiss.

ENTERTAINMENT

Palm Springs Follies (Map p254; ☎ 760-327-0225; www.psfollies.com; 128 S Palm Canyon Dr; tickets $50-92; ☺ Nov-May) This Ziegfeld Follies–style revue includes music, dancing, showgirls and comedy. The twist? Many of the performers are as old as the theater – all are over 50 years of age, some into their 80s. But this is no amateur hour: in their heyday, many of these old-timers hoofed it alongside Hollywood and Broadway's biggest, who occasionally guest star.

Toucan's Tiki Lounge (Map p254; ☎ 760-416-7584; www.toucanstikilounge.com; 2100 N Palm Canyon Dr) A couple of miles north of Arenas, this locals' hangout has something for everyone: tropical froufrou, bingo mavens, karaoke, drag revues, smoking patio and dance floor. It's packed on weekends.

SHOPPING

Modern Way (Map p254; ☎ 760-320-5455; 745 N Palm Canyon Dr) The largest, oldest and most stylin' consignment shop for collectors of modern furniture.

Collectors Corner (Map p252; ☎ 760-346-1012; 71280 Hwy 111, Rancho Mirage) Antiques, vintage clothing, jewelry and furniture draw enthusiastic shoppers from across the Coachella Valley, where well-heeled retirees, and their propensity to pass on to the next world, mean shelves are constantly replenished.

GETTING THERE & AWAY
AIR

Palm Springs International Airport (PSP; Map p254; ☎ 760-318-3800; www.palmspringsairport.com; 3400 E Tahquitz Canyon Way) is a 10-minute drive northeast of downtown.

TRAIN

Amtrak (☎ 800-872-7245; www.amtrak.com) serves the unstaffed and kinda creepy North Palm Springs Station (Map p252), about 5 miles north of downtown Palm Springs. Trains are often late.

LEFT LANE MUST TURN LEFT

COREY WISE

Palm Springs has many buildings in the desert modernist architectural style

LUCIANO LEON/ALAMY

Revelers at Burning Man

↘ IF YOU LIKE...

If you like the **Coachella Valley Music & Arts Festival** (p251) we think you'll enjoy these eclectic desert events:

- **Burning Man** (www.burningman.com; admission $210-300) For one week at the end of August, Burning Man explodes onto the sunbaked Black Rock Desert, and Nevada sprouts a third major population center – Black Rock City. An experiential art party (and alternative universe) that climaxes in the immolation of a towering stick figure, Burning Man is a whirlwind of outlandish theme camps, dust-caked bicycles, bizarre bartering, costume-enhanced nudity and a general relinquishment of inhibitions.

- **Badwater** (www.badwater.com) A 135-mile ultramarathon from Badwater Basin (p263) up to Whitney Portal, near Lone Pine and Mt Whitney (p246), it's staged in mid-July at the suicidal height of summer.

- **Death Valley '49ers** (www.deathvalley49ers.org) In early November, this historical encampment takes place at Furnace Creek (p263), featuring cowboy poetry, campfire sing-alongs, a gold-panning contest and a Western art show. Show up early to watch the pioneer wagons come thunderin' in.

- **Joshua Tree Music Festival** (☎ 877-327-6265; www.joshuatreemusicfestival.com; 1-day pass $50-80, 3-day pass $140) Over a long weekend in May, this family-friendly indie-music fest grooves out at Joshua Tree Lake Campground. It's followed by a soulful roots celebration in mid-October.

JOSHUA TREE NATIONAL PARK

Joshua Tree National Park straddles the transition zone between the Colorado Desert and the higher, cooler Mojave Desert, where Joshua trees (actually tree-sized yuccas) grow. Lower down, the desert is characterized by cacti, particularly prickly green cholla, and ocotillos, whose octopus-like tentacles shoot out crimson flowers in spring. Wildflowers bloom at varying elevations between February and

April. In winter it can snow at higher points, such as Keys View (5185ft).

The mystical quality of this stark, boulder-strewn landscape has inspired many artists, most famously the band U2, which named its 1987 album *The Joshua Tree*. The park's wonderfully shaped rocky outcroppings also draw world-class climbers, who know 'J-Tree' as the best place to climb in California.

INFORMATION

Admission to **Joshua Tree National Park** (☎ 760-367-5500; www.nps.gov/jotr; 7-day entry pass per car/bicycle $15/5; ⏱ 24hr) includes a map/brochure and the seasonal *Joshua Tree Guide*.

There are no facilities inside the park except restrooms, so gas up and bring food and plenty of water. In the park, cell-phone coverage is almost nonexistent, but there's an emergency-only telephone at the Intersection Rock parking lot by Hidden Valley Campground.

TOURIST INFORMATION

Cottonwood Visitor Center (Map p252; www.nps.gov/jotr; Cottonwood Spring Rd; ⏱ 9am-3pm)

Joshua Tree Visitor Center (Map p252; www.nps.gov/jotr; Park Blvd, south of Hwy 62, Joshua Tree; ⏱ 8am-5pm)

Oasis Visitor Center (Map p252; www.nps. gov/jotr; National Park Blvd, Twentynine Palms; ⏱ 8am-5pm)

SIGHTS

Behind the Oasis Visitor Center, near the park's northern entrance, the natural **Oasis of Mara** (Map p252) has the original 29 palm trees for which the nearby town is named. They were planted by Serrano tribespeople, who named this 'the place of little springs and much grass.' The Pinto Mountain Fault, a small branch of the San Andreas, runs through the oasis, as does a 0.5-mile, wheelchair-accessible nature trail with labeled desert plants.

In the center of the park, the most whimsically dramatic conglomeration of rocks is known as the **Wonderland of Rocks**, where designated picnic areas, pull-offs and campgrounds give everyone a chance to clamber on the giant boulders. East of Queen Valley, travelers with 4WD vehicles or mountain bikes can detour onto **Geology Tour Road**, an 18-mile field trip down into and around Pleasant Valley, where the forces of erosion, earthquakes and ancient volcanoes combine.

Joshua trees grow throughout the upper area of the park, including right along Park Blvd, but some of the biggest trees are found in **Covington Flats**, along a dirt road that ends with views of Palm Springs, the Morongo Basin and the mountains. Much more easily reached, about a 20-minute drive south of Park Blvd, **Keys View** overlooks the entire Coachella Valley and the San Bernardino Mountains. You can clearly observe the San Andreas fault system from here.

ACTIVITIES

HIKING

Leave the car behind to appreciate Joshua Tree's trippy lunar landscapes. Try to hike early or late in the day, to avoid the worst heat. To protect plants and the cryptobiotic soil crust that keeps the desert from blowing away, always stay on established trails.

If you're short on time, amble along the 1.3-mile loop out to **Barker Dam**, which passes a little lake and a rock incised with Native American petroglyphs. Then stretch your legs on the 1.7-mile trail around **Skull Rock** (Map p252) and other cool boulder pile-ups in the Wonderland of Rocks.

To escape the crowds, take the 3-mile round-trip hike to **Fortynine Palms Oasis** (Map p252), an up-and-down trail starting near Indian Cove, or the fairly flat 7.2-mile round-trip trek out to **Lost Palms Oasis** (Map p252), starting from Cottonwood Spring.

ROCK CLIMBING

From boulders to cracks to multipitch faces, there are more than 8000 established routes, many accessed off Park Blvd. If you're going bouldering, rent crash pads from **Joshua Tree Outfitters** (Map p252; ☎ 760-366-1848, 888-366-1848; www.joshuatreeoutfitters.com; 61707 Twentynine Palms Hwy, Joshua Tree; ☼ 9am-5pm Thu-Tue).

SLEEPING

There are nine **NPS campgrounds** (www.nps.gov/jotr/planyourvisit/camping.htm; tent & RV sites $10-15) in the park.

Joshua Tree Inn (Map p252; ☎ 760-366-1188; www.joshuatreeinn.com; 61259 Twentynine Palms Hwy, Joshua Tree; r $85-155; ✗ ☜) Alt-country pioneer and 1970s rock legend Gram Parsons overdosed in this large U-shaped motel; his fans still flock here to stay in Room 8. Other famous blast-from-the-past guests include Robert Plant, Keith Richards and Emmy Lou Harris. Retro digs have beamed ceilings and country-kitsch furnishings. The communal area features a rock fireplace.

our pick **Spin & Margie's Desert Hide-a-Way** (Map p252; ☎ 760-366-9124; www.deserthideaway.com; 6920-6923 Sunkist Rd, Joshua Tree; ste $125-160; ✗ ☜) Boldly colorful, snappy-looking suites each have their own kitchen, TV/VCR and stereo at this delightful hacienda-style inn, where unusual design motifs include corrugated tin, old license plates and cartoon art. Knowledgeable, gregarious owners ensure a relaxed visit.

EATING & DRINKING

our pick **Crossroads Cafe & Tavern** (Map p252; ☎ 760-366-5414; 61715 Twentynine Palms Hwy, Joshua Tree; mains $6-11; ☼ 6:30am-8pm Thu-Tue; **V**) An eclectic-looking joint with a treehugger-friendly atmosphere, the much-loved Crossroads dishes up homemade breakfast hashes, fresh sandwiches, fruit smoothies and dragged-through-the-garden salads that make both omnivores and vegans happy.

JT Country Kitchen (Map p252; ☎ 760-366-8988; 61768 Twentynine Palms Hwy, Joshua Tree; mains $6-10; ☼ 6:30am-3pm) This roadside shack serves down-home cookin': eggs, pancakes, biscuits with gravy, sandwiches and…what's this? Cambodian noodles and salads? Delish.

Ricochet (Map p252; ☎ 760-366-1898; 61705 Twentynine Palms Hwy, Joshua Tree; ☼ 7am-3pm Mon & Tue, 7am-5pm Wed-Sat, 9am-2pm Sun) Friendly lasses rule the roost at this espresso and juice bar, wine and beer shop, and recycled clothing store. Daily specials from the bakery and kitchen at the back sell out quickly. Diehard urbanites can buy the *New York Times* here.

ANZA-BORREGO DESERT STATE PARK

Enormous and little developed, Anza-Borrego Desert State Park comprises almost a fifth of San Diego County and extends almost all the way to Mexico, making it the largest state park in the USA outside Alaska. It covers 640,000 acres – over 40% of the land in the California state park system. This untamed desert claims some of SoCal's most spectacular scenery and wildlife, with untrammeled backcountry byways to explore, all within easy reach of the retro-flavored resort town of Borrego Springs.

Depending on winter rains, wildflowers bloom brilliantly, albeit briefly, in

Anza-Borrego starting in late February, making a striking contrast to the subtle earth tones of the desert. Call the **Wildflower Hotline** (☎ 760-767-4684) for updates. The average daily maximum temperature in July is 107°F (42°C), but it can reach 125°F (52°C).

INFORMATION

The excellent **Anza-Borrego Desert State Park Visitor Center** (☎ 760-767-4205; www.parks.ca.gov; 200 Palm Canyon Dr, Borrego Springs; ☽ 9am-5pm Thu-Mon Oct-May, 9am-5pm Sat & Sun Jun-Sep) is built partly underground. Park entry fees ($8 per vehicle per day) are required only for entering campgrounds, to access trails or to go picnicking.

SIGHTS

To find out which roads require 4WD vehicles or are currently impassable, check the signboard inside the state park visitors center.

East of Borrego Springs, a 4-mile dirt road, sometimes passable without 4WD, diverges south from County Rte S22 out to **Fonts Point**, a spectacular panorama over the Borrego Valley to the west and the Borrego Badlands to the south. You'll be amazed when the desert seemingly drops from beneath your feet.

ACTIVITIES

Borrego Palm Canyon Nature Trail, a popular 3-mile loop trail that starts near the Borrego Palm Canyon Campground, passes a palm grove and waterfall, a delightful oasis in the dry, rocky countryside that's favored by bighorn sheep. The plucky **Maidenhair Falls Trail** starts from the Hellhole Canyon Trailhead, south of the visitors center on County Rte S22, and climbs 3 miles each way past several palm oases to a seasonal waterfall that supports bird life and a variety of plants.

The 0.5-mile **Narrows Earth Trail**, about 4.5 miles east of Tamarisk Grove along Hwy 78, is an amateur geologist's walk in a fault zone. Look for low-lying, brilliant-red chuparosa shrubs, which attract hummingbirds.

WITOLD SKRYPCZAK

The untamed beauty of Anza-Borrego Desert State Park

MOJAVE NATIONAL PRESERVE

Controversially created as part of the 1994 California Desert Protection Act, this lonely, windswept preserve contains 1.6 million acres of 'singing' sand dunes, Joshua trees, volcanic cinder cones and the ruins of Native American, military and mining settlements. Solitude and serenity are the big draws, often with bighorn sheep, desert tortoises, jackrabbits and coyotes as your only companions. Daytime temperatures hover above 100°F (38°C) during summer, then hang around 50°F (10°C) in winter, when snowstorms are not unheard of.

INFORMATION

Admission to the **Mojave National Preserve** (☎ 760-252-6100; www.nps.gov/moja; ☽ 24hr) is free.

SIGHTS & ACTIVITIES

Visible to the south from I-15, **Cima Dome** is a 1500ft hunk of granite spiked with volcanic cinder cones and crusty out-

croppings of basalt left by lava. At one point the number of cones is so great that they're protected as **Cinder Cones National Natural Landmark**. This anciently charred landscape is best viewed from a distance.

On Black Canyon Rd, east of Kelso-Cima Rd via unpaved Cedar Canyon Rd, is the **Hole-in-the-Wall** formation. These vertical walls of rhyolite tuff (pronounced toof), which look like Swiss-cheese cliffs made of unpolished marble, are the result of a powerful prehistoric volcanic eruption that blasted rocks across the landscape. On the 0.5-mile Rings Trail, metal rings lead down through a narrow slot canyon, once used by Native Americans to escape 19th-century ranchers.

The heart of the preserve is the palm-fringed **Kelso Depot Visitor Center** (☎ 760-252-6108; Kelbaker Rd, Kelso; ☽ 9am-5pm), inside a gracefully restored 1920s railway depot. Stop by to watch the 12-minute park orientation film and peruse in-depth museum exhibits that explore the multicultural and natural history

Wildflowers, Death Valley National Park

KRISTIN PILJAY

of the desert, from Native American days to the arrival of the Union Pacific Railroad in 1905.

DEATH VALLEY

Death Valley National Park, the largest national park in the continental USA, covers an enormous area – more than 5000 sq miles – that includes other valleys and mountain ranges to the north. The name itself evokes all that is harsh, hot and hellish in the deserts of the imagination, a punishing, barren and lifeless place of Old Testament severity. But Death Valley is full of life. Inside this crazy-quilted geological playground you'll find giant sand dunes, mosaic marbled canyons, boulders that appear to race across the sunbaked desert floor, extinct volcanic craters, palm-shaded oases and dozens of rare wildlife species that exist nowhere else in the world.

Peak tourist season is during the cooler winter months and in spring when wildflowers bloom. From late February until early April, all accommodations for over 100 miles are booked solid for weeks, campgrounds fill before noon and people wait for hours to see Scotty's Castle. With a reliable, air-conditioned car, a summer trip is possible, but only if you sightsee in the early morning and late evening, spending the hottest part of the day by a pool or at cooler higher elevations.

HISTORY

Shoshone tribespeople lived in the Panamint Range for centuries, visiting the valley every winter to gather acorns, hunt waterfowl, catch pupfish in marshes and cultivate small areas of corn, squash and beans. After Death Valley National Monument was created by the federal government in 1933, the tribe was forced to move several times, eventually restricted to a 40-acre village site near Furnace Creek, which they still occupy. In 2000 President Clinton signed an act transferring 7500 acres of land back to the Timbisha tribe, creating the first Native American reservation inside a US national park.

The fractured geology of Death Valley left many minerals accessible, and in the late 1800s miners here sought gold, silver, copper and lead. The most successful mining operation was the Harmony Borax Works, which extracted borate, a mineral historically used to make everyday household detergents. The valuable stuff was transported out of Death Valley in wagons pulled by 20-mule teams and hauled over 165 miles to a railway stop near Boron, a grueling 10-day trip. By the late 1920s, most mining activities had ceased.

ORIENTATION & INFORMATION

Not all entrances to **Death Valley National Park** (☎ 760-786-3200; www.nps.gov/deva; 7-day entry pass per car/bicycle $20/10; ☉ 24hr) have a staffed fee-collection station, but you're still expected to self-register and pay for an entry permit to display on your vehicle's windshield.

You'll find gas stations with 24-hour credit-card pumps at Furnace Creek and Panamint Springs. Stovepipe Wells Village, a 35-minute drive northwest of Furnace Creek, has a gas station, general store and ATM.

Furnace Creek Visitor Center (☎ 760-786-3200; Hwy 190, Furnace Creek; ☉ 8am-5pm; ☝) Sells books and maps, offers free informational handouts (available online) and screens a 15-minute slide show.

Scotty's Castle Visitor Center (☎ 760-786-2392; North Hwy; ☉ 9am-4:30pm summer, 8:30am-5pm rest of year) Has exhibits from the castle's museum-worthy collection.

DEATH VALLEY & AROUND

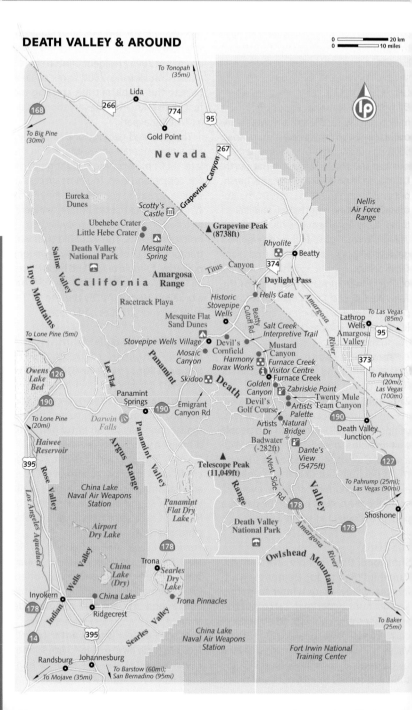

0 |————————| 20 km
0 |————————| 10 miles

To Tonopah (35mi)

Lida

266

774

168

95

To Big Pine (30mi)

Gold Point

N e v a d a

267

Eureka Dunes

Nellis Air Force Range

Scotty's Castle

Ubehebe Crater
Little Hebe Crater

Grapevine Peak (8738ft)

Grapevine Canyon Rd

Death Valley National Park

Mesquite Spring

Rhyolite

Beatty

Saline Valley

Amargosa Range

Titus Canyon

374

Daylight Pass

C a l i f o r n i a

Inyo Mountains

Racetrack Playa

Historic Stovepipe Wells

Hells Gate

Amargosa River

To Las Vegas (85mi)

Lathrop Wells

Amargosa Valley

95

To Lone Pine (5mi)

Mesquite Flat Sand Dunes

Stovepipe Wells Village

Beatty Cutoff Rd

Salt Creek Interpretive Trail

Mosaic Canyon

Devil's Cornfield

Mustard Canyon

373

To Pahrump (20mi); Las Vegas (100mi)

Owens Lake Bed

126

Lee Flat

Panamint

Harmony Borax Works

Skidoo

Furnace Creek
Visitor Centre

Furnace Creek

190

To Lone Pine (20mi)

Panamint Springs

190

Emigrant Canyon Rd

Golden Canyon

Death

Zabriskie Point

Twenty Mule Team Canyon

Darwin Falls

Devil's Golf Course

Artists Palette

190

Haiwee Reservoir

395

Panamint Valley

Artists Dr

Natural Bridge

Death Valley Junction

Argus Range

Badwater (-282ft)

Dante's View (5475ft)

127

China Lake Naval Air Weapons Station

Telescope Peak (11,049ft)

West Side Rd

To Pahrump (25mi); Las Vegas (90mi)

Airport Dry Lake

Panamint Flat Dry Lake

Valley

Shoshone

Amargosa River

Los Angeles Aqueduct

Wells Valley

China Lake (Dry)

Trona

178

Death Valley National Park

178

Rose Valley

Searles Dry Lake

Owlshead Mountains

Inyokern

China Lake

Trona Pinnacles

To Baker (25mi)

Ridgecrest

178

14

395

Searles Valley

China Lake Naval Air Weapons Station

Fort Irwin National Training Center

Randsburg Johannesburg

To Barstow (60mi); San Bernardino (95mi)

To Mojave (35mi)

Indian Wells Valley

SIGHTS
In summer, stick to paved roads (dirt roads can quickly overheat vehicles) and strictly limit your exertions (eg hiking).

BADWATER & FURNACE CREEK
In a park filled with Mother Nature's oddities, the strangest place may be **Badwater**, officially the lowest elevation point in the Western Hemisphere (282ft below sea level). Here you can walk out onto a boardwalk over a constantly evaporating bed of salty, mineralized water that's otherworldly in its beauty.

As you drive back north on Hwy 178, gaze west across the valley floor at the **Devil's Golf Course**, filled with lumps of crystallized salt. Further north is the **Artists Drive**, a one-way scenic loop that passes alluvial fans, where streams have left deposits at the mouths of side canyons, and the **Artists Palette** of colorful exposed minerals and volcanic ash.

Take a break at shady Furnace Creek Ranch. The **Borax Museum** (☎ 760-786-2345; admission free; ⏱ 10am-5pm Oct-May) will tell you all about the once-valuable stuff, with a collection of pioneer-era stagecoaches and wagons out back. The Furnace Creek Visitor Center, with its small **museum** of natural and human history, is up the road. A short drive further north, a short interpretive trail leads in the footsteps of late-19th-century Chinese laborers and through the adobe ruins of **Harmony Borax Works**, where you can take a side trip through twisting **Mustard Canyon**.

At the end of the day, backtrack to **Dante's View** (5475ft). This panoramic vision of an inferno of badlands is gorgeously hued at sunset. En route, detour through **Twenty Mule Team Canyon**, a one-way driving and mountain-biking loop through an ancient lakebed that will make you feel like an ant. Heading back down toward the valley, it's a short walk out to **Zabriskie Point**, where you can scramble down into the eroded badlands.

STOVEPIPE WELLS VILLAGE
En route from Furnace Creek to Stovepipe Wells, keep an eye out for a camera-icon

JOHNNY HAGLUND
Devil's Golf Course, Death Valley National Park

sign and a roadside pull-off on your right, where you can walk out (as long as it's not too hot) into the Sahara-like **Mesquite Flat sand dunes**. On the other side of the road, look for the **Devil's Cornfield**, full of arrow weed clumps. Just west of **Stovepipe Wells Village**, the site of Death Valley's original 1920s tourist resort, a 3-mile gravel side road leads to **Mosaic Canyon**, where you can hike, then crawl through a polished marble slot canyon.

Further southwest, Emigrant Canyon Rd detours off Hwy 190, passing the turnoff to **Skidoo**, a mining ghost town that went bust and where the silent movie *Greed* was filmed in 1923. This turnoff travels along a graded high-clearance gravel road to jaw-dropping Sierra Nevada views.

SCOTTY'S CASTLE

Walter E Scott, alias 'Death Valley Scotty,' was the quintessential tall-tale teller who captivated people with his fanciful stories of gold. His most lucrative friendship was with Albert and Bessie Johnson, insur-ance magnates from Chicago. Despite knowing that Scotty was a freeloading liar, they bankrolled the construction of this elaborate Spanish-inspired villa. Restored to its 1930s appearance, the historic house has sheepskin drapes, carved California redwood, handmade tiles, elaborately wrought iron, woven Shoshone baskets and a bellowing pipe organ upstairs.

For the full story on **Scotty's Castle** (☎ 760-786-2392; adult/child $11/6; ☒ grounds 7:30am-5:30pm summer, 8:30am-6pm rest of year, tours 9am-4:30pm summer, 9am-5pm rest of year), take one of the guided 'Living History' tours. All tickets are first-come, first-served, and there can be a long wait (or they may sell out completely).

Nearly 3000ft above sea level, and noticeably cooler than the valley floor, the castle's palm-shaded lawns make for a picturesque escape from the midday heat. Three miles west of the castle, turn off the main road to visit 770ft-deep **Ubehebe Crater**, formed by the explosive meeting of fiery magma and cool groundwater.

JOHN ELK III

Tour Scotty's Castle, Death Valley National Park

ACTIVITIES

HIKING

Avoid hiking in summer, except on higher-elevation mountain trails, which may be snowed over in winter.

On Hwy 190, just north of Beatty Cutoff Rd, is the half-mile **Salt Creek Interpretive Trail**; in late winter or early spring, rare pupfish splash in the stream alongside the boardwalk. A few miles south of Furnace Creek is **Golden Canyon**, where a self-guided interpretive trail winds for a mile up to the now-oxidized iron cliffs of **Red Cathedral**. With a good sense of orientation, you can keep going up to **Zabriskie Point** for a hardy 4-mile round-trip. Before reaching Badwater, stretch your legs with a 1-mile round-trip walk to the **Natural Bridge**.

The park's most demanding summit is **Telescope Peak** (11,049ft), with views that plummet down to the desert floor, which is two Grand Canyons deep! The 14-mile round-trip trail climbs 3000ft above Mahogany Flat, off upper Wildrose Canyon Rd.

GOLF

For novelty's sake, you can play a round at historic **Furnace Creek Golf Course** (☎ 760-786-2301; Hwy 190, Furnace Creek; greens fees $30-55), the world's lowest-elevation course (18 holes, par 70), redesigned by Perry Dye in 1997. Players claim the below-sea-level setting helps them set personal records. Well, it can't hurt, right?

SLEEPING

There are nine **NPS campgrounds** (www. nps.gov/deva/planyourvisit/camping.htm; tent & RV sites $12-18) inside the park. In summer, it's too hot to camp on the valley floor.

Stovepipe Wells Village (☎ 760-786-2387, reservations 303-297-2757, 888-786-2387; www.stovepipewells.com; Hwy 190, Stovepipe Wells Village; RV sites with hookup $30, r $80-120; ♨ ♿ 👤) It may be just a roadside motel with a small pool, but it has more quirky character than Furnace Creek. Renovated motel rooms (no phones or TVs) are spacious, and definitely the valley's best bargain. Pets OK.

Furnace Creek Ranch (☎ 760-786-2345, reservations 303-297-2757, 800-236-7916; www.furnacecreekresort.com; Hwy 190, Furnace Creek; cabins $130-162, motel r $162-213; ♨ ♿ 👤) Tailor-made for families, this dusty, Old West–style ranch is a short walk from the general store and restaurants. Not as peaceful as Stovepipe Wells Village, it has only ordinary cabins and motel rooms, but more facilities, such as a children's playground, tennis courts and a natural-spring-fed swimming pool.

Furnace Creek Inn (☎ 760-786-2345, reservations 303-297-2757, 800-236-7916; www.furnacecreekresort.com; Hwy 190, Furnace Creek; r $330-443, ste $438-458; ♨ ♿) At this elegant hilltop adobe hotel built in 1927, Mission-style buildings are spread among California-fan-palm-shaded garden terraces. Elemental, almost Zen-like rooms with cable TV are overpriced, but the serenity is priceless. There's a warm-springs outdoor swimming pool with jaw-dropping valley views, plus tennis courts.

EATING & DRINKING

Toll Road Restaurant (☎ 760-786-2387; Stovepipe Wells Village, Hwy 190; mains breakfast & lunch $10-15, dinner $12-25; ☯ breakfast, lunch & dinner; 👤) Above-par cowboy cooking happens inside this ranch house with fireplace. Native American blankets and rickety wooden chairs and tables make it feel like the Old West. At dinner, expect beef brisket, an unlimited salad bar and key lime pie for dessert. Next door, the divey Bad Water Saloon (open 4:30pm to

Telescope Peak from across a salt pan at Death Valley National Park

WITOLD SKRYPCZAK

11pm) has Skynyrd on the jukebox and a pool table.

Panamint Springs Resort (☎ 775-482-7680; www.deathvalley.com; Hwy 190, Panamint Springs; mains $10-32; ⏲ breakfast, lunch & dinner; 🛜) Barely inside the park's western boundary, a winding 30-mile drive southwest of Stovepipe Wells Village, this friendly outback cafe cooks up three square meals a day, with outdoor barbecues in summer. Crack open a microbrew and toast the panoramic views from the front porch.

Furnace Creek Inn (☎ 760-786-3385; Hwy 190, Furnace Creek; mains lunch $14-18, dinner $25-38; ⏲ breakfast, lunch & dinner mid-Oct–mid-May) At the elegant inn atop the oasis, reserve a table in the formal dining room (strict dress code applies), or keep things casual at the sociable bar, where you can order from the same menu of so-so Southwestern fare like fried cactus and pork tamales. Sunset cocktails and decent wines are served on the outdoor patio.

GETTING THERE & AROUND

Gas is expensive in the park, so fill up your tank beforehand.

CENTRAL & SOUTHERN CALIFORNIA COAST

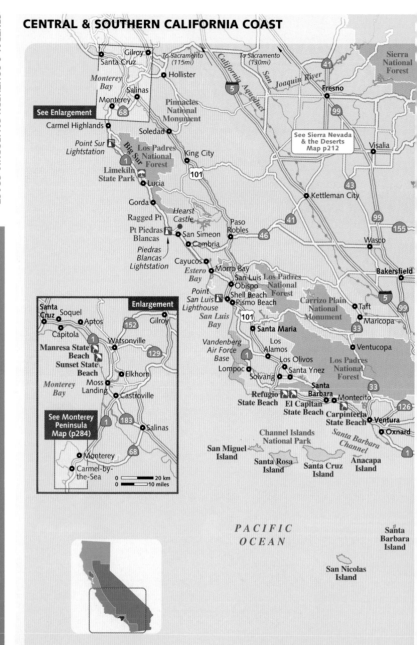

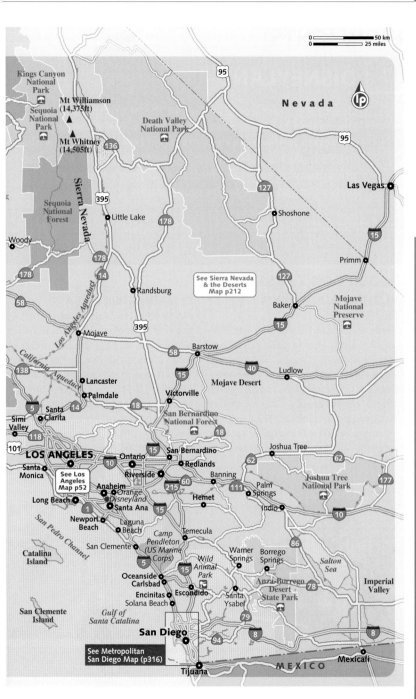

CENTRAL & SOUTHERN CALIFORNIA COAST

HIGHLIGHTS

HIGHLIGHTS

1 | DISNEYLAND

One of the most iconic images of the entire United States, Disneyland has seen more visitors than just about any attraction in the world (over 600,000,000 since its inception in 1955). Perhaps the largest existential experiment on the philosophy of entertainment, Walt Disney's theme park has truly changed the way the globe thinks about fun.

⬊ OUR DON'T MISS LIST

❶ DISNEY CALIFORNIA ADVENTURE

While Disneyland itself gets top billing, its sister theme park next door can be an even bigger crowd-pleaser, especially for older kids and teens who prefer a bit more roller coaster rather than Sleeping Beauty. Over $1 billion has been poured into a 2012 grand re-opening, which will include a racecar ride (the most expensive theme-park ride ever built).

❷ MAIN STREET, USA

Modeled after Walt Disney's home-town of Marceline, Missouri (look for a Marceline Hotel), and in ¾ scale to make it more kid-friendly, Main Street, USA is the gateway to the magic kingdom. If you need to rest tired little feet or want a quick break in the shade, pop into Main Street Cinema for early Mickey films (including his debut, *Steamboat Willie*).

Clockwise from top: Treasure Room, Pirates of the Caribbean ride; Downtown Disney; California Screamin' roller coaster

CENTRAL & SOUTHERN CALIFORNIA COAST

HIGHLIGHTS

❸ DISNEY CHARACTER MEALS

Have you ever wanted to meet Ariel the Little Mermaid, Winnie the Pooh, Captain Hook or even Mickey himself? How about dining with them? Five restaurants across the Disney parks and resorts serve up costumed characters along with their buffet meals throughout the day. Hint: have your child bring a toy or game and his or her favorite character is likely to stick around a bit longer.

❹ DISNEY'S GRAND CALIFORNIAN HOTEL

If you've saved this long for a once-in-a-lifetime family trip to Disneyland, you might as well do it in style. A direct entrance straight into California Adventure and a quick stroll to Disneyland mean you can catnap in your own hotel room during the day.

❺ BLUE BAYOU

In the middle of New Orleans Square lies this nondescript restaurant specializing in Cajun and Creole cuisine. Yeah, yeah, yeah...but it's *inside* the Pirates of the Caribbean ride! Perpetually bathed in a Louisiana twilight, fireflies sparkle and frogs creak while ride-goers float past below.

↘ THINGS YOU NEED TO KNOW

Technology meets Mickey Before arriving, download a Disneyland smartphone app to gauge wait times and locate your favorite characters in real time **Best time to go** May and September are the prime visiting months, for crowd and weather control **For full details on Disneyland, see p306**

HIGHLIGHTS

2

⬎ FIND PEACE IN BIG SUR

Even city slickers will feel a moment of Zen calm here. While there is no town
called Big Sur, the stretch of central California coastline (p292) is worthy of an
ode (just ask all the poets and artists who have called the area home for generations). California condors fly above fields of wildflowers while otters and tourists
co-exist along an impossibly beautiful rocky shoreline.

3

⬎ HISTORIC MONTEREY

Two hundred years ago, Ah-nold would have governated from Monterey
(p282), not Sacramento. The first capital of Spanish and then Mexican California,
Monterey is the West Coast's most historic city. With adobe buildings from the
1770s and a fishing history worthy of a John Steinbeck novel, you'd want to visit
Monterey even if wasn't home to one of the world's top aquariums.

↘ 17-MILE DRIVE

The ultimate pay-per-view drive. Wind your way past upscale golf courses, 30-million-dollar houses and hotels and spas worthy of kings and queens to get to the real attraction of the 17-Mile Drive (p289): the stunning Monterey pines and feral coastline that make the entrance fees worth it. Stop by the golf compound for sandwiches or ice cream.

↘ LAGUNA BEACH

Orange County's most relaxed beach town (p312) has just about everything you'd want in a casual seaside vacation – great shopping, cliff-top restaurants, myriad art galleries, romantic inns and the world-renowned summer arts performance Pageant of the Masters and its accompanying Festival of Arts (see p47).

↘ SAN DIEGO ZOO

Part teaching center, part botanical garden and part conservation organization, this zoo (p317) is a hit with all age groups. Hint: arrive before 11am when the animals are feeding and usually at their most active.

CENTRAL & SOUTHERN CALIFORNIA COAST

HIGHLIGHTS

2 DOUGLAS STEAKLEY; 3 RICHARD CUMMINS; 4 ROBERTO GEROMETTA; 5 PAUL KENNEDY; 6 RICHARD CUMMINS

2 Big Sur (p292); 3 Fisherman's Wharf (p285), Monterey; 4 Lone Cypress Tree, 17-Mile-Drive (p289); 5 Laguna Beach (p312); 6 Peacock, San Diego Zoo (p318)

BEST...

⬊ LIGHTHOUSES

- **Surfing Museum** (p280) When Santa Cruz loses a lighthouse, it gains a surf museum.
- **Monterey Maritime Museum** (p285) Get up close to an 1887 Fresnel lighthouse lens.
- **Point Pinos Lighthouse** (p288) Guiding sailors off the coast of Pacific Grove since 1855.
- **Piedras Blancas Lightstation** (p295) Come for the historic lighthouse, stay for the elephant seals, peregrine falcons and otters.
- **Point San Luis Lighthouse** (p295) The extra effort getting here is worth it for the sweeping views.

⬊ BEACHES

- **Santa Cruz Beach Boardwalk** (p280) The oldest wooden roller coaster on the West Coast.
- **Pfeiffer Beach** (p293) Big Sur's most dramatic beach.
- **East Beach** (p303) Santa Barbara's downtown, kid-friendly beach.

- **Laguna Beach** (p312) Just steps away from Laguna's art galleries, restaurants and dramatic cliffs.
- **La Jolla Cove** (p324) Charming sliver of beach with great tide pools.

⬊ CHARMING DOWNTOWNS

- **Pacific Grove** (p288) Historic downtown.
- **Carmel** (p291) Galleries, upscale boutiques and fairy-tale cottages attract shoppers, art collectors and dogs.
- **San Luis Obispo** (p296) Hip college town with a revitalized city center pedestrianized area.

⬊ FARMERS MARKETS

- **Old Monterey Marketplace** (p288) California produce, international street food and fun performers.
- **San Luis Obispo** (p296) Huge agricultural street party every Thursday.
- **Santa Barbara** (p305) Taste the sunshine in local grapes and olives.

LEFT: HANAN ISACHAR; RIGHT: RICK GERHARTER

Left: Plenty of berries to buy, Santa Barbara Farmers Market (p305); Right: Santa Cruz Beach Boardwalk (p280)

THINGS YOU NEED TO KNOW

⬇ VITAL STATISTICS

- **Area codes** ☎ Monterey and Northern Central Coast 831; ☎ Santa Barbara and Southern Central Coast 805; ☎ Orange County 657, 714 and 949; ☎ San Diego 619
- **Best time to visit** April through May, and September through October (summer months can be overcast, especially in northern Central California)

⬇ CITIES IN A NUTSHELL

- **Anaheim** (p306) Home to Mickey Mouse.
- **Santa Cruz** (p278) Hippies, surfers, artists and college students chill in this seaside university town.
- **Monterey** (p282) More history than any other California town; Monterey's downtown and Bay Aquarium are top in their class.
- **Santa Barbara** (p300) The most pleasant climate in the US where red-tiled roofs add an air of romance.
- **San Diego** (p314) SeaWorld and the zoo will delight youngsters, while beaches and historic districts will delight parents.

⬇ ADVANCE PLANNING

- **Two months before** Look up festivals and events around the state.
- **One month before** Book your Disneyland package and hotel rooms.
- **Two weeks before** Break in your boots for all of the hiking you'll do around Big Sur.

⬇ RESOURCES

- **Monterey Bay Aquarium** (www.montereybayaquarium.org) Tickets, info on exhibits and detailed sustainable seafood listings.
- **Big Sur California** (www.bigsurcalifornia.org) Information on lodging, restaurants and parklands.
- **Disneyland** (disneyland.disney.go.com) *Everything* you'd ever want to know about the Magic Kingdom.
- **San Diego Info** (www.sandiego.org) Official information.

⬇ GETTING AROUND

- **Walking** Several downtowns are quite walkable, including San Luis Obispo, Monterey, Santa Barbara and Old Town San Diego.
- **Bus** Public transportation can be iffy, but Amtrak runs extremely comfortable buses to most destinations in Central California.
- **Amtrak** Its *Coast Starlight* route runs between Los Angeles, Santa Barbara, San Luis Obispo and Salinas (near Monterey).
- **Car** Your best bet for Big Sur, Pacific Grove and Orange County.

⬇ BE FOREWARNED

- **Costs** The Central and Southern California Coast can be quite an expensive destination for accommodations.

CENTRAL & SOUTHERN CALIFORNIA COAST ITINERARIES

GREAT OUTDOORS Three Days

Start in **(1) Monterey** (p282), where whale-watching or kayaking is a must in the world-famous Monterey Bay. Then pay your way into **(2) 17-Mile Drive** (p289) to see ridiculously beautiful beaches backed with Monterey pines. Head toward **(3) Point Lobos State Reserve** (p291), especially in June or July when the wildflowers bloom. Spend the rest of your two days in **(4) Big Sur** (p292), hopping between beach waterfalls, redwood groves and hiking trails.

SAN DIEGO FOR KIDS Five Days

The southern quarter of California is a dream for youngsters. A must-see for kids (and adults) is the **(1) San Diego Wild Animal Park** (p325), a game-changer on the zoo market where the animals roam free and the people are fenced off. Alternate with a quiet day by stopping by the **(2) New Children's Museum** (p317), where parents will dig the modern-art vibe and the naptime-and-apple-juice-set will love the hands-on exhibits. Get a very good night's sleep then make the trek up to **(3) Legoland** (p326), 30 minutes north of San Diego, where all ages will love building with Lego and watching what the world's Lego-masters can do with plastic bricks. Also check out **(4) Mission Beach** (p323), where older kids will enjoy stretching their legs cycling or in-line skating. The pièce de résistance is **(5) SeaWorld** (p322), where trained orcas, splashy water rides and cotton candy make for a child's dream day.

COASTAL ROMANCE One Week

Start your romantic journey in charming (1) Monterey (p282) on a double-kayak tour of the Monterey Bay. Stay a few nights at a waterfront B&B in (2) Pacific Grove (p288), once called the most romantic city in the country by *Life* magazine. Make sure you enjoy a meal at Passionfish (p290). Walk hand-in-hand down the streets of (3) Carmel-by-the-Sea (p291), where cozy restaurants and romantic hotels make this a popular destination for lovebirds. For prime picnicking spots, continue down the wild coast along (4) Big Sur (p292). For a splurge, stay at Post Ranch Inn (p296), where you have your pick between an ocean-front suite or the world's most upscale tree house. If you'd like a bit more hot pink and campiness with your romance, head to (5) San Luis Obispo (p296) and the Madonna Inn (p300), where you can stay in themed rooms like 'Merry' (lest your love life has been woefully short of pink glitter wallpaper) or 'Caveman' (yeah, we don't want to know).

The nearby seaside towns are a bit further off the beaten track, but Cambria (p299) and Morro Bay (p299) are both fabulous quiet spots to watch the sunset together. Most folks think of (6) Disneyland (p306) as a kids' paradise, but thousands of couples get married or spend a honeymoon here every year. Check into the Disney Grand Californian Hotel (p311), the most lavishly romantic of the Disney properties.

DISCOVER CENTRAL & SOUTHERN CALIFORNIA COAST

Beautiful white sandy beaches hosting surfer dudes and chicks? Check. Historic downtowns lined with art galleries and one-of-a-kind shops? Double check. Disneyland, SeaWorld and the San Diego Zoo? Yep. It's officially a California vacation.

Central California starts in flower-power Santa Cruz, meandering past the incomparable Monterey Bay Aquarium and through collegiate San Luis Obispo and swanky Santa Barbara, while Southern California stretches from swish Orange County to climate-controlled San Diego. And then there's the natural beauty: towering sand dunes, mossy redwood forests where hot springs beckon, and rolling golden hills with ripening vineyards. Big Sur's rugged wilderness is home to poets, artists, California condors and migrating humpback whales, while the small towns each have their own flavor: romantic Pacific Grove, 'Surf City, USA' Huntington Beach, San Diego's historic and charming neighborhoods. Gas up the convertible, slip your feet into a pair of flip flops and stay a few weeks.

MONTEREY BAY

Monterey Bay is the constant backdrop to life around the peninsula. Along its half-moon coastline, you'll find miles of often-deserted beaches and small towns bubbling over with idiosyncratic character. Even more diverse is the bay itself, protected as the Monterey Bay National Marine Sanctuary, one of the richest and most varied marine environments anywhere on the planet.

SANTA CRUZ

pop 56,925

Anchoring the north end of Monterey Bay, Santa Cruz is counterculture central, a touchy-feely place famous for its leftie-liberal-socialist politics and live-and-let-live ideology – except when it comes to dogs (not allowed off-leash or downtown), parking (meters run seven days a week) and Republicans (allegedly shot on sight). The City Council spends more of its time debating whether medical marijuana dispensaries should be allowed than figuring out ways to help downtown's homeless population.

Local politics aside, Santa Cruz is a crazy-fun city with a carnival-esque downtown. On the waterfront is the famous beach boardwalk and, in the hills, the University of California, Santa Cruz (UCSC). Plan to hang out for a half day, but to truly appreciate the aesthetic of jangly skirts, crystal pendants and waist-length Rastafarian dreadlocks, you'll need to stay longer.

ORIENTATION

Santa Cruz stretches along the coast, blending into Capitola, a low-key beach town, and Aptos beyond. The meandering San Lorenzo River divides the town into a sort of yin and yang. Pacific Ave is downtown's main street. Hwy 1 from the north leads onto Mission St; Hwy 17, the main route from the San Francisco Bay

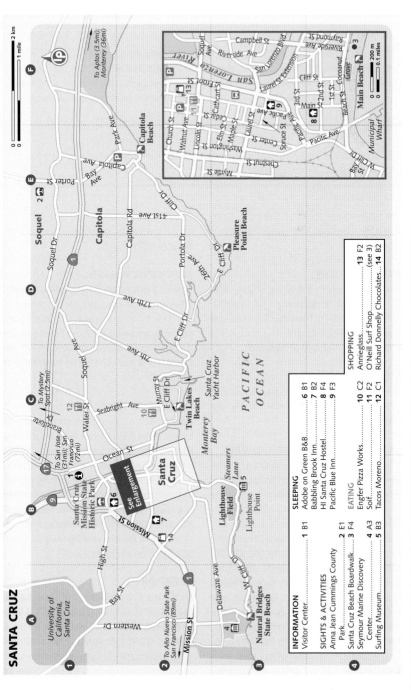

SANTA CRUZ

INFORMATION
Visitor Center.............................. **1** B1

SIGHTS & ACTIVITIES
Anna Jean Cummings County
Park.................................... **2** E1
Santa Cruz Beach Boardwalk..... **3** F4
Seymour Marine Discovery
Center................................. **4** A3
Surfing Museum......................... **5** B3

SLEEPING
Adobe on Green B&B................. **6** B1
Babbling Brook Inn..................... **7** B2
HI Santa Cruz Hostel.................. **8** F4
Pacific Blue Inn.......................... **9** F3

EATING
Engfer Pizza Works...................... **10** C2
Soif.. **11** F2
Tacos Moreno............................ **12** C1

SHOPPING
Annieglass.................................. **13** F2
O'Neill Surf Shop..................... (see 3)
Richard Donnelly Chocolates... **14** B2

WHAT THE...?

A kitschy old-fashioned tourist trap, the Mystery Spot (☎ 831-423-8897; www.mysteryspot.com; 465 Mystery Spot Rd; admission $5; ⊙ 10am-6pm Mon-Fri, 9am-7pm Sat & Sun Jun-Aug, 10am-5pm daily Sep-May; 🕭) has scarcely changed since the day it opened in 1940. On this steeply sloping hillside, compasses point crazily, mysterious forces push you around, and buildings lean at weird angles. Yes, it's silly, but it's also classic Santa Cruz. Make reservations or risk being stuck waiting for a tour. It's 3 miles north of downtown: take Water St east to Market St, turn left and continue on Branciforte Dr into the hills. Parking costs $5. Don't forget your souvenir bumper sticker!

Area, turns into Ocean St. The UCSC campus is uphill, about 2.5 miles northwest of downtown.

INFORMATION

Visitor Center (☎ 831-425-1234, 800-833-3494; www.santacruz.org; 1211 Ocean St; ⊙ 9am-5pm Mon-Fri, 10am-4pm Sat, 11am-3pm Sun; 🖳 🛜) Free courtesy phones for checking availability of lodgings.

SIGHTS

Go strolling, shopping and freak-watching along downtown's Pacific Ave, a 10-minute walk from the beach.

SANTA CRUZ BEACH BOARDWALK

The 1907 boardwalk (☎ 831-423-5590; www.beachboardwalk.com; admission free, per ride $2.25-4.50, all-day pass $30; ⊙ seasonal hr vary; 🕭) is the West Coast's oldest beachfront amusement park. It has a glorious old-school Americana vibe, the smell of cotton candy mixes with the salt air, punctuated by the squeals of kiddos hanging upside down on carnival rides. The half-mile-long Giant Dipper, a vintage 1924 wooden roller coaster, and the 1911 Looff carousel are National Historic Landmarks. When you're feeling dizzy, don your flip-flops and plop down your towel on the beach outside. On summer

Friday nights, tune in to free concerts by rock veterans you may have thought were already dead.

MUNICIPAL WHARF

You can drive the length of the wharf, where restaurants, gift shops and barking sea lions compete for attention. Some shops rent poles and fishing tackle if you're keen to join those waiting patiently for a bite. The views here are first rate.

WEST CLIFF DRIVE

Bordered by a paved recreation path, this scenic road follows the cliffs southwest of the wharf. Lighthouse Point overlooks Steamers Lane, one of the top – and most accessible – surfing spots in California. The lighthouse is home to a tiny surfing museum (☎ 831-420-6289; www.santacruzsurfingmuseum.org; 701 W Cliff Dr; donation requested; ⊙ noon-4pm Thu-Mon early Sep-early Jul, 10am-5pm Wed-Mon early Jul-early Sep).

SLEEPING

HI Santa Cruz Hostel (☎ 831-423-8304, 888-464-4872; www.hi-santacruz.org; 321 Main St; dm $25-28, r $60-100; ⊙ reception 8-11am & 5-10pm; 🖳) This lovely hostel occupies several century-old cottages surrounded by flowering gardens. It's just two blocks from the beach, a 10-minute walk from downtown. Most rooms have shared bath. One bummer: the 11pm curfew. Limited parking costs $1.

ourpick **Adobe on Green B&B** (☎ 831-469-9866; www.adobeongreen.com; 103 Green St; r incl breakfast $149-199; ☎) Peace and quiet are the mantras here, just a three-block walk from Pacific Ave. Your hosts are practically invisible but their thoughtful touches are everywhere: stylish amenities inside spacious, solar-powered rooms, and breakfast spreads featuring fresh, organic fare.

Pacific Blue Inn (☎ 831-600-8880; http://pacificblueinn.com; 636 Pacific Ave; r incl breakfast $175-225; ☎) This laidback courtyard B&B near downtown keeps an ecoconscious focus, from energy-efficient lighting and water-saving fixtures to renewable and recycled building materials. Clean-lined rooms have pillow-top beds, fireplaces and flat-screen TVs with DVD players. Free loaner bikes.

Babbling Brook Inn (☎ 831-427-2437, 800-866-1131; www.innbythesea.com; 1025 Laurel St; r incl breakfast $209-289; ☐ ☎) With meandering gardens and towering trees, this streamside inn gathers together private rooms in small satellite buildings, decorated with a nod to French-provincial style. Most have gas fireplaces, some have Jacuzzis, and all have feather beds.

EATING

ourpick **Tacos Moreno** (☎ 831-429-6095; 1053 Water St; dishes $2-6; ☼ 11am-8pm) Who cares how long the line is, even at lunchtime when you and every other surfer is starving? You're guaranteed to find *taquería* heaven here, from marinated pork, chicken and carne asada soft tacos to supremely stuffed burritos.

Soif (☎ 831-423-2020; 105 Walnut Ave; small plates $4-15, mains $20-23; ☼ 5-10pm Mon-Thu, 5-11pm Fri & Sat, 4-10pm Sun) Part wine shop, part wine bar and restaurant, Soif is where *bon vivants* flock for a heady selection of 50 international wines by the glass paired with a sophisticated, seasonally driven, often organic Euro-Cal menu. Expect gastronomic creativity like squid salad with

---

SANTA CRUZ FOR KIDS

Near Natural Bridges State Beach, the **Seymour Marine Discovery Center** (☎ 831-459-3800; www2.ucsc.edu/seymourcenter; off Delaware Ave; adult/child 4-16yr $6/4; ☼ 10am-5pm Jun-Aug, 10am-5pm Tue-Sat & noon-5pm Sun Sep-May, tours 1pm, 2pm & 3pm daily; ⛹) is part of UCSC's Long Marine Laboratory. Kid-friendly interactive exhibits include touchable tidepools, aquarium tanks and a ginormous blue-whale skeleton outside.

If it's too cold for the beach or your kids aren't up for a roller coaster, ride the **Roaring Camp Railroad** (☎ 831-335-4484; www.roaringcamp.com; round-trip fares adult/child 3-12yr from $20/14; ☼ seasonal hr vary; ⛹), which operates standard-gauge trains from the beach boardwalk up to Felton, 6 miles north of Santa Cruz, where narrow-gauge trains continue up into the redwood forests.

Local moms and dads call the area's best playground, **Anna Jean Cummings County Park** (☎ 831-454-7956; 461 Old San Jose Rd, north of Soquel Dr, Soquel; admission free; ☼ 8am-dusk; ⛹), 'Blue Balls Park' after several giant blue balls that appear to be rolling uphill. It's a 10-minute drive east of Santa Cruz, off the Bay/Porter exit from Hwy 1.

cucumber gazpacho or crispy duck breast with redcurrant gastrique.

Engfer Pizza Works (☎ 831-429-1856; 537 Seabright Ave; pizzas $8-23; ✹ 4-9:30pm Tue-Sun; ⓹) Inside an old factory, Engfer crafts addictive wood-fired pizzas using housemade dough and sauces. The specialty 'no-name' pizza is like a giant salad on roasted bread. There's even a vegan pie. Play ping-pong and sip draft microbrews while you wait.

SHOPPING

Downtown abounds with locally owned stores – never mind the Gap.

O'Neill Surf Shop (☎ 831-459-9230; 400 Beach St; ✹ 10am-5pm Mon-Fri, 10am-6pm Sat & Sun) If you can't make it to the Capitola mothership, check out the boardwalk branch of this homegrown, internationally renowned brand of surf wear and gear. Graffiti-art fleece hoodie, anyone?

Annieglass (☎ 831-427-4620; 110 Cooper St; ✹ 10am-6pm Mon-Sat, 11am-5pm Sun) Handcrafted sculptural dinnerware and home accents sold in ultrachic New York

department stores are made right here in wackadoodle Santa Cruz. Go figure.

Richard Donnelly Chocolates (☎ 831-458-4214; 1509 Mission St; ✹ 10:30am-6pm Tue-Fri, noon-6pm Sat & Sun) The Willy Wonka of Santa Cruz makes chocolates on a par with those in the big city. This guy is an alchemist! Try the cardamom truffles.

MONTEREY

pop 28,800

Working-class Monterey is all about the sea. What draws many tourists is the world-class aquarium that overlooks Monterey Bay National Marine Sanctuary, which extends from north of San Francisco's Golden Gate Bridge all the way south beyond Hearst Castle. Once the USA's largest marine sanctuary, it protects dense kelp forests and a stunning variety of marine life, including seals, sea lions, dolphins and whales. Meanwhile, the city itself possesses the best-preserved historical evidence of California's Spanish and Mexican periods, with many restored adobe buildings. An afternoon's wander

Cannery Row, Monterey

DOUGLAS STEAKLEY

ENORMOUS E-SEALS

Nearly extinct by the late 19th century, northern elephant seals have made a remarkable comeback along California's coast, most famously at Año Nuevo State Reserve north of Santa Cruz. These days a larger, more easily accessible colony of 'e-seals' hangs around Piedras Blancas, including at a well-signposted boardwalk viewpoint 4.8 miles northwest of Hearst Castle, where you'll find interpretive panels and blue-jacketed volunteers from the Friends of the Elephant Seal (☎ 805-924-1628; www.elephantseal.org).

During peak winter season, upward of 15,000 elephant seals seek shelter in the coves and beaches along this stretch of coast. On sunny days the seals pretty much 'lie around like banana slugs,' in the words of one volunteer. The behemoth bulls engage in mock – and sometimes real – combat, all the while making odd guttural grunts, as their harems of females and young pups look on. You wouldn't think it from just watching them snooze on the sand, but elephant seals can dive deeper (nearly a mile) and for longer (over an hour) than any other mammal.

Always observe elephant seals from a safe distance and do not approach or otherwise harass these unpredictable wild animals. Some of the mature bulls weigh over 2 tons – about the same as those SUVs whizzing by on Hwy 1 – and, despite their enormous size, they can move faster on the sand than any human can.

Here's a quick seasonal viewing guide:

- **November and December** Bull seals arrive at the beach, followed by juveniles and mature females already pregnant from last winter's breeding season.
- **January through March** Pregnant seals give birth, peaking in February; after delivering, females mate with the waiting and rather anxious males, who then depart for feeding migrations.
- **April and May** Females wean pups and leave to feed themselves; pups teach themselves how to swim and eventually leave as well.
- **June through October** Seals of all ages return to molt, with females arriving in early summer and males in late summer and early fall.

through the town's historic quarter promises to be more edifying than time spent in the tourist ghettos of Fisherman's Wharf and Cannery Row. A snorkeling excursion on the bay? Even better.

SIGHTS
CANNERY ROW

Back in John Steinbeck's day, Cannery Row was the epicenter of the sardine-canning industry that was Monterey's lifeblood in the first half of the 20th century. A stinky, hardscrabble melting pot, the area's grit and energy were immortalized in Steinbeck's novel *Cannery Row*. Sadly, there's precious little evidence of that time now, except for the Cannery Workers Shacks at the base of flowery Bruce Ariss Way. This small row of even-smaller houses depicts the

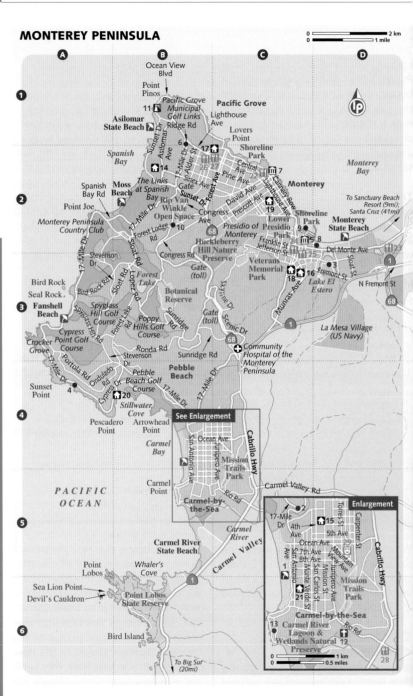

MONTEREY PENINSULA

stark and strenuous lives led by Filipino, Japanese and Spanish laborers during the cannery's heyday. A bronze **bust** of the Pulitzer prize–winning writer sits at the bottom of Prescott Ave, just steps from the unabashedly commercial experience that his row has devolved into. It's chockablock with touristy restaurants and souvenir shops hawking T-shirts and saltwater taffy.

THE WHARVES
Like its larger namesake in San Francisco, **Fisherman's Wharf** is a tacky tourist trap at heart. It's the jumping-off point for whale-watching expeditions (see right) and deep-sea fishing trips. The refreshingly authentic **Municipal Wharf II** is a short walk east. There, fishing boats bob

and sway, painters work on their watercolor canvases and seafood purveyors hawk fresh catches.

MARITIME MUSEUM
Dive right into Monterey's naval history, from the days of early European explorers through the 20th century, at this nifty **museum** (☎ 831-372-2608; www .montereyhistory.org; 5 Custom House Plaza; admission free; ☺ 10am-5pm Tue-Sun). Highlights of the seafaring collection include the Fresnel lens from Point Sur Lightstation, a ship-in-a-bottle collection, and displays on Monterey's salty past, particularly the rise and rapid fall of the sardine business.

ACTIVITIES
A must for fans of kick-ass playgrounds, **Dennis the Menace Park** (☎ 831-646-3860; 777 Pearl St; ☺ 10am-dusk, closed Tue Sep-May; ☉) was the brainchild of Hank Ketcham, the classic comic-strip creator. This ain't your standard dumbed-down playground, suffocated by Big Brother's safety regulations. With lightning-fast roller slides, towering climbing walls and hedge mazes, even adults can't resist playing.

WHALE-WATCHING
You can spot whales off the coast of Monterey year-round. Gray whales pass by from mid-December to April, while the season for blue and humpback whales runs from late April through November. Book ahead for basic, three-hour boat tours with **Monterey Bay Whale Watch** (☎ 831-375-4658; http://gowhales.com; 84 Fisherman's Wharf; adult/child 4-12yr from $36/25) and **Monterey Whale Watching** (☎ 831-372-2203, tickets 800-979-3370; www. montereywhalewatching.com; 96 Fisherman's Wharf; adult/child 3-12yr $40/30).

SIGHTS & ACTIVITIES		
Carmel Beach	1	C5
Carmel Gate (toll)	2	C5
Dennis the Menace Park	3	D3
Lone Cypress	4	A4
Maritime Museum	5	C2
Monarch Grove Sanctuary	6	B1
Monterey Bay Aquarium	7	C2
Monterey Bay Kayaks	8	D2
Monterey Bay Whale Watch	9	C2
Monterey Whale Watching	(see 9)	
Pacific Grove Gate (toll)	10	B2
Point Pinos Lighthouse	11	B1
San Carlos de Borroméo de Carmelo Mission	12	D6
Tor House	13	C6

SLEEPING		
Asilomar Conference Grounds	14	B2
Carmel Wayfarer Inn	15	D5
Casa Munras	16	C3
Centrella Inn	17	C2
Colton Inn	18	C3
Jabberwock	19	C2
Lodge at Pebble Beach	20	B4
Sea View Inn	21	C6

EATING		
First Awakenings	22	C2
Monterey's Fish House	23	D2
Montrio Bistro	24	C2
Old Monterey Marketplace	25	C3
Passionfish	26	B2
Red House Cafe	27	C2
Rio Grill	28	D6

ENTERTAINMENT		
Forest Theater	29	D5

DOUGLAS STEAKLE

Visitors taking in the underwater displays, Monterey Bay Aquarium

MONTEREY BAY AQUARIUM

Monterey's most mesmerizing experience is a visit to the ginormous aquarium, built on the site of what was once the city's largest sardine cannery. All forms of aquatic creatures are on display, from kid-tolerant sea stars and slimy sea slugs to animated sea otters and surprisingly nimble 800lb tuna. But the aquarium is more than an impressive collection of glass tanks – thoughtful placards underscore the bay's ecological, cultural and historical contexts.

Every minute, upward of 2000 gallons of seawater is pumped into the three-story kelp forest, re-creating as closely as possible the natural conditions you see out the windows to the east. The large fish of prey are at their charismatic best during mealtimes; divers hand-feed at 11:30am and 4pm. More giggle-inducing are sea-otter feeding and training sessions at 10:30am, 1:30pm and 3:30pm. Otherwise, the otters can often be seen basking in the Great Tidepool outside the aquarium, where they are readied for reintroduction to the wild.

Even new-agey music and the occasional infinity-mirror illusion don't detract from the appeal of the Jellies Gallery, where jellyfish show off their mysterious, diaphanous beauty. To see hammerhead sharks, fish and other sea creatures that outweigh you many times over, ponder the awesome Outer Bay tank. Nearby you can explore the Secret Lives of Seahorses. Throughout the aquarium there are touch pools, where you can get close to sea cucumbers, bat rays and various tide-pool creatures. Tots will go nuts in the interactive, bilingual Splash Zone, where blackfooted penguin colony feedings happen at 10:30am and 3pm.

Things you need to know: ☎ 831-648-4888, tickets 866-963-9645; www.monterey bayaquarium.org; 886 Cannery Row; adult/child 3-12yr $30/18; ⏰ 9:30am-6pm Mon-Fri, 9:30am-8pm Sat & Sun May-Sep, 10am-6pm daily Oct-Apr; 🛜 ♿

KAYAKING

For kayak rentals and weekend instruction courses, head to **Monterey Bay Kayaks** (☎ 831-373-5357, 800-649-5357; www.monterey baykayaks.com; 693 Del Monte Ave; kayak rentals per day from $30, tours adult/child 3-12yr from $50/30; ✆ 9am-7pm). It also leads family-oriented and natural-history tours, including sunset paddles around the bay and full-moon trips to Elkhorn Slough.

SLEEPING

Book ahead for summer visits – the festivals and events listed above can sell out the town remarkably early. Inexpensive chain motels cluster along Munras Ave, just south of downtown, and on N Fremont St, a couple of miles east of downtown off Hwy 1. To avoid the tourist circus of Cannery Row, consider staying in Pacific Grove (p288).

Colton Inn (☎ 831-649-6500, 800-848-7007; www.coltoninn.com; 707 Pacific St; r incl breakfast $100-325; �=) Downtown, this champ of a motel prides itself on cleanliness and friendliness, and has earned a solid base of repeat guests. There's no pool and zero view, but staff loan out DVDs and there's even a sauna.

Jabberwock (☎ 831-372-4777, 888-428-7253; www.jabberwockinn.com; 598 Laine St; r incl breakfast $169-299; ☐ �=) High atop a hill and barely visible through a shroud of foliage, this 1911 Craftsman house hums a playful *Alice in Wonderland* tune through its seven immaculate rooms with names like the Brillig, which flaunts gorgeous hand-painted wallpaper and bay views. All in all, a sublime place to celebrate your un-birthday.

Casa Munras (☎ 831-375-2411, 800-222-2446; www.hotelcasamunras.com; 700 Munras Ave; d $169-319; ☐ �= ☒ ☀) Built around an adobe hacienda once owned by a 19th-century Spanish colonial don, this historic downtown boutique hotel has chic modern rooms with lofty beds and fireplaces. Splash in the heated outdoor pool then unwind with a sea-salt scrub in the spa.

OURPICK Sanctuary Beach Resort (off Map p284; ☎ 831-883-9478, 877-944-3863; www.

Sea lions, Monterey Bay

LAWRENCE WORCESTER

thesanctuarybeachresort.com; 3295 Dunes Dr, off Hwy 1 exit Reservation Rd, Marina; r $189-369; 🌐 ⛟ ♿ ⛲) Be lulled to sleep by the surf at this low-lying retreat hidden in the sand dunes north of Monterey. Timeshare townhouses hold petite rooms with gas fireplaces and kitchenettes, plus binoculars to borrow for whale-watching. The beach is an off-limits nature preserve, but there are other beaches and hiking trails nearby.

EATING

Escape Cannery Row for Lighthouse Ave, lined with budget-friendly ethnic eateries serving everything from Hawaiian barbecue to Middle Eastern kebabs, or head over to Pacific Grove. The weekly **Old Monterey Marketplace** (☎ 831-655-8070; www.oldmonterey.org; ⏱ 4-8pm Thu) farmers market takes over downtown's Alvarado St.

ourpick **First Awakenings** (☎ 831-372-1125; 1st fl, American Tin Cannery, 125 Ocean View Blvd; mains $5-11; ⏱ 7am-2pm Mon-Fri, 7am-2:30pm Sat & Sun; ♿) Sweet or savory, but always from scratch, breakfasts and lunches merrily weigh down sunny tables at this hideaway cafe inside an outlet mall near the aquarium. Try the gigantic blueberry wheat-germ pancake – you'll only need one!

Montrio Bistro (☎ 831-648-8880; 414 Calle Principal; mains $14-38; ⏱ 4:30-10pm Sun-Thu, to 11pm Fri & Sat; ♿) It's fitting that Montrio occupies the old firehouse, because this place is hot. Euro-Cal dishes are concocted from mostly organic, market-driven and sustainable local ingredients. Despite its hip interior – think leather walls and iron trellises – the tables still have butcher paper and fat crayons for kids.

Monterey's Fish House (☎ 831-373-4647; 2114 Del Monte Ave, mains $14-40; ⏱ lunch 11:30am-2pm, dinner 5-9pm) Ten bucks says

you're the only nonlocal in the joint. Dig into spanking-fresh seafood with the occasional Asian twist while being watched over by photos of Sicilian fishermen. Even though it's a casual joint – Hawaiian shirts seem to be *de rigueur* for gentlemen – reservations are essential.

GETTING THERE

Monterey is 120 miles south of San Francisco via inland Hwys 101 and 156. From Santa Cruz, it's less than an hour's drive south along coastal Hwy 1.

PACIFIC GROVE
pop 14,700

Founded as a Methodist summer retreat in 1875, Pacific Grove (aka PG) is a tranquil community that maintained a quaint, holier-than-thou attitude well into the 20th century – the selling of liquor was illegal up until 1969, making it California's last 'dry' town. Today, leafy streets are lined by stately Victorian homes, making PG a welcome respite from the touristy Monterey-Carmel hubbub. Its charmingly compact downtown lies along Lighthouse Ave.

SIGHTS & ACTIVITIES

Aptly named **Ocean View Boulevard** affords fine views from Lovers Point west to Point Pinos. There the road becomes the again appropriately monikered **Sunset Drive**, with numerous turn-outs where you can enjoy the pounding surf, rocky outcrops and teaming tidepools. The entire route is ideal for walking or cycling – we think it surpasses the 17-Mile Drive (see opposite) for beauty, and it's free.

At the northwestern end of Lighthouse Ave, on the tip of the peninsula, historic **Point Pinos Lighthouse** (☎ 831-648-5716; www.pgmuseum.org; donation requested; ⏱ 1-4pm Thu-Mon) is the oldest continuously operating lighthouse on the West Coast. It has been warning ships off this hazardous point since 1855. Inside are exhibits on its history and its failures: local shipwrecks. The lighthouse grounds provide excellent whale-watching between December and April.

If you're in town during monarch butterfly season (roughly October through February), the best place to see them

⬎ DRIVING TOUR: 17-MILE DRIVE
What to See

Pacific Grove and Carmel are linked by the spectacularly scenic 17-Mile Drive, which meanders through Pebble Beach, a private resort and residential area that epitomizes the peninsula's jaw-dropping wealth. It's no chore staying within the 25mph limit – every curve in the road reveals another postcard-worthy vista, especially when wildflowers bloom. If you're driving, expect to share the road with cyclists, some quite wobbly on their wheels.

Using the free map provided at toll booths, you can easily pick out landmarks such as **Spanish Bay**, where explorer Gaspar de Portolá dropped anchor in 1769; treacherously rocky **Point Joe**, which in the past was often mistaken for the entrance to Monterey Bay and thus became the site of several shipwrecks; and **Bird Rock**, a haven for seals, too. The ostensible pièce de résistance of the drive is the **Lone Cypress**, the trademarked symbol of the Pebble Beach Company that perches on a seaward rock. Over 250 years old, the tree is now reinforced with wire supports, which fortunately aren't that visible in photographs.

Besides the coast, the real attractions here are the world-famous **golf courses**, including at Pebble Beach, which hosts February's **AT&T Pebble Beach National Pro-Am** (www.attpbgolf.com), a famous golf tournament mixing pros and celebrities. It's easy to picture Don Cheadle driving down the spectacular 18th hole for a victory. The **Lodge at Pebble Beach** (☎ 831-647-7500, 800-654-9300; www.pebblebeach.com; r from $695; ✕ ▯ 🛜 ▥) brags about its world-class spa, restaurants and extravagant shops. Even if you're not a trust-fund baby, you can still soak up the rich atmosphere in the resort's art-filled public spaces.

The Route

Open sunrise to sunset, entry to the 17-Mile Drive is controlled by the **Pebble Beach Company** (☎ 831-647-7500; www.pebblebeach.com; per vehicle $9.25, bicycles free). There are five gates; for the most scenic stretch, enter the Pacific Grove Gate off Sunset Dr and exit at the Carmel Gate.

Cycling the drive is enormously popular, but try to do so during the week when traffic isn't as heavy. There's no shoulder on the road, so keep your wits about you. On weekends the flow of bikes goes primarily north to south.

Time & Mileage

This route, which actually measures slightly less than 17 miles these days, could take anywhere from an hour up to a half day, if you stop to mosey around.

cluster is at the **Monarch Grove Sanctuary** (☎ 831-648-5716; off Ridge Rd; admission free; dawn-dusk), a thicket of eucalyptus trees off Lighthouse Ave.

SLEEPING & EATING

PG has no shortage of froufrou B&Bs in gingerbread Victorian houses. Midrange motels shelter off Lighthouse and Asilomar Aves, near the peninsula's western edge.

Asilomar Conference Grounds (☎ 831-372-8016, 866-654-2878; www.visitasilomar.com; 800 Asilomar Ave; r incl breakfast $115-185;) This thickly forested state-park lodge boasts buildings designed by architect Julia Morgan, of Hearst Castle (see p297) fame. The historic rooms are tiny and thin-walled but charming nonetheless. The lodge's rec room offers free wi-fi, fireside reading nooks, ping-pong and pool tables, and bicycle rentals.

Centrella Inn (☎ 831-372-3372, 800-233-3372; www.centrellainn.com; 612 Central Ave; r incl breakfast $129-229;) For a romantic night inside a Victorian seaside mansion, this turreted National Historic Landmark is dreamy, with enchanting gardens and a player piano. Some of the stately rooms have fireplaces, clawfoot tubs and kitchenettes. Rates include afternoon refreshments and around-the-clock cookies.

Red House Cafe (☎ 831-643-1060; 662 Lighthouse Ave; breakfast & lunch $5-12, dinner $13-16; 8:30-11am Sat & Sun, 11am-2pm & dinner from 5pm Tue-Sun;) Always crowded with locals, this 1895 shingled house dishes up comfort food with delightful haute touches, from cinnamon-raisin brioche French toast for breakfast to blue cheese soufflés and grilled lamb at dinner. Exceptional French tea list.

our pick **Passionfish** (☎ 831-655-3311; www.passionfish.net; 701 Lighthouse Ave; mains $17-24; dinner) Fresh, sustainable seafood is artfully presented in any number of inventive ways, though the seasonally inspired menu also carries slow-cooked meats and vegetarian dishes. The earth-tone decor is sparse, with tables squeezed close together. A stellar wine list is temptingly priced at retail, and there are dozens of

DOUGLAS STEAKLEY

Springtime is picturesque in the valleys around Carmel-by-the-Sea

Chinese teas to pick from. Reservations recommended.

CARMEL-BY-THE-SEA

pop 3928

With impressive coastal frontage, upper-crust boutique shopping and borderline fanatical devotion to its canine residents, Carmel simply glows with smugness. Springing to life as a seaside resort in the 1880s – surprisingly, given that the beach is nearly always clouded over with fog – Carmel attracted famous artists and writers such as Sinclair Lewis and Jack London. Although artistic indulgence survives in the town's 100-plus galleries, sky-high property values have long since obliterated its salt-of-the-earth bohemia.

Today, fairy-tale Comstock cottages, with their characteristic stone chimneys and pitched gable roofs, dot the town. Local bylaws forbid neon signs and billboards; even payphones, garbage cans and newspaper vending boxes are picturesquely shingled. Buildings have no street numbers, so addresses always specify the block and the street, and/or the nearest intersection.

SIGHTS & ACTIVITIES

Escape the shopping blitzkrieg to amble through tree-lined streets on the lookout for domiciles charming and peculiar. The Hansel-and-Gretel houses at Torres St and Ocean Ave are just how you'd imagine them, while a home at 13th Ave and Monte Verde St is covered in bark. A wicked, cool house in the shape of a ship, made from stone and salvaged ship parts, is near 6th Ave and Guadalupe St. There's more – go find 'em.

Though not always sunny, **Carmel Beach** is still a gorgeous white-sand crescent, where pampered puppies excitedly run off-leash.

SAN CARLOS DE BORROMÉO DE CARMELO MISSION

About a mile south of downtown, this gorgeous Spanish colonial **mission** (☎ 831-624-1271; www.carmelmission.org; 3080 Rio Rd; adult/child 7-17yr $6.50/2; �

9:30am-5pm Mon-Sat, 10:30am-5pm Sun) is an oasis of calm and solemnity, ensconced by flowering gardens. Its stone basilica is filled with original art, while a separate chapel protects the tomb of California mission founder Junípero Serra. The original Monterey mission was established by Serra in 1769, but poor soil and the corrupting influence of military troops quickly motivated the move to Carmel.

TOR HOUSE

Even if you've never heard of the 20th-century poet Robinson Jeffers, a pilgrimage to the structures he built with his own hands – **Tor House** (☎ 831-624-1813; www.torhouse.org; 26304 Ocean View Ave; adult/child 12-17yr $7/2; �

tours 10am-3pm Fri & Sat) and the Celtic-inspired Hawk Tower – offers fascinating insight into both the man and the ethos of the Carmel he embodied, not to mention a host of intriguing architectural aspects. A porthole in Hawk Tower, which is visible from the street, came from the wrecked ship that carried Napoleon from Elba. The only way to see inside is on a tour (advance reservations required).

POINT LOBOS STATE RESERVE

About 4 miles south of town, **Point Lobos** (☎ 831-624-4909; http://pt-lobos.parks.state.ca.us; off Hwy 1; per car $10; �

8am-30min after sunset) has a dramatically rocky coastline. It takes its name from the Punta de los Lobos Marinos, or the 'Point of the Sea Wolves,' named by the Spanish for the howls of the resident sea lions. The full perimeter hike is 6 miles, but several short walks take in the wild scenery. Favorite destinations include **Bird Island**, **Sea Lion Point** and **Devil's Cauldron**, a whirlpool that gets splashy at high tide.

SLEEPING

Carmel Wayfarer Inn (☎ 831-624-2711, 800-533-2711; www.carmelwayfarerinn.com; cnr 4th Ave & Mission St; r incl breakfast $110-210; 🛜 🐾) None of the charming courtyard rooms or suites in this 1920s apartment complex are quite the same. Some have delightfully retro kitchens and sunset views. Rates include afternoon wine-and-cheese tastings.

Sea View Inn (☎ 831-624-8778; www.seaviewinncarmel.com; Camino Real btwn 11th & 12th Aves; r incl breakfast $120-195; 🛜) An intimate retreat away from downtown; here cozy fireside nooks are tailor-made for reading or taking afternoon tea. The cheapest country-style rooms are short on cat-swinging space, but it's a short walk over to the beach.

EATING

Rio Grill (☎ 831-625-5436; 101 Crossroads Blvd, off Hwy 1 exit Rio Rd; dinner mains $10-37; 🕑 11:30am-9pm Mon-Thu, 11:30am-10pm Fri & Sat, 10:30am-9pm Sun; 🔥) At this jazzy bistro, local ingredients find their destiny in flavorful Southwestern, Southern and Cal-Italian dishes. The fire-roasted artichoke and oakwood-smoked baby back ribs will have you licking your fingers.

ENTERTAINMENT

Forest Theater (☎ 831-626-1681; www.foresttheaterguild.org; cnr Mountain View Ave & Santa Rita St; tickets $7-25; 🕑 Apr-Jul) Musicals, drama, comedies and film screenings take place at this enchanting outdoor performance venue, dating from 1910 and anchored by enormous fire pits.

BIG SUR

Much ink has been spilled extolling the raw beauty and energy of this stretch of land shoehorned between the Santa Lucia Range and the Pacific Ocean, but nothing quite prepares you for your first glimpse of the craggy, unspoiled coastline. Big Sur is more a state of mind than a place you can pinpoint on a map. It has no traffic lights, banks or strip malls, and when the sun goes down, the moon and stars are the only streetlights – that is, if summer's dense fog hasn't extinguished them already.

ORIENTATION & INFORMATION

Visitors often wander into businesses along Hwy 1 and ask, 'How much further to Big Sur?' In fact, there is no town of Big Sur as such, though you may see the name on maps. The little commercial activity is concentrated between Andrew Molera State Park to the north and Pfeiffer Big Sur State Park to the south. Sometimes called 'The Village,' this stretch has the post office and the most shops, restaurants and lodgings.

Pick up the comprehensive free *Big Sur Guide*, published by the **Big Sur Chamber of Commerce** (☎ 831-667-2100; www.bigsurcalifornia.org; 🕑 9am-1pm), at local businesses and tourist spots. Just south of Pfeiffer Big Sur State Park, the **Big Sur Ranger Station** (☎ 831-667-2315; Hwy 1; 🕑 8am-4:30pm) has information and maps for all state parks, the Los Padres National Forest and Ventana Wilderness. South of the Nacimiento-Fergusson Rd turn-off, the US Forest Service (USFS) **Pacific Valley Ranger Station** (☎ 805-927-4211; Hwy 1; 🕑 8:30am-4:30pm) has limited recreational information.

Road and emergency services here are distant – in Monterey to the north or

Cambria to the south. Fill up the tank beforehand, and be careful.

SIGHTS & ACTIVITIES

All of the following are along Hwy 1, listed north to south. Unless otherwise noted, all of Big Sur's state parks are open from 30 minutes before sunrise until 30 minutes after sunset, with 24-hour access for campers. If you pay the entrance fee for one park, you get in free to any others that day – just hang on to your receipt or self-registration payment stub.

ANDREW MOLERA STATE PARK

Named for the farmer who first planted artichokes in California, this oft-overlooked **park** (☎ 831-667-2315; per car $10), 3 miles further south, enjoys a remote and wild setting, with lots of wildlife and great beachcombing. A quarter-mile trail leads from the campground to a beautiful beach where the Big Sur River meets the ocean. **Molera Horseback Tours** (☎ 831-625-5486, 800-942-5486; http://molerahorseback tours.com; Mar-Nov) offers guided trail rides to the beach (from $40). Learn more about endangered California condors at the park's barn-sized **Big Sur Discovery Center** (☎ 831-620-0702; www.ventanaws.org; admission free; 9am-4pm Fri-Sun;), which leads guided condor-watching tours (per person from $50). You can watch wildlife techs at work in the **bird-banding lab** (sunrise-noon Fri-Sun Apr-May & Sep-Oct, sunrise-noon Thu & Sat Jun-Aug) next door.

PFEIFFER BIG SUR STATE PARK

Four miles further south past the village, **Pfeiffer Big Sur State Park** (☎ 831-667-2315; per car $10;) is Big Sur's largest state park, named after the first European settlers who arrived in 1869. There are miles of pristine hiking trails winding through the redwood groves. The most popular walk – to 60ft-high **Pfeiffer Falls**, a delicate cascade that usually runs from December to May – is an easy, kid-friendly 1.4-mile round-trip.

PFEIFFER BEACH

Just west of Pfeiffer Big Sur State Park, this phenomenal, crescent-shaped **beach**

DOUGLAS STEAKLEY

Little Sur River, Big Sur

HOLGER LEUE

Life is bliss at the Post Ranch Inn (p296), Big Sur

(☎ 831-667-2315; per car $5; ☽ 6am-sunset; 🐾) is notable for its huge double rock formation through which waves crash with life-affirming power. It's often windy, and the surf is too dangerous for swimming. Dig down into the wet sand – it's purple! To get there from Hwy 1 south, drive 0.5 miles past Big Sur Ranger Station, then make a sharp right onto Sycamore Canyon Rd, marked by a yellow sign that says 'narrow road.' Follow it for over 2 miles down to the parking lot.

HENRY MILLER LIBRARY
A denizen for 17 years, Henry Miller wrote, 'It was here in Big Sur I first learned to say Amen!' A living memorial, alt-cultural center and bookshop, the nonprofit Henry Miller Library (☎ 831-667-2574; www.henrymiller.org; Hwy 1; donation requested; ☽ 11am-6pm Wed-Mon; 🖳 📶) is the art and soul of Big Sur bohemia, but was never Miller's home. Inside you'll find all of Miller's written works, many of his paintings and an eye-popping collection of Big Sur and Beat generation

material, including copies of the top 100 books Miller claimed most influenced him. Stop by for a browse, some coffee and good conversation. Check the website for upcoming community events including live-music concerts, open-mic nights and outdoor film series. The library is just south of Nepenthe restaurant (p296), over 3 miles south of Pfeiffer Big Sur State Park.

JULIA PFEIFFER BURNS STATE PARK
Named for another Big Sur pioneer, this park (☎ 831-667-2315; per car $10; ☽ 8am-7pm) hugs both sides of Hwy 1. At the entrance, you'll find picnic grounds along McWay Creek. The highlight is California's only coastal waterfall, McWay Falls, which drops 80ft straight into the sea – or onto the beach, depending on the tide. We dare you to take fewer than a dozen photos. To reach the waterfall viewpoint, take the short Overlook Trail west of the parking lot and cross beneath Hwy 1.

SLEEPING

Big Sur Campground & Cabins (☎ 831-667-2322; www.bigsurcamp.com; 47000 Hwy 1; campsites $35-60, cabins $88-360; 🐾) Popular with RVers, this well-run private campground has dozens of tent and RV sites with hookups, and also some small tent and A-frame cabins shaded by redwoods, right on the river. It's also got coin-op laundry and hot-shower facilities, a playground and general store.

Deetjen's Big Sur Inn (☎ 831-667-2377; www.deetjens.com; 48865 Hwy 1; r $80-200) Nestled among redwoods and wisteria along Castro Creek, this enchanting conglomeration of rustic, thin-walled rooms and cottages was constructed by Norwegian immigrant Helmuth Deetjen in the 1930s. Some rooms are warmed by wood-burning fireplaces. Cheaper ones share bathrooms, but all book up far in advance.

Treebones Resort (☎ 877-424-4787; www.treebonesresort.com; 71895 Hwy 1, off Willow Creek Rd; d incl breakfast $155-245; 🐾 👶) Don't let the word 'resort' throw you. Yes, it's got an ocean-view hot tub and heated pool, but when was the last time you slept in a yurt? Expect sumptuous quilt-covered beds, sink vanities and redwood decks, but little privacy. Common bathrooms with showers are a quick stroll away near the main lodge. It's just north of Gorda, in southern Big Sur.

Big Sur Lodge (☎ 831-667-3100, 800-424-4787; www.bigsurlodge.com; 47225 Hwy 1; d $209-369; 🐾) What you're paying for here is the supremely peaceful location, tucked away inside the redwood forest of Pfeiffer Big Sur State Park. Throwback duplex

---

DETOUR: PIEDRAS BLANCAS & POINT SAN LUIS LIGHTHOUSES

Although many lighthouses still freckle the California coast, few offer such a historically evocative seascape as **Piedras Blancas Lightstation** (☎ 805-927-7361; www.piedrasblancas.org; adult/child 6-17yr $10/5; ⏰ tours 10am Tue, Thu & Sat). Picturesquely, everything looks much the way it did when the first lighthouse keepers helped ships find safe harbor around the whaling station at San Simeon Bay. Federally designated an outstanding natural area, the grounds of this 1875 lighthouse – incidentally, one of the tallest on the West Coast – have been painstakingly replanted with native vegetation. Knowledgeable volunteers lead walking tours of the property as they chat about marine wildlife, Native American culture and the maritime history of this lonely, windswept coastal spot. Tours currently meet at 9:45am at the old Piedras Blancas Motel, 1.5 miles north of the lightstation. Call ahead to confirm current schedules.

Ready for an adventure? Visiting the Victorian-era **Point San Luis Lighthouse** (☎ 805-546-4904; www.sanluislighthouse.org; hike-in admission adult/child under 12yr $5/free), now surrounded by a nuclear power plant, can be a challenge. At press time, the only ways to reach this extremely windy point were by joining a van tour ($20 per person, reservations required – call ☎ 805-540-5771) or hiking a rocky, strenuous 3.5-mile round-trip trail. Guided hikes led by Pacific Gas & Electric docents depart at 9am most Saturday mornings (children must be at least nine years old). Make reservations online at least two weeks in advance, bring plenty of water and expect to return to the harbor parking lot around noon or 1pm.

bungalows each have a deck or balcony; pricier ones may have kitchenettes and/or wood-burning fireplaces. Guests enjoy free admission to all of Big Sur's state parks.

Post Ranch Inn (☎ 831-667-2200, 800-527-2200; www.postranchinn.com; Hwy 1; d incl breakfast $550-2185; ❄ 🖥 📶 🐾) The last word in luxurious coastal getaways, the legendary Post Ranch pampers guests with elite lodgings featuring slate spa tubs, private decks, fireplaces and even walking sticks for those coastal hikes. The mountain-view tree houses built on stilts do have a bit of sway.

EATING

Big Sur River Inn (☎ 831-667-2700; Hwy 1; breakfast & lunch $8-19, dinner $17-37; ❄ breakfast, lunch & dinner) This roadside inn has a woodsy old supper-club feel with a deck overlooking a creek that teems with throaty frogs. The wedding reception-quality food is classic American, with breakfast the most reliable bet.

ourpick **Nepenthe** (☎ 831-667-2345; 48510 Hwy 1; mains $14-37; ❄ 11:30am-4:30pm & 5-10pm, to 10:30pm Jul 4-Labor Day) Nepenthe comes from a Greek word meaning 'isle of no sorrow.' Indeed, it'd be hard to feel blue while sitting on the cliff-top ocean-view terrace. The food, while sometimes tasty (try the renowned Ambrosia burger), is secondary to the view and Nepenthe's place in history – Orson Welles and Rita Hayworth bought the place in 1944.

SAN LUIS OBISPO

pop 42,960

Almost exactly midway between LA and San Francisco, San Luis Obispo (aka SLO) has long been the classic stopover point for those making the journey along the coast. With no must-see attractions, SLO might not seem to warrant much time. But not only does it make an ideal base

for coastal explorations, it's one of those small cities that doles out urban pleasures and rural charm in equal measure. Nestled at the base of the Santa Lucia foothills and a grape's throw from a thriving wine industry, SLO gets high marks for livability – to wit: drive-throughs are illegal downtown. California Polytechnic State University (Cal Poly) students keep the streets buzzing during the school year.

SIGHTS

Those satisfyingly reverberatory bells you'll hear emanate from **Mission San Luis Obispo de Tolosa** (☎ 805-543-6850; www.missionsanluisobispo.org; 751 Palm St; donation requested; ❄ 9am-4pm). The fifth of the California missions, it was established in 1772 and named for a French saint. Nicknamed the 'Prince of the Missions,' the modest church has an unusual L-shape and whitewashed walls with Stations of the Cross. Tame exhibits depict everyday life during the Chumash and Spanish periods.

Outside, **Mission Plaza** is a shady oasis ringed by restored adobes and fountains overlooking the creek. Look for the **Moon Tree**, a coast redwood grown from a seed that journeyed on board Apollo 14's lunar mission. Nearby the creek, which has shady walking trails, the **San Luis Obispo Art Center** (☎ 805-543-8562; www.sloartcenter.org; 1010 Broad St; admission free; ❄ 11am-5pm Wed-Mon) showcases local artists and traveling exhibits from around California.

FESTIVALS & EVENTS

SLO's renowned **farmers market** (☎ 805-541-0286; ❄ 5-9pm Thu; 👪) turns downtown's Higuera St into a giant street party. In the midst of the requisite organic, locally grown fruit and veggie stands and barbecues belching smoke, witness garage bands, salvation peddlers,

BEVERLY & WOODWARD PAYNE ANDERSON

Aerial view of Hearst Castle

⤴ HEARST CASTLE

The most important thing to know is that William Randolph Hearst (1863–1951) did not live like Charles Foster Kane in *Citizen Kane*. Not that Hearst wasn't bombastic, conniving and larger than life, but the moody recluse of Orson Welles' movie he was not. Hearst never called his 165-room monstrosity a castle, preferring its official name *La Cuesta Encantada* (The Enchanted Hill) or more often simply calling it 'the ranch.' From the 1920s to the '40s, Hearst and his long-time mistress Marion Davies (Hearst's wife refused to grant him a divorce) entertained here, seeing a steady stream of the era's biggest movers and shakers. Invitations were highly coveted, but Hearst had his quirks – he despised drunkenness, and guests were forbidden to speak of death.

It's a wondrous, historic (Winston Churchill penned anti-Nazi essays here in the 1930s), over-the-top homage to material excess perched high on a hill, and a visit is a must. Architect Julia Morgan based the main building, or Casa Grande, on the design of a Spanish cathedral, and over decades catered to Hearst's every design whim, deftly integrating the spoils of his fabled European shopping sprees (ancient artifacts, entire monasteries etc) into the whole. The estate sprawls out over acres of bountiful, landscaped gardens (and, at the time, the world's largest private zoo), accentuated by shimmering pools and fountains, and statues from ancient Greece and Moorish Spain.

Much like Hearst's construction budget, the castle will devour as much of your time as you let it. To see anything of this state historical monument, you have to take a tour. For most of the year, you'll need tour reservations. In peak summer months and for magical sunset living-history and winter holiday tours, you'll need reservations at least a week or two in advance. Before you leave, or if someone fell down on reservation duty, visit the museum in the back of the visitors center and watch the 40-minute documentary film about the castle and Hearst's life inside the five-story-high National Geographic Theater.

Things you need to know: ☎ information 805-927-2020, reservations 800-444-4445; www.hearstcastle.com; adult/child from $24/12

political signature-collectors, balloon-animal twisters and more free entertainment, intentional or otherwise.

SLEEPING

Motels cluster along the northeastern end of Monterey St near Hwy 101 and by the Hwy 101 exit for Hwy 1 at Santa Rosa St.

HI Hostel Obispo (☎ 805-544-4678; www.hostelobispo.com; 1617 Santa Rosa St; dm $24-27, r with shared bath from $45; ☀ reception 8-10am & 4:30-10pm; 🖥 ☎) In a converted Victorian house on a tree-lined street by the train station, this solar-powered hostel has a garden patio and indoor games room. Kitchen scraps go to the owner's chickens, linens are line-dried and bikes can be rented. Simply put, you can feel the love. No credit cards.

Peach Tree Inn (☎ 805-543-3170, 800-227-6396; www.peachtreeinn.com; 2001 Monterey St; r incl breakfast $80-200; 🗱 🖥 ☎) Friendly, folksy motel rooms (most with air-con) look mighty inviting, especially those right by the creek or with rocking chairs on wooden porches overlooking the grassy lawns, eucalyptus trees and rose gardens. The hearty breakfast comes with homemade breads.

San Luis Creek Lodge (☎ 805-541-1122, 800-593-0333; www.sanluiscreeklodge.com; 1941 Monterey St; r incl breakfast $135-249; 🗱 ☎) Squeezed between neighboring motels, this boutique inn has spacious rooms with divine beds (some have gas fireplaces and jetted tubs) in whimsically mismatched buildings evoking Tudor, arts-and-crafts and Southern Plantation styles. Fluffy robes, DVDs, chess sets and board games are free for guests to borrow.

Petit Soleil (☎ 805-549-0321, 800-876-1588; www.petitsoleilslo.com; 1473 Monterey St; d incl breakfast $149-289; ☎) This French-themed, gay-friendly 'bed *et* breakfast' charms many travelers, who enjoy the evening wine tastings. Each converted motel room is whimsically decorated according to its name and several – including Chocolat – feature hand-painted murals. Expect some street noise.

RICHARD CUMMINS

Mission San Luis Obispo de Tolosa (p296)

BRENT WINEBRENNER

Pismo Beach pier

⬎ IF YOU LIKE...

If you like San Luis Obispo (p296) and its perfect climate, we think you'll like the small towns and beach communities in the surrounding Central Coast. From north to south:

- **Cambria** Here's the contest you'll play over in your mind while here: Which do I love more, the antique- and B&B-filled downtown, or watching the sunset over the white sand beaches? For dinner, stop by **Robin's** (☎ 805-927-5007; www.robinsrestaurant.com; 4095 Burton Dr, Cambria; lunch mains $10-14, dinner mains $17-26; ⏲ 11am-10pm), where pistachio-vinaigrette-topped heirloom tomato salads set the scene for lobster enchiladas and portobello lasagna.

- **Cayucos** When the name of the town is Spanish for 'canoe,' you know you're in a Southern California town that's serious about its beaches. The main drag of amiable, slow-paced Cayucos calls to mind an Old West frontier town, while a block to the west, surf's up. At the north end of town, fronting a broad beach, is the blissfully uncommercialized, knock-kneed pier, built in 1875 – today, it's favored by fishers and newbie surfers.

- **Morro Bay** In a romantic-seaside-town cage fight, Morro Bay would more than hold its own against Cambria these days. Morro Bay's natural harbor paved the way for a fishing industry that continues to this day. Bird-watching, kayak tours, and frequent otter and seal sightings all surround the eponymous rock that heralds the last of the extinct Seven Sisters volcanoes before the great Pacific.

- **Pismo Beach** It's hard to believe that Clam City and its absorbed twin city Shell Beach were once seedy. Now, these family-friendly beach towns balance great seafood with laid-back atmosphere. On Pismo Beach proper, check out the views of the dunes to the left and Port San Luis lighthouse to the right.

...AND NOW FOR SOMETHING TOTALLY DIFFERENT

'Oh, my!' is just one of the more printable exclamations overheard at the Madonna Inn (☎ 805-543-3000, 800-543-9666; www.madonnainn.com; 100 Madonna Rd; r $179-449; 🅿 ♿). You'd expect a place like this in Vegas, not SLO, but here it is, in all its campy, over-the-top extravagance. Japanese tourists, vacationing Mid-Westerners and irony-loving San Francisco hipsters adore the 109 themed rooms – including Yosemite Rock, Caveman and hot-pink Sugar & Spice. Check out photos of the rooms online, or wander the halls and spy into ones being cleaned. The urinal in the men's room is a bizarre waterfall. But the best reason to stop here? Old-fashioned cookies from the fairy-tale-esque bakery.

EATING

Mo's Smokehouse BBQ (☎ 805-544-6193; 1005 Monterey St; mains $7-19; 🕙 11am-9pm Mon-Wed, to 10pm Thu-Sun; ♿) Sink your tush into an antique chair before sinking your teeth into some authentic 'cue, hickory-smoked on the premises. You order at the counter, so it's a good option for those short on time. The championship ribs are lip-smacking.

Novo (☎ 805-543-3986; 726 Higuera St; small plates $6-22, dinner mains $16-32; 🕙 11am-10pm Mon-Thu, 11am-midnight Fri & Sat, 10am-10pm Sun) Novo proffers hit-or-miss Mediterranean, Brazilian and Asian-inspired tapas, with an eye toward freshness and artful presentation. Choose from dozens of international beers, wines or sakes as you savor the view from the creek-side decks.

DRINKING

Higuera St downtown is ground zero for student-centric bars and nightlife.

Creekside Brewing Co (☎ 805-542-9804; 1040 Broad St) Kick back at a sunnyside patio table above the creek near Mission Plaza. It's got its own brews on tap, plus bottled Belgian beers. On Mondays, all pints are just three bucks.

Taste (☎ 805-269-8279; 1003 Osos St) At this high-ceilinged co-op wine-tasting room, take the enomatic wine-dispensing sys-

tem for a spin with a Riedel glass in hand, then pick up an Edna Valley winery map and go straight to the source.

ENTERTAINMENT

Sunset Drive-In (☎ 805-544-4475; 255 Elks Lane, off Hwy 1 exit Madonna Rd; adult/child 5-11yr $6/2) Never made out at a drive-in? Here's your chance. The movies are mindless Hollywood blockbusters but the bags of popcorn are bottomless.

GETTING THERE & AROUND

A half-mile east of downtown, **Amtrak** (1011 Railroad Ave) runs the daily Seattle–LA *Coast Starlight* and twice-daily *Pacific Surfliner,* heading south to Santa Barbara ($30, 2¾ hours), LA ($37, 5¾ hours) and San Diego ($55, 8½ hours). Several daily Thruway buses link to more-frequent regional trains.

From SLO's train station, **Greyhound** (1023 Railroad Ave) has a few daily buses to LA ($38, 5½ hours) via Santa Barbara ($27, 2¼ hours), and to San Francisco ($48, seven hours).

SANTA BARBARA
pop 85,680

A 90-minute drive north of LA, Santa Barbara basks smugly in its apparent perfection. Nicknamed the American

Riviera, it's blessed with freakishly good weather and a backdrop of mountains to complement its oceanic foreground. What's apparent as soon as you arrive is the city's iconic architecture. After a 1925 earthquake leveled downtown, planners chose to go with a Mediterranean-style rebuild, thus the city's trademark red-tile roofs, whitewashed adobe walls and waving palm trees. And no one can deny the appeal of the beaches that line the city tip to toe either. Just ignore those pesky oil derricks out to sea.

INFORMATION

Visitor Center (☎ 805-965-3021; www. santabarbaraca.com; 1 Garden St; ☾ 9am-5pm Mon-Sat, 10am-5pm Sun; 🖳 📶) Offers maps and themed self-guided touring brochures.

SIGHTS
THE WATERFRONT

At its southern end, State St runs into **Stearns Wharf**. Built in 1872 and once partly owned by tough-guy actor Jimmy Cagney, it's the West Coast's oldest continuously operating wooden pier. There's 90 minutes of free parking right on the wharf with validation from any shop or restaurant.

West alongside the yacht harbor, the interesting **Santa Barbara Maritime Museum** (☎ 805-962-8404; www.sbmm.org; 113 Harbor Way; adult/child 1-5yr/child 6-17yr $7/2/4, free 3rd Thu of the month; ☾ 10am-5pm Thu-Tue, to 6pm Jun-Aug; ♿) examines the city's briny history with memorabilia, hands-on and virtual-reality exhibits, and a movie theater.

The biodiesel, bright yellow-painted **Lil' Toot water taxi** (one-way fare adult/child under 13yr $4/1) shuttles between Stearns Wharf and the harbor every half hour from noon to 6pm daily.

SANTA BARBARA COUNTY COURTHOUSE

Built in Spanish-Moorish revival style, the magnificent 1929 **courthouse** (☎ 805-962-6464; www.santabarbaracourthouse.org; 1100 Anacapa St; admission free; ☾ 8am-5pm Mon-Fri,

Santa Barbara's Mediterranean-style architecture

LEE FOSTER

10am-4:30pm Sat & Sun, tours 2pm Mon-Sat & 10:30am Mon, Tue & Fri) is an absurdly beautiful place to be on trial (or get married). Marvel at the hand-painted ceilings, tiles from Tunisia and Spain, gorgeously kept grounds and the best view of the city

from El Mirador, the *Vertigo*-esque clock tower. Peek into the second-floor mural room depicting California's colonial history and also glimpse the law library, with its vaulted blue ceiling covered in golden stars. You're free to explore on your own

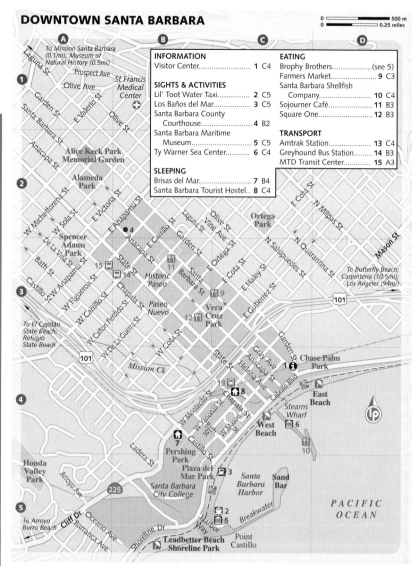

DOWNTOWN SANTA BARBARA

0 — 500 m
0 — 0.25 miles

INFORMATION
Visitor Center........................ 1 C4

SIGHTS & ACTIVITIES
Lil' Toot Water Taxi............... 2 C5
Los Baños del Mar.................. 3 C5
Santa Barbara County
  Courthouse........................ 4 B2
Santa Barbara Maritime
  Museum............................ 5 C5
Ty Warner Sea Center........... 6 C4

SLEEPING
Brisas del Mar........................ 7 B4
Santa Barbara Tourist Hostel.. 8 C4

EATING
Brophy Brothers..................(see 5)
Farmers Market..................... 9 C3
Santa Barbara Shellfish
  Company........................ 10 C4
Sojourner Café.................... 11 B3
Square One........................ 12 B3

TRANSPORT
Amtrak Station.................... 13 C4
Greyhound Bus Station........ 14 B3
MTD Transit Center............. 15 A3

but the best way to see the courthouse is on a free guided tour.

MISSION SANTA BARBARA

Nicknamed the 'Queen of the Missions,' Mission Santa Barbara (☎ 805-682-4713; www.sbmission.org; 2201 Laguna St; adult/child 6-15yr $5/1; ☏ 9am-4:30pm) sits on a hilltop perch northwest of downtown. It's the only California mission to have twin bell towers, as well as the sole one to have escaped secularization under Mexican rule. It has been occupied without interruption by Franciscans since its founding in 1786, although the pink sandstone church dates only from 1820. Outside is a moody cemetery where an estimated 4000 Chumash tribespeople lie buried in unmarked graves.

ACTIVITIES
BEACHES

Equipped with a playground, East Beach is a long, sandy stretch between Stearns Wharf and Montecito. It's Santa Barbara's most popular beach. Chic but narrow Butterfly Beach, at its eastern end, is near the Biltmore hotel.

Between Stearns Wharf and the harbor, West Beach has calm water and is popular with tourists. Los Baños del Mar (☎ 805-966-6110; 401 Shoreline Dr; admission $6; ☏ call for hr; ⛱) is a municipal outdoor heated-pool complex for recreational and lap swimming. On the other side of the harbor, Leadbetter Beach is a good spot for beginner surfers and windsurfers. Climbing the stairs on the west end takes you to Shoreline Park, with picnic tables and awesome kite-flying conditions. Further west near the junction of Cliff Dr and Las Positas Rd, Arroyo Burro Beach County Park, aka Hendry's, offers romps for kids and dogs and has free parking, a restaurant and a bar.

SANTA BARBARA FOR KIDS

- **Santa Barbara Maritime Museum** (p301) Peer through a periscope, reel in a virtual fish or check out the model ships.
- **Ty Warner Sea Center** (☎ 805-962-2526; 211 Stearns Wharf; www.sbnature.org; adult/child 2-12yr $8/5; ☏ 10am-5pm; ⛱) Touch tide-pool critters and crawl through a surge-tank tunnel.
- **Carpinteria State Beach** (see below) Long sandy beach with gentle waves.
- **Museum of Natural History** (☎ 805-682-4711; www.sbnature.org; 2559 Puesta del Sol Rd; adult/child 3-12yr $10/6; ☏ 10am-5pm; ⛱) Giant skeletons and a petite planetarium captivate kids' imaginations.

Twelve miles southeast of Santa Barbara, Carpinteria State Beach (per car $10; ☏ 7am-sunset; ⛱) has calm waters for swimming, wading and tidepooling. About 25 miles northwest of the city, Refugio State Beach (per vehicle $10; ☏ 8am-sunset) is a popular surf spot. It's connected by a recreational cycling path to El Capitán State Beach (per car $10; ☏ 8am-sunset; ⛱), perched on low bluffs 3 miles east. All state beaches are signposted off Hwy 101; call ☎ 805-968-1033 for closure updates.

CYCLING

The Cabrillo Blvd beachfront bike path runs for 3 miles along the water, between Andrée Clark Bird Refuge and Leadbetter Beach. Wheel Fun (☎ 805-966-2282; www.wheelfunrentals.com; 23 E Cabrillo Blvd & 22 State St; bike rental per hr from $8; ☏ 8am-8pm) rents bikes and silly-looking

RICHARD CUMMINS

Del Mar Beach, San Diego

↘ IF YOU LIKE...

If you like the beaches of **Santa Barbara** (p300) or **La Jolla** (p324), we think you'll also like the following:

- **Huntington Beach** Officially now known as Surf City, USA, the Orange County suburb is 8.5 miles of quintessential Southern California beach, surf competitions and chill vibes. Become one with the locals at **Zack's Pier Plaza** (☎ 714-536-0215; www.zackshb.com; 405 Pacific Coast Hwy, Huntington Beach; lessons from $75), where lifeguard-certified surfing instructors teach you to hang ten.

- **Newport Beach** The upscale Orange County suburb is as famous for its ritzy homes ($15 million, anyone?) as it is for its surprisingly relaxed beach. The 6-mile-long Balboa Peninsula has two piers, stretches of white sandy beach and a renowned body-surfing spot at the end, the Wedge.

- **Solana Beach** For a seaside neighborhood, it's hard to beat Solana Beach. Just north of Del Mar and metropolitan San Diego, the relaxed town is a far cry from the crowds of SeaWorld. Soak up the beach sun or pick up a few items for your house in the **Cedros Design District** (Cedros Ave), where home-furnishings stores, antique shops and clothing boutiques share space with casual bars and restaurants.

- **Del Mar** Swanky Del Mar is now known as much for ugly dogs and fast horses as it is for its gorgeous beaches. The **Del Mar Racetrack & Fairgrounds** (☎ 858-755-1141; www.sdfair.com; 2260 Jimmy Durante Blvd, Del Mar; entrance from $5; ☺ races mid-Jul–early Sep, fair late Jun–early Jul) hosts thoroughbred racing and the San Diego State Fair (home to the famous ugly-dog contest).

surreys (quadracycles). The **Santa Barbara Bicycle Coalition** (www.sbbike.org) offers free printable self-guided road-cycling tours online.

SLEEPING

Prepare for sticker shock: basic rooms command over $200 in summer. Don't just show up and expect to find cheap accommodations at the last minute, especially not on weekends. For decent mid-range motels and hotels, follow Hwy 101 south to Carpinteria (12 miles) or Ventura (30 miles).

Santa Barbara Tourist Hostel (☎ 805-963-0154; www.sbhostel.com; 134 Chapala St; dm $28-35, r $79-95; 🖳 📶) Traveling strangers, roaring trains and a rowdy bar just steps from your door – it's either the perfect country-and-western song or this low-slung bungalow, which feels like a grungy college dorm, next to the Amtrak station.

ourpick El Capitan Canyon (☎ 805-685-3887, 866-352-2729; 11560 Calle Real, Goleta; tents with shared bath $155, cabins from $225; 📶 🔲 ♿) A 20-minute drive northbound up Hwy 101, El Capitan is for those who love to camp but hate to wake up with dirt under their nails. Safari tents are rustic. Creekside cabin amenities vary – some come with fireplaces, kitchenettes, soaking tubs and sleeping lofts – but all have divine beds. You can borrow bikes to pedal over to the beach.

Brisas del Mar (☎ 805-966-2219, 800-468-1988; www.sbhotels.com; 223 Castillo St; r incl breakfast $170-265; 🖳 📶 🔲) Big kudos for all the freebies (DVDs, afternoon wine and cheese, evening milk and cookies) and the new Mediterranean-style front section, although the motel wing is unlovely. The hotel's respectable sister properties, some also near the beach, are lower-priced.

EATING

Santa Barbara's **farmers market** (☎ 805-962-5354; cnr Cota & Santa Barbara Sts; ⏰ 8:30am-12:30pm Sat) also stages a Tuesday afternoon version along the 500 and 600 blocks of State St.

Santa Barbara Shellfish Company (☎ 805-966-6676; 230 Stearns Wharf; dishes $5-15; ⏰ 11am-9pm) 'From sea to skillet to plate'

best describes this end-of-the-wharf crab shack that's more of a counter joint. Great lobster bisque and ocean views, and the same location for 25 years.

Sojourner Café (☎ 805-965-7922; 134 E Cañon Perdido; mains $7-14; ⏰ 11am-11pm Mon-Sat, to 10pm Sun) Hippie Soj has been doing its all-natural, mostly meatless magic since 1978. Globally flavored vegetarian-friendly comfort food sometimes borders on bland, though the gingered tofu wonton pillows are tasty. The dessert list is mostly vegan (though you'd never guess it).

Brophy Brothers (☎ 805-966-4418; 119 Harbor Way; mains $8-20; ⏰ 11am-10pm Sun-Thu, to 11pm Fri & Sat) The seafood at this always-bustling harbor hangout is so fresh that you half expect it to have leapt straight out of the ocean. Show up at sunset, grab an ocean-view table on the outdoor deck or sit inside at the boisterous bar to knock back Bloody Marys.

ourpick Square One (☎ 805-965-4565; 14 E Cota St; mains $14-25; ⏰ 5:30-9pm Tue-Sun) A postmodern Californian menu reaches stratospheric heights of inventiveness, piquing even jaded palates with the likes of seafood seviche with grapefruit gelée or squid-ink ravioli in a delicate sea-urchin broth. Sculpted desserts are sweetly challenging. Svelte wine bar.

GETTING THERE & AROUND

Greyhound (☎ 805-965-7551; 34 W Carrillo St) has daily bus services to LA ($18, three hours) and San Francisco ($60, nine hours), the latter via San Luis Obispo ($27, 2¼ hours).

Santa Barbara is a stop on the daily Seattle–LA *Coast Starlight,* run by **Amtrak** (209 State St). *Pacific Surfliner* regional trains frequently head south to LA ($25, three hours) and San Diego ($47, six hours), and twice daily north to San Luis Obispo ($30,

DETOUR: FOXEN CANYON WINE TRAIL

Santa Barbara's wine country, made up of the Santa Maria and Santa Ynez Valleys, unfurls along winding country lanes amid oak-dotted rolling hills that stretch for miles. The 2004 indie hit movie *Sideways* was both a blessing and a curse: local winemakers have found international acclaim, but also huge crowds and tour buses. Free self-guided touring maps from the Santa Barbara County Vintners' Association (www.sbcountywines.com) are available at every winery, most found inside the triangle of Hwys 101, 246 and 154. The beautiful Foxen Canyon Wine Trail (www.foxencanyonwinetrail.com; Foxen Canyon Rd) curves north of Los Olivos for nearly 30 miles. Seek out big-shouldered giants such as Firestone and Fess Parker or hidden gems like Zaca Mesa, producing Rhône varietals; Foxen, with its corrugated metal-roofed tasting barn; Rancho Sisquoc, where grapevines sprawl across an early-20th-century ranch; or cult winemaker Kenneth Volk. Most tasting rooms are open at least 10am to 4pm daily, keeping shorter hours in winter; tasting fees average $10 to $20, maybe including a souvenir glass.

2¾ hours). Additional Thruway bus services link Santa Barbara with SLO.

ORANGE COUNTY

Although it's 34 independent cities, Orange County (OC) identifies itself as a county more than any other in Southern California.

Indulgent TV shows from *The OC* to *Real Housewives* have cemented the county's reputation as a place seething with the spoiled and the rich, and Angelenos poke fun at their southern neighbors. 'Behind the Orange Curtain' is a vague reference to the county's brand of conservatism, an amalgam of Christian fundamentalism, materialism, libertarianism and anti-immigrantism. Orange County hurls it right back, with some justification. Laguna Beach supports a flourishing arts community, and the OC's cultural institutions – and beaches – are some of America's best.

INFORMATION

The knowledgeable folks at the Anaheim/ Orange County Visitor & Convention Bureau (☎ 714-765-8888; www.anaheimoc.org;

800 W Katella Ave, Anaheim; ☼ 8am-5pm Mon-Fri) can help plan your OC visit.

DISNEYLAND RESORT

Mickey is one lucky mouse. Created by animator Walt Disney in 1928, he caught a ride on a multimedia juggernaut (film, TV, publishing, music, merchandising and theme parks) that has made him an international superstar. Plus, he lives in the Happiest Place on Earth, a slice of 'imagineered' hyperreality where the streets are always clean, the employees – called cast members – are always upbeat, and there's a parade every day of the year. It would be easy to hate the guy but, since opening the doors to his Disneyland home in 1955, he's been a thoughtful host to millions of guests. For the kids and families who visit every year, Disneyland remains a magical experience.

HISTORY

During the 1990s, Anaheim, the city surrounding Disneyland, undertook a staggering $4.2-billion revamp and expansion, cleaning up rundown stretches where hookers once roamed and establishing the first police force in the US devoted specifically to guarding tourists. The cornerstone of the five-year effort was the addition of a second theme park in February 2001, Disney California Adventure (DCA). Adjacent to the original park, it pays tribute to the state's cultural history and its most famous landmarks. Also added was Downtown Disney, an outdoor pedestrian mall. The ensemble is called the Disneyland Resort.

Roads near the park have been widened, landscaped and given the lofty name 'the Anaheim Resort.' In 2008 Anaheim GardenWalk opened on Katella Ave within walking distance of the park. This outdoor mall, though lacking personality, brings a welcome, much-needed array of sit-down restaurants to the Disney-adjacent neighborhood.

TICKETS & OPENING HOURS

Both parks are open 365 days a year, but hours can vary. During peak season (mid-June to early September) Disneyland's hours are usually 8am to midnight. The rest of the year it's open from 10am to 8pm or until 10pm. DCA closes at 10pm in summer, earlier in the off-season. For hours and parade schedules, call ☎ 714-781-4565 or check www.disneyland.com.

One-day admission to Disneyland or DCA costs $76 for adults, and $68 for children aged three to nine. A Parkhopper ticket (for both parks in one day) costs $94/84 per adult/child. Two- to six-day passes per adult/child range from $151/136 to $256/230, valid for up to a 13-day period.

The free FASTPASS system pre-assigns boarding times for about a dozen attractions. Get tickets from FASTPASS machines near the ride entrances, show up at the time printed on the ticket, and go to the FASTPASS line. There's still a wait, but it'll be much shorter. Note that you can get only one FASTPASS at a time.

DISNEYLAND

Upon entering **Disneyland** (☎ recorded info 714-781-4565, live assistance 714-781-7290; www.disneyland.com; ♿) you're funneled onto Main Street, USA. Main Street ends in the Central Plaza, from which all the 'lands' extend (Frontierland, Tomorrowland etc).

MAIN STREET, USA

Fashioned after Walt's hometown of Marceline, MO, bustling Main Street, USA resembles a classic turn-of-the-20th-century all-American town. It's an idyllic, relentlessly cheerful representation complete with barbershop quartet, penny arcades, ice-cream shops and a steam train.

©DISNEY ENTERPRISES, INC.

Sleeping Beauty Castle, Disneyland

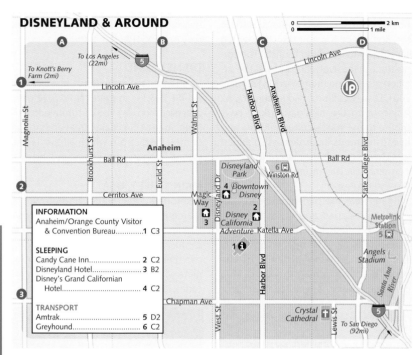

DISNEYLAND & AROUND

INFORMATION
Anaheim/Orange County Visitor
& Convention Bureau.............1 C3

SLEEPING
Candy Cane Inn.......................2 C2
Disneyland Hotel......................3 B2
Disney's Grand Californian
Hotel....................................4 C2

TRANSPORT
Amtrak...................................5 D2
Greyhound..............................6 C2

If you're visiting on a special occasion, stop by City Hall to pick up oversized buttons celebrating birthdays, anniversaries and those 'Just Married.' There's also an Information Center here. Nearby there's a station for the **Disneyland Railroad**, a steam train that loops the park and stops at four different locations.

There's plenty of shopping along Main Street, but you can save that for the evening as the stores remain open after the park's attractions close. Main Street ends in the **Central Plaza**, the hub of the park from which the eight different lands (such as Frontierland and Tomorrowland) can be reached. **Sleeping Beauty Castle** lords over the plaza, its towers and turrets fashioned after Neuschwanstein, the Bavarian castle owned by Mad King Ludwig. One difference? The roof here was placed on backward.

Pay attention to the cool **optical illusion** along Main Street. As you look from the entrance, up the street toward Sleeping Beauty Castle, everything looks big and far away. When you're at the castle looking back, everything looks closer and smaller. This effect is known as forced perspective, a technique used on Hollywood sets where buildings are constructed at a decreasing scale to create an illusion of height or depth.

TOMORROWLAND
The future looks different than imagineered in 1955, the year Tomorrowland opened, so in 1998 this 'land' was revamped to honor three timeless futurists: Jules Verne, HG Wells and Leonardo da Vinci. Rumble through an underwater earthquake and look for Nemo from inside a sub in the **Finding Nemo**

Submarine Voyage, which debuted in 2007. **Space Mountain**, one of the park's signature attractions and one of the best roller coasters in America, is still hurtling through complete darkness at frightening speeds nearby. The **monorail**, which

WITOLD SKRYPCZAK

The Danish-style wonderland of Solvang

◥ IF YOU LIKE...

If you like the pure, unadulterated joy of **Disneyland** (p306) we think you'll also enjoy these vacation destinations:

- **Knott's Berry Farm** A smaller, quainter neighbor of Disneyland, this **theme park** (☎ 714-220-5200; www.knotts.com; 8039 Beach Blvd, Buena Park; adult/child $53/24; ☼ from 10am; ♿) is just 4 miles northwest of Anaheim off I-5. It claims to be America's first theme park, dating from 1934 when Walter Knott's boysenberries (a loganberry-blackberry-raspberry hybrid) and his wife Cordelia's fried-chicken dinners attracted crowds of local farmhands. By 1940 Mr Knott had built an imitation ghost town to keep their guests entertained, which gave way to carnival rides.
- **Solvang** In the early 1900s, Danish pioneers set up camp near Santa Barbara, re-creating their architecture and culture. Today, windmills, pastries and souvenirs are most of what's left – a wonderland of kitsch. The Danish Disneyland of wine country serves up the Central Coast's best dessert – the gooey *ebelskiver* – fruit- or chocolate-filled pancake balls.
- **Balboa Island** The streets here are still largely lined with tightly clustered cottages built in the 1920s and '30s. Chocolate-covered frozen bananas, a beachfront Ferris wheel 'Fun Zone' and dozens of shops and restaurants make for a fabulous day trip from Laguna Beach or Disneyland. Take the adorable **ferry** (☎ 949-673-1070; www.balboaislandferry.com; adult/child $1/0.50, car & driver $2; ☼ 6am-2am). Around Christmas, check out the boat parade, or the local competition that pits mansion owners with animatronic animals against waterfront condos with Vegas-style lighting.

travels a 2.5-mile round-trip route between Downtown Disney and the park, stops here.

FANTASYLAND

Located behind Sleeping Beauty Castle, Fantasyland is filled with characters from classic children's stories, such as Dumbo the Elephant and Peter Pan. Kids love whirling around the **Mad Tea Party** ride, while fans of old-school attractions enjoy **Mr Toad's Wild Ride**, a loopy jaunt through London in an open-air jalopy. As for the classic **'it's a small world'** attraction, the public's response has long been ambivalent: 'That song is so annoying. And those kids are creepy. I just hope they never change it.' But they did change it in 2009 – despite protests by purists – so recognizable Disney characters are interspersed among the international array of animatronic singing children.

FRONTIERLAND

In the wake of the successful *Pirates of the Caribbean* movies, Tom Sawyer Island –

the only attraction in the park personally designed by Uncle Walt – was re-imagined as **Pirate's Lair on Tom Sawyer Island**, and now honors Tom in name only. After a raft ride to the island, guests wander among rowing pirates, cannibal cages, ghostly apparitions and buried treasure. Somewhere, Injun Joe is smiling. The rest of Frontierland gives a nod to the rip-roarin' Old West.

ADVENTURELAND

Adventureland loosely derives its style from Southeast Asia and Africa. The hands-down highlight is the jungle-themed **Indiana Jones Adventure**. Enormous Humvee-type vehicles lurch and jerk as they re-create stunts from the famous film trilogy. (Look closely at Indie during the ride: is he real or Audio-Animatronics?) Nearby, little ones love climbing the stairways of **Tarzan's Treehouse**.

NEW ORLEANS SQUARE

New Orleans was Walt and his wife Lillian's favorite city, and he paid tribute

Indiana Jones Adventure ride, part of Adventureland, Disneyland

©DISNEY ENTERPRISES, INC./LUCASFILM LTD

to it by building this charming square. **Pirates of the Caribbean**, the longest ride in Disneyland (17 minutes) and the 'inspiration' for the movies, opened in 1967 and was the first addition to the park after Walt Disney's death. Real human skeletons from the UCLA Medical Center were used as props when the attraction first opened because the artificial versions didn't look real enough. Elements from the movies have now been incorporated.

At the **Haunted Mansion**, '999 happy haunts' – spirits and goblins, shades and ghosts – evanesce while you ride in the Doom Buggy through web-covered graveyards of dancing skeletons. The Disneyland Railroad stops at New Orleans Square.

CRITTER COUNTRY

Tucked behind the Haunted Mansion, Critter Country is home to both Winnie the Pooh and **Splash Mountain**, a flume ride through the story of Brer Rabbit and Brer Bear, based on the controversial film *Song of the South*. Right at the big descent, a camera snaps your picture. Some visitors lift their shirts, earning the ride the nickname 'Flash Mountain.' The photos are usually destroyed, but a few years ago some made their way on to the internet.

DISNEY CALIFORNIA ADVENTURE

DCA covers more acres than Disneyland, feels less crowded, and has a mix of attractions and straightforward amusement-park-style rides.

The **Hollywood Pictures Backlot** includes a mishmash of building styles. You'll do a serious double-take where a forced-perspective sky-and-land mural makes it look like the street keeps going. The 183ft-tall **Twilight Zone Tower of Terror** is essentially a drop down an elevator chute in a haunted hotel. The **California Screamin'** roller coaster covers 10 acres, while the **Toy Story Mania** ride feels as if you're in a video game; 3-D glasses give you the illusion of throwing pies and breaking plates to score points.

SLEEPING & EATING

Candy Cane Inn (☎ 714-774-5284, 800-345-7057; www.candycaneinn.net; 1747 S Harbor Blvd; r $99-189; P ⚡ 🛜 📺) Adjacent to Disneyland's main gate, *this* might actually be the happiest place around. Guests rave about its sparkling pool and spotless (if a bit cramped) rooms, complimentary continental breakfast and gorgeous gardens.

Disneyland Hotel (☎ 714-778-6600; 1150 Magic Way; r $255-345; P ⚡ 🖥 📺 👶) The park's original hotel, with a whopping 969 rooms, hasn't lost its appeal, though its three towers feel a bit retro-mod these days. Turn off the lights in your room and Tinker Bell's pixie dust glows in the dark on the walls. The Never Land–themed pool has a 110ft waterslide, and kids can play aboard Captain Hook's Pirate Ship. *Sweet.*

our pick **Disney's Grand Californian Hotel** (☎ 714-635-2300; 1600 S Disneyland Dr; r from $550; P ⚡ 🖥 🛜 📺 👶) Timber beams rise majestically above the cathedral-like lobby of this six-story monument to the American arts-and-crafts movement. Cushy amenities include triple-sheeted beds, custom bedspreads and bathrobes, and a spa. At night kids wind down with bedtime stories by the lobby's giant stone hearth. Worth visiting even if you don't stay here.

Each of Disney's 'lands' has cafeteria-style eating options, and all Disney restaurants have kids' menus. Call **Disney Dining** (☎ 714-781-3463) to make reservations and enquire about character dining – Disney characters work the dining room and greet kids during meals. The

Downtown Disney shopping district has dozens of choices from fast food to fine dining.

GETTING THERE & AWAY

The Anaheim Resort is off I-5, about 30 miles south of Downtown LA; exit Disneyland Dr. Enter the 'Mickey & Friends' parking structure from southbound Disneyland Dr at Ball Rd (the largest parking structure in the world, with room for 10,300 vehicles). Parking costs $12.

See p85 for bus services from Los Angeles International Airport.

Two blocks from Disneyland, **Greyhound** (☎ 714-999-1256; 100 W Winston Rd) runs frequent departures to/from Downtown LA ($10, 40 minutes).

Amtrak (☎ 714-385-1448; www.amtrak.com; 2150 E Katella Ave) trains stop next to Angels Stadium. Tickets to/from LA's Union Station are $12 (40 minutes).

GETTING AROUND

Many hotels and motels have free shuttles to Disneyland and other area attractions.

Anaheim Resort Transit (ART; ☎ 714-563-5287; www.rideart.org) provides a frequent bus service between Disneyland and nearby hotels. Before boarding pick up an all-day pass ($4) at kiosks or online. Otherwise it's $3 per one-way trip.

LAGUNA BEACH

pop 23,700

Secluded down a long canyon and ensconced in wooded hillsides, seaside cliffs, pristine beaches and azure waves, Laguna Beach boasts one of OC's prettiest stretches of coast.

Artist Norman St Clair 'discovered' Laguna around 1910, and soon other artists influenced by French impressionism, who came to be known as the *plein air* school, were setting up camp. By the late 1920s, more than half of the town's 300 residents were artists. Real-estate prices make such ratios impossible these days, but the town's artistic heart still beats vigorously. Public sculpture graces the streets and parks, dozens of galleries feature local artists, and the city hosts several renowned festivals.

ANGUS OBORN

Crescent Bay, Laguna Beach

Laguna is also the center of the OC's gay scene. Although the legendary Boom Boom Room club has closed, West St Beach remains a popular summer meeting place.

ORIENTATION & INFORMATION

Laguna's beach stretches for 7 miles, but the downtown 'Village' – beguiling shops, restaurants and bars, many hidden in courtyards and funky shacks – occupies about a quarter-mile stretch along three parallel streets: Broadway, Ocean Ave and Forest Ave. S Coast Hwy runs south from the Village, parallel to the water, and N Coast Hwy runs north of the Village.

Pick up info, maps and guides at **Laguna Beach Visitors Bureau** (☎ 949-497-9229, 800-877-1115; www.lagunabeachinfo.com) 252 Broadway (✢ 10am-4pm Mon-Fri); 381 Forest Ave (✢ 10am-5pm Mon-Sat, noon-4pm Sun).

SIGHTS & ACTIVITIES

Laguna has 30 public beaches and coves. Though many are hidden from view by multimillion-dollar homes, most are accessible by stairs off S Coast Hwy; just look for 'beach access' signs.

Main Beach has volleyball and basketball courts and a playground, and is the best beach for swimming. Northwest of Main Beach, the area is too rocky to surf; tide pooling is best. Tiny **Brown's Park** (551 S Coast Hwy), more of a sculpture-lined garden alley, dead-ends in a deck overlooking Main Beach.

Just northwest of Main Beach, the grassy, bluff-top **Heisler Park** has sweeping views of the craggy coves and deep blue sea. Drop down below the park to **Diver's Cove**, a deep, protected inlet popular with snorkelers and, of course, divers.

Gallery hoppers: on S Coast Hwy, there's a gallery at least every couple of blocks. Of special note is the site of the first 'Whaling Wall,' now a gallery of the marine artist **Wyland** (☎ 949-376-8000; www.wyland.com; 509 S Coast Hwy), whose 100 (and counting) murals of whales adorn buildings worldwide.

The **Laguna Art Museum** (☎ 949-494-8971; www.lagunaartmuseum.org; 307 Cliff Dr; adult/child under 12yr/student $15/free/12; ✢ 11am-5pm, occasional extended hours) has changing exhibits usually featuring California artists, plus a permanent collection heavy on California landscapes and vintage photographs.

SLEEPING & EATING

Rates here are for high season (late May to early September) and can fall steeply at other times.

Pacific Edge Hotel (☎ 949-494-8566, 866-932-2896; www.pacificedgehotel.com; 647 S Coast Hwy; r from $149; P ⚏ 🖵 🛜 🐾) This cluster of beachside buildings boasts a combined 130 rooms renovated with mid-century furniture and candy colors. About half have ocean views, and many are suites with kitchenettes. Kick back on your deck with brewskis and watch the sun set, or borrow lounge chairs and umbrellas for the hotel's stretch of private beach.

Tides Inn (☎ 949-494-2494, 888-777-2107; www.tideslaguna.com; 460 N Coast Hwy; r $175-285; 🖵 🐾) This 21-room place is a bargain for Laguna, especially considering its location three blocks north of the town center, the bend-over-backwards service and comfortable rooms – though some bathrooms are minuscule. Certain rooms have kitchenettes and ocean views. The three rooms on the road can be noisy.

Casa Laguna Inn & Spa (☎ 949-494-2996, 800-233-0449; www.casalaguna.com; 2510 S Coast Hwy; r from $280; P ⚏ 🖵 🛜 🐾) On a terraced acre of gardens on the south side of town sits this gorgeous 1920s

DETOUR: SAN JUAN CAPISTRANO

Famous the world over for the swallows that return from their winter migration on the same day every year, the town of San Juan Capistrano is also home to the 'jewel of the California missions.'

Located about 10 miles southeast and inland of Laguna Beach, the Mission San Juan Capistrano (☎ 949-234-1300; www.missionsjc.com; 31882 Camino Capistrano; adult/child/senior $9/5/8; 🕒 8:30am-5pm) was built around a series of 18th-century arcades, each of which enclose charming fountains and lush gardens that range from rose to cactus to water lilies, and are often awash in monarch butterflies. The whitewashed Serra Chapel is considered the oldest building in California and is the only chapel still standing in which Padre Junípero Serra (the founder) gave Mass.

To celebrate the swallows' return from their Argentine sojourn, the city puts on the Festival of the Swallows every year on March 19. Calling the ceilingless Great Stone Church 'the American Acropolis' is a bit of a stretch, but in its walls is where the beloved swallows make their summer home until around October 23.

From Laguna Beach, take OCTA bus 1 south to K-Mart Plaza, then connect to bus 191/A in the direction of Mission Viejo, which drops you near the mission ($2, about one hour). Drivers should exit I-5 at Ortega Hwy and head west for about a quarter of a mile.

mission-style B&B. Each of the 22 compact rooms is uniquely furnished, but all feature seven layers of bedding; the fastidious attention to detail continues from the gourmet breakfast to the evening drinks. Watch the sun set from the ocean-view tub. A great couple's getaway.

Taco Loco (☎ 949-497-1635; 640 S Coast Hwy; dishes $2.60-12.25; 🕒 11am-midnight Sun-Thu, 11am-2am Fri & Sat; V) This taco stand accomplishes the near impossible: good-for-you Mexican food that doesn't suck. A hippie vibe pervades the plastic garden chairs and simple ceramic tables for munching tacos, burritos and quesadillas with fillings from mushroom and tofu to blackened swordfish.

Mozambique (☎ 949-715-7777; 1740 S Coast Hwy; dinner mains $18-39; 🕒 4-10pm Mon-Thu, 4pm-midnight Fri & Sat, 11am-10:30pm Sun) African-inspired cuisine as exotic as its name: Durban lamb curry, chicken or shrimp in piquant peri-peri sauce and

steaks rubbed in special house spices. Most mains are under $30 and are also served upstairs under the chic black-and-white striped canopy of the Shebeen bar.

GETTING THERE & AROUND

To reach Laguna Beach from I-405, take Hwy 133 (Laguna Canyon Rd) southwest. Laguna is served by OCTA bus 1, which runs along the coast from Long Beach to San Clemente.

Parking is a perpetual problem. Hoard your quarters. Traffic is slow in town in summer, especially on weekend afternoons.

SAN DIEGO

California's second-largest city and America's eighth largest, San Diego doesn't seduce like San Francisco or thrill like LA, but life here is so persistently pleasant, what with 70 miles of coastline and the nation's most enviable climate, that you won't care much. Small wonder that San Diegans shamelessly yet endearingly promote their hometown as 'America's Finest City.'

For visitors, San Diego bursts with world-famous attractions: the zoo, SeaWorld, Legoland and the museums of Balboa Park (one of the nation's largest urban parks) just for starters. In the heart of downtown is the always-buzzing Gaslamp Quarter, ideal for listening to a live band or dancing 'til the wee hours. Miles of urban beaches reach their apex in the ritzy, picturesque enclave of La Jolla, which boasts pride of place on San Diego's coast. Plus, there's a burgeoning culinary scene.

SIGHTS
DOWNTOWN

Just south of the city's stretch of skyscrapers lies the historic Gaslamp Quarter. Closer to the bay and near the city's mammoth convention center looms Petco Park, San Diego's baseball stadium, which has helped seal downtown's re-newal. To the west lies the Embarcadero district, a fine place for a bay-front jog alongside historic battleships. A short walk north lands you in Little Italy, where mom-and-pop eateries alternate with high-end design stores.

GASLAMP QUARTER

Founded in 1867, the Gaslamp Quarter has, almost since its inception, catered to the vices of travelers. During San Diego's Gold Rush of the 1870s, the neighborhood quickly degenerated into a string of saloons, bordellos, gambling halls and opium dens. In San Diego's postwar boom, the Victorian and beaux-arts buildings were left to molder while the rest of downtown was razed and rebuilt. When developers started to eye the area in the early 1980s, preservationists organized to save the old brick and stone facades from the wrecking ball.

These days, the Gaslamp Quarter is again the focus of the city's nightlife, though of a significantly tamer variety; much of the business comes from

WITOLD SKRYPCZAK

San Diego's Gaslamp Quarter

METROPOLITAN SAN DIEGO

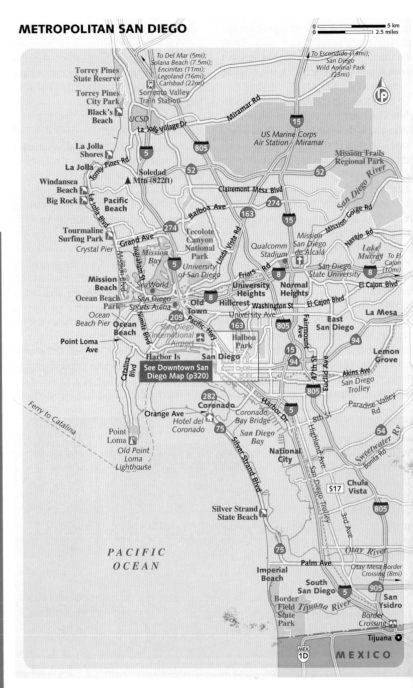

0 ——————— 5 km
0 ——————— 2.5 miles

To Del Mar (5mi);
Solana Beach (7.5mi);
Encinitas (11mi);
Legoland (16mi);
Carlsbad (22mi)

To Escondido (14mi);
San Diego
Wild Animal Park
(23mi)

Torrey Pines
State Reserve

Torrey Pines
City Park

Black's
Beach

Sorrento Valley
Train Station

UCSD

La Jolla Village Dr

US Marine Corps
Air Station - Miramar

Miramar Rd

Mission Trails
Regional Park

La Jolla
Shores

Torrey Pines Rd

La Jolla

Soledad
Mtn (822ft)

Clairemont Mesa Blvd

San Diego River

Windansea
Beach

Big Rock

La Jolla Blvd

Pacific
Beach

Balboa Ave

Mission Gorge Rd

Tourmaline
Surfing Park

Crystal Pier

Grand Ave

Ingraham St

Mission Blvd

Tecolote
Canyon
National
Park

Linda Vista Rd

Qualcomm
Stadium

Mission
San Diego
de Alcalá

Navajo Rd

Lake
Murray

To El
Cajon
(10mi)

Mission
Bay

University
of San Diego

San Diego
State University

El Cajon Blvd

Mission
Beach

SeaWorld

San Diego
Sports Arena

Friars Rd

University
Heights

Normal
Heights

El Cajon Blvd

La Mesa

Ocean Beach
Park

Ocean
Beach Pier

Nimitz Blvd

Old
Town

Hillcrest

Washington St

University Ave

Fairmount Ave

East
San Diego

Point Loma
Ave

Ocean
Beach

209

Pacific Hwy

San Diego
International
Airport

163

Balboa
Park

805

94

Lemon
Grove

Catalina Blvd

Harbor Is

San Diego

See Downtown San
Diego Map (p320)

15

94

8th St

Highland Ave

15th Ave

Euclid Ave

Akins Ave

San Diego
Trolley

Paradise Valley
Rd

282

Coronado

Orange Ave

Hotel del
Coronado

75

Coronado
Bay Bridge

San Diego
Bay

Harbor Dr

5

805

Sweetwater Rv

Bonita Rd

54

Ferry to Catalina

Point
Loma

Old Point
Loma
Lighthouse

Silver Strand Blvd

National
City

San Diego Trolley

3rd Ave

S17

Chula
Vista

805

PACIFIC
OCEAN

75

Silver Strand
State Beach

Otay River

Palm Ave

Otay Mesa Border
Crossing (8mi)

Imperial
Beach

South
San Diego

5

905

San
Ysidro

Border
Field
State
Park

Tijuana River

Border
Crossing

Tijuana

MEX
1D

MEXICO

conventioneers at the nearby convention center and, especially on weekend nights, hordes of visitors flash their plastic money (and plastic cleavages).

NEW CHILDREN'S MUSEUM
San Diego's **New Children's Museum** (Map p320; ☎ 619-233-8792; www.thinkplay create.org; 200 W Island Ave; adult/senior over 65yr/child over 1yr $10/5/10; 10am-4pm Mon, Tue, Fri & Sat, 10am-6pm Thu, noon-4pm Sun;) is new both chronologically (opened 2008) and conceptually. Installations are designed by artists, so tykes can learn principles of movement and physics while simultaneously being exposed to art and working out the ants in their pants. Exhibits change every 18 months or so, but if we mention a climbing wall covered with graffiti art, a pillowfight in a room with mattress-like walls and human-powered 'legway' scooters, do you get the idea?

LITTLE ITALY
Italian immigrants, mostly fishers, began settling this rise of land just up from San Diego Bay in the 19th century. The community had its heyday in the 1920s, when Prohibition opened up new 'business opportunities' (read 'bootlegging'). Although construction of I-5 tore apart Little Italy's cultural fabric, the hardiest of the old family businesses have survived and, thanks to the city's recent urban renaissance, gained new clientele. Now old-world grocery stores alternate with slick cafes and high-end boutiques.

EMBARCADERO
The 100ft masts of the square-rigger *Star of India* will help you spot the **Maritime Museum** (Map p320; ☎ 619-234-9153; www.sdmaritime.com; 1492 N Harbor Dr; adult/child 6-17yr/senior over 62yr $14/8/11; 9am-8pm, to 9pm late May-early Sep;). Launched in

1863, the tall ship plied the England–India trade route and carried immigrants to New Zealand. The museum takes you on a journey through the history of water voyage, plus a fair amount of navy stuff.

The main attraction, though, is the **USS Midway Museum** (Map p320; ☎ 619-544-9600; www.midway.org; Navy Pier; adult/child 6-17yr/senior over 62yr/student $17/9/13/13; 10am-5pm;) aboard the Navy's longest-serving aircraft carrier (1945–91). A self-guided audiotour takes in berthing spaces, galley, sick bay and, of course, the flight deck with its restored aircraft, including an F-14 Tomcat. Allow at least two hours. Parking costs from $5.

BALBOA PARK
After receiving her botany degree in 1881, Kate O Sessions came to San Diego as a teacher but soon began working as a horticulturist, establishing gardens for the fashionable homes of the city's emerging elite. In 1892, in need of space for a nursery, she suggested to city officials that they allow her the use of 30 acres of city-owned Balboa Park in return for planting 100 trees a year and donating 300 others for placement throughout San Diego. The city agreed, and within a decade Balboa Park had shade trees, lawns, paths and flowerbeds. Today it's one of the country's finest urban parks, with flower gardens and shaded walks, tennis courts and swimming pools, museums and theaters, a velodrome, golf courses, an outdoor organ and one of the world's great zoos. The park is also the city's premier cultural center, with a cluster of theaters and museums along the El Prado promenade.

EL PRADO
Originally built for the 1915–16 Panama-California Exposition, these Spanish

colonial buildings are particularly beautiful in the morning and evening. The original exposition halls, which were mostly constructed out of stucco, chicken wire, plaster, hemp and horsehair, were only meant to be temporary. However, they proved so popular that, over the years, they have been gradually replaced with durable concrete replicas. The complex houses a number of museums.

CALIFORNIA BUILDING & MUSEUM OF MAN

As you enter Balboa Park via Laurel St, you cross the picturesque Cabrillo Bridge under an archway and into an area called the California Quadrangle, home to the **Museum of Man** (Map p320; ☎ 619-239-2001; www.museumofman.org; Plaza de California; adult/child 6-12yr/child 13-17yr & senior $10/5/7.50; ◷ 10am-4:30pm), which specializes in Native American artifacts from the American Southwest. The California Building's richly decorated **Tower of California** has become a symbol of San Diego itself. The museum exhibits world-class pottery, jewelry, baskets and other artifacts of cultures as diverse as the Maya, ancient Egyptians and Native Americans of the Southwest.

SAN DIEGO MUSEUM OF ART

The city's largest **museum** (Map p320; ☎ 619-232-7931; www.sdmart.org; Plaza de Panama; adult/child 6-17yr/student/senior over 65yr $10/4/7/8; ◷ 10am-5pm Tue-Sat, noon-5pm Sun, to 9pm Thu) has no truly famous works in its permanent collection, but includes a decent survey of European masters from the Renaissance to modernism, as well as some noteworthy American landscape paintings and Asian art. It was designed by San Diego architect William Templeton Johnson in the 16th-century Spanish style. The facade is particularly ornate, with sculptures depicting Spanish artists. The **Sculpture Garden** has pieces by Alexander Calder and Henry Moore.

TIMKEN MUSEUM OF ART

Distinctive for *not* being in imitation Spanish style, the **Timken** (Map p320; ☎ 619-239-5548; www.timkenmuseum.org; 1500 El Prado; admission free; ◷ 10am-4:30pm Tue-Sat, 1:30-4:30pm Sun) houses a significant collection of works by Rembrandt, Rubens and El Greco. There's also a remarkable selection of Russian icons. The museum is named after the Timken family, who rode to fame and fortune on the invention of the roller bearer used in horse-drawn carriages.

SPRECKELS ORGAN PAVILION

Heading south from Plaza de Panama, you can't miss the extravagantly curved colonnade that provides shelter for one of the world's largest **outdoor organs**. Donated by the Spreckels family of sugar fame, the organ has 4400 pipes, the smallest the size of a pencil and the largest nearly 32ft long. Free concerts are held at 2pm on Sunday afternoons and 7:30pm on Monday evenings from mid-June to August.

SAN DIEGO ZOO

If it slithers, crawls, stomps, swims, leaps or flies, chances are you'll find it in this justifiably world-famous **zoo** (Map p320; ☎ 619-231-1515; www.sandiegozoo.org; 2920 Zoo Dr; adult/child 3-11yr $28.50/18.50, with guided bus tour & aerial tram ride $35/26; ◷ from 9am, closing times vary; P ♿) on some 100 acres in northern Balboa Park. It's home to more than 3000 animals – representing more than 800 species – in a beautifully landscaped setting, including the new 7.5 acre Elephant Odyssey.

The zoo shines for its pioneering methods of housing and displaying animals to mimic their natural habitats, leading to a revolution in zoo design and, so the argument goes, to happier animals. The zoo also plays a major role in the protection of endangered species.

OLD TOWN

In 1769 Junípero Serra and Gaspar de Portolá established the first Spanish settlement in California on **Presidio Hill**, overlooking the valley of the San Diego River, though it was later moved to a more ready source of water. Until the 1860s, the cluster of wood and adobe buildings here, just below Presidio Hill, pretty much was San Diego. Today this area is called Old Town, and it's good for those who need to quell their beach-guilt with a spot of history.

Statue at the Museum of Man, Balboa Park

RICHARD CUMMINS

Old Town State Historic Park Visitors Center (☎ 619-220-5422; Wallace St; 🕙 10am-5pm) houses a California history slide show and a neat model of Old Town. Several guided tours of Old Town leave daily in summer. Other buildings around Old Town Plaza are a mix of historic and commercial: old dentist's office, tinsmith, shops selling candles and moccasins, early courthouse and Wells Fargo Bank, and the Casa de Estudillo, the adobe home of an early commandant.

Two blocks from the Old Town perimeter sits **Whaley House** (☎ 619-297-7511; 2482 San Diego Ave; admission $5; 🕙 10am-10pm in summer, to 4:30pm rest of year), the city's oldest brick building, having served as courthouse, theater and private residence. In the 1960s it was officially certified as haunted by the US Department of Commerce. Inside, the period furniture is watched over by knowledgeable costumed docents. Ask one of them about the theater's slanted stage.

El Campo Santo Cemetery, between Arista and Conde Sts on San Diego Ave, is a tiny, touching cemetery dating back to the earliest Spanish settlers. One grave near the gate was so placed because the man, 'Jesus the Indian,' died while 'completely drunk.' The construction of San Diego Ave accidentally covered many resting spots, so you may notice some medallions marking grave sites embedded in the street.

The walk from Old Town along Mason St to Presidio Hill (now Presidio Park) rewards you with views of the bay. On the site of the original mission stands the handsome **Serra Museum** (☎ 619-297-3258; 2727 Presidio Dr; adult/child 6-17yr/student/senior $5/2/4/4; 🕙 irregular hr), which highlights life during the city's rough-and-tumble early period.

DOWNTOWN SAN DIEGO

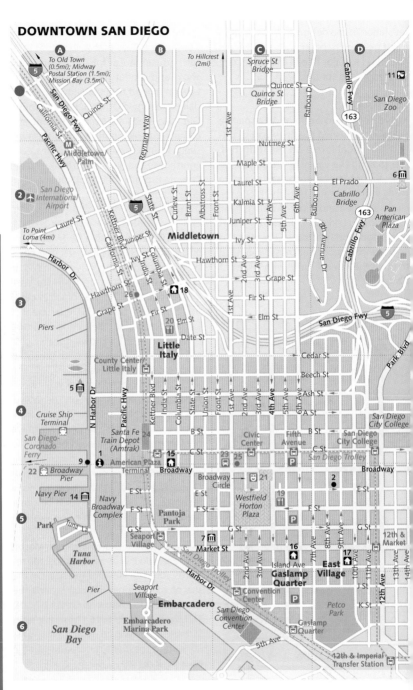

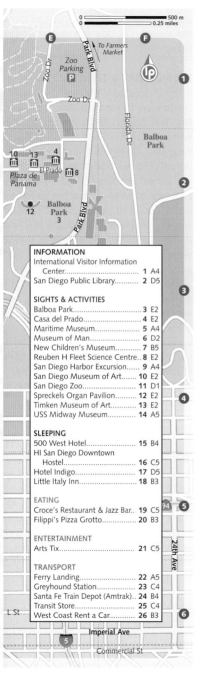

INFORMATION
International Visitor Information
Center..................................... 1 A4
San Diego Public Library........... 2 D5

SIGHTS & ACTIVITIES
Balboa Park..................................3 E2
Casa del Prado............................4 E2
Maritime Museum.......................5 A4
Museum of Man.........................6 D2
New Children's Museum...........7 B5
Reuben H Fleet Science Centre..8 E2
San Diego Harbor Excursion...... 9 A4
San Diego Museum of Art.......10 E2
San Diego Zoo..........................11 D1
Spreckels Organ Pavilion.........12 E2
Timken Museum of Art...........13 E2
USS Midway Museum.............14 A5

SLEEPING
500 West Hotel........................15 B4
HI San Diego Downtown
Hostel.................................16 C5
Hotel Indigo...........................17 D5
Little Italy Inn...........................18 B3

EATING
Croce's Restaurant & Jazz Bar.. 19 C5
Filippi's Pizza Grotto................20 B3

ENTERTAINMENT
Arts Tix....................................21 C5

TRANSPORT
Ferry Landing..........................22 A5
Greyhound Station..................23 C4
Santa Fe Train Depot (Amtrak)..24 B4
Transit Store............................25 C4
West Coast Rent a Car...........26 B3

The Old Town Transit Center, on the trolley line at Taylor St, is a stop for the Coaster commuter train, the San Diego Trolley (orange and blue lines) and buses 4 and 5 from downtown. Free parking lots surround the park.

UPTOWN, HILLCREST & NORTH PARK

Uptown consists roughly of the triangle north of downtown, east of Old Town and south of Mission Valley. As you head north from downtown along the western side of Balboa Park, you arrive at a series of bluffs that, in the late 19th century, became San Diego's most fashionable neighborhood – only those who owned a horse-drawn carriage could afford to live here. Known as Bankers Hill after some of the wealthy residents, these upscale heights had unobstructed views of the bay and Point Loma before I-5 went up.

As you head northward toward Hillcrest, detour across the 375ft **Spruce St Footbridge** (off Map p320), a 1912 suspension bridge built over a deep canyon between Front and Brant Sts. The nearby **Quince St Bridge** (Map p320), between 3rd and 4th Aves, is a wood-trestle structure built in 1905 and refurbished in 1988.

Just up from the northwestern corner of Balboa Park, you hit **Hillcrest**, the heart of Uptown. The neighborhood began its life in the early 20th century as a modest middle-class suburb, and it has evolved into a well-tended bohemian neighborhood with a large gay population. The **Hillcrest Gateway**, a neon sign that arches over University Ave at 5th Ave, marks the center of the action: coffeehouses, thrift shops and excellent restaurants in all price ranges. Hillcrest's **farmers market** (off Map p320; 5th Ave, cnr Normal & Lincoln Sts; ☺ 9am-1pm Sun) is tops for people-watching.

The bohemian vibe continues as you head east on University Ave to 30th St, where the North Park neighborhood is to San Diego what Brooklyn has become to New York City: an enclave of young bohemians making the world a better place through food, art and music. There are no sights per se here, but it's worth a stroll or a night out.

CORONADO

Directly across the bay from downtown San Diego, protecting the harbor from the ocean, Coronado is a civilized escape from the jumble of the city or the humble of the beaches. Follow the tree-lined, manicured median strip of Orange Ave toward the commercial center, Coronado Village, around the Hotel del Coronado. Then park your car; you won't need it again until you leave.

The story of Coronado is in many ways the story of that hotel. When the 'Hotel Del' was built in 1888, it was designed to 'be the talk of the western world.' While that's surely an exaggeration these days, the Del has plenty of lore to go along with its 26 acres of grounds overlooking an impossibly white beach. Its main building is a sprawling timber palace with billowing turrets, dramatic ballrooms and nearly 700 rooms, all connected by a maze of dark corridors, bright courtyards, and elegantly carved stairways.

Alternatively, the hourly **Coronado Ferry** (**☎ 619-234-4111; www.sdhe.com; adult/child under 4yr $3.25/free; 9am-10pm**) shuttles between the Broadway Pier on San Diego's Embarcadero to the ferry landing at the foot of Orange Ave in Coronado, from where it's about 1.5 miles to the Village. At the ferry landing, **Bikes & Beyond** (**☎ 619-435-7180; rental per hr/day from $7/30; 9am-8pm, call for seasonal hr**) is the most convenient place that rents out bicycles, or you can catch the hourly bus 904 to the rest of the island.

MISSION BAY & THE BEACHES

In the 18th century, the mouth of the San Diego River formed a shallow bay when the river flowed and a marshy swamp when it didn't – the Spanish called it False Bay. After WWII, a rare combination of civic vision and coastal engineering turned the swamp into a 7-sq-mile playground, with 27 miles of shoreline and 90 acres of public parks. The river was channeled to the sea, the bay was dredged and millions of tons of sludge were used to build islands, coves and peninsulas.

The attractions of Mission Bay run the gamut from luxurious resort hotels to free outdoor activities. Kite flying is popular in Mission Bay Park, beach volleyball is big on Fiesta Island, and there's delightful cycling and in-line skating on the miles of smooth bike paths. Sailing, windsurfing and kayaking dominate the waters in northwest Mission Bay.

SEAWORLD

Along with the zoo, **SeaWorld** (**Map p316; ☎ 619-226-3901, 800-257-4268; www.seaworld.com/seaworld/ca; 500 SeaWorld Dr; adult/child 3-9yr $65/55; 9am-11pm Jul–mid-Aug, shorter hr rest of year;**) is one of San Diego's most popular attractions. There's no denying that SeaWorld has an overtly commercial feel, with corporate logos slapped on every available surface, but it's entertaining and it can even be educational.

The biggest draws are live-animal shows, particularly Believe, featuring Shamu, the world's most famous killer whale, and his killer whale amigos who leap, dive and glide. Some may find the presentation a little, well, awww, but the animals induce awe. Dolphin shows are also popular. Avoid marked 'soak zones' near the tanks or you will get wet. There are also zoo-like animal exhibits, such as petting pools where you can touch the slippery surface of a dolphin or manta ray, along with a few amusement-park-style rides, such as the Journey to Atlantis flume. Lines can be long in summer and around holidays.

By car, take SeaWorld Dr off the I-5 less than a mile north of where it intersects with I-8. Parking is $12. Take bus 9 from Old Town.

MISSION BEACH & PACIFIC BEACH

Between the South Mission Jetty and Pacific Beach Point stretch 3 miles of pure, unadulterated SoCal beach scene. **Ocean Front Walk** bristles with joggers, in-line skaters and cyclists – the perfect place for scantily clad, pretty-people watching. Back from the beach, Mission Blvd consists of block after block of surf shops, burger joints and beer busts. Down at the Mission Beach end, beach bums pool their resources to rent small houses and apartments for the summer season.

The surf is good for beginners, bodyboarders and bodysurfers.

The family-style amusement park **Belmont Park** (☎ 858-488-0668; www.belmontpark.com; admission free) has been at the southern end of Mission Beach since 1925. One of the highlights is the classic wooden **Giant Dipper roller coaster** (admission $6; ⏰ from 11am). Check its website for the latest on opening hours.

Up in Pacific Beach (PB) the activity spreads further inland, especially along **Garnet Ave**, with bars, restaurants and vintage-clothing stores. At the ocean end of Garnet Ave, **Crystal Pier** is worth a gander. Built in the 1920s, it's still home to a cluster of rustic cabins built out over the waves.

Tourmaline Surfing Park, at the far northern end of the beach, is particularly popular with longboarders.

To get around, consider renting a bike or in-line skates. **Cheap Rentals** (☎ 800-941-7761, 858-488-2453; www.cheap-rentals.com;

EDDIE BRADY

The walrus is just one of the water creatures on show at SeaWorld

3689 Mission Blvd; ☼ 9am-7pm daily Mar-Aug, to 5pm Mon-Fri Sep-Feb) has low prices and rents out everything from bikes and skates (per hour/day $5/15) to surf equipment and baby joggers; it also accepts advance reservations.

LA JOLLA

Though technically part of San Diego, La Jolla feels a world apart because of both its conspicuous wealth and its location above San Diego's most photogenic stretch of coast.

LA JOLLA COASTLINE

A wonderful walking path skirts the La Jolla shoreline for half a mile. Its western end is at the **Children's Pool**, where a jetty protects the beach from big waves. Atop Point La Jolla, at the path's eastern end, **Ellen Browning Scripps Park** is a tidy expanse of green lawns and palm trees, with views of **La Jolla Cove** to the north. The cove's gem of a beach provides access to some of the best snorkeling around.

Experienced surfers can head to **Windansea Beach**, 2 miles south of downtown (take La Jolla Blvd south and turn west on Nautilus St). If you can brave the ire of the locals, you'll find that the surf's consistent peak works best at medium to low tide. You'll find a more civilized welcome immediately south at **Big Rock**, California's version of Hawaii's Pipeline.

LA JOLLA SHORES

Called 'the Shores,' this area northeast of La Jolla Cove is where La Jolla's cliffs meet the wide, sandy beaches that stretch north to Del Mar. To reach the **beach**, take La Jolla Shores Dr north from Torrey Pines Rd and turn west onto Av de la Playa. The waves here are gentle enough for beginner surfers, and kayakers can launch from the shore without much problem.

Some of the best beaches in the county are north of the Shores in **Torrey Pines City Park**, which covers the coastline from the Salk Institute up to the Torrey Pines

Seals make themselves at home on the beaches of La Jolla, San Diego

EDDIE BRADY

MARK NEWMAN

Cheetah, San Diego Wild Animal Park

SAN DIEGO WILD ANIMAL PARK

Since the early 1960s, the San Diego Zoological Society has been developing the **Wild Animal Park**, an 1800-acre, open-range zoo where herds of giraffes, zebras, rhinos and other animals roam the open valley floor. For an instant safari feel, board the Journey to Africa tram ride, which tours you around the second-largest continent in under half an hour.

Elsewhere, animals are in enclosures so naturalistic it's as if the humans are guests, and there's a petting enclosure and animal shows; pick up a map and schedule. Special programs, like a 'photo caravan,' zip-lining and even sleep-overs (yowza!) are available for an additional fee. A combined ticket for unlimited visits to both San Diego Zoo and the Wild Animal Park within a five-day period costs $60/43 per adult/child.

The park's just north of Hwy 78, 5 miles east of I-15 from the Via Rancho Pkwy exit. Plan a 45-minute transit by car from San Diego, except in rush hour when that figure can double. Parking is $9. For transit information contact **North San Diego County Transit District** (☎ 619-233-3004, from North County 800-266-6883; www.gonctd.com).

Things you need to know: off Map p316; ☎ 760-747-8702; www.sandiegozoo.org; 15500 San Pasqual Valley Rd, Escondido; adult/child 3-11yr $28.50/18.50, incl tram $35/26; from 9am, closing times vary;

State Reserve. **Torrey Pines Gliderport**, at the end of Torrey Pines Scenic Dr, is the place for hang gliders and paragliders to launch themselves into the sea breezes that rise over the high cliffs. Tandem flights are available if you can't resist trying it.

SLEEPING

Wherever you're looking to stay, San Diego has a variety of lodgings across all budget categories. If you're staying in Ocean Beach, near the flight path of San Diego International Airport, you might wish to bring earplugs. Always

⚓ DETOUR: LEGOLAND

Legoland California (☎ 760-918-5346; www.legoland.com/california; 1 Legoland Dr, Carlsbad; adult/child 3-12yr $65/55; ⏱ opens 10am, closing hours vary, closed most Tue & Wed Sep-May; ♿) is a fantasy environment built largely of those little colored plastic blocks. Many rides and attractions are targeted to elementary schoolers: a junior 'driving school,' a jungle cruise lined with Lego animals, pedaling wacky 'sky cruiser' cars on a track, and fairy-tale, princess, pirate, adventurer and dino-themed escapades. Sign up budding scientists (age 10 and over) on arrival at the park for an appointment for Mindstorms, where they can make computerized Lego robots. There are also lots of low-thrill activities like face painting.

ask about discounts; some are available only online.

Ocean Beach International Hostel (☎ 619-223-7873, 800-339-7263; www.california hostels.com; 4961 Newport Ave, Ocean Beach; dm $17-24; 🖳 🛜) OBI Hostel is a friendly, laid-back place popular with Europeans, and only a couple of blocks from the water. Perks include complimentary transport from the airport or bus and train stations, and free breakfast and wi-fi. Private rooms are first-come, first-served.

HI San Diego Downtown Hostel (Map p320; ☎ 619-525-1531, 888-464-4872, ext 156; www.sandiegohostels.org; 521 Market St, Gaslamp Quarter; dm/d/tr members $25/55/78, nonmembers $28/58/81; 🖳 🛜) Centrally located in the Gaslamp Quarter, this HI facility is conveniently near to public transportation and nightlife, and has a wide range of rooms. It provides a make-your-own pancake breakfast and has 24-hour access.

ourpick **500 West Hotel** (Map p320; ☎ 619-234-5252, 866-315-4251; www.500westhotel.com; 500 W Broadway, Downtown; s/d/tw with shared bath $59/69/79; 🖳 🛜) Inside the elegant beaux-arts former YMCA (the Y gym is still in the building; guests pay $5 per day for access), this place is almost too good to be true – tiny rooms are decked out with playful modern furniture, flat-screen TVs

and platform beds. The catch: bathrooms are shared, though they're private once you get inside and they are cleaned fastidiously round the clock.

Little Italy Inn (Map p320; ☎ 619-230-1600, 800-518-9930; www.littleitalyinn.com; 505 E Grape St, Little Italy; r $89-199; ✲ 🛜) It may lie in the shadow of the I-5, but this utterly charming boutique hotel manages to pull off 'urban getaway,' regardless. Staff go out of their way to make you feel at home, and the 23 uniquely decorated rooms are all tastefully appointed, with luxuries like plush bathrobes. Most rooms have private bathrooms, and others boast indulgent in-room spa bathrooms. Stylish continental breakfast included. Note: rooms facing Grape St are subject to traffic noise.

Park Manor Suites (☎ 619-291-0999, 800-874-2649; www.parkmanorsuites.com; 525 Spruce St, Hillcrest; r from $139; 🅿 🖳 🛜) This gay-friendly place, facing Balboa Park and a reasonable walk to central Hillcrest, used to be an apartment building, meaning mostly large rooms with kitchens and vast closets. Staff call the room decor 'old world,' though we'd say 'old' – take your pick. Breakfast is served on the top floor, with sweeping downtown-to-ocean views.

Hotel Indigo (Map p320; ☎ 619-727-4000, 877-846-3446; www.hotelindigo.com/sandiego; 509

9th Ave, Downtown; r from $200; 🛏 💻 🛜 🐾) San Diego's first hotel to be Leadership in Energy and Environmental Design–certified green, the Indigo (opened 2009) proves that environmentally friendly can still be comfy. This pet-friendly property has green roofs, sustainable materials in its construction, windows that open (there's a concept!) and cheery design motifs inspired by local waters and California poppies. Bonus: when the Padres are playing, you get to watch the game from your room or the roof deck.

La Valencia (☎ 858-454-0771, 800-451-0772; www.lavalencia.com; 1132 Prospect St, La Jolla; r from $295; P 💻 🛜 🍴) Publicity stills of Lon Chaney, Lillian Gish and Greta Garbo line the hallways of this 1926 landmark: pink-walled, Mediterranean-style, and designed by William Templeton Johnson. Among its 116 rooms, the ones in the main building are rather compact (befitting the era), but villas are spacious and, in any case, the property wins for Old Hollywood romance. If you don't stay, consider lifting a toast – and a pinkie – to the sunset from its Spanish-revival lounge, La Sala. Parking is $25.

Hotel del Coronado (☎ 619-435-6611, 800-468-3533; www.hoteldel.com; 1500 Orange Ave, Coronado; r from $380; P 💻 🛜 🍴) San Diego's iconic hotel, the Del provides more than a century of history, tennis courts, spa, shops, splashy restaurants, manicured grounds and a white-sand beach. Some rooms are in a 1970s seven-story building; book the original building. Parking is $25. For more on the Del's history, see p322.

EATING & DRINKING

Downtown restaurants tend to cater to conventioneers and businessfolk, but that doesn't mean you have to sacrifice in quality or atmosphere. You'd expect – and you'll find – Italian cuisine in Little Italy, hoppy, happy places in Hillcrest and high-toned dining in La Jolla. But don't overlook Old Town, touristy though it may be, for Mexican fare, and North Park is an up-and-coming neighborhood bubbling with eager gourmets.

CHEYENNE ROUSE

Welcome to Legoland (p326), Carlsbad

CENTRAL & SOUTHERN CALIFORNIA COAST

SAN DIEGO

Bread & Cie (☎ 619-683-9322; 350 University Ave, Hillcrest; pastries $2.50-5, sandwiches $7-8; ☷ 7am-7pm Mon-Fri, to 6pm Sat, 8am-6pm Sun; P) This clattery, chattery cafeteria-size bakery-deli makes the best bread around (with flavors like lemon sage, anise and fig, and caramelized onion), and carries a limited assortment of gourmet sandwiches. It's an excellent spot to eavesdrop on locals, especially in the mornings. The name 'Cie' is pronounced 'sea.'

Big Kitchen (☎ 619-234-5789; 3003 Grape St, South Park; mains $4-9.50; ☷ 7am-2pm Mon-Fri, 7:30am-3pm Sat & Sun; ☷) The heart and soul of funky South Park, just to the east of Balboa Park at 30th Ave, Big Kitchen welcomes all to its enclave of food, art, music and civic bonhomie. The omelets are stupendous, as is the challah French toast, and there's a whole page of breakfast combos named after regulars, including Whoopi Goldberg, who used to wait tables here.

Old Town Mexican Cafe (☎ 619-297-4330; 2489 San Diego Ave, Old Town; dishes $3-14; ☷ 7am-midnight) Watch the staff turn out fresh tortillas in the window while you wait for a table. Besides breakfast (great *chilaquiles* – soft tortilla chips in mole), there's a big bar (try the Old Town ultimate margarita) and rambling dining room serving famous *machacas* (shredded pork with onions and peppers).

Filippi's Pizza Grotto (Map p320; ☎ 619-232-5095; 1747 India St, Little Italy; dishes $5-17; ☷ 9am-10pm Sun & Mon, 9am-10:30pm Tue-Thu, 9am-11:30pm Fri & Sat; ☷) There are often lines out the door for Filippi's old-school Italian cooking (pizza, spaghetti and ravioli) served on red and white-checked tablecloths in the dining room. The front of the shop is an excellent Italian deli.

Hash House a Go Go (☎ 619-298-4646; 3628 5th Ave, Hillcrest; breakfast $8-16; ☷ 7.30am-2pm Tue-Fri, 7.30am-2.30pm Sat-Mon, dinner

Tue-Sun) This buzzing bungalow makes biscuits and gravy straight outta Carolina; towering eggs Benedict, large-as-your-head pancakes and – wait for it – hash seven different ways. Come hungry. Eat your whole breakfast and you may not need dinner.

our pick Urban Solace (☎ 619-295-6464; 3823 30th St, North Park; lunch $8-16, dinner $9-18; ☷ 11:30am-10pm Mon-Thu, 11:30am-11pm Fri, 5-11pm Sat, 5-9pm Sun) You know those hip young gourmets in North Park? Here's where you'll find them, reveling in creative comfort food: meat loaf of ground lamb, fig, pine nuts and feta; mac and cheese with duck confit; chicken and dumplings. The setting's surprisingly chill for such great eats; maybe it's the cocktails, like a mojito made with bourbon.

Croce's Restaurant & Jazz Bar (Map p320; ☎ 619-233-4355; 802 5th Ave, Downtown; breakfast & lunch $7-19, dinner $23-35; ☷ 5:30pm-midnight Mon-Fri, 10am-midnight Sat & Sun) This sizzling restaurant is a pioneer of the Gaslamp. It's also Ingrid Croce's tribute to her late husband, singer Jim Croce. The contemporary American menu hits few false notes, as do the musicians who perform nightly at the jazz bar.

our pick Whisknladle (☎ 858-551-7575; 1044 Wall St, La Jolla; dishes $9-30; ☷ lunch & dinner) This newcomer has earned plenty of kudos for its 'Slow Food' preparations of local, farm-fresh ingredients, served on a breezy covered patio. The menu changes daily, but it's always clever. So are the cocktails (the London's Burning mixes gin and jalapeño water).

ENTERTAINMENT

Check the San Diego *Reader* or the Thursday edition of the San Diego *Union-Tribune* for the latest happenings around town. **Arts Tix** (Map p320; sdartstix.com; 3rd Ave & Broadway, Downtown; ☷ 11am-6pm Tue-Thu,

10am-6pm Fri & Sat, 10am-5pm Sun), in a kiosk on Broadway outside Horton Plaza, has half-price tickets for same-day evening or next-day matinee performances and discounted tickets to all types of other events.

GETTING THERE & AWAY

AIR

All major US carriers serve **San Diego International Airport** (SAN; Lindbergh Field; Map p316; ☎ 619-400-2400; www.san.org; 3665 N Harbor Dr), about 3 miles west of downtown; plane-spotters can experience the thrill of watching jets come in for a landing over Balboa Park. If coming from LA, air fares fluctuate and it may be less expensive to travel by bus or train. Ground transportation may also makes more sense after allowing for check-in times for the 30-minute flight.

TRAIN

Amtrak trains arrive at and depart from the lovely **Santa Fe Train Depot** (Map p320; 1050 Kettner Blvd) at the western end of C St. Amtrak's *Pacific Surfliner* runs several

times daily to LA ($34, three hours) and Santa Barbara ($47, six hours).

GETTING AROUND

Car is the main mode of transport, but you can reach most places on public transportation. Local buses and trolley lines are run by the **Metropolitan Transit System** (MTS; ☎ 619-233-3004, 24hr recorded info 619-685-4900; www.sdmts. com), and several other bus companies serve surrounding areas. All sorts of local public-transportation tickets, maps and information are available from the **Transit Store** (Map p320; ☎ 619-234-1060; 102 Broadway; 🕑 9am-5pm Mon-Fri).

TO/FROM THE AIRPORT

Bus 992 ('the Flyer,' $2.25) operates at 10- to 15-minute intervals between the airport and downtown, with stops along Broadway. Buses leave between 5am and 1am and make several stops before heading north on Harbor Dr to the airport.

Airport shuttles such as **Super Shuttle** (☎ 800-974-8885; www.supershuttle.com) charge

Old Town State Historic Park (p319)

RICHARD CUMMINS

about $13 to downtown, but these tend to travel at their own pace, often making stops en route. If you're going to the airport, call the shuttle a day ahead. The taxi fare to downtown from the airport is $10 to $15.

BOAT

San Diego Harbor Excursion (☎ 619-234-4111; www.sdhe.com; one way $3.25) runs hourly ferries between Broadway Pier in San Diego's Embarcadero and the San Diego Convention Center and Coronado. It also operates a water taxi (☎ 619-235-8294; per person $7; ⏰ 9:30am-8pm Mon-Fri, 9:30am-10pm Sat & Sun) connecting San Diego, Coronado and other shore points, by reservation.

CAR

All the big-name rental companies have convenient desks at the airport. The western terminal at the airport has free direct phones to a number of car-rental companies – you can call several and then get a courtesy bus to the company of your choice.

For contact details of the big-name rental companies, including Avis, Budget and Hertz, see p392. Some of the smaller, independent companies – such as West Coast Rent a Car (Map p320; ☎ 619-544-0606; 834 W Grape St) in Little Italy – may have lower rates and offer more relaxed conditions. Ecoconscious travelers can try LA-based Simply Hybrid (p393).

TAXI

Taxi flag fall is $2.40, plus $2.60 for each additional mile. Some established companies:
San Diego Cab (☎ 619-226-8294)
Yellow Cab (☎ 619-234-6161)

TRAIN

A commuter train service, the Coaster, leaves Santa Fe Train Depot (Map p320) and runs up the coast to North County, with stops including Solana Beach, Encinitas, Carlsbad and Oceanside. In the city of San Diego, it stops at the Sorrento Valley station (where there's a connecting shuttle to UCSD) and Old Town. Tickets

San Diego Bay, Embarcadero and Downtown

WITOLD SKRYPCZAK

Old Town Trolley, San Diego

RICHARD CUMMINS

are available from vending machines at stations, payable with cash, Visa, MasterCard and most debit cards. Fares range from $5 to $6.50 depending on distance. There are about 20 trains daily in each direction Monday to Friday, 10 on Saturday and none on Sunday.

Bicycles are permitted on board Coaster trains.

For information, contact **Regional Transit** (☎ 619-233-3004, from North County 511; http://transit.511sd.com).

TROLLEY

Municipal trolleys (not to be confused with Old Town Trolley tourist buses) operate on three main lines. From the transit center across from the Santa Fe Train Depot, Blue Line trolleys go south to San Ysidro (Mexico border) and north to the Old Town Transit Center. The Green Line runs from Old Town east through Mission Valley including to Mission San Diego de Alcalá. The Orange Line connects the Convention Center with the rest of downtown, but otherwise it's less useful for visitors. Trolleys run between about 4:15am and 1am daily at 15-minute intervals during the day, and every 30 minutes in the evening. The Blue Line continues limited all-night service on Saturday. Fares are $2.50 per ride, valid for two hours from the time of purchase at vending machines on the station platforms.

For information, contact **MTS** (☎ 619-233-3004, 24hr recorded info 619-685-4900; www.sdmts.com).

ARTS & POP CULTURE

DAVID PEEVERS

California is the place to be for aspiring artists

Thanks to the movie industry, perhaps no other city can claim the pop-cultural influence that Los Angeles exerts worldwide. Meanwhile, writers and musicians have been seeking inspiration in gritty LA and bohemian San Francisco for decades. Southern California in particular has proved to be fertile ground for new architectural styles.

CINEMA & TELEVISION

California's major export – film – is a powerful presence in the lives of not only Americans but people around the world. Images of California are distributed far beyond its borders, ultimately reflecting back upon the state itself. With increasing regularity, Hollywood films feature California as both a setting and a topic and, in some cases, almost as a character.

Today, the high cost of filming in LA has sent location scouts beyond the San Fernando Valley (where most movie and TV studios are found) and north of the border to Canada, where they're welcomed with open arms in 'Hollywood North.' A few production companies are still based in the Bay Area, including Pixar Animation Studios, Francis Ford Coppola's American Zoetrope and George Lucas' Industrial Light & Magic, made up of high-tech gurus who produce computer-generated special effects for Hollywood blockbusters.

LITERATURE

Californians read more than movie scripts: they make up the largest market for books in the US, and read more than the national average. Skewing the curve is bookish San

Francisco, with more writers, playwrights and book purchases per capita than any other US city.

The West Coast has long drawn artists and writers, and today California's resident literary community is as strong as ever with such talent as: Alice Walker, Pulitzer prize–winning author of *The Color Purple* (1982); progressive feminist poet Adrienne Rich; Chilean-American novelist Isabel Allende; Amy Tan, author of such popular fiction as *The Joy Luck Club* (1989); Maxine Hong Kingston, coeditor of the landmark anthology *The Literature of California* (2000); Dave Eggers, the hipster behind *McSweeney's* quarterly literary journal; and Michael Chabon, author of the Pulitzer prize–winning *The Amazing Adventures of Kavalier and Clay* (2000).

Few writers nail California culture as well as Joan Didion. She's best known for her collection of essays, *Slouching Towards Bethlehem* (1968), which takes a caustic look at 1960s flower power and Haight-Ashbury. Tom Wolfe also put '60s San Francisco in perspective with *The Electric Kool-Aid Acid Test* (1968), which follows Ken Kesey's band of Merry Pranksters, who began their acid-laced 'magic bus' journey near Santa Cruz. Charles Bukowski's semiautobiographical novel *Post Office* (1971) captures down-and-out Downtown LA. Richard Vasquez' *Chicano* (1971) takes a dramatic look at LA's Latino barrio.

Back in the 1930s, San Francisco and LA became the capitals of the pulp detective novel, often made into classic noir films. Dashiell Hammett (*The Maltese Falcon,* 1930) made San Francisco's fog a sinister character. The king of hard-boiled crime writers was Raymond Chandler (*The Big Sleep,* 1939), who thinly disguised Santa Monica as shadowy Bay City. A renaissance of noir crime fiction has been masterminded by James Ellroy (*LA Confidential,* 1990) and Walter Mosley (*Devil in a Blue Dress,* 1990), whose Easy Rawlins detective novels are set in LA's South Central 'hood.

MUSIC

From smoky jazz clubs that once filled San Francisco's North Beach to hard-edged West Coast rap and hip-hop born in South Central LA, California has rocked the world.

In the 1960s, Jim Morrison and The Doors busted onto the Sunset Strip, and San Francisco launched the psychedelic-rock revolution with big-name acts such as the Grateful Dead and Janis Joplin. The late '70s and early '80s saw the birth of California's

CALIFORNIA IN FOCUS

ARTS & POP CULTURE

⤜ BEHIND THE CURTAIN

Learn about the world of film and TV production while touring a working studio. Reservations recommended; bring photo ID.

Paramount Pictures (off Map p71; ☎ 323-956-1777; www.paramountstudios.com/special-events/tours.html; 5555 Melrose Ave, Hollywood; tours $40; ☯ Mon-Fri) The only remaining studio in Hollywood proper runs two-hour tram tours of its lot, by reservation only.

Warner Bros Studios (Map p71; ☎ 818-972-8687; www.wbstudiotour.com; 3400 Riverside Dr, Burbank; tours $48; ☯ Mon-Fri) This authentic behind-the-scenes look kicks off with a greatest hits video (*Rebel Without a Cause, Harry Potter* etc) before you travel by mini-tram to sound stages, backlot sets, and costumes and set building departments.

own brand of punk, including the LA-based bands X and Black Flag, and the Dead Kennedys in San Francisco. The funk-punk sound of the Red Hot Chili Peppers exploded out of LA in the late '80s, while the early '90s generated pop punksters blink-182 in San Diego and Green Day in the Bay Area.

LA today is the hotbed for West Coast rap and hip-hop. At the turn of the 21st century, the Bay Area was producing underground artists and birthed the 'hyphy movement,' a reaction against the increasing commercialization of hip-hop.

ARCHITECTURE

California's architecture, a fruitful jumble of styles, is as diverse as the state's population. The late 18th and early-19th centuries saw the construction of Spanish colonial missions built with materials that were on hand: adobe, limestone and grass, and during the mid-19th-century Gold Rush, California's nouveau riche started constructing grand mansions. Victorian architecture, especially the showy Queen Anne style, is most prevalent in NorCal cities such as San Francisco.

Simplicity was the hallmark of the arts-and-crafts style, a reaction against the mass production of the industrial revolution. Modernism has characteristics such as boxlike building shapes, open floor plans, plain facades and abundant glass, and was adapted to residential houses that reflected SoCal's see-and-be-seen culture. More recently, postmodernism sought to reemphasize the structural form of the building and the space around it; examples in LA include Richard Meier's Getty Center (p66) and Frank Gehry's Walt Disney Concert Hall (p65).

VISUAL ARTS

Pristine, poolside SoCal aesthetics competed with San Francisco's love of rough-and-readymade 1950s Beat collage, 1960s psychedelic Fillmore posters, earthy

SABRINA DALBESIO

The Grateful Dead house, at 710 Ashbury St, is distinctive of the architecture of the Haight (p108), San Francisco

THE BEST

SABRINA DALBESIO

San Francisco Museum of Modern Art (p100)

BIG CITY ART MUSEUMS

- **San Francisco Museum of Modern Art (SFMOMA)** (p100)
- **Getty Center, Los Angeles** (p66)
- **LACMA, Los Angeles** (p72)
- **MH de Young Fine Arts Museum, San Francisco** (p102)

'70s funk and beautiful-mess punk, and '80s graffiti and skate culture. Today, the California contemporary art scene brings all these influences together with muralist-led social commentary, California's cutting-edge technology, and an obsessive dedication to craft. From this new-media milieu emerged San Francisco–raised Matthew Barney, who debuted his *Cremaster Cycle* videos at SFMOMA (p100). In LA, the Museum of Contemporary Art (p65) puts on provocative and avant-garde shows. To see Californian art at its most exciting and experimental, don't miss the alternative gallery scene in Culver City and converted warehouses of LA's Chinatown, and check out the indie art spaces in San Francisco's Mission District and laboratory-like galleries and museums in Yerba Buena Arts District.

CALIFORNIA IN FOCUS

ARTS & POP CULTURE

THEATER

In your California dream you were discovered by a movie talent scout, but most Californian actors get their start in theater. Home to about 25% of the nation's professional actors, LA is the second-most influential city in America for theater, and San Francisco has been the US hub for experimental theater since the 1960s.

DANCE

In LA and San Francisco, dance has always leaned toward the experimental and the avant-garde, with Martha Graham, Alvin Ailey and Bella Lewitzky pioneering new movements in Los Angeles. LA's American Repertory Dance Company is dedicated to keeping alive the legacy of early-20th-century modern dances, including those by San Francisco dance pioneer Isadora Duncan. Founded in 1933, internationally renowned San Francisco Ballet (p116) is America's oldest resident professional ballet company and still draws dancers from all over the globe and commissions international works.

CALIFORNIA IN FOCUS

BEACHES & OUTDOOR ACTIVITIES

BEACHES & OUTDOOR ACTIVITIES

ANGUS OBORN

Crescent Bay, Laguna Beach (p312)

Californians know they're spoiled silly with spectacular natural riches, so they express their gratitude by taking every chance to hit the trails, hop into the saddle or grab a paddle. Now it's your turn: go kayaking under sea arches and along rocky coastlines, launch your paraglider off a cliff and float over the glistening ocean, spot a whale breaching off the bow of your boat or make your California dreamin' come true with a surfing lesson. This state may be where car and mall culture gained a foothold, but the wise among us know that in reality, it's all about the great outdoors.

SWIMMING

If lazing on the beach and taking quick dips in the Pacific is what you've got in mind, look to Southern California (SoCal). Northern California waters are unbearably cold year-round, with a dangerously high swell in places and rocky beaches that make swimming uninviting. Once you get far enough south, let's say Santa Barbara, the beaches become golden and sandy, and the weather and the waters turn balmy. By the time you hit Los Angeles, Orange County (aka 'the OC') and San Diego, you'll find SoCal beach culture in full swing – at least during summer. SoCal beaches can be chilly and too stormy for swimming in winter.

The biggest hazards along the coast are riptides and dangerous ocean currents. Obey all posted signs on beaches. If you get caught in a riptide, which pulls you away from shore, don't fight it or you'll get exhausted and drown. Instead, swim parallel to the shoreline and, once the current stops pulling you out, swim back to shore.

WINDSURFING & KITESURFING

Experienced windsurfers tear up the waves up and down the coast, while newbies (or those who want a mellower ride) skim along calm bays and protected beaches. There's almost always a breeze, with the best winds from April through October, but the water is cold year-round and, unless you're a polar bear, a wet suit is a necessity. Any place that has good windsurfing has good kiteboarding. Look for surfers doing aerial acrobatics while parachute-like kites propel them over the waves.

ANTHONY PIDGEON

THE BEST

Getting ready to surf, La Jolla (p324)

SURF BEACHES

- **Surfrider, Malibu** (p61)
- **Steamers Lane, Santa Cruz** (p280)
- **La Jolla Shores, La Jolla** (p324)
- **Leadbetter Beach, Santa Barbara** (p303)

SURFING

Surf's up! Are you down? Even if you never set foot on a board – and we, like, totally recommend that you do, dude – there's no denying the influence of surfing on every aspect of California beach life. Invented by Pacific Islanders, surfing first washed ashore in 1907, when business tycoon Henry Huntington invited Irish Hawaiian surfer George Freeth to LA to help promote real-estate developments – California has never been the same since.

The state has plenty of easily accessible world-class surf spots, with the lion's share in SoCal. You won't find many killer spots north of the San Francisco Bay Area, but if your travels take you up there, check out www.northerncaliforniasurfing.com. Famous surf spots southbound include Mavericks, past Half Moon Bay; Steamers Lane (p280) in Santa Cruz; Rincon Point, outside Santa Barbara; Surfrider (p61) in Malibu; and Trestles, south of San Clemente in the OC. All are point breaks, known for their consistently clean, glassy, big waves.

Generally speaking, the most powerful swells arrive in winter (especially at Mavericks, world-famous for its big-wave surfing competition), while early summer sees the flattest conditions (except at Trestles, which still goes off then) but also warmer waters. Bring or rent a wet suit.

Check **Surfline** (www.surfline.com) for conditions and webcams.

SCUBA DIVING & SNORKELING

All along the coast, rocky reefs, shipwrecks and kelp forests teem with sea creatures ready for their close-up. Santa Catalina Island and Channel Islands National Park are hot spots for diving and snorkeling. Thanks to the Monterey Bay National Marine Sanctuary, Monterey Bay (p278) offers year-round, world-renowned diving and snorkeling, though you'll need to don a wet suit. Nearby Point Lobos State Reserve (p291) is another diving gem. North of San Francisco, dive boats depart from windy Bodega Bay (p148).

KAYAKING

Few watersports are as accessible or as much fun for the whole family as kayaking. Prior experience is rarely necessary. Lots of rental outfitters can be found along the Central Coast, for example in Morro Bay, whose waters are protected by a gorgeous 4-mile sand spit, and from Monterey north to Santa Cruz, especially around Elkhorn Slough. Sausalito (p140) in Marin County is a mere paddle's-length away from San Francisco's skyline, while sheltered Tomales Bay at Point Reyes National Seashore (p146) and Bodega Bay (p148) are also popular spots. As you head further up the chilly north coast, various small towns offer challenging put-in points for experienced sea kayakers. On the Redwood Coast, you can take a scenic spin around Humboldt Bay, Trinidad Cove or Humboldt Lagoons State Park, with outfitters in Eureka (p162) and Arcata (p164). Meanwhile, SoCal's warmer waters beckon sea kayakers to Santa Catalina Island and Channel Islands National Park offshore, and San Diego's Mission Bay (p322) and La Jolla (p324).

WHALE-WATCHING

During summer, majestic gray whales feed in the Arctic waters between Alaska and Siberia, and every October they start moving south down the Pacific coast to the sheltered lagoons of the Gulf of California in Mexico's Baja California. While there, pregnant whales give birth to calves weighing up to 1500lb (who go on to live up to 60 years, grow to 50ft in length and weigh up to 40 tons). Around mid-March, these whales turn around and head back to the Arctic. Luckily for us, during their 12,000-mile round-trip, these whales pass just off the California coast.

Mothers tend to keep newborn calves closer to shore for safety, so your best chances of catching a glimpse may be during the whales' northbound migration. You can try your luck from shore (free, but you're less likely to see anything and are more removed from the action) or by taking a boat cruise. A few of the best dockside spots from which to point

DOUGLAS STEAKLEY

Humpback whale, Monterey Bay (p282)

JOHN ELK III

Vernal Falls, Yosemite National Park (p229)

CALIFORNIA IN FOCUS

BEACHES & OUTDOOR ACTIVITIES

your binoculars include Point Reyes Lighthouse (p147), Point Pinos Lighthouse (p288) on the Monterey Peninsula, and Cabrillo National Monument at San Diego's Point Loma.

HIKING

California is perfect for exploring on foot, whether you've got your heart set on peak-bagging in the Sierra Nevada, trekking to desert palm-tree oases, rambling among the world's tallest, largest or most ancient trees, or simply heading for a coastal walk accompanied by booming surf. The best trails are generally found among the jaw-dropping scenery in national and state parks, national forests and wilderness areas. You can choose from an infinite variety of routes, from easy, interpretive nature walks negotiable by wheelchairs and baby strollers to multiday backpacking routes through rugged wilderness. Parks and forests almost always have a visitors center or ranger station with clued-in staff to offer route suggestions, trail-specific tips and weather forecasts. The most popular trails may be subject to daily quotas and require wilderness permits.

CAMPING

All across California, campers are absolutely spoiled for choice. Pitch a tent beside alpine lakes and streams with views of snaggle-toothed Sierra Nevada peaks, along gorgeous strands of southern California sand or on the wilder, windswept beaches of the north coast. Take shelter underneath redwoods, the tallest trees on earth, from south of San Francisco north to the Oregon border. Inland, deserts are magical places to camp, especially next to sand dunes on full-moon nights.

To reserve sites at national parks and on federal lands, use **Recreation.gov** (☎ 518-885-3639, 877-444-6777; www.recreation.gov). For California state parks, East Bay regional parks and private campgrounds statewide, check out **ReserveAmerica** (☎ 916-638-5883, 800-444-7275; www.reserveamerica.com).

ROCK CLIMBING

Rock hounds can test their mettle on world-class climbs on the big walls and granite domes of Yosemite National Park (p229), where the climbing season runs from April through October. In the warmest summer months, climbers move camp from the Yosemite Valley to Tuolumne Meadows, off Tioga Rd, which also has good bouldering. In SoCal, Joshua Tree National Park (p256) is another climbing mecca, with over 8000 established routes ranging from boulders and cracks to multipitch faces; the climbing season runs year-round, but beware of blistering summer heat. Both of these national parks are excellent places to try the sport for the first time; outdoor outfitters offer guided climbs and instruction, costing from $120 per day. Other prime spots for bouldering and rock climbing include Bishop in the Eastern Sierra; Sequoia & Kings Canyon National Parks (p236), south of Yosemite; and outside Truckee, near Lake Tahoe.

CYCLING & MOUNTAIN BIKING

Top up those tires and strap on that helmet! California is outstanding cycling territory, whether you're off for a leisurely spin by the beach, an adrenaline-fueled mountain ride or a multiday cycling tour along the Pacific Coast Hwy.

> **THE BEST**

LEE FOSTER

Lake Tahoe Rim Trail, Lake Tahoe (p222)

LONG-DISTANCE WALKS

- **Pacific Crest Trail** (PCT; www.pcta. org) A 2650-mile journey from Mexico to Canada.
- **John Muir Trail** A 211-mile route linking Yosemite Valley and Mt Whitney along the backbone of the Sierra Nevada.
- **Tahoe Rim Trail** (www.tahoerimtrail. org) For 150 miles, trace the footsteps of early pioneers, Basque shepherds and Washoe tribespeople for inspirational views of the mountains and Lake Tahoe.

With few exceptions, mountain biking is not allowed in wilderness areas or on trails in national or state parks, but you may usually cycle on paved or dirt roads that are open to cars. Mountain bikers are allowed on single-track trails in national forests and Bureau of Land Management (BLM) land, but must yield to hikers and stock animals.

WHITE-WATER RAFTING

California has scads of mind-blowing rivers, and feeling their surging power is like taking a thrilling ride on nature's roller coaster. Sure, there are serene floats suitable for picnics with grandma and the kiddies, but then there are others. White-water giants swelled by the snowmelt that rip through sheer canyons. Roaring cataracts that hurtle you through chutes where gushing water compresses through a 10ft gap between menacing boulders. Pour-overs, voracious hydraulics, endless Class III-IV standing waves wrenching at your shoulders as you scream and punch on through to the next onslaught. Your thoughts are

MARK NEWMAN

Rock-climber, Joshua Tree National Park (p256)

reduced to two simple words: 'survive' and 'damn!' Too much for you? Between these two extremes run myriad others suited to the abilities of any wannabe river rat.

HANG GLIDING & PARAGLIDING

For a memorable, fly-like-a-bird experience – and perhaps the most expensive 20 minutes of your life so far – you can't beat gliding. Very roughly speaking, paragliding is to hang gliding as a plane is to a hot-air balloon.

Some of the most unbelievable vistas and best gliding schools are found on the California coast. A tandem flight (the only kind you can do as a first-timer) either paragliding or hang gliding costs $150 to $200 a pop, with the former on the cheaper side of the spectrum. Most companies won't allow kids under 12 to take the leap.

Popular gliding spots include Torrey Pines Gliderport (p325) in La Jolla, north of San Diego, and Santa Barbara. Even if you have no intention of going up yourself, you can swing by and watch the fun. For more gliding locations up and down the California coast, check www.caoutdoors.com for listings.

CALIFORNIA IN FOCUS

CALIFORNIA CUISINE

CALIFORNIA CUISINE

California-style meatloaf sandwich

JERRY ALEXANDER

California cuisine has risen to an art form in the Golden State. In an age where chefs now vie with movie stars for fame, any California foodie worth their weight in Meyer lemon–infused French sea salt knows the difference between arugula and radicchio. What's come to represent California cuisine need not be fancy; a good surfer-worthy fish taco is just as coveted as a roasted quail, drizzled with raspberry coulis. In California, it's all about the ingredients.

If not for the hundreds of cultures and nationalities who have immigrated to California over the past 200 years, Californians might never eat. Fusion dominates menus, from kimchi tacos to vegan soul food. You'll find that California cooks are generous about sharing credit with the local producers who provide the stellar ingredients – many cheesemakers, wineries, farms, ranches and fisheries are credited by name on California menus, like actors in a film.

REGIONAL CUISINE
LOS ANGELES
Most of California's produce is grown in the hot, irrigated Central Valley, south of the Bay Area, but road-tripping foodies tend to bolt through this sunny stretch of fast-food speed traps to reach Los Angeles in time for dinner. Authenticity-trippers know exactly where to go: directly to Koreatown for tender *kalbi* (marinated barbecued beef short ribs) and strong *soju* (barley spirits), East LA for tacos *al pastor* (with marinated fried

pork) and margaritas on the rocks, and Little Tokyo for sashimi faceted like diamonds and palate-purifying *junmai* sake.

SAN FRANCISCO

Although San Francisco ballooned from a sleepy cove of 800 people in 1849 to a Gold Rush boomtown of 25,000 by 1850, at that time there was only one woman per 100 men – but there were hundreds of eateries, ranging from ubiquitous Chinese noodle shops to struck-it-rich French fine dining. The first Italian restaurant in America opened in San Francisco's North Beach in 1886, serving the ever-popular cioppino (Dungeness crab stew).

Even 160 years after that boom went bust, there's still one restaurant for every 28 San Franciscans – that's 10 times more than any other North American city. All that competition keeps chefs innovating and prices lower than you'd find for equivalent dining experiences elsewhere. Chinese, Mexican, French and Italian restaurants remain perennial local favorites, along with more recent San Francisco crazes for sushi, tandoori and pho (Vietnamese noodles). San Francisco has more award-winning chefs per capita than any other US city (sorry, New York). Today the busiest SF tourist attraction is no longer the Golden Gate Bridge, but the local, sustainable, seasonal bounty at the San Francisco Ferry Building Farmers Market (p120).

THE BAY AREA & NORTHERN CALIFORNIA

Just as influential (or more) as San Francisco, the Bay Area and Northern California has changed the way the world looks at food. California Cuisine was perfected in Berkeley at Alice Waters' iconic Chez Panisse (p134), and world-renowned food writer and expert Michael Pollan is a journalism professor at nearby UC Berkeley.

Scratch any food trend's surface and you'll likely find it happening in the Bay Area and Northern California. Marin County, one of the wealthiest in the United States, can afford to make sustainable and organic food a priority. In Sausalito, Fish (p142) and the restaurant at Cavallo Point (p142) use a majority of organic produce and meat.

WINE COUNTRY

George Yount (of Yountville fame) was the first Napa resident to plant a few grapes in the 1830s, and before the 20th century, there were already almost 150 wineries in the region. The climate and soil were a perfect mix for agriculture, and the natural hot springs around Calistoga brought tourists in from San Francisco. Even before Prohibition, the Wine Country was

▶THE BEST

SABRINA DALBESIO

Tagliatelle at Delfina (p112)

NEIGHBORHOOD SPOTS IN SAN FRANCISCO

- **Delfina** (p112)
- **La Taquería** (p110)
- **La Boulange** (p111)
- **Magnolia Brewpub** (p111)
- **Molinari's Delicatessen** (p114)

CALIFORNIA IN FOCUS

CALIFORNIA CUISINE

THE BEST

BRENT WINEBRENNER

Fresh fish is often on the menu in California

GOURMET HOT SPOTS IN NORTHERN CALIFORNIA

- La Petite Rive, Elk (p152)
- Cafe Beaujolais, Mendocino (p154)
- Restaurant 301 at Hotel Carter, Eureka (p163)
- Folie Douce, Arcata (p166)

cemented as a destination for folks with a taste for the good life.

By the 1930s Sonoma was supplying excellent jack cheese to accompany local wine; local chefs had more unusual pairings in mind. Chef Thomas Keller transformed Yountville's saloon-turned-restaurant French Laundry (p192) into an international foodie landmark in 1994, showcasing local produce and casual elegance in multicourse feasts. Other chefs eager to make their names and fortunes among free-spending wine-tasters flocked to the area, and some great options are featured in the Wine Country chapter (p175). If you'd like to learn a thing or two about cooking, you can sign up for day or weekend courses, or a full-time chef training program at the Culinary Institute of America (p192) in St Helena.

SIERRA NEVADA & THE DESERTS

Outside of the Palm Springs area, the eastern half of California doesn't offer quite as much California cuisine dining options as do the coastal regions. While most of the state's food comes from the farmlands around Sacramento, Fresno and Bakersfield, most of these ingredients are sautèed, poached and consumed west of the breadbasket region.

We're not sure if it's a good or bad sign, but our favorite restaurant in the Sierra Nevada mountain range is at a gas station. Every skier or hiker worth his or her weight in a pair of telemarks has an almost cultlike devotion to the Whoa Nellie Deli (p243), where you can fill up on wild boar ribs, mushroom bisque and unleaded.

CENTRAL & SOUTHERN CALIFORNIA COAST

In towns like Monterey (p282), Santa Barbara (p300) and San Luis Obispo (p296), you are a stone's throw from one of the most productive agricultural regions in the world. Spanish and Italian

THE BEST

JERRY ALEXANDER

Refined dining options abound in Guerneville

WINE COUNTRY RESTAURANTS

- Wine Spectator Greystone Restaurant at the Culinary Institute of America (p194)
- Market (p194)
- girl & the fig (p201)
- Farmhouse Inn (p193)

visitors will recognize the gently sloping hills and Mediterranean climate as the perfect conditions to grow all sorts of yummy treats – olives, lemons, arugula, sunflowers etc.

Dining out in Orange County can be an adventure. Taco trucks near the beach allow you to eat lunch with sandy bare feet and sunburned shoulders, while swank dining can rival LA but with a better view (and less smog). If you've promised to eat all your vegetables, you can even dine with a giant mouse (see Disney Character Meals, p271).

In the past few decades, San Diego (p314) has developed a strong culinary voice. Where to eat is as important as what to eat, as each neighborhood has its own feel, from the old-school vibe at Filippi's Pizza Grotto (p328) in Little Italy to the chorizo date fritters at Whisknladle (p328) in La Jolla.

FARMERS MARKETS

A dying trend in the 1960s and '70s, the California farmers market rebounded in the 1990s faster than John Travolta's career. Farmers markets all across the country have more than tripled in the past 20 years, and nowhere is this more apparent (or tasty) than in the organic produce capital of the country, California. Over 40% of America's organic fruit and vegetables are grown in California (over 430,000 acres) and the immediacy of high-quality produce at farmers markets has helped fuel the organic industry.

Although it's nearly impossible to find a 'bad' farmers market along the coast, several in California stand out for their excellence or quirkiness, and some small towns are worth a road trip just for their markets. At Central California's San Luis Obispo farmers market (p296), the Thursday night social event is as much a food fair where you can gorge on strawberry-filled churros, pork barbecue and beloved

Farmers market, San Luis Obispo (p296)

LEE FOSTER

THE BEST

RICHARD CUMMINS

Fresh strawberries for sale at a farmers market

FARMERS MARKETS

- **LA's Original Farmers Market** (p73)
- **San Luis Obispo** (p296)
- **Arcata** (p164)
- **Hillcrest, San Diego** (p321)

roasted corn. Find radishes and peaches at our favorite farmers market in neo-hippie Arcata (p164), which we love for its commitment to organic, sustainable produce as well as the angora bunny lady (www.sherityler.com), who sells hats and scarves made from the angora bunnies she brings with her each Saturday morning to the town square market (or buy her rabbit-urine fertilizer).

COOKING COURSES

Some high-end cookware shops like **Williams-Sonoma** (www.williams-sonoma.com) and **Sur la Table** (www.surlatable.com) offer introductory cooking classes.

Balboa Park Food & Wine School (☎ 619-557-9441; www.balboawinefood.com; 1549 El Prado, San Diego; from $45) Quickie demonstrations, hands-on classes and wine tastings with local chefs.

California Sushi Academy (☎ 310-231-4499; www.sushi-academy.com; 1131 Nebraska Ave, LA; from $80) Apprentice in the art of finessing raw fish, either for a day or a 12-week professional course. Also has sake tasting.

Cavallo Point Cooking School (☎ 888-651-2003; www.cavallopoint.com; 601 Murray Circle, Fort Baker, Sausalito; from $55) Seasonal, sustainable-themed cooking classes and tastings featuring farmers-market fare and local chefs.

BRENT WINEBRENNER

Many types of international cuisine are available in Santa Barbara, including Japanese sushi

Culinary Institute of America (CIA; ☎ 800-888-7850; www.ciachef.edu; 2555 Main St, St Helena; classes from $95, demonstrations and flavor bar tastings from $15) Demonstration and hands-on classes in Sonoma wine country. Also offers culinary tasting day trips.

Laguna Culinary Arts (☎ 949-494-0745; www.lagunaculinaryarts.com; 845 Laguna Canyon Rd, Laguna Beach; from $85) Home-chef classes occasionally indulge in wine pairings.

FOOD & WINE FESTIVALS

Of course, almost every wine country, county fair and farm town has its own festival or food competition, too. For more epicurean celebrations, see the destination chapters. Here are just a few of our faves:

San Francisco Chronicle Wine Competition (☎ 415-391-2000; www.winejudging.com) The world's stiffest competition of American wines, with gourmet food and drink vendors galore. Held in February.

Rhône Rangers Grand Wine Tasting (☎ 800-467-0163; www.rhonerangers.org) Scores of American Rhône-style wine producers, with artisanal food producers from the Bay Area. Held in San Francisco in March.

California Strawberry Festival (☎ 888-288-9242; www.strawberry-fest.org) Family-fun festival with recipe cook-offs and star chefs' demos. Held near Ventura in May.

Castroville Artichoke Festival (☎ 831-633-2465; www.artichoke-festival.org) Classic car show, 3D 'agro-art' sculptures and a wine expo. Held near Monterey in May.

Cooking for Solutions (☎ 866-963-9645; www.montereybayaquarium.org) Celeb chefs show how to cook using sustainably farmed ingredients. Held in Monterey in May.

California Festival of Beers (☎ 805-544-2266; www.hospiceslo.org/beerfest) All profits go to charity at this brewmeisters' summit. Held near San Luis Obispo in May.

Organic Planet Festival (☎ 707-445-5100; www.organicplanetfestival.com) Live entertainment, all-natural food vendors and the world's largest organic salad. Held in Eureka in August.

California Avocado Festival (☎ 805-684-0038; www.avofest.com) The world's largest vat of guacamole – 'nuff said. Held near Santa Barbara in October.

CALIFORNIA IN FOCUS

CALIFORNIA CUISINE

◥**THE BEST**

JERRY ALEXANDER

Mexican food is a fresh and tasty option

FOODIE WEBSITES

- **www.cafarmersmarkets.com** Find a farmers market in any town in California; there are 80 in Los Angeles county alone.

- **www.chowhound.com** A website 'for those who live to eat.' Come here to ask locals about hot foodie issues, such as where to find the tastiest taco trucks in San Francisco.

- **www.opentable.com** A fast and easy way to make free online reservations at hundreds of restaurants in California.

- **www.happycow.net** Free online directory of vegetarian, vegan and veg-friendly restaurants and health-food stores.

❧ THE BEST

SABRINA DALBESIO

Blueberry pancakes at Greens (p111), San Francisco

RESTAURANTS FOR VEGETARIANS

- Greens (p111)
- Ravens (p154)
- Sojourner Café (p305)
- Ubuntu (p193)

Pismo Beach Clam Festival (☎ 805-773-4382; www.pismochamber.com) Chowder cook-offs, a kids' clam dig and plenty of fried mollusks. Held near San Luis Obispo in October.

San Diego Bay Wine & Food Festival (☎ 877-808-9463; www.worldofwineevents.com) Tastings, wine-maker dinners, classes and demos. Held at various locations in November.

VEGETARIANS & VEGANS

Chefs elsewhere often gripe about catering to vegetarians, but California produce is fresh and flavorful enough to be a menu scene-stealer, and doesn't need to be hidden under slabs of meat or heavy sauces. California may have more vegetarians and vegans per capita than any other state, but outside the Bay Area, Northern California and greater LA, strictly vegetarian restaurants are few and far between. Take heart: vegetarians may go to virtually any proper sit-down restaurant in California and order a satisfying meal from the regular menu. Most restaurants have obligatory vegetable pasta dishes, salads, portobello-mushroom burgers, baked squash and eggplant, pilafs and rice bowls. Dishes of steamed, mixed vegetables dressed with olive oil or an emulsion sauce are popular, and cooks do astonishing things with tofu. Many Chinese and Mexican restaurants offer vegetarian dishes – just ask to make sure lard isn't used.

FAMILY TRAVEL

©DISNEY ENTERPRISES, INC

Mickey Mouse Fountain, Disneyland

(Tiny) hands down, California has got to be one of the most child-friendly vacation spots on the planet. The kids will already be begging to go to Disneyland, Universal Studios, SeaWorld, the San Diego Wild Animal Park and Fisherman's Wharf. Get those over with (you may well enjoy them, too) and then introduce them to many other worlds. SoCal's 'endless summer' of sunny skies and warm temperatures lends itself to outdoor activities too numerous to mention, and then there's Yosemite, the redwoods and Lake Tahoe.

Sometimes no organized activity is even needed. We've seen kids from Washington, DC, thrill at catching their first glimpse of a palm tree, and 11-year-olds with sophisti-cated palates in bliss over their first heirloom tomatoes at a farmers market or shrimp dumplings at a dim-sum palace. The upshot: if the kids are having a good time, their parents are doing the same.

DESTINATIONS
LOS ANGELES

Los Angeles does entertainment right. This dedication to *fun* – plus acres and acres of public parks, wide-open beaches and plenty of space to run around – is what makes LA such a (surprisingly) kid-friendly city.

Kids old enough to appreciate movies will love Universal Studios Hollywood (p72); adjacent Universal CityWalk makes a colorful meal stop. Children also thrill at get-ting their picture taken beside the star of their favorite celebrity on Hollywood Blvd;

FAMILY TRAVEL

❯ THE BEST

Tidal pool at Monterey Bay Aquarium (p286)

PLACES TO EXPAND KIDS' MINDS

- **California State Railroad Museum** (p248)
- **Exploratorium** (p104)
- **Monterey Bay Aquarium** (p286)
- **Happy Isles Nature Center** (p231)
- **Big Sur Discovery Center** (p293)
- **Griffith Observatory** (p69)

the hand-, foot- and wand-prints of the young stars of the Harry Potter movies were recent additions near Grauman's Chinese Theatre (p67). To see the cast of *Ice Age* (albeit in their former real-life selves), visit the Page Museum at the La Brea Tar Pits (p73).

Downtown's ethnic neighborhoods are a treat for little sophisticates. In Chinatown, pick up touristy knickknacks or make a wish in a fountain. Stop nearby at Empress Pavilion (p78) for dim sum or a streetside shop for boba tea (with black 'pearls' of tapioca). Mexican-themed Olvera St (p64), LA's oldest street, mixes kitsch with quality. LA's Original Farmers Market (p73) allows little ones to taste food from around California, and the world.

SAN FRANCISCO

Folks are usually surprised to find out San Francisco has the lowest number of children for any city in the country (hovering around 14%). In turn, it's not a terribly child-friendly city for living, and traveling can be somewhat challenging. Independent restaurants in San Francisco can give parents the cold shoulder (profit margins go down

Hands-on at the Exploratorium (p104), San Francisco

☜ THE NITTY GRITTY

- **Change facilities** Available in most public locations such as malls and rest stops.
- **Cots** Many hotels offer cots for kids for a nominal fee or no cost.
- **Diapers (nappies)** Readily available at grocery stores and even most convenience stores.
- **Health** California retains a very high standard of health and clean facilities.
- **Highchairs** Almost ubiquitous in casual restaurants; call ahead at upscale places.
- **Strollers** Available to rent at Disneyland and SeaWorld.
- **Transportation** On buses, parents hold children on laps. Car seats are required for children under 6.

considerably with child patrons), but kids are so rare, your well-behaved ones might just get doted upon.

San Francisco has plenty of tourist attractions for kids. Just running around Golden Gate Park (p88) and feeding ducks or spotting the buffalo herd will keep children entertained for hours. Sensory illusions and a Tactile Dome make the Exploratorium (p104) one of the most inventive hands-on museums for children. Hint: bring crumbs to feed the swans at the neighboring Palace of Fine Arts (p104) afterwards. The area around Pier 39 (p103) and Fisherman's Wharf (p103) is pure joy with barking seals, clam chowder in a bread bowl, a carousel and plenty of kitschy shops and amusements.

Remember Mark Twain's saying about the coldest winter, and bundle everyone up accordingly. Scarves and a warm winter coat wouldn't be overkill most summer days, and sweaters are a must, even during the day.

WINE COUNTRY

You wouldn't think Wine Country would be an appropriate destination for kids. And, for the most part, you'd be right. There are several very notable exceptions, however. The hot springs and mineral pools of Calistoga (p194) can be a hoot for older kids, and precocious teenagers will enjoy the mother-daughter specials Wine Country spas often advertise during the winter. Plus, the area around Calistoga is just plain fun, including a geyser (p196) and an African safari (p197) with cheetah, giraffes and lemurs.

THE BAY AREA & NORTHERN CALIFORNIA

Of all of the regions in California, the northern coast is probably the most romantic. B&Bs along the coasts of Sonoma and Mendocino probably host more baby-making weekends than babies.

However, the further reaches of Northern California are part of what makes life on this planet worth living. The call of wild beaches and statuesque redwoods just might be enough to keep little ones from irritating their siblings for the entire five-hour drive north from the Bay Area. If you're going to camp anywhere in California, under a canopy of ancient redwoods isn't a bad choice. Dozens of redwood groves, drive-through

CALIFORNIA IN FOCUS

FAMILY TRAVEL

THE BEST

LEE FOSTER

Furnace Creek Inn (p265), Death Valley

SLEEPING OPTIONS FOR KIDS

- **Clair Tappaan Lodge** (p228)
- **Curry Village** (p235)
- **El Capitan Canyon** (p305)
- **Furnace Creek Inn** (p265)
- **Dr Wilkinson's Motel & Hideaway Cottages** (p195)

trees and well-marked trails in Redwood State and National Parks (p168) ensure the whole family can enjoy at least a day or two of redwood-hopping.

Just staying in the Bay Area offers countless opportunities for younger folk. Cross a few bridges and you're in a whole other world from San Francisco. In the upper-crust bucolic area around Marin County, the Marin Headlands are a draw for hikers and ocean lovers, and its Marine Mammal Center (p140) allows visitors to witness injured and sick marine mammals being nursed back to health.

SIERRA NEVADA & THE DESERTS

Take your children to Yosemite (p229) for a trip into nature they will undoubtedly never forget. River rafting down energetic rapids, hiking below the playful beauty of the waterfalls, ranger talks for kids, and the extremely small likelihood of actually getting eaten by a bear...kids have a tendency to discover a love for nature here. (That is, if you're not in Yosemite Valley on a weekend in July, with 12,000 other nature-loving kids.)

Kids of all ages love the Palm Springs Aerial Tramway (p250), whose cars rotate ever so slowly as they ascend nearly 6000 vertical feet up the San Jacinto Mountains. Temperatures at the top are up to 40°F lower than on the desert floor; in cooler months, bring warm clothing and snow gear (the latter can be rented).

In Death Valley National Park (p261), the lowest place on Earth, quirky kid-friendly attractions and a gorgeous desert landscape make the area popular with families, but remember to keep kids out of the midday sun in summer; temperatures often hover above 120°F.

CENTRAL & SOUTHERN CALIFORNIA

Go ahead, just try to visit Disneyland (p306) and not enjoy yourself. Walt Disney's vision of an amusement park where both children and adults could enjoy themselves has taken shape like nothing the world has ever seen.

But simple pleasures also abound along the Southern or Central California coast. Buy a $4 shovel and pail and head to the beach. Which one? You could start your way at La Jolla Cove (p324), stop in Santa Barbara (p300) to stroll Stearns Wharf (p301) pier and the nearby West Beach, and end your trip with a roller-coaster ride on the Santa Cruz Beach Boardwalk (p280). And we haven't even gotten started with SeaWorld (p322), the San Diego Zoo (p318) or San Diego Wild Animal Park (p325), or the Monterey Bay Aquarium (p286).

HISTORY

JERRY ALEXANDER

Paiute people in traditional dress, Lake Tahoe

THE FIRST PEOPLES

Immigration is hardly a new phenomenon here, since people have been migrating to California for millennia. Archaeological sites indicate this geographical region was first inhabited soon after people migrated across the long-gone land bridge from Asia during an ice age at least 20,000 years ago. Many archaeological sites have yielded evidence, from large middens of seashells along the beaches to campfire sites on the Channel Islands, that people have been living along this coast for around 8000 years.

Archaeological evidence paints a clear picture of the diversity of indigenous peoples living here at the time of first European contact. Native peoples spoke over 60 different languages and numbered as many as 300,000. They mostly lived in small groups, often migrating with the seasons from the coast up into the mountains. Acorn meal was their dietary staple, supplemented by small wild game and seafood.

A NEW WORLD FOR EUROPEANS

Following the conquest of Mexico in the early 16th century, the Spanish turned their attention toward exploring the edges of their new empire. In 1542 the Spanish crown engaged Juan Rodríguez Cabrillo, a Portuguese explorer and retired conquistador,

25,000 BC – 10,000 BC	6000 BC	1542
Earliest known humans cross over the Bering Strait from Asia.	Date of earliest petroglyphs (rock art) found at Lava Beds National Monument near Mt Shasta.	Juan Rodríguez Cabrillo becomes the first European to 'discover' California.

THE BEST

Mastodon skeleton, La Brea Tar Pits (p73), Los Angeles

PLACES FOR ANCIENT HISTORY

- La Brea Tar Pits (p73)
- Redwood trees (p122)
- Petroglyphs at Lava Beds National Monument (p174)
- Petrified Forest (p196)
- Devils Postpile (p246)

to lead an expedition up the West Coast to find the fabled golden land beyond Mexico's west coast.

When Cabrillo sailed into San Diego Bay in 1542, he and his crew became the first Europeans to see mainland California. Staring back at them from shore were the Kumeyaay – to learn more about this coastal tribe, visit San Diego's Museum of Man (p318). Cabrillo's ships sat out a storm in the harbor, then sailed northward. They made a stop at the Channel Islands where, in 1543, Cabrillo fell ill, died and was buried. The expedition continued as far as Oregon, but returned with no evidence of a sea route to the Atlantic, a city of gold or islands of spice. The unimpressed Spanish authorities forgot about California for the next 50 years.

The English privateer Sir Francis Drake sailed up the California coast in 1579. He missed the entrance to San Francisco Bay, but pulled in near what is now called Point Reyes (p146) to repair his ship, which was bursting with the weight of plundered Spanish silver. He claimed the land for Queen Elizabeth, named it Nova Albion (New England) and left for other adventures, starting with journeying north up the Pacific Coast to Alaska.

THE MISSION PERIOD

Around the 1760s, as Russian ships came to California's coast in search of sea-otter pelts, and British trappers and explorers spread throughout the West, King Carlos III of Spain grew worried that these other newcomers might pose a threat to Spain's claim. Conveniently for the king, the Catholic Church was anxious to start missionary work among the indigenous peoples, so church and state combined forces to found missions inside presidios (military forts).

Ostensibly, the presidios' purpose was to protect the missions and deter foreign intruders. The idea was to have Native American converts live inside the missions, learn trade and agricultural skills, and ultimately establish pueblos (small towns). But these garrisons created more threats than they deterred, as the soldiers aroused local hostility by raiding Native American camps to sexually assault and kidnap women. Not

1579	1769	1821
English explorer Sir Francis Drake stops by Marin County, staking out a claim for England.	Padre Junípero Serra establishes the first of 21 missions along the 650-mile El Camino Real.	Mexico wins independence from Spain, taking over rule of Alta (Upper) California after Spain's 52-year reign.

only were the presidios militarily weak, but their weaknesses were well known to Russia and Britain, and didn't strengthen Spain's claims to California.

Ultimately, the mission period was pretty much a failure. The Spanish population remained small; the missions achieved little more than mere survival; foreign intruders were not greatly deterred; and more Native Americans died than were converted. Most of California's missions are still standing today, though a few are in ruins. Beautifully restored Mission San Juan Capistrano (p314) is among California's original chain of 21 missions, the earliest of which were founded by peripatetic Franciscan priest Junípero Serra.

FROM MEXICO TO MANIFEST DESTINY

When Mexico gained independence from Spain in 1821, many of the new nation's people looked to California to satisfy their thirst for private land. By the mid-1830s the Spanish missions had been secularized, with a series of Mexican governors doling out hundreds of free land grants, or ranchos, that were largely given over to livestock to supply a profitable trade in hide and tallow. The new landowners, called rancheros or Californios, quickly prospered and became the social, cultural and political heavyweights of Alta (Upper) California.

American explorers, trappers, traders, whalers, settlers and opportunists showed increasing interest in California, seizing on prospects that the rancheros ignored. Some of the Americans who started businesses converted to Catholicism, married locals and assimilated into Californio society. Impressed by California's potential wealth and

CALIFORNIA IN FOCUS

HISTORY

RICHARD CUMMINS

Mission San Juan Capistrano (p314)

1840s	1846	1849
Chinese immigrants are recruited to build the growing railroad business.	The Mexican-American War begins; drunk Californians in Sonoma declare independence, which lasts for 22 days.	The Gold Rush is in full-swing; San Francisco gains 10 times the population and 100 times the bars.

RICHARD CUMMINS

Mission Santa Barbara (p303)

THE BEST

CALIFORNIA MISSION BUILDINGS

- **Mission Santa Barbara** (p303)
- **Mission San Juan Capistrano** (p314)
- **San Carlos de Borroméo de Carmelo Mission** (p291)
- **Mission San Luis Obispo de Tolosa** (p296)

hoping to fulfill the promise of Manifest Destiny (the USA's imperialist doctrine to extend its borders from coast to coast), US President Andrew Jackson sent an emissary to offer the financially strapped Mexican government $500,000 for California in 1835. Though American settlers were by then showing up by the hundreds, especially in Northern California, Jackson's emissary was tersely rejected.

In 1836 Texas had seceded from Mexico and declared itself an independent republic. On May 11, 1846, the US declared war on Mexico following disputes over the former's annexation of Texas. By July, US naval units occupied every port on the California coast, including Monterey, the capital of Alta California. When US troops captured Mexico City in September 1847, ending the war, the Mexican government had little choice but to cede much of its northern territory to the US. The Treaty of Guadalupe Hidalgo, signed on February 2, 1848, turned over what is now California, Nevada, Utah and parts of Arizona, New Mexico, Colorado and Wyoming to the US. Two years later, California was admitted as the 31st state of the United States.

THERE'S GOLD IN THEM THAR HILLS

By remarkable coincidence, gold was discovered at Sutter's Creek, about 120 miles northeast of San Francisco, little more than a week before the signing of the Treaty of Guadalupe Hidalgo that ended the Mexican-American War. By 1849, surging rivers of wagon trains were creaking into California filled with miners, pioneers, savvy entrepreneurs, outlaws and prostitutes, all seeking their fortunes.

Population growth and overnight wealth stimulated every aspect of California life, from agriculture and banking to construction and journalism. But mining damaged the land: hills were stripped bare, erosion wiped out vegetation, streams silted up and mercury washed down rivers into San Francisco Bay. San Francisco became a hotbed of gambling, prostitution, drink and chicanery, giving rise to its moniker 'the Barbary Coast,' whose last vestiges live on today in the strip joints in SF's North Beach neighborhood (p108).

1869	1892	1906
The transcontinental railroad is complete; California sees its first train arrive from the East Coast.	John Muir founds the Sierra Club after helping establish Yosemite as a national park.	A 7.9 earthquake and resulting fire destroys much of San Francisco.

CALIFORNIA IN FOCUS

HISTORY

RICHES FROM RAILROADS, FARMS & OIL FIELDS

Opening the floodgates to massive migration into the West, the transcontinental railroad drastically shortened the trip from New York to San Francisco from two months to five days, profitably linking markets on both coasts. Los Angeles was not connected to the transcontinental railroad until 1876, when Southern Pacific Railroad laid tracks from San Francisco south to the fledgling city.

By this time, rampant speculation had raised land prices in California to levels no farmer or immigrant could afford; the railroad brought in products that undersold goods made in California; and some 15,000 Chinese laborers – no longer needed for railroad construction – flooded the labor market. A period of unrest ensued, which culminated in anti-Chinese discrimination and the federal 1882 Chinese Exclusion Act banning Chinese immigration. The act was not repealed until 1943.

RICHARD CUMMINS

Marshall Gold Discovery State Historic Park (p248)

PLACES TO EXPERIENCE THE GOLD RUSH

- Bodie State Historic Park (p241)
- Sonoma (p199)
- Marshall Gold Discovery State Historic Park (p248)
- San Francisco's North Beach (p108)

Much of the land granted to the railroads was sold in big lots to speculators who also acquired, with the help of corrupt politicians and administrators, a lot of the farmland intended for new settlers. A major share of the state's agricultural land thus became consolidated as large holdings in the hands of a few city-based landlords, establishing the pattern (which continues to this day) of industrial-scale 'agribusiness' rather than small family farms. These big businesses were well placed to provide the substantial investment and the political connections required to bring irrigation water to the farmland. They also solidified an ongoing need for cheap farm labor.

In the absence of coal, iron ore or abundant water, heavy industry developed slowly in California, though the 1892 discovery of oil in central Los Angeles by Edward Doheny stimulated the development of petroleum processing and chemical industries. By the year 1900, California was producing 4 million barrels of oil per year and the population of LA had doubled to over 100,000 people.

1911	1927	1928
Hollywood's first film is shot.	San Francisco inventor Philo Farnsworth transmits the first successful TV broadcast of...a straight line.	*The Jazz Singer* is released as the first feature-length 'talkie' movie. The worldwide demand for films brings a boom to Hollywood

GROWING INTO THE 20TH CENTURY

The population, wealth and importance of California increased dramatically throughout the 20th century. The great San Francisco earthquake and fire of 1906 decimated the city, but it was barely a hiccup in the state's development. The revolutionary years in Mexico, from 1910 to 1921, caused a huge influx of immigrants from south of the border, reestablishing Latino communities that had been smothered by Anglo dominance. Meanwhile, SoCal's oil industry boomed in the 1920s and Hollywood entered its so-called 'Golden Age,' which lasted through the 1950s.

The Great Depression saw another wave of immigrants, this time from the impoverished Great Plains states of the Dust Bowl. Outbreaks of social and labor unrest led to rapid growth of the Democratic Party in California, as well as trade unions for blue-collar workers. Many of the Depression-era public works projects sponsored by the federal government had lasting benefits, from San Francisco's Bay Bridge to the restoration of historic missions statewide, notably Mission La Purísima Concepción near Santa Barbara.

WWII had a major impact on California. Women were co-opted into wartime factory work and proved themselves in a range of traditionally male jobs. Anti-Asian sentiments resurfaced, many Japanese Americans were interned, and more Mexicans crossed the border to fill labor shortages. Some military servicepeople who passed through California liked the place so much that they returned to settle after the war. In the post-war decade, the state's population jumped by 40%, reaching 13 million by 1955.

▶ THE BEST

RYAN MILLER/GRAMMY MUSEUM

Grammy Museum (p67), Los Angeles

HISTORY MUSEUMS

- **California State Railroad Museum** (p248)
- **Emigrant Trail Museum** (p228)
- **Grammy Museum** (p67)
- **Museum of the American West** (p67)
- **Manzanar National Historic Site** (p246)

RADICALS, TREND-SETTERS & TECHNOLOGY

Unconstrained by tradition, California has long been a leader in new attitudes and social movements. During the affluent postwar years of the 1950s, the Beat movement in San Francisco's North Beach railed against the banality and conformity of suburban life, instead choosing bohemian coffeehouses for jazz, poetry and pot.

1939	1955	1962
Hewlett-Packard is formed in Dave Packard's garage in Palo Alto.	Disneyland opens to guests; remains the only Disney property designed by Walt himself.	César Chávez organizes migrant laborers into what will eventually become the United Farm Workers.

When the postwar baby boomers came of age, many took up where the Beat generation left off, heeding 1960s countercultural icon Timothy Leary's counsel to 'turn on, tune in, and drop out.' Their revolt climaxed in San Francisco's Haight District (p108) during the 1967 'Summer of Love.' Sex, drugs and rock-and-roll ruled the day. With the foundation for social revolution already laid, gay liberation exploded in San Francisco in the '70s. Today San Francisco remains one of the world's most exuberantly gay cities – just take a stroll through the Castro District (p108).

In the 1980s and '90s, California catapulted to the forefront of the healthy lifestyle, with more aerobics classes and self-actualization workshops than you could shake a shaman's stick at. In-line skating, snowboarding and mountain biking rose to fame here first.

As digital technology continually reinvents our world view, California has also led the world in developing computer technology. In the 1950s, Stanford University needed to raise money to finance postwar growth, so it built an industrial park and leased space to high-tech companies like Hewlett-Packard, which formed the nucleus of Northern California's Silicon Valley. In 1971 Intel invented the microchip, and in 1976 Apple invented the first personal computer. In the fat years of the late 1990s, companies nationwide jumped on the dot-com bandwagon following the exponential growth of the web. Many reaped huge overnight profits, fueled by misplaced optimism, only to crash with equal velocity at the turn of the millennium.

DAVID RYAN

Collapsed apartment building after the 1989 earthquake, San Francisco

CALIFORNIA IN FOCUS

HISTORY

1967	1978	1989
San Francisco's Summer of Love kicks off the hippie movement.	San Francisco elects the nation's first openly gay politician, Harvey Milk (assassinated later that year).	The Bay Area is hit by the 7.1 Loma Prieta earthquake during the 'Bay Bridge' World Series.

CALIFORNIA IN FOCUS

OUTLOOK FOR THE 21ST CENTURY

No place in America was more affected by the demise of the dot-coms in 2000 than California. That same year also brought widespread power shortages and rolling blackouts to California, which were caused by Enron's illegal manipulation of markets. But before the truth came out, Republican malcontents fingered then-Governor Gray Davis and called for a special recall election that ousted him.

Enter Arnold Schwarzenegger – Californians will always forgive a movie star more easily than a politician. Although a Republican, Schwarzenegger's actions during his first term suggested that he intended to govern from California's political center, notably when it came to environmental issues. He fought to pass legislation that helped California lead the nation in cutting greenhouse emissions, even as US President and fellow Republican George W Bush rejected the Kyoto Protocol.

In 2006 Schwarzenegger won another gubernatorial term, and San Francisco congresswoman Nancy Pelosi became the Speaker of the House in Washington DC. But the next year saw the start of the unraveling subprime mortgage-lending crisis, which triggered the US stock market crash of 2008 and caused the entire nation to sink into a recession. Massive unemployment devastated California, once the world's sixth-largest economy. By 2009 the state was so broke that it issued IOU slips to creditors. The 'Governator' played hardball during the budget crisis, making massive cuts to social services, education and state parks funding.

HISTORY

2003	2004	2009
Governor Gray Davis is recalled; the 'Governator' Arnold Schwarzenegger replaces him.	The most anticipated IPO in history, Google shares start at $85 (reaching $700 just a few years later).	Michael Jackson dies in LA.

LAND & WILDLIFE

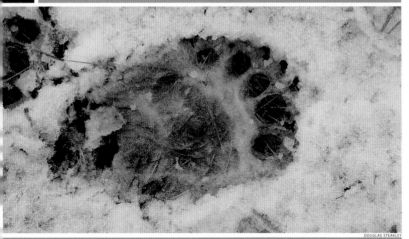

DOUGLAS STEAKLEY

Footprint of a black bear, Yosemite National Park (p229)

From soaring snowcapped peaks, to scorching deserts and dense forests, California is home to a bewildering variety of ecosystems and animals. In fact the state not only has the highest biodiversity in North America, it has more types of climate and more types of soils than nearly any location in the world. California is one of few places in the world with a Mediterranean climate, characterized by dry summers and mild wet winters favored by unique plants and animals.

THE LAND

The third-largest state after Alaska and Texas, California covers more than 160,000 sq miles and is larger than the UK. It is bordered to the north by Oregon, to the south by Mexico, with Nevada and Arizona on its eastern border, and 840 miles of glorious Pacific shoreline on the west. Its cool northern border stands at the same latitude as Rome, Italy, while the arid southern border is at the same latitude as Tel Aviv, Israel.

GEOLOGY & EARTHQUAKES

California is an exceedingly complex geological landscape formed from fragments of rock and earth crust scraped together as the North American continent drifted westward over hundreds of millions of years. Crumpled coast ranges, the downward-bowing Central Valley and the still-rising Sierra Nevada all provide evidence of gigantic forces exerted as the continental and ocean plates crushed together. This changed about 25 million years ago, when the plates stopped colliding and started sliding against

THE BEST

JOHN ELK III

The majestic Mt Shasta (p170)

IMPRESSIVE PEAKS

- **Mt Whitney** (p247) 14,505ft
- **Mt Shasta** (p170) 14,162ft
- **Telescope Peak, Death Valley** (p265) 11,049ft
- **Mammoth Mountain, Mammoth Lakes** (p244) 11,053ft
- **Half Dome, Yosemite National Park** (p231) 8842ft

each other, creating the San Andreas Fault. Because this contact zone doesn't slide smoothly, it rattles California with an ongoing succession of tremors and earthquakes.

MOUNTAINS & VALLEYS

Much of the California coast is fronted by rugged, little-explored coastal mountains that capture winter's water-laden storms. San Francisco divides the coastal ranges roughly in half: the foggy north coast remains sparsely populated, while the central and south coasts have a balmy climate, sandy beaches and lots of people.

On their eastern flanks, the coastal ranges subside into gently rolling hills that give way to the sprawling Central Valley. Further east looms California's most prominent topographic feature, the world-famous Sierra Nevada. At 400 miles long and 50 miles wide, it's one of the largest mountain ranges in the world and a vast wilderness areas with 13 peaks over 14,000ft.

DESERTS

All lands east of the Sierra crest are dry and desertlike, receiving less than 10in of rain a year. Areas in the northern half of the state, especially on the elevated Modoc Plateau of northeastern California, are a cold desert blanketed with hardy sagebrush shrubs and pockets of juniper trees. Temperatures increase to the south, with a prominent transition occurring when you descend from Mammoth into Bishop and Owens Valley. This hot desert (the Mojave Desert) includes Death Valley, one of the hottest places on earth.

Southern California is a hodgepodge of small mountain ranges and desert basins. Mountains on the eastern border of the Los Angeles Basin continue southward past San Diego and down the spine of northern Baja California, while the Mojave Desert of the southern Sierra Nevada morphs into the Colorado Desert around the Salton Sea. This entire region is dry and rocky, mostly devoid of vegetation except for pockets of desert-adapted shrubs, cacti and Joshua trees.

WILDLIFE

Much of California is a biological island cut off from the rest of North America by the soaring heights of the Sierra Nevada and, as on other 'islands' in the world, evolution creates unique plants and animals under these conditions. As a result, California ranks first in the nation for its number of endemic plants, amphibians, reptiles, freshwater fish and mammals. Even more impressive, 30% of all the plant species found in the US, 50% of all the bird species and 50% of all the mammal species occur in California.

ANIMALS

Many types of birds, including ducks and geese, either pass through California or linger through the winter, making the state one of the top destinations in North America for bird-watchers. Year round, the best places to see birds are the state's beaches, estuaries and bays, where herons, cormorants, shorebirds and gulls gather.

Black bears are one of the most magnificent animals found in California. These burly omnivores feed on berries, nuts, roots, grasses, insects, eggs, small mammals and fish, but can become a nuisance around campgrounds and mountain cabins where food is not properly stored.

The coast of California is blessed with a fantastic assortment of marine mammals, including one of the few whale migrations in the world that can be easily viewed from land or nearshore boats. It also offers many chances to see sleek seals, bulky sea lions and mammoth 3000lb elephant seals.

PLANTS

California is a land of superlatives: the tallest (coastal redwoods approaching 380ft), the largest (giant sequoias of the Sierra Nevada 38ft across at the base), the oldest (bristlecone pines of the White Mountains that are almost 5000 years old) and the smallest (a pond-dwelling plant that measures a fraction of a tenth of an inch).

Water is an overriding issue for many of California's plants because there is almost no rain during the prime growing season. Desert areas begin their peak blooming in March, with other lowland areas of the state producing abundant wildflowers in April.

DOUGLAS STEAKLEY

Sea otters, Monterey Bay (p278)

CALIFORNIA IN FOCUS

LAND & WILDLIFE

CALIFORNIA IN FOCUS

SHOPPING

SHOPPING

CHRISTINA LEASE

Shop 'til you drop in Beverly Hills, Los Angeles (p84)

New York, Paris, Milan...to many, California is next. Starting in the 1920s, costume designers began flocking to Hollywood to style the stars (previously, actresses had simply dressed themselves). One designer, Gilbert Adrian, who dressed the likes of Greta Garbo, Judy Garland and Joan Crawford, opened atelier 'Gowns by Adrian' for wealthy Angeleno women. Soon thereafter, a style industry was born.

While Los Angeles is the obvious choice for fashion, San Francisco's boutiques and vintage shops have earned a very respectable reputation as a shopping destination (besides, San Franciscans will tell you it's about *style* not fashion). However, what we love about California shopping is it's not all about fashion boutiques in the big cities, it's also about the home-made bagpipe kit you'll find in Mendocino (p152), the cheese and wine markets in Napa (p186) or the hand-forged wrought-iron pot racks at the Ferndale Blacksmith Shop (p162).

REGIONAL SHOPPING

California has a diverse range of destinations to suit most every shopping style. From trendy mainstream boutiques in Los Angeles and San Francisco, to same-price-as-my-car art galleries in Carmel and Laguna Beach, and chain and gift stores just about everywhere, California is a shopper's dream.

LOS ANGELES

In Los Angeles, *the* places to shop are Robertson Blvd (p84) and Melrose Ave (p84) in West Hollywood, and Rodeo Drive in Beverly Hills (p84). Other areas worth checking

THE BEST

Cannery Row (p283), Monterey

TOWNS TO SHOP FOR ART

- **Carmel** (p291)
- **Monterey** (p282)
- **Los Angeles** (p51)
- **Laguna Beach** (p312)

out include Third St Promenade in Santa Monica, to do some celebrity-spotting at Fred Segal and the like, and Venice Beach Boardwalk, for its array of hippie stalls. In Los Angeles, shopping is a serious pastime, and you're buying a window into a lifestyle. Go ahead, just try to spend two hours shopping in LA without running into a mid-level celebrity. And think: these folks pay people to tell them where to shop, and they're here. Dress nicely, pretend you don't notice the blonde paying for sunglasses in front of you just starred on *The Bachelorette*, and you'll fit right in.

SAN FRANCISCO

San Francisco is a city of neighborhood cliques, and nowhere is this more obvious than in its shopping. For hipster threads or cheap resale, head to Valencia Street and the Mission District (p108). Find big box department stores and well-known chains at malls or in Union Square (p100). For quirky boutiques and boho vintage, check out Hayes Valley.

WINE COUNTRY

In Wine Country, the big draw is – surprise – buying wine. Each town has its own version of a gift shop selling local wines, olive oils, cheese and picnic supplies, or hand-

Loyal Army (p117) in The Haight, San Francisco

CALIFORNIA IN FOCUS

SHOPPING

CALIFORNIA IN FOCUS

SHOPPING

THE BEST

RICK GERHARTER

Nancy Boy (p117), San Francisco

ONE-OF-A-KIND NORCAL SHOPPING OPTIONS

- **Lark in the Morning** (p155)
- **Blacksmith Shop & Gallery, Ferndale** (p162)
- **Nancy Boy** (p117)
- **Telegraph Avenue area** (p132)

made items. The excellent gift shop at the Culinary Institute of America (p192) has the benefit of 100 years of kitchen-supply-buying expertise.

THE BAY AREA & NORTHERN CALIFORNIA

While Berkeley is known for its left-wing vendors parked along Telegraph Avenue (p132), each town along the coast – from Marin to Humboldt – has at least a handful of unique shops, many with handmade and local products. Our favorites are Ferndale (p159), the town square in Arcata (p164) and the imminently walkable village of Mendocino, where you can find a hand-carved djembe drum or a banjolele (a banjo ukelele, of course) at Lark in the Morning (p155).

SUSTAINABLE TRAVEL

JOHN ELK III

Redwood National Park (p168)

CALIFORNIA IN FOCUS

SUSTAINABLE TRAVEL

California has the largest human population of any state and the highest projected growth rate in the nation, putting a tremendous strain on California's many precious resources. Although California is in many ways a success story, development and growth have come at great environmental cost. Some cities are greener than others, but some standouts are Arcata, Hopland, Santa Barbara and San Francisco.

You can reduce your carbon footprint while you travel and help fight California's air pollution problems by using public transportation to get around, rather than flying or driving. Amtrak's *Coast Starlight* and *Pacific Surfliner* (p394) routes reward carbon-conscious travelers with epic scenery. Although riding Greyhound buses (p391) lacks the romance of the rails, you'll definitely meet a diverse cross-section of Californians to give you insight into the real 'state of the state,' something drivers cocooned inside their cars won't get. Some cities offer car-free tourism discount incentives, like in Santa Barbara, to encourage bus-hopping or rail-riding weekenders and ambitious long-distance cyclists alike.

For sustainable travel options, including ecofriendly hotels, lodges and inns, see our GreenDex (p414), which lists environmentally, socially and culturally responsible places that travelers can support. Our GreenDex also includes restaurants that serve seasonal, organic produce and are committed to sourcing their food from local vendors, a trend that has caught on across the state. If you're cooking for yourself, there are farmers markets in many cities and even rural towns.

CALIFORNIA IN FOCUS

SUSTAINABLE TRAVEL

ENVIRONMENTAL ISSUES

Starting in 1849, Gold Rush miners tore apart the land in their frenzied quest for the 'big strike,' ultimately sending more than 1.5 billion tons of debris, and uncalculated amounts of poisonous mercury, downstream into the Central Valley where streams became so clogged that the California Supreme Court ruled in 1884 against then-common mining practices.

Water, or the lack thereof, has always been at the heart of California's epic environmental struggles and catastrophes. Damming of the Tuolumne River at Hetch Hetchy (inside the supposedly protected Yosemite National Park) so that San Francisco could have drinking water was reputed to have caused California's greatest environmental champion, John Muir, to die of grief. Likewise, the diversion of water to the Los Angeles area has contributed to the destruction of Owens Lake and its fertile wetlands, and the degradation of Mono Lake.

Tourism development contributes to perennial water shortages, but some hotels have taken steps to reduce water waste, including installing low-flush toilets and encouraging guests to request that their bedsheets and towels are not changed daily. A

THE BEST

HANNAH LEVY

Golden Gate Bridge (p99), San Francisco

CAR-FREE JOURNEYS

- **Walking over the Golden Gate Bridge, San Francisco** (p99)
- **Biking to Napa Valley vineyards for wine tasting** (p185)
- **Riding Amtrak's Coast Starlight trains** (p394)
- **Ascending the Palm Springs Aerial Tramway** (p250)

WITOLD SKRYPCZAK

The distinctive tufa towers at Mono Lake (p242)

CALIFORNIA IN FOCUS

SUSTAINABLE TRAVEL

DOUGLAS STEAKLEY
Joshua Tree National Park (p256)

few hotels have done away with toiletries in plastic bottles, hanging bulk dispensers in bathrooms instead.

Although air quality in California has improved markedly over the past two decades, it's still the worst in the country. Auto exhaust and fine particles generated by the unending turning of vehicle tires, along with industrial emissions, are the chief culprits. An even greater health hazard is ozone, the principal ingredient in smog, which makes sunny days in Los Angeles and the Central Valley look hazy. But there's hope. Cities sometimes offer car-free tourism incentives, as in Santa Barbara (go to www.santabarbaracarfree.org), and low-emission vehicles are rapidly becoming one of the most sought-after types of car in the state, as high gas costs keep many of the larger gas-guzzling vehicles off the road.

NATIONAL & STATE PARKS

The majority of Californians rank outdoor recreation as vital to their quality of life, and the amount of preserved lands has grown due to several important pieces of legislation passed since the 1960s, including the landmark 1976 California Coastal Act, which saved the coastline from further development, and the controversial 1994 California Desert Protection Act, which angered many ranchers, miners and off-roaders.

Unfortunately, many of California's national parks are being loved to death. Overcrowding severely impacts the environment, and it's increasingly difficult to balance public access with the natural state of parks. Try visiting in the shoulder seasons (ie not summer) and flee the paved roads and parking lots for rugged backcountry. Lesser-known parks, especially in the northern mountains and southern California deserts, may go relatively untouched most of the year, which means you won't have to reserve permits, campsites or accommodations months in advance.

THE WAY OF LIFE

Huntington Beach (p304), Orange County

MICAH WRIGHT

The rest of America shakes its head in wonder at California, never quite sure how to categorize it. It's best not to try, since the Golden State is forever reinventing itself. Remember, this is the place that gave the world both hippies *and* Ronald Reagan.

REGIONAL IDENTITY

It's best to think of California as two states: Southern California (SoCal) and Northern California (NorCal, *not* NoCal). Although nobody can agree on exactly where to draw the line between the two, it falls somewhere between San Francisco, with its liberal-minded hipsters, and Los Angeles, the glitzy but tarnished 'City of Angels.'

In any case, believe everything you've ever heard about Californians, so long as you realize the stereotypes are always exaggerated. Sure, tweens snap chewing gum in the shopping malls of the San Fernando Valley north of LA, blond surfers shout 'Dude!' across San Diego beaches, hippies and Rastafarians gather for drum circles in San Francisco's Golden Gate Park, and tree huggers toke on joints in the North Coast woods but, all in all, it's hard to peg the population. Bear in mind that the following explorations of identity merely address trends, not hard-and-fast rules.

In the Bay Area, the politics are liberal and the people open-minded, with a strong live-and-let-live ethic and an often passionate devotion to the outdoors. San Francisco is more of a melting pot, but there aren't a lot of lower-income citizens since rents are so high. The East Bay, Alameda County, which covers Oakland and Berkeley, has more ethnic diversity.

The hard-to-classify Central Coast, with its smaller pockets of population, starts near wacky, left-of-center Santa Cruz and stretches all the way south to surreally beautiful,

STEPHEN SAKS

Santa Cruz Beach Boardwalk (p280)

THE BEST

PLACES TO PEOPLE-WATCH

- **Arcata** (p164)
- **Coachella Valley Music & Arts Festival** (p251)
- **San Francisco Ferry Building** (p98)
- **Santa Cruz** (p278)
- **Venice Beach** (p61)

sexily posh Santa Barbara. Along the way, Hwy 1 winds past working-class Monterey, made famous in John Steinbeck's novels; the bohemian Big Sur coast; the conservative upper-crust villages of Carmel-by-the-Sea and Cambria, where the 'newly wed and nearly dead' have multimillion-dollar homes; and the laid-back, liberal college town of San Luis Obispo, midway between SF and LA.

LA has a reputation for racial tension, possibly because it's so much more diverse. Yet the unease also likely reflects the disparity between haves and have-nots, for example, from Beverly Hills and South Central. Composed of dozens of independent cities, it's impossible to generalize about LA, but one thing is for sure: almost everybody drives. You're nothing – and sometimes nowhere – without a car.

Between LA and San Diego lies Orange County, aka 'the OC,' where beautifully bronzed, buff bodies soak up rays on the sands. The politics 'behind the Orange Curtain' are notably conservative. The conservative politics extend south to San Diego, partly due to its sizeable military population.

POPULATION

California ranks as the most populous state in the US, with over 36 million residents. The state has more than double the US average population density, with 217 people per square mile. In fact, 25% of California residents live in LA County alone. California is one of the fastest-growing states, with three million new residents just since 2000. Its racial makeup continues to shift: Hispanic, Latino and Asian populations steadily increase, while Caucasians (non-Hispanic) decline. At least one in four California residents is foreign-born (including Governor Schwarzenegger) and 40% speak a language other than English at home, primarily Spanish.

CALIFORNIA IN FOCUS

THE WAY OF LIFE

WINE & MICROBREWS

JERRY ALEXANDER

Harvesting grapes, Napa Valley (p186)

From the liquid-courage-inspired Bear Flag Revolt against Mexico in the 1840s to 'vinotherapy' spa treatments in the 2010s, California and the fermented beverage have had a long and storied history. Napa is just one of 107 American Viticultural Areas (AVAs). Well-regarded wine regions now stretch from Mendocino to Santa Barbara, and wine tourism is the second most popular attraction in California (number one is Disneyland).

Beer is also popular, with breweries popping up all over California. San Diego is now second to Portland's designation as America's 'beervana' with 16 microbreweries. While the sixth largest brewery in the United States (Sierra Nevada Brewing Co) is based in Chico, one of the country's smallest legal brewpubs is run from a basement behind a garage in San Francisco, promoted via Twitter.

WINE

Padre Junípero Serra, the father of the California missions, was also the father of California wine; the first grapes planted in California were his, in 1769. By 1900, California wine was on menus all over the United States. California's international victory was heralded 76 years later when Stag's Leap Cabernet Sauvignon and Chateau Montelena's Chardonnay, both hailing from the Napa Valley, beat French rivals at the 1976 Judgment of Paris. Since then, California vintages have merited international attention.

🍷 WINE REGIONS

Looking to blaze your own wine-tasting path? Venture out to these off-the-beaten-path destinations:

- **Livermore Valley** (www.lvwine.org) This East Bay community is less than 30 minutes from downtown Oakland, and has over 40 wineries.
- **Mendocino County** (www.truemendocinowine.com) Not far from Napa and Sonoma, follow back roads for stellar syrah and riesling.
- **Santa Cruz Mountains** (www.scmwa.com) Some of California's oldest, most revered winemakers hide among the redwoods, a mecca for pinot noir.
- **Paso Robles** (www.pasowine.com) California's fastest-growing wine region crafts superb zinfandel and cabernet sauvignon just north of San Luis Obispo.
- **Edna Valley** (www.slowine.com) Crisp chardonnay and smoky syrah vintages, just south of San Luis Obispo.
- **Santa Ynez & Santa Maria Valleys** (www.sbcountywines.com) Starting from Los Olivos north of Santa Barbara, wander along the Foxen Canyon Wine Trail (p306).

WINE-TASTING BASICS

Wine-tasting in California is ridiculously easy. Vineyards are a dime a dozen, from the famous Napa Valley (p186) and Sonoma (p197) to the itty-bitty small town areas and, these days, to urban vineyards. (In the increasingly ritzy Livermore Valley, you can now buy a $1-million-plus tract home with an accompanying personal vineyard.) Most wineries have tasting rooms, many with posted open hours for the public.

'Flights' include four to six different wines. Napa wineries charge $10 to $40 per flight. In Sonoma Valley, tastings cost $5 to $10, often refundable with purchase. You must be 21 to taste. To avoid burnout, visit no more than three wineries per day. Most open daily from 10am or 11am to 4:30pm or 5pm, but call ahead if you've got your heart set, or absolutely want a tour, especially in Napa, where law requires that some wineries accept visitors only by appointment. Alternatively, book a tour with a private company or driver who will make all of the arrangements. If you're buying, ask if the winery has a wine club, which is usually free to join and provides discounts.

Zoning in Napa prohibits picnicking at most wineries, but every place in Sonoma allows it. Just remember to buy a bottle of your host's wine.

🍷 THE BEST

Castello di Amorosa (p188)

EMILY RIDDELL

SMALL WINERIES

- **Frog's Leap** (p186)
- **Castello di Amorosa** (p188)
- **Gundlach-Bundschu** (p197)

CALIFORNIA IN FOCUS

GREAT MICROBREWERIES IN SAN DIEGO

Our favorite breweries and microbreweries in San Diego county include the following:

- **Karl Strauss Brewery & Grill** (www.karlstrauss.com) Downtown (☎ 619-234-2739; 1157 Columbia St; mains $9-29; ☼ hrs vary); La Jolla (☎ 858-551-2739; cnr Wall St & Herschel Ave; mains $9-29; ☼ hrs vary) San Diego meets Bavaria at this longtime favorite, where wait staff will help you out with which beer to pair with your food. Go on Thursday 'cask nights.'
- **Pacific Beach Ale House** (☎ 858-581-2337; www.pbalehouse.com; 721 Grand Ave, Pacific Beach; mains $9-25; ☼ 11am-2am) Contempo-cool setting and a huge menu including lobster mac and cheese, steamed clams and bistro meat loaf.
- **Pizza Port** (☎ 760-720-7007; www.pizzaport.com; 571 Carlsbad Village Dr, Carlsbad; pizzas $8-23; ☼ 11am-11pm; Ⓥ) Rockin' and raucous barn of a space with surf art and 'anti-wimpy' pizzas to go with the signature 'Sharkbite Red' brew.

WINE & MICROBREWS

MICROBREWS

While wine is *de rigueur* for many Californians, beer is the favorite beverage by volume. California's first brewery opened in the rough-and-tumble Gold Rush streets of 1849 San Francisco. By 1852, the city had 350 bars; about one for every 100 citizens. Over the past few decades, Californian microbreweries have catapulted beer onto the 'crisp, with a nose of sweet orange and rye' crowd.

These days, there are well over 100 breweries and microbreweries in California. Most restaurants carry at least two or three local brews, and a few even offer beer flights (including the Magnolia Brewpub on Haight Street, in San Francisco; see p111).

↘ DIRECTORY & TRANSPORTATION

↘ **DIRECTORY**	**378**	INTERNET ACCESS	385
ACCOMMODATIONS	378	LEGAL MATTERS	386
ACTIVITIES	379	MAPS	386
CLIMATE CHARTS	379	PETS	387
COURSES	379	TIME	387
DANGERS & ANNOYANCES	379	TOURIST INFORMATION	387
DISCOUNT CARDS	382	TOURS	387
FESTIVALS & EVENTS	382	TRAVELERS WITH DISABILITIES	388
GAY & LESBIAN TRAVELERS	382	WOMEN TRAVELERS	389
HOLIDAYS	383	↘ **TRANSPORTATION**	**389**
INSURANCE	383	GETTING THERE & AWAY	389
INTERNATIONAL VISITORS	383	GETTING AROUND	390

DIRECTORY
ACCOMMODATIONS

Lodging in California is expensive and reservations are recommended year-round. Accommodations in this book fall into one of three categories: budget (double rooms less than $100); midrange ($100 to $185); and top end (over $185). Rates are generally highest in summer. They spike even higher around major holidays such as Memorial Day, Independence Day and Labor Day, when minimum-night stays often apply. Be aware, too, that room prices along the Central and Southern California Coast can be higher than other areas of California. Prices listed in this guide reflect peak-season rates but don't include accommodation taxes of 10% to 16%, unless otherwise stated.

You can almost always do better than the published rates, particularly midweek or during the off-season (ie winter). Always ask about discounts, packages and promotional rates. Also check the web: some lodgings give better rates if you book online. Auto-club members get discounts at many motels and some hotels, which may also publish discount coupons in flyers available at highway rest areas, gas stations and tourist information offices (or online at www.roomsaver.com).

More and more properties are providing wi-fi ( ), handy if you travel with a laptop. Accommodations that provide internet access for travelers without their own computers are indicated in this guide with an internet ( ) icon. Lodgings that cater to families are marked with the child-friendly ( ) icon. For ecofriendly accommodations, turn to the GreenDex (p414).

If you smoke, ask about the availability of smoking rooms. Many lodgings in California are exclusively nonsmoking. In Southern California, nearly all lodgings have air-con but in Northern California, where it's hot, the opposite is true. If it matters, inquire when making reservations.

If you book over the phone, get a confirmation number, and always ask about the cancellation policy before you give your credit-card number. If you plan to arrive late in the evening, call to reconfirm on the day of arrival. Hotels may overbook but if you've guaranteed the reservation with a credit card, they should accommodate you somewhere else. If they don't, squawk.

Where available, we have listed a property's toll-free reservation number. If you're having trouble finding accommodations, consider booking online with travel agencies like **Orbitz** (www. orbitz.com), **Travelocity** (www.travelocity.com) and **Expedia** (www.expedia.com), or travel discounters **Hotels.com** (www.hotels.com), **Hotwire** (www.hotwire.com) and **Priceline** (www.priceline.com).

B&BS

If you want an atmospheric, often romantic, alternative to impersonal motel or hotel rooms, stay at a B&B. They're typically in restored old houses with floral wallpaper and antique furnishings, and charge well over $100 per couple. Rates normally include breakfast, but rooms with TV and

---

⤷ BOOK YOUR STAY ONLINE

For more accommodations reviews and recommendations by Lonely Planet authors, check out the online booking service at www.lonelyplanet.com. You'll find the true, insider lowdown on the best places to stay. Reviews are thorough and independent. Best of all, you can book online.

telephone are the exception, not the rule; some may share bathrooms. Most B&Bs require advance reservations, though some will accommodate the occasional drop-in guest. Smoking is prohibited. A two- or three-night minimum stay usually applies. Many belong to the **California Association of Bed & Breakfast Inns** (☎ 800-373-9251; www.cabbi.com).

CAMPING

Campgrounds abound in California, with most open year-round. Facilities vary widely. Primitive campgrounds usually have toilets, fire pits, picnic benches and sometimes drinking water; they're most common in national forests and on Bureau of Land Management (BLM) land. State and national park campgrounds are usually better equipped, featuring flush toilets and sometimes hot showers and RV hookups. Overnight fees range from under $5 for walk-in, tent-only 'envirosites' up to $65 for developed beachfront campsites with hookups. For a complete list of state-park campgrounds and overnight fees, browse www.parks.ca.gov.

MOTELS & HOTELS

Motels surround a parking lot and usually have some sort of a lobby. Hotels provide extra services and amenities, but these can be expensive. If you walk in without reservations, always ask to see a room before paying for it, especially at motels.

Rooms are often priced by the size and number of beds in a room, rather than the number of occupants. A room with one double or queen-size bed usually costs the same for one or two people, while a room with a king-size bed or two beds costs more. There is often a surcharge for a third or fourth person. 'Suites' may simply mean oversized rooms, not necessarily two separate rooms, so ask.

As a rule, motels offer the best lodging value for the money. Rooms won't often win design awards, but they're usually comfortably furnished and cleanish. Amenities vary, but expect a telephone, TV, alarm clock and private bathroom. Some provide an in-room minifridge, coffeemaker and microwave.

ACTIVITIES

California offers all kinds of activities for outdoor enthusiasts, from surfing and kayaking to whale-watching and hiking. Most outdoor outfitters provide instruction and hand-holding for newbies, or they'll simply rent equipment for do-it-yourself types. Co-op retailer **REI** (☎ 253-891-2500, 800-426-4840; www.rei.com) sells and rents outdoor-activity equipment and offers lessons, workshops and adventure tours. In Southern California, also try **Adventure 16** (☎ 619-283-2362; www.adventure16.com).

CLIMATE CHARTS

For advice about seasonal travel in California, see p44. For climate charts, see p380.

COURSES

The big three coastal cities – San Francisco, LA and San Diego – are the best places to take a class. Grab a local alternative weekly newspaper for current listings of drop-in classes. For cooking courses, see p348.

DANGERS & ANNOYANCES

By and large, California is not a dangerous place. The most publicized problem is violent crime, but this is pretty much confined to areas not on the itinerary of most visitors. Traffic accidents pose a potential danger and, of course, there is always the dramatic, albeit unlikely, possibility of a

DIRECTORY

ACTIVITIES

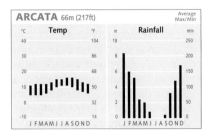

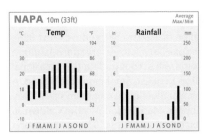

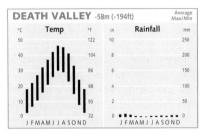

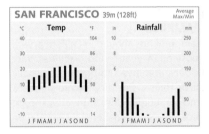

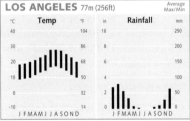

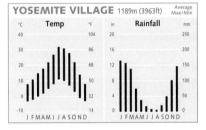

natural disaster, such as an earthquake. Prepare for the worst, but expect the best.

CRIME

Most cities have 'bad' neighborhoods to avoid, particularly after dark. In the destination chapters, the Dangers & Annoyances sections provide some details. If you're worried, quiz hostel and hotel staff, locals and police about the latest no-go zones.

If you find yourself in a neighborhood where you'd rather not be, look confident. Don't keep stopping to look at your map, and hail a taxi if you can. Use ATMs during daylight hours in well-trafficked areas. Exercise caution in parking lots and garages, especially at night. If your car is bumped from behind by another vehicle in a remote area, keep going to a well-lit public place like a police or gas station.

If you're accosted by a mugger, there's no 100% recommended plan of action. Don't carry valuables or an excess of cash, and don't put it all in the same pocket, wallet or bag. Keep some money separate, and hand it over fast – it's better than getting attacked. Muggers are not too happy to find their victims penniless.

That said, don't obsess about crime. Just protect yourself as best you can.

EARTHQUAKES

Earthquakes happen frequently in California, but most are so tiny they can only be detected by sensitive seismological instruments. If you're caught in a serious earthquake, stand inside a doorway or get under a desk or table. Protect your head and stay clear of windows, mirrors or anything that might fall. Don't head for elevators or go running into the street. If you're in a shopping mall or large public building, expect the alarm and/or sprinkler systems to come on.

If outdoors, get away from buildings, trees and power lines. If you're driving, pull over to the side of the road away from bridges, overpasses and power lines; stay inside the car until the shaking stops. If you're on a sidewalk near buildings, duck into a doorway to protect yourself from falling bricks, glass and debris. Prepare for aftershocks. Use the telephone only if absolutely necessary. Turn on the radio and listen for news bulletins.

SWIMMING
Popular beaches are patrolled by lifeguards, but even so some of them can be dangerous places to swim. The biggest hazards are riptides and dangerous ocean currents. Obey all posted signs on beaches. If you get caught in a riptide that carries you away from the shore, don't panic and try to swim against the current, or you'll quickly get exhausted and drown. Instead, try to swim parallel to the shoreline and once the current stops pulling you out, swim back to shore.

WILDLIFE
Never feed or approach wild animals, because it causes them to lose their innate fear of humans, which in turn makes them more aggressive, and eventually they may have to be killed. Feeding or otherwise harassing specially protected wildlife is a crime, subject to huge fines. Black bears are often attracted to campgrounds where they may find food, trash and any other scented items left out on picnic tables or stashed in tents and cars. Always use bear-proof boxes where they're provided.

Attacks on humans by mountain lions – also called cougars or pumas – are rare. Stay calm if you encounter a mountain lion, pick up small children, stand your ground – unless you've cornered the animal, in which case give it an escape route – and appear as large (and confident) as possible by raising your arms or grabbing a stick. If the lion gets aggressive or attacks, fight back, shout and throw objects at it.

Snakes and spiders are found throughout California, not just in wilderness areas, but they prefer warmer inland areas. Attacks or fatalities are exceedingly rare; the following descriptions are necessarily general. If you get bitten, seek medical attention immediately.

Watch your step when hiking as rattlesnakes may bask in the middle of the trail. Most rattlesnakes have roughly diamond-shaped patterns along their backs. Bites are rarely fatal; antivenin is available in most hospitals. Always wear hiking boots and, if you're worried, stomp your feet and stay out of thick underbrush and tall grass.

Scorpions spend their days under rocks or woodpiles. The long stinger curving up and around the back is characteristic of these animals. Stings can be very painful but almost never fatal; however, bear in mind that small children are at highest risk.

The most dangerous spider is the black widow. The female has a small, round body marked with a red hourglass shape under its abdomen. She makes very messy webs, so avoid these, as the normally shy spider will bite only if harassed. The bite emits neurotoxins; they're painful but rarely fatal.

The large (up to 4in long) and hairy tarantula looks much worse than it is – it very rarely bites, and then usually only when it is roughly handled. The bite is not fatal, although it is quite painful and can cause infections.

DISCOUNT CARDS

Available at universities and student-oriented travel agencies, an International Student Identity Card (ISIC; www.isic.org) entitles you to some discounts on transportation and admission to sights and attractions. For nonstudents under 26, the International Youth Travel Card (IYTC) offers some of the same savings. If you're a US student, always carry your school or university ID card. Registered students can also buy the Student Advantage Card (☎ 877-256-4672; www.studentadvantage.com; 1-year card $20) for worthwhile discounts on trains, buses, airfares and shopping.

People over the age of 62 (sometimes 55 or 60) often qualify for the same discounts as students; any ID showing your birth date should suffice as proof of age. Members of the American Association of Retired Persons (AARP; ☎ 888-687-2277; www.aarp.org; 1-year membership $12.50), an advocacy group for those aged 50 years and older, qualify for small discounts on hotels, car rentals, attractions and entertainment venues.

For tourists, local discount cards include the Go San Diego Card (www.gosandiegocard.com; adult/child from $65/50), the Go Los Angeles Card (www.golosangelescard.com; adult/child from $60/50) and CityPass (www.citypass.com; adult/child from $59/39) valid for San Francisco, Hollywood or Southern California. These discount passes will save you money only if you're doing lots of sightseeing in a short time, however.

FESTIVALS & EVENTS

Check with local visitor information centers or chambers of commerce, or contact the California Travel & Tourism Commission (p387) for even more current events. See also Calendar (p46), and Holidays (see opposite page).

GAY & LESBIAN TRAVELERS

The mayor of San Francisco declared same-sex marriage legal in 2004, but statewide voters overturned it in 2008. So make no mistake, bigotry persists. Californians tend to be tolerant, although there have been cases of bashings even in metropolitan areas. In small towns, 'tolerance' may come down to a don't-ask-don't-tell policy. The age of sexual consent, regardless of gender or sexual orientation, is 18.

San Francisco has its famed Castro District (p108); San Diego's hottest gay neighborhood is Hillcrest (p321); and in LA it's West Hollywood (p69) and Silver Lake (p67). All three cities have gay and alternative newspapers that cover what's going on and provide contact information for local GLBT organizations.

Damron (www.damron.com) publishes the classic gay travel guides, but they're advertiser-driven and sometimes outdated. Check out OutTraveler (www.outtraveler.com), Gay.com (www.gay.com/travel) and PlanetOut (www.planetout.com/travel) for loads of online travel information. Purple Roofs (www.purpleroofs.com) lists gay-owned and gay-friendly hotels, B&Bs and inns statewide.

If you're looking for a gay mechanic or florist, consult the Gay & Lesbian Yellow Pages (www.gayyellow.com). For counseling or referrals, call the GLBT National Hotline (☎ 888-843-4564; www.glnh.org; 1-9pm Mon-Fri, 9am-2pm Sat).

HOLIDAYS

Thanksgiving and Christmas are the biggest holiday travel times, when you'll overpay for airfares and still be squeezed onto an overbooked flight. On the upside, people usually spend these holidays with family, so city hotels stand nearly empty and may offer fantastic room rates. On summer holiday weekends (ie Memorial Day, Fourth of July, Labor Day), everywhere is crowded and overpriced.

On the following national holidays, banks, schools and government offices (including post offices) close, and transportation, museums and other services operate on a Sunday schedule. Holidays falling on a weekend are usually observed the following Monday.

New Year's Day January 1

Martin Luther King Jr Day 3rd Monday in January

Presidents' Day 3rd Monday in February

Memorial Day last Monday in May

Independence Day July 4 (aka Fourth of July)

Labor Day 1st Monday in September

Columbus Day 2nd Monday in October

Veterans' Day November 11

Thanksgiving Day 4th Thursday in November

Christmas Day December 25

Colleges usually take a one- or two-week 'spring break' in March or April, when many beach hotels and resorts, especially in SoCal, raise their rates. For students of all ages, summer vacation runs from June to August, making these the busiest travel months in California.

INSURANCE

No matter how long you're traveling for, it's smart to buy travel insurance. Worldwide travel insurance is available at www.lonelyplanet.com/travel_services. You can buy, extend and claim online anytime – even if you're already on the road.

At minimum you'll need coverage that includes treatment for medical emergencies. The best policies also extend to the worst possible scenario, such as an accident that requires hospitalization and a return flight home. Medical care in California is prohibitively expensive and some providers demand payment up-front. Be sure to keep all receipts and documentation so you can make a claim later. Some policies ask you to phone a call center for an immediate assessment of your problem before seeking medical care. Some also specifically exclude 'dangerous activities' such as scuba diving and motorcycling. US citizens should check with their medical insurer at home to see if they already have coverage in California.

Also consider coverage for luggage theft or loss and trip cancellation. If you already have a home-owner's or renter's policy, see what it will cover and consider getting supplemental insurance to cover the rest. If you have prepaid a large portion of your trip, cancellation insurance may be a worthwhile expense. If you're driving, you must carry liability insurance, offered by car-rental agencies and some credit cards (see p392).

INTERNATIONAL VISITORS
ENTERING THE COUNTRY

Getting into the USA can be a bureaucratic nightmare, depending on your country of origin, as the rules keep changing. All travelers should double-check current visa and passport regulations *before* coming to the USA. For updated information, check the website of the **US Department of State** (http://travel.state.gov/visa) and the travel section of the **US Customs & Border Protection** (www.cbp.gov) website.

The Department of Homeland Security (DHS) registration program, US-VISIT (www.dhs.gov/us-visit), currently includes 327 ports of air, land and sea entry. For foreign visitors (excluding, for now, most Canadian and some Mexican citizens), registration consists of having a digital photo taken and electronic (inkless) fingerprints made of each index finger; the process takes less than a minute.

PASSPORTS & VISAS

Currently, most Canadian citizens arriving from anywhere in the Western hemisphere are exempt from visa requirements. However, a Canadian passport, cross-border Trusted Traveler Program card or an enhanced driver's license or photo ID that complies with the USA's Western Hemisphere Travel Initiative (WHTI) is now required. For details, consult www.cbp.gov.

All visitors to the USA from other countries must have a machine-readable passport that is valid for six months longer than their intended stay and meets current US standards. If your passport was issued after October 26, 2006, it must be an e-Passport with a digital photo and an integrated RFID chip containing biometric data. For more information, consult www.cbp.gov.

Currently under the Visa Waiver Program (VWP), citizens of the following countries may enter the USA without a visa for stays of 90 days or fewer (no extensions allowed): Andorra, Australia, Austria, Belgium, Brunei, Czech Republic, Denmark, Estonia, Finland, France, Germany, Hungary, Iceland, Ireland, Italy, Japan, Latvia, Liechtenstein, Lithuania, Luxembourg, Malta, Monaco, the Netherlands, New Zealand, Norway, Portugal, San Marino, Singapore, Slovakia, Slovenia, South Korea, Spain, Sweden, Switzerland and the UK.

Under the VWP program, you must have a passport that meets current US standards and either a round-trip or onward ticket to any foreign destination, other than a territory bordering the US (ie Mexico and Canada). This ticket must be nonrefundable in the USA. You must also get approval from the Electronic System for Travel Authorization (ESTA) in advance. Register online with DHS at https://esta.cbp.dhs.gov at least 72 hours before arrival. Once travel authorization is approved, your registration is valid for two years.

All other foreign visitors must obtain a visa from a US consulate or embassy in their own country, a process that costs at minimum a nonrefundable $131, involves a personal interview and can take several weeks; apply at home as early as possible.

CUSTOMS REGULATIONS

You may import duty free 1L of alcohol, if you're over 21; 200 cigarettes (one carton) or 50 cigars (not Cubans), if you're over 18; and $100 worth of gifts ($800 for US citizens). Amounts in excess of $10,000 in cash, traveler's checks, money orders and other cash equivalents must be declared. Unless you're curious about US jails, don't even think about bringing in illegal drugs, drug paraphernalia, firearms or other weapons. For full details and the latest regulations, contact US Customs & Border Protection (☎ 703-526-4200, 877-227-5511; www.cbp.gov).

California is an important agricultural state. To prevent the spread of pests and diseases, certain food items (including meats, fresh fruit and vegetables) may not be brought into the state. If you drive into California across the border from Mexico or the adjacent states of Oregon, Nevada and Arizona, you may have to stop for a quick vehicle inspection by California Department of Food and Agriculture officials.

EMBASSIES & CONSULATES

Most foreign embassies are in Washington, DC, but many countries have consular offices in LA and San Francisco. To get in touch with an embassy in Washington, DC, call that city's directory assistance (☎ 202- 555-1212). For more foreign consulates in California, click to www.sos.ca.gov/business/ibrp/consulates.htm.

Australia Los Angeles (Map p79; ☎ 310-229-2300; Century Plaza Towers, 31st fl, 2029 Century Park E); San Francisco (☎ 415-536-1970; 575 Market St, Suite 1800)

Canada Los Angeles (Map p68; ☎ 213-346-2700; 550 S Hope St, 9th fl); San Francisco (☎ 415-834-3180; 580 California St, 14th fl)

France Los Angeles (Map p79; ☎ 310-235-3200; 10390 Santa Monica Blvd, Suites 115 & 410); San Francisco (☎ 415-397-4330; 540 Bush St)

Germany Los Angeles (Map p79; ☎ 323-930-2703; 6222 Wilshire Blvd, Suite 500); San Francisco (☎ 415-775-1061; 1960 Jackson St)

Ireland San Francisco (☎ 415-392-4214; 100 Pine St, Suite 3350)

Italy Los Angeles (Map p62; ☎ 310-820-0622; 12400 Wilshire Blvd, Suite 300); San Francisco (☎ 415-931-4924; 2590 Webster St)

Japan Los Angeles (Map p68; ☎ 213-617-6700; 350 S Grand Ave, Suite 1700); San Francisco (☎ 415-777-3533; 50 Fremont St, Suite 2300)

Mexico Los Angeles (☎ 213-351-6800; 2401 W 6th St); San Francisco (☎ 415-354-1700; 532 Folsom St)

Netherlands Los Angeles (Map p62; ☎ 877-388-2443; 11766 Wilshire Blvd, Suite 1150)

New Zealand Los Angeles (Map p52; ☎ 310-566-6555; 2425 Olympic Blvd, Suite 600e)

South Africa Los Angeles (Map p79; ☎ 310-651-0902; 6300 Wilshire Blvd, Suite 600)

Spain Los Angeles (off Map p79; ☎ 323-938-0158; 5055 Wilshire Blvd, Suite 860); San Francisco (☎ 415-922-2995; 1405 Sutter St)

UK Los Angeles (Map p62; ☎ 310-481-0031; 11766 Wilshire Blvd, Suite 1200); San Francisco (☎ 415-617-1300; 1 Sansome St, Suite 850)

It's important to realize what the embassy of the country of which you are a citizen can and can't do. Generally speaking, it won't be much help in emergencies if the trouble you're in is remotely your own fault. Remember, you're bound by local laws and embassy officials won't be sympathetic if you've committed a crime in California, even if such actions are legal in your own country. If you have all your money and documents stolen, they will assist you in getting a new passport, but forget about a loan for onward travel.

INTERNET ACCESS

California leads the world in internet technology, so it's pretty easy to stay connected. This guide uses the internet icon (🖳) wherever public internet terminals are available and the wi-fi icon (📶) to denote wireless internet access, whether free or fee-based.

There are internet cafes in cities and towns, charging $3 to $12 per hour for online access. Better cybercafes and full-service copy shops like FedEx Office (☎ 800-463-3339; www.fedex.com) also provide stations for printing digital-camera photos and/or burning photo CDs. At public libraries, internet terminals and wi-fi access are typically free but may be subject to registration requirements, time limits, queues and slow connections, with access to some websites blocked; out-of-state visitors must sometimes pay a nominal fee. Most coffee shops, including Starbucks, and some airports, bars and even museums have wi-fi hot spots, either free or for an hourly/daily access fee.

Many motels and most hotels provide guests with high-speed internet connections (sometimes wired, but increasingly wireless) and/or a place to log on to the internet, such as a self-serve lobby terminal or full-fledged business center. Fees range from nothing to more than $10 per day. These days, you can even connect in the woods: private campgrounds and RV parks increasingly offer wi-fi, as do dozens of state parks (www.parks.ca.gov), usually near to the ranger station or in campgrounds and picnic areas.

If you're visiting from abroad, remember that you will need an AC adapter and a plug adapter for US sockets. Both are sold in larger electronics stores such as **Best Buy** (☎ 888-237-8289; www.bestbuy.com).

See p45 for useful California travel websites.

LEGAL MATTERS

If you are stopped by the police for any reason, there is no system of paying fines on the spot. Attempting to pay the fine to the officer may lead to a charge of attempted bribery. There is usually a 30-day period to pay a fine. For traffic offenses, the police officer will explain the options to you. Most matters can be handled by mail.

If you are arrested for more serious offenses, you have the right to remain silent and are presumed innocent until proven guilty. There is no legal reason to speak to a police officer if you don't wish. All persons who are arrested are legally allowed the right to make one phone call. If you don't have a lawyer, friend or family member to help you, call your embassy. The police will give you the number upon request. If you can't afford a lawyer, a public defender will be appointed to you free of charge.

At bars, restaurants, nightclubs and liquor stores, you may be asked for photo ID to prove you are of legal age to buy and consume alcohol. Stiff fines, jail time and other penalties can be incurred for driving under the influence (DUI) of alcohol or drugs. A blood-alcohol content of 0.08% or higher is illegal. Penalties for DUI range from license suspension and fines to jail time. It is also illegal to carry open containers of alcohol inside a vehicle, even if they are empty. Containers that are full and sealed may be carried, but if they have ever been opened, they must be stored in the trunk.

During holidays and festive events, police roadblocks are sometimes set up to deter DUI. Officers can give roadside sobriety checks to assess if you've been drinking or using drugs. If you fail, they'll require you to take a breath, urine or blood test to determine the level of alcohol in your body. Refusing to be tested is treated the same as taking and failing the test. If you're in a group, choose a 'designated driver' who agrees not to consume alcohol or drugs.

In California, possession of less than 1oz of marijuana is a misdemeanor, punishable by up to one year in jail, though first-time offenders may be eligible for community service and counseling. Possession of any other illegal drug, including cocaine, heroin, ecstasy, hashish or more than an ounce of weed, is a felony, punishable by lengthy jail sentences. For foreign visitors, it's grounds for deportation.

MAPS

Visitors centers and chambers of commerce stock basic local and regional maps, often free. Gas stations, convenience shops and bookstores sell low-cost folding maps of local areas that include street-name indexes. Members of automobile associations can obtain free maps from local offices. For a map atlas, the gold standard is Benchmark Press' *California Road & Recreation Atlas* (www.benchmark maps.com; $24.95), which shows *every* road in the state, as well as campgrounds, trailheads, ski areas and hundreds of other points of interest. For detailed trail and topographical maps, stop by state and national park visitors centers, USFS ranger stations or outdoor retailers like REI (☎ 800-426-4840; www.rei.com). The best topo maps are published by the US Geological Survey (USGS; ☎ 877-275-8747; www.usgs.gov), available online. For GPS and laptop users, National Geographic (☎ 800-962-1643; www.natgeomaps.com) publishes the Topo! series of outdoor recreation mapping software, with a complete CD-ROM set available for California ($100).

PETS

Traveling with your canine companion is no more difficult in California than in the rest of the USA. Look for the 🐾 icon, highlighting pet-friendly businesses in the destination chapters. For general travel tips and even more dog-friendly accommodations, restaurants, beaches and off-leash parks, browse www.dogfriendly.com.

Many motels and hotels have pet-friendly accommodations, although these are often smoking rooms and pets may never be left unattended; a nightly surcharge (ranging from nominal to outrageously expensive) and maximum weight restrictions may apply. Dogs are sometimes welcome on outdoor patios or at sidewalk tables at restaurants and cafes, but ask first. Dogs are not usually allowed on public transportation or inside shops, though exceptions may be made for 'pocket pooches' being toted around in designer handbags, especially in chi-chi neighborhoods.

Few beaches allow dogs, and then usually only if they're leashed; check posted signs carefully. If you're planning to visit state or national parks, consider leaving Fido at home – dogs are rarely, if ever, allowed on hiking trails, and may not be left alone tied up at public campgrounds. Never leave your pet unattended inside a locked vehicle with the windows rolled up – temperatures inside can quickly become lethal.

TIME

California is in the Pacific time zone, eight hours behind GMT/UTC. Daylight Saving Time (DST), when clocks move ahead one hour, runs from the second Sunday in March to the first Sunday in November.

TOURIST INFORMATION

The California Travel & Tourism Commission (☎ 916-444-4429, 877-225-4367; www.visitcalifornia.com) has an excellent website packed with useful pretrip planning information, plus a free downloadable annual visitors' guide. It also maintains 12 regional California Welcome Centers (CWC; www.visitcwc.com). Staff dispense maps and brochures and can help with accommodations. Look for the CWC in San Francisco (p94). There are also CWCs located at Pismo Beach (p299) on the Central Coast, and Arcata (p164) on the North Coast. Local tourist information offices are listed throughout the destination chapters.

TOURS

For city tours and guided outdoor activities that you can sign up for after arrival in California, see the destination chapters.
Backroads (☎ 510-527-1555, 800-462-2848; www.backroads.com) Bicycling, hiking, kayaking and multisport tours of the California coast, with deluxe camping and inn stays.
Elderhostel (☎ 978-323-4141, 800-454-5768; www.elderhostel.org) Nonprofit organization offers 'learning adventures' throughout California for active travelers aged 55 and up.

Green Tortoise (☎ 415-956-7500, 800-867-8647; www.greentortoise.com) Budget-minded trips for independent travelers utilizing converted sleeping-bunk buses; the 'Coastal Crawler' route connects San Francisco and LA.

Trek America (☎ 800-873-5872; www.trek america.com) This outfit offers outdoors-focused trips for small groups along the coast, including camping and visits to national parks.

TRAVELERS WITH DISABILITIES

If you have a physical disability, California can be an accommodating place. The Americans with Disabilities Act (ADA) requires that all public buildings (including hotels, restaurants, theaters and museums) be wheelchair-accessible, and buses and trains must have wheelchair lifts. Telephone companies are required to provide relay operators (available via TTY numbers) for the hearing impaired. Many banks now provide ATM instructions in Braille or via earphone jacks for hearing-impaired customers, and you'll find audible crossing signals at many intersections.

Larger chain motels and hotels often have specially equipped rooms and suites for guests with disabilities. If you're worried about stairs, ask about the availability of an elevator, especially at independent lodgings. Major car-rental agencies offer hand-controlled vehicles and vans with wheelchair lifts at no extra charge, but you must reserve them well in advance. **Wheelchair Getaways** (☎ 800-642-2042; www.wheelchairgetaways.com) rents out wheelchair-accessible vans in San Francisco, LA and San Diego.

All major airlines, Greyhound buses and Amtrak trains will assist travelers with disabilities, as long as you notify them 48 hours in advance. Service animals (such as guide dogs) are allowed to accompany passengers, but you must have documentation. Airlines and Greyhound buses accept wheelchairs as checked baggage, while Amtrak allows standard wheelchairs on trains. On Amtrak, travelers with documented disabilities receive discounts off regular fares when booking in person or by phone.

Most national and some state parks and recreation areas have paved, graded-dirt or boardwalk nature trails. For free admission to national parks, US citizens and permanent residents with permanent disabilities can get a free 'America the Beautiful Access Pass. **California State Parks** (☎ 916-445-8949; http://access.parks.ca.gov/) has a detailed online accessibility guide with a searchable regional directory. The **California State Coastal Conservancy** (☎ 510-286-1015; www.scc.ca.gov) offers free downloadable wheelchair riders' guides to the San Francisco Bay Area and the LA and Orange County coasts.

For local access guides, contact visitor information centers listed throughout the destination chapters. Other helpful resources for travelers with disabilities:

Access-Able Travel Source (☎ 303-232-2979; www.access-able.com) General travel website with useful tips and links, including the Travelin' Talk Network.

Disabled Sports USA Far West (☎ 530-581-4161; www.dsusafw.org; annual membership $25) Organizes adaptive sports and outdoor recreation programs.

Mobility International USA (☎ 541-343-1284; www.miusa.org) Advises disabled travelers on mobility issues and runs educational international-exchange programs.

Moss Rehabilitation Hospital (☎ 800-225-5667; www.mossresourcenet.org/travel.htm) Extensive links and tips for accessible travel.

WOMEN TRAVELERS

California is a reasonably safe place to travel, even if you're flying solo. Just use the same common sense as you would anywhere. The website www.journeywoman.com facilitates women exchanging travel tips and links to helpful resources. The booklet 'Her Own Way,' published by the Canadian government, is filled with general travel tips, useful for any woman; click to www.voyage.gc.ca, then under Resources select Publications and download the PDF.

Planned Parenthood (☎ 800-230-7526; www.plannedparenthood.org) offers referrals to low-cost women's health clinics throughout California. If you are sexually assaulted, consider contacting a rape-crisis center before calling the police, unless you are in immediate danger, in which case call ☎ 911. Not all police have as much sensitivity training and/or experience in assisting sexual assault survivors, whereas rape crisis-center staff will actively advocate on your behalf and act as a link to other community services, including hospitals and the police. Telephone books have listings of local rape-crisis centers, or contact the 24-hour **National Sexual Assault Hotline** (☎ 800-656-4673; www.rainn.org). Alternatively, go straight to a hospital emergency room.

TRANSPORTATION

GETTING THERE & AWAY

Flights and tours can be booked online at www.lonelyplanet.com/travel_services.

AIR

Domestic airfares vary hugely depending on the season, day of the week, length of stay and flexibility of the ticket for changes and refunds. Still, nothing determines fares more than demand, and when business is slow, airlines lower fares to fill seats. Airlines are competitive and at any given time any one of them could have the cheapest fare. Expect less fluctuation with international fares.

International passengers arriving in Los Angeles disembark at the Tom Bradley International Terminal of **Los Angeles International Airport** (LAX; ☎ 310-646-5252; www.lawa.org/lax), 19 miles southwest of Downtown. Most international flights to the San Francisco Bay Area land at **San Francisco International Airport** (SFO; ☎ 650-821-8211, 800-435-9736; www.flysfo.com), 15 miles south of downtown. Bay Area airports in **Oakland** (OAK; ☎ 510-563-3300; www.flyoakland.com) and **San Jose** (SJC; ☎ 408-277-4759; www.sjc.org) are important domestic gateways with limited international services. **San Diego International Airport** (SAN; ☎ 619-400-2400; www.san.org), aka Lindbergh Field, has flights to Canada and Mexico.

Smaller regional airports mainly for domestic travel:

Arcata/Eureka Airport (ACV; ☎ 707-839-5401; http://co.humboldt.ca.us/aviation) On the North Coast.

Bob Hope Airport (BUR; ☎ 818-840-8840; www.burbankairport.com) In Burbank.

Jack McNamara Field Airport (CEC; ☎ 707-464-7229; www.co.del-norte.ca.us) In Crescent City.

John Wayne Airport (SNA; ☎ 949-252-5200; www.ocair.com) In Orange County.

Long Beach Airport (LGB; ☎ 562-570-2600; www.longbeach.gov/airport) In LA County.

Monterey Peninsula Airport (MRY; ☎ 831-648-7000; www.montereyairport.com) On the Central Coast.

San Luis Obispo County Regional Airport (SBP; ☎ 805-781-5205; www.sloairport.com) On the Central Coast.

Santa Barbara Municipal Airport (SBA; ☎ 805-967-7111; www.flysba.com) On the Central Coast.

LAND

BUS

The main national bus carrier, Greyhound (☎ 800-231-2222; www.greyhound.com), operates to cities and towns in California from around the US. See p391 for information about domestic fares, seating and reservations.

CAR & MOTORCYCLE

Though each US state legislates its own rules of the road, there's little variation. For advice about driving in California, see p392.

TRAIN

Amtrak (☎ 800-872-7245; www.amtrak.com) operates a fairly extensive rail system throughout the US. Trains are comfortable, if slow, and equipped with dining and lounge cars on long-distance routes. Fares vary according to the type of train and seating. You can travel in reserved or unreserved coach seats, business class or first class, which includes sleeping compartments.

GETTING AROUND

AIR

If you have limited time and want to cover great distances quickly, fly. Depending on the departure airport, destination, time of year and booking date, air travel can be less expensive than bus, train or rental car.

Flights between the Bay Area and Southern California take off every hour from 6am to 10pm from SFO and OAK. It's possible to show up at the airport, buy your ticket and hop on, though competitive fares require advance purchase, and you'll have to set aside time to contend with security lines. Flights to smaller airports can be fairly pricey, because fewer airlines compete on these routes.

BICYCLE

Bicycling California requires a high level of fitness and focused awareness. Coastal highways climb up and down wind-blown bluffs above the ocean and along narrow stretches of winding road with fast-moving traffic. Nonetheless, bicyclists are

⚐ CLIMATE CHANGE & TRAVEL

Every form of transport that relies on carbon-based fuel generates CO_2, the main cause of human-induced climate change. Modern travel is dependent on aeroplanes and while they might use less fuel per kilometre per person than most cars, they travel much greater distances. It's not just CO_2 emissions from aircraft that are the problem. The altitude at which aircraft emit gases (including CO_2) and particles contributes significantly to their total climate change impact. The Intergovernmental Panel on Climate Change believes aviation is responsible for 4.9% of climate change – double the effect of its CO_2 emissions alone.

Lonely Planet regards travel as a global benefit. We encourage the use of more climate-friendly travel modes where possible and, together with other concerned partners across many industries, we support the carbon offset scheme run by ClimateCare. Websites such as climatecare.org use 'carbon calculators' that allow people to offset the greenhouse gases they are responsible for with contributions to portfolios of climate-friendly initiatives throughout the developing world. Lonely Planet offsets the carbon footprint of all staff and author travel.

fairly common, and the ride is incredibly rewarding. Cars pose the greatest hazard.

You can rent bikes by the hour, day, week or month. Buy them new at specialty bicycle shops, sporting-goods stores or outdoor outfitters like co-op REI (☎ 800-426-4840; www.rei.com), or used at flea markets and from notice boards at hostels and universities. Also check online bulletin boards like Craigslist (www.craigslist.org).

Cyclists must follow the same rules of the road as vehicles, but don't expect drivers to always respect your right of way. Bicycling is permitted on all roads and highways – even along freeways if there's no designated alternative, such as a smaller parallel route (all mandatory exits are marked). The Adventure Cycling Association (☎ 406-721-1776, 800-775-2453; www.adv-cycling.org) is an excellent source for bicycle touring maps covering the entire Pacific Coast.

If you tire of pedaling, some local buses are equipped with bike racks; call the transportation company to check. To transport bikes on airplanes, Greyhound buses and Amtrak trains, contact the respective company to ask about reservations, excess-baggage surcharges and whether you'll need to disassemble the bike and box it.

For coastal cycling enthusiasts, perhaps the best-kept secret is those specially designated 'hike & bike' campsites available at some California State Parks. There you can roll (or walk) right into your campsite and set up a tent for just $5 to $10 per night.

San Francisco, Arcata, Santa Cruz, San Luis Obispo and Santa Barbara rank among California's most bike-friendly communities. The California Department of Transportation website (www.dot.ca.gov/roadsandtraffic.html) has links to cycling advocacy groups statewide. For more inspiration and practical information for recreational cycling and mountain biking, see p342.

To avoid all-too-common bicycle theft, use a good, heavy-duty lock. Always wear a helmet – they're mandatory for anyone under 18. Ensure you have proper lights and reflective clothing at night. Carry water and a repair kit for flats.

BOAT

You can't travel around California by boat, although there are a few public ferry services, including to Santa Catalina Island, off the Los Angeles and Orange County coasts, and Channel Islands National Park, offshore from Ventura County. Also, commuter ferries operate throughout the San Francisco Bay Area.

BUS

Often the cheapest way to get around California, Greyhound (☎ 800-231-2222; www.greyhound.com) runs several daily buses along highways between coastal cities, stopping at some smaller towns along the way. Frequency of service varies, but the most popular routes operate every hour or so, sometimes around the clock.

As a rule, Greyhound buses are reliable, cleanish and comfortable, with air-con, barely reclining seats, onboard lavatories and no smoking on board. Sit toward the front, away from the bathroom. Long-distance buses stop for meal breaks and driver changes every few hours, usually at fast-food restaurants or truck stops.

Bus stations are dreary places, often in sketchy urban areas. In small towns, where there is no station, buses stop in front of a specific business – know exactly where and when the bus arrives, be obvious as you flag it down, and be prepared to pay with exact change.

TRANSPORTATION

GETTING AROUND

It's easiest to buy tickets online with a major credit card, and then pick them up by showing photo ID at the bus terminal's ticket counter. You can also buy tickets over the phone or through an agent. For tickets by mail, order at least 10 business days in advance.

For the lowest fares, buy tickets online at least seven days in advance. Also check the Greyhound website for special promotional deals. Children aged two to 11 get 40% off; seniors over 62 qualify for 5% discounts. Students who have a Student Advantage Discount Card (see p382) receive 15% off regular fares, or 10% with any valid student ID. If you're traveling with friends or family, Greyhound's companion fares allow up to three additional travelers to get 50% off with a minimum three-day advance purchase.

CAR & MOTORCYCLE

Neither buses nor trains access large swaths of California's coast, so plan on driving if you want to visit small towns, isolated beaches or far-flung forests. Independence costs you, since rental rates and gas prices will eat a good chunk of a travel budget.

DRIVER'S LICENSE

Foreign visitors may legally drive a car in the USA for up to 12 months using their home driver's license. However, an International Driving Permit (IDP) will simplify the car-rental process, especially if your license doesn't have a photo or isn't written in English. To drive a motorcycle, you will need either a valid US state motorcycle license or a specially endorsed IDP.

INSURANCE

Liability insurance is required by law, but is not automatically included in California rental contracts because some Americans are covered for rental cars under their personal car-insurance policies. If you're not already covered, expect to pay about $15 per day. Insurance against damage to the car itself, called Collision Damage Waiver (CDW) or Loss Damage Waiver (LDW), costs an additional $15 or so per day, usually with an initial deductible of $100 to $500 for any repairs.

Some credit cards cover CDW for rentals of up to 15 days, provided you charge the entire cost of the rental to the card. But if there's an accident, you may have to pay the car-rental agency first, and then seek reimbursement from the credit-card company. There may also be exceptions that are not covered, such as 'exotic' rentals (eg 4WDs, convertibles). Check with your credit-card company in advance.

RENTAL

Most international car-rental agencies have desks at major airports, in all coastal cities and some smaller towns. For rates and reservations, go online or call toll-free:
Alamo (☎ 877-222-9075; www.alamo.com)
Avis (☎ 800-331-1212; www.avis.com)
Budget (☎ 800-527-0700; www.budget.com)
Dollar (☎ 800-800-3665; www.dollar.com)
Enterprise (☎ 800-261-7331; www.enterprise.com)
Fox (☎ 800-225-4369; www.foxrentacar.com)
Hertz (☎ 800-654-3131; www.hertz.com)
National (☎ 877-222-9058; www.nationalcar.com)
Rent-A-Wreck (☎ 877-877-0700; www.rent-a-wreck.com)
Thrifty (☎ 800-847-4389; www.thrifty.com)

Car Rental Express (www.carrentalexpress.com) rates and compares independent agencies, and is especially useful for searching out cheaper long-term rentals.

Some major car-rental agencies, including Avis, Budget and Hertz, now offer 'green' fleets of hybrid rental cars, as does LA-based **Simply Hybrid** (☎ 323-653-0011, 888-359-0055; www.simplyhybrid.com).

MOTORCYCLES

Motorcycle rentals and insurance are not cheap, especially if you've got your eye on a Harley-Davidson. Expect to pay from $100 to $175 per day (excluding taxes and fees), depending on the rental location, size of the bike and length of the rental. Rates sometimes include helmets, unlimited miles and liability insurance; collision insurance (CDW) costs extra.

Motorcycle rental agencies in California:
Dubbelju Motorcycle Rentals (☎ 415-495-2774, 866-495-2774; www.dubbelju.com; 698a Bryant St, San Francisco) Rents BMWs, Triumphs and Harley-Davidson motorcycles and Yamaha scooters.

Eagle Rider (☎ 310-536-6777, 888-900-9901; www.eaglerider.com) Has 12 outlets in California, including in LA, San Diego and San Francisco; one-way rental surcharge from $150 to $300.

RECREATIONAL VEHICLES

Gas-guzzling RVs remain popular with California travelers despite high fuel prices. It's easy to find campgrounds with electricity and water hookups, but in big cities, RVs are nothing but a nuisance, because there are few places to park or plug them in. Although cumbersome to navigate, they do solve transportation, accommodation and cooking needs in one fell swoop.

RV rental agencies with branches in California:
Cruise America (☎ 480-464-7300, 800-671-8042; www.cruiseamerica.com)
El Monte RV (☎ 562-483-4956, 888-337-2214; www.elmonterv.com)
Happy Travel Campers (☎ 310-675-1335, 800-370-1262; www.camperusa.com) Main base is located in LA.

ROAD CONDITIONS & HAZARDS

Drivers should watch for stock and deer on coastal highways. Hitting a large animal at 55mph will total your car, kill the animal and perhaps seriously injure you as well. Thick fog may also impede driving – slow down, and if it's too soupy, pull off the road. Watch out for fallen rocks, which can damage or even disable your car if struck. For statewide road conditions contact **Caltrans** (☎ 800-427-7623; www.dot.ca.gov).

Hwy 1 hugs the coastal bluffs along dramatic stretches of coastline, particularly between San Luis Obispo and Big Sur, and north of San Francisco. Not for the faint of heart, these precarious cliffsides often wash out in winter. Caltrans always seems to be repairing Hwy 1, and every couple of years, stretches close for months at a time. Hwy 101 north of Leggett (where Hwy 1 ends) is particularly prone to slides where it runs between the Eel River Gorge and unstable slopes.

When you see signs that read, 'Expect long delays 40 miles ahead,' or 'Hwy 1 closed north of Hearst Castle,' heed their warnings but don't panic. They sometimes overstate the situation to deter unnecessary travel. If you have hotel reservations, call the innkeeper. Local folk *always* know precisely what's happening with Hwys 1 and 101, which may be their only connections to the outside world.

ROAD RULES

The *California Driver Handbook* and *California Motorcycle Handbook* explain everything you need to know about driving here. They're available free from any Department of Motor Vehicles (DMV) office or download the PDFs from www.dmv.ca.gov.

Talking on a handheld cell (mobile) phone while driving is illegal in California; use a handsfree device (ie Bluetooth headset) instead. Drivers, front-seat passengers and children under 16 must wear a seatbelt at all times. Children under six years old, or those weighing less than 60lb, must ride in approved child-safety seats; most car-rental agencies rent these for around $10/50 per day/week, though you must reserve them when booking. All motorcyclists must wear helmets.

In winter months along the coast, avoid high-mountain inland routes unless you have a 4WD vehicle. If it's raining on the coast in January, chances are it's snowing in the mountains. Chains may be required at any time. Take note of weather forecasts.

Californians drive on the right-hand side of the road. On interstate highways, the speed limit is sometimes raised to 70mph. Unless otherwise posted, the speed limit is 65mph on freeways, 55mph on two-lane undivided highways, 35mph on major city streets and 25mph in business and residential districts and near schools. It's forbidden to pass a school bus when its lights are flashing.

Unless otherwise posted, you may turn right on red after stopping, so long as you don't impede intersecting traffic, which has the right of way. You may also make a left on red at two intersecting one-way streets. At four-way stop signs, cars proceed in the order in which they arrived. If two cars arrive simultaneously, the one on the right has the right of way. When in doubt, just politely wave the other person ahead.

When emergency vehicles (ie police, fire or ambulance) approach, pull over and get out of their way. On freeways you may pass slower cars on either the left or the right lane, but try to pass on the left. If two cars are trying to get into the same central lane, the one on the right has priority. Carpool lanes marked with

a diamond symbol are reserved for cars with multiple passengers. Fines for driving in these lanes without the minimum number of passengers are prohibitively stiff.

California has strict anti-littering laws. If you are seen throwing anything from a vehicle onto the roadway, you may be fined up to $1000. Littering convictions are shown on your driving record the same as other driving violations. When parking read all posted regulations and pay attention to colored curbs, or you may be towed.

LOCAL TRANSPORTATION

California's major cities all have local bus, cable-car, trolley, train, light-rail and/or subway systems. Larger coastal towns and counties operate commuter-bus systems, usually with limited evening and weekend services. Inexpensive water taxis ply San Diego, Long Beach and Santa Barbara harbors. For local transportation details, see the destination chapters.

TRAIN

Amtrak (☎ 800-872-7245; www.amtrak.com) operates intra-California routes, with Thruway buses providing connections to smaller towns. Sometimes you'll only spend an hour on the train, then four hours on a bus, but it's more civilized than Greyhound.

Valid for seven days of travel within a 21-day period, Amtrak's California Rail Pass (per adult/child $159/80) can be used on *Pacific Surfliner* trains, the *Coast Starlight* within California, and most connecting Thruway bus services. Buy passes online, by phone or in person. You must make separate seat reservations for each leg of travel.

⬊ BEHIND THE SCENES

THE AUTHORS
BETH KOHN

Coordinating author, This Is California, California's Top 25
Experiences, California's Top Itineraries, San Francisco, Wine
Country, Sierra Nevada & the Deserts, California in Focus

A lucky long-time resident of San Francisco, Beth lives to be
playing outside or splashing in big puddles of water. For this
guide, she biked the Bay Area and Lake Tahoe–area byways,
crossed off her first California 14er, dodged pesky wildfires
and selflessly soaked in hot springs – for research purposes,
of course. She is an author for Lonely Planet's *California* and
Yosemite, Sequoia & Kings Canyon National Parks guides, and
you can also see more of her work at www.bethkohn.com.

Author thanks A big thanks to Suki Gear for signing me up, and to Sasha Baskett for
answering every single question imaginable. Alex Leviton receives the coveted disco-
dancing-under-duress award, and Claude Moller gets his usual hugs.

ALEX LEVITON

Coordinating author, Planning Your Trip, Los Angeles, The
Bay Area & Northern California, Central & Southern California
Coast, California in Focus, Directory & Transportation

Alex was born and raised in Southern California, lived in
Humboldt County for seven years and has a graduate degree
in journalism from UC Berkeley. When not living or traveling
abroad or in her adopted second state of North Carolina, Alex
has called San Francisco or Oakland home for a dozen or so years.
She's been on, oh, no less than six gazillion road trips throughout
the state, from the ghost town of Bodie to the wine country's
Culinary Institute. Alex's usual haunts are Italy and the American

South, so she was thrilled to write about her favorite places since childhood: the Los Angeles beaches where she grew up, the redwoods and Monterey Bay.

Author thanks An enormous debt of gratitude goes to D Gregg Doyle, Central California expert, urban planner and traveling companion extraordinaire. Thanks to my Orange County connection, Jennifer Brunson. In the Melbourne office, props goes to Sasha Baskett and her helpful explanations. And, of course, thanks to my coauthor Beth Kohn. Go, Team Disco!

ALEXIS AVERBUCK
North Coast, Northern Mountains

Alexis Averbuck was born in Oakland but since childhood has been on serial walkabout. Her early jaunts had her road-tripping through Europe and living in Hong Kong, India and Sri Lanka. Soon thereafter she was bitten by the travel-writing bug and covered places as disparate as Guatemala, Italy and Thailand. Now Alexis lives in Hydra, Greece, so for this research trip she returned to her home state to further explore the back roads of beautiful northern California. Despite having lived in Antarctica for a year and crossed the Pacific by sailboat, Alexis still adores the Mendocino coast. She's also a painter – see her work at www.alexisaverbuck.com.

AMY C BALFOUR
Orange County, San Diego Area

To ensure that readers get the full California experience, Amy has explored the Gaslamp Quarter in the rain, surprised a Wolf's guenon in the San Diego Zoo, worn a cardboard crown at Medieval Times, and spied on guests at the naughty Ivy Hotel from a nearby condo (hey, they left the blinds open). For the last few years she's also had fun hiking, biking and four-wheeling all over the SoCal backcountry. She wrote Lonely Planet's *Los Angeles Encounter* and contributed to *Coastal California*, *Los Angeles & Southern California* and *California Trips*. She's written for *Backpacker*, *Every Day with Rachael Ray*, *Redbook*, *Southern Living*, *Women's Health* and the *Los Angeles Times*.

ANDREW BENDER
Los Angeles, Orange County, San Diego

Yet another Lonely Planet author with an MBA, this native New Englander first came to Los Angeles after B-school to work in film production, but he ended up leaving the industry to do what every MBA (and production dude) secretly dreams of: traveling and writing about it. These days you can see his writing and photography in the *Los Angeles Times*, *Forbes*, *SilverKris* (Singapore Airlines in-flight magazine), over a dozen Lonely Planet titles including *Los Angeles & Southern California*, and at www.andrewbender.com. When not on the road he can be seen biking the beach in Santa Monica, discovering the next greatest ethnic joint and scheming over ways to spoil his nieces and nephews.

SARA BENSON
Central Coast, The Deserts

Born in the cornfields outside Chicago, Sara jumped on a plane to the West Coast after college with just one suitcase and $100 in her pocket. She landed in San Francisco and has bounced around the state ever since, including the Sierra Nevada, Los Angeles and San Luis Obispo County. Sara is also an avid outdoor enthusiast. Her travel writing has featured on popular websites and in magazines and newspapers from coast to coast, including the *Los Angeles Times, San Francisco Chronicle*, *Las Vegas Review-Journal* and *National Geographic Adventure*. Already the author of 30 travel and nonfiction books, Sara has written Lonely Planet's *Las Vegas* and *Las Vegas Encounter* guides and contributed to *California Trips*.

ALISON BING
San Francisco, The Bay Area

Author, arts commentator and adventurous eater Alison Bing was adopted by California 17 years ago. By now she has done everything you're supposed to do here and a few things you're definitely not, including talking up LA bands in San Francisco bars and falling in love on the 7 Haight bus. Alison holds a graduate degree in international diplomacy, which she regularly undermines with opinionated commentary in magazines, newspapers, public radio and more than 20 books.

NATE CAVALIERI
Gold Country, Central Valley

Nate Cavalieri fell hard for Sacramento (what some call the *other* California) the first summer he lived there: it was hotter than hell, the AM station played plenty of Merle Haggard and on a clear day the cool, jagged caps of the Sierras broke up the eastern horizon to suggest the perfect escape plan. His previous titles with Lonely Planet include *Chicago*, *Puerto Rico* and *Volunteer: A Traveler's Guide to Making a Difference Around the World*. He writes about music and travel and lives with his partner and proofreader, Florence.

JOHN A VLAHIDES
San Francisco, Wine Country

John Vlahides lives in San Francisco. He's a former luxury-hotel concierge and member of the prestigious Les Clefs d'Or, the international union of the world's elite concierges. He is cofounder of the travel site 71miles.com, and appears regularly on television and radio; watch some of his travel videos on lonelyplanet.tv. John spends his free time singing with the San Francisco Symphony, sunning on the beach beneath the Golden Gate Bridge, skiing the Sierra Nevada and touring California on his motorcycle.

THIS BOOK

This 1st edition of *Discover California* was coordinated by Beth Kohn and Alex Leviton, and researched and written by Alexis Averbuck, Amy C Balfour, Andrew Bender, Sara Benson, Alison Bing, Nate Cavalieri, Beth Kohn, Alex Leviton and John A Vlahides. Alison Bing also researched and wrote the Golden Gate Park highlight (p88). This guidebook was commissioned in Lonely Planet's Oakland office, and produced by the following:

Commissioning Editor Suki Gear
Coordinating Editor Martine Power
Coordinating Cartographer Hunor Csutoros
Coordinating Layout Designer Jacqui Saunders
Managing Editors Sasha Baskett, Annelies Mertens
Managing Cartographers David Connolly, Alison Lyall
Managing Layout Designers Indra Kilfoyle, Celia Wood
Assisting Editors Ali Lemer, Katie O'Connell, Susan Paterson, Dianne Schallmeiner, Jeanette Wall
Assisting Cartographers Mark Griffiths, Andy Rojas

BEHIND THE SCENES

THIS BOOK

BEHIND THE SCENES

SEND US YOUR FEEDBACK

We love to hear from travelers — your comments keep us on our toes and help make our books better. Our well-travelled team reads every word on what you loved or loathed about this book. Although we cannot reply individually to postal submissions, we always guarantee that your feedback goes straight to the appropriate authors, in time for the next edition. Each person who sends us information is thanked in the next edition and the most useful submissions are rewarded with a free book.

To send us your updates — and find out about Lonely Planet events, newsletters and travel news — visit our award-winning website: lonelyplanet.com/contact.

Note: we may edit, reproduce and incorporate your comments in Lonely Planet products such as guidebooks, websites and digital products, so let us know if you don't want your comments reproduced or your name acknowledged. For a copy of our privacy policy visit lonelyplanet.com/privacy.

THIS BOOK

Cover Research Naomi Parker
Internal Image Research Jane Hart

Thanks to Glenn Beanland, Jessica Boland, Sabrina Dalbesio, Chris Girdler, Michelle Glynn, Martin Heng, Craig Kilburn, Darren O'Connell, Alison Ridgway, Averil Robertson, Rebecca Skinner

Internal photographs p4 Venice Beach, Los Angeles, Richard Cummins; p10 Dog in convertible, VanNess Ave, San Francisco, Sabrina Dalbesio; p12 Yosemite Valley viewed from Inspiration Point, Yosemite National Park, Feargus Cooney; p31 Avenue of the Giants, Humboldt Redwoods State Park, Emily Riddell; p39 Coastal poppies line the road through Big Sur, Jan Stromme; p3, p50 Harbor Grill, Santa Monica Pier, Los Angeles, Richard Cummins; p3, p87 Mural in the Castro District, San Francisco, Richard l'Anson; p3, p121 Pigeon Point Lighthouse, Hwy 1, Thomas Winz; p3, p175 Vineyard, Oakville, Napa Valley, Jerry Alexander; p3, p211 Hiker at Hetch Hetchy, Yosemite National Park, Lee Foster; p3, p267 Newport Beach, Orange County, Richard Cummins; p332 Vineyard, Dutch Canyon, Napa Valley, Jerry Alexander; p377 Cable car on California St, San Francisco, Angus Oborn

All images are copyright of the photographer unless otherwise indicated. Many of the images in this guide are available for licensing from Lonely Planet Images: www.lonelyplanetimages.com.

NOTES

NOTES

↘ INDEX

17-Mile Drive 273, 289, *273*

A

accommodations 42, 378-9, *see also individual locations*
activities 338-43, 379, *see also individual activities*
agricultural development 359
Ahwahneechee people 229
air pollution 371
air travel 389, 390
  air fares 389
  airports 389
  travel to/from California 389
  travel within California 390
Alabama Hills 247
Alcatraz Island 90, 100, *90*, *100*
American River 217, 248, *217*
Amtrak 25, 394, *25*
amusement parks
  Belmont Park 323
  Disney California Adventure 311
  Disneyland 270-1, 307-11
  Knott's Berry Farm 309
  Legoland 326
  Pacific Park 61
  Santa Cruz Beach Boardwalk 280
  Universal Studios Hollywood 54, 72
Andrew Molera State Park 293
animals 365
Año Nuevo State Reserve 136
Anza-Borrego Desert State Park 258-9, *251*, *259*
Aquarium of the Pacific 74, *74*
aquariums, *see also* wildlife

sanctuaries, zoos
  Aquarium of the Pacific 74
  Monterey Bay Aquarium 20, 286
  SeaWorld 322-3
  Seymour Marine Discovery Center 281
Arcata 164-8, **164**, *165*
Arcata Community Forest 123, 165
architects
  Gehry, Frank 65
  Meier, Richard 66
  Morgan, Julia 297
architecture 41, 336
area codes, *see inside front cover*
Armstrong Redwoods State Reserve 206, *208*
art galleries, *see* galleries
arts 334-7, *see also* literature, music, visual arts
Asian Art Museum 102
ATMs 42
Auburn State Recreation Area 248
Avenue of the Giants 123, 156-7, *31*, *122*, *157*

B

Badwater 263
Baker Beach 106
Balboa Island 309
Balboa Park 317, *319*
Bay Area Discovery Museum 141
Bay Area & Northern California 121-74, **129**, **131**, **138**, **158**
Bay Model Visitor Center 141
Bay to Breakers 46, 107-8
beaches 338-43, *see also* surfing, swimming
  Baker Beach 106

Cambria 299
Carmel Beach 291
Cayucos 299
Centerville Beach 160
Del Mar 304
Hermosa Beach 70
Huntington Beach 304
La Jolla 324
Laguna Beach 21, 313
Los Angeles 58
Lost Coast 172
Malibu 28, 61
Manhattan Beach 70
Miwok Beach 150
Muir Beach 145
Navy Beach 242
Newport Beach 304
Ocean Beach 106
Palos Verdes 70
Pfeiffer Beach 293-4
Pismo Beach 299
Portuguese Beach 150
Salmon Creek Beach 150
San Pedro 70
Santa Barbara 303
Schoolhouse Beach 150
Shell Beach 150
Solana Beach 304
Sonoma Coast State Beach 149-50
Stinson Beach 145
Stump Beach 151
swimming safety 381
beer 374-6
Beetle Rock Education Center 239
Belmont Park 323
Berkeley 130-5, **132**, **134**
bicycle travel, *see* cycling
Big Basin Redwoods State Park 137

000 Map pages
000 Photograph pages

Big Sur 272, 292-6, 15, 39, 272
bird-watching
    Arcata Marsh & Wildlife Sanctuary 165
    Big Sur 293
boat travel 391
boating 103, *see also* canoeing, kayaking, whitewater rafting
Bodega Bay 148-9, 148
Bodie State Historic Park 241-2, 241
books 45, *see also* literature
breweries 376
Broad Contemporary Art Museum 72
Burning Man 256, 256
bus travel
    to/from California 390
    within California 391-2
bushwalking, *see* hiking
business hours, *see inside front cover*
'butterfat' mansions 160

C
cable cars 91, 91
California Academy of Sciences 88, 102, 88, 99
California Building 318
California cuisine 15, 23, 344-50
California Palace of the Legion of Honor 106-7
Calistoga 179, 194-6, 179, 194
Cambria 299
camping 341
Cannery Row 283, 282, 367
canoeing, *see also* boating, kayaking, whitewater rafting
    Guerneville 206
    Healdsburg 209
    Mendocino 153
    Mono Lake 242

car travel 392-4, *see also* driving tours
    car rental 392-3
    driver's licenses 392
    insurance 392
    recreational vehicles (RVs) 393
    road conditions 393
    road rules 393-4
Carmel-by-the-Sea 291-2, 290
Carnaval 108
Carson Mansion 163
casinos 224
Castro District, the 108, **115**, 87, 108
Castro Theatre 108, 99
cathedrals, *see* churches & cathedrals
Cayucos 299
Cedar Grove Village 238-9
Central & Southern California Coast 267-331, **268-9**, **277**
ceramics 141
Charles M Schulz Museum 208, 207
children, travel with 351-4
    Bay Area & Northern California 126
    Los Angeles 58
    San Francisco 92
    Santa Barbara 303
    Santa Cruz 281
    South Lake Tahoe 225
    Wine Country 180
Chinatown 108
Chinese New Year 46, 107, 46
Christmas Boat Parade 49
churches & cathedrals
    Cathedral of Our Lady of the Angels 65
    First Church of Christ Scientist 133
cinema 334
City Lights (bookstore) 94, 91
City of Ten Thousand Buddhas 156
climate 44, 379, 380
Coachella Valley 250-5, **252-3**

Conservatory of Flowers 89, 103, 89
consulates 385
Convict Lake 243
cooking courses 348-9
    Healdsburg 209
    Sonoma 201
costs 42
courses 379, *see also* cooking courses
Covington Flats 257
credit cards 42
crime 380
Crystal Cave 240, 240
Culinary Institute of America 176
Culinary Institute of America at Greystone 192
culture 334-7
customs regulations 384
cycling 342, 390-1, 56
    Bodega Bay 148
    Los Angeles 74-5
    Mammoth Lakes 244
    Mendocino 153
    Prairie Creek Redwoods State Park 169
    San Francisco 103
    Santa Barbara 303-4
    Sausalito 141-2
    Sonoma 201
    South Bay Bicycle Trail 56, 61

D
dance 337
dangers 379-82, 393
Death Valley National Park 19, 216, 261-6, **262**, 19, 216, 260, 263, 264, 266
Del Mar 304, 304
desert environment 364
Deserts, the 211-22, 250-66, **212-13**, **221**
dessert spots 40-1
Devils Postpile National Monument 246

INDEX

D-G

Devil's Golf Course 263, *263*
Día de los Muertos 49
disabilities, travelers with 388
discounts 382
Disney California Adventure 311
Disneyland 16, 270-1, 307-11, *16*, *270*, *271*, *307*, *310*, *351*
Disneyland Resort 306-12, **308**
Diver's Cove 313
diving 313, 339
Donner Lake 227-8
Donner Memorial State Park 228
Donner Party 227
Drake, Sir Francis 146, 356
drinks 374-6, *see also* wine
driver's licenses 392
driving, *see* car travel, driving tours
driving tours 41, *see also* car travel, itineraries
  17-Mile Drive 289
  Avenue of the Giants 157
  Deserts, the 218
  Foxen Canyon Wine Trail 306
  Sierra Nevada 218
drugs, possession of 386
Dyerville Giant 157

E
earthquakes 42, 363-4, 380-1
Eastern Sierra 241-7
El Prado 317-18
electricity 42
elephant seals 283
Elk 152
embassies 385
Emerald Bay State Park 226, *216*, *226*
emergencies 43, *see also inside front cover*
environmental issues 370-1
Eureka 162-3, *163*
events, *see* festivals

000 Map pages
000 Photograph pages

exchange rates, *see inside front cover*
Exploratorium 104, 106, *352*

F
family travel 351-4
Fannette Island 226
farmers markets 347-8, *see also* markets, shopping
  Arcata 164
  Los Angeles 61, 73
  San Diego 321
  San Francisco 120, *40*, *120*
  San Luis Obispo 296, 298, *347*
Ferndale 125, 159-62, *125*, *160*
Ferry Building Marketplace 98
Festival of Arts & Pageant of the Masters 47, *47*
festivals 46-9, 382, *see also* music festivals
  Badwater 256
  Burning Man 256
  Carnaval 108
  Death Valley '49ers 256
  Festival of the Swallows 314
  food 349-50
  Humboldt County Fair 161
  Kinetic Grand Championship 160, 161, 166
  Palm Springs 251
  San Francisco 107-8
  SF Gay Pride Month 108
  wine 349-50
films 45
First Night 49
Fisherman's Wharf 103-4, **105**
fishing
  Bodega bay 149
  Twin Lakes 243
Fleet Week 48
food 15, 23, 40, 344-50, *see also* cooking courses
  festivals 349-50
Fort Point National Historic Site 106

Founders Grove 157
Foxen Canyon Wine Trail 306
French Laundry 192, *193*
Furnace Creek 263

G
galleries, *see also* museums
  Bergamot Station Arts Center 61
  Gallery of Functional Art 61
  Getty Center 66
  Ren Brown Collection Gallery 149
  San Luis Obispo Art Center 296
gardens, *see* parks & gardens
Gaslamp Quarter 315-17, *315*
gay travelers 382
  San Francisco 118
  San Francisco Pride 47
  SF Gay Pride Month 108
Gehry, Frank 65
General Grant Grove 238
General Sherman Tree 239
geography 363-4
geology 363-4
Gerstle Cove Marine Reserve 151
Getty Center 56, 66, *56*, *66*
Getty Villa 56, 66
Giant Forest 239, *218*
Glacier Point 214, 231, *214*
Gold Country 26, 247-9, *26*
Gold Rush 358
Golden Gate Bridge 22, 99-100, *22*, *370*
Golden Gate Park 18, 88-9, 102-3, *89*, *88*, *89*, *99*
golf courses
  Death Valley National Park 265
  Palm Springs 250
  Trump National Golf Course 70
Grammy Museum 67, *65*, *360*
Grand Central Market 80, *81*
Grauman's Chinese Theatre 55, 67, *55*, *65*
Great Depression 360

Griffith Observatory 57, 69, 57
Griffith Park 67, 69
Gualala 150
Guerneville 205-7

H

Haight, the 108, **102**, 336
hang gliding 343
Hawk Hill 137
Healdsburg 208-10, **209**, **210**
Hearst Castle 28, 297, **28**, **297**
Hearst, William Randolph 297
Heath Ceramics 141
Heavenly 222, **224**
Heavenly Gondola 224
Henry Miller Library 294
Hermosa Beach 70, **70**
Hetch Hetchy 215, 233, **211**
Highway 1 15, 147-55
Highway 101 155-6
hiking 40, 341, 342
  Alabama Hills 247
  Anza-Borrego Desert State
    Park 259
  Arcata Marsh & Wildlife
    Sanctuary 165
  Bodega Head Trail 148
  Death Valley National Park 265
  Griffith Park 75
  Humboldt Redwoods State
    Park 157, 159
  John Muir Trail 233, 342
  Joshua Tree National Park
    257-8
  June Lake Loop 243
  Kings Canyon National Park
    238-9
  Kortum Trail 150
  Lava Beds National
    Monument 174
  Malibu Creek State Park 75
  Mammoth Lakes 244
  Mojave National Preserve 260-1
  Mt Hollywood Hiking Trail 67
  Mt Tamalpais 172

Muir Woods National
    Monument 144
  Pacific Crest Trail 342
  Palm Springs 251
  Prairie Creek Redwoods State
    Park 169
  Redwood National Park 168
  Robert Louis Stevenson State
    Park 197
  Runyon Canyon 75
  Salt Point State Park 151
  Sequoia National Park 239-40
  Shasta-Trinity National Forest
    170
  South Lake Tahoe 224-5
  South Tufa Reserve 242
  Stinson Beach 145
  Tahoe Rim Trail 342
  Yosemite National Park 233
history 355-62
holidays 44, 383
Hollywood 19, 54-5, **71**
Hollywood Bowl 83
Hollywood Christmas Parade 49
Hollywood Walk of Fame 55, 67,
  19, **32**, **55**
Hopland 155-6
horseback riding
  Big Sur 293
  Bodega Bay 148
hot springs
  Calistoga 179, 195
  Ukiah 156
hot-air ballooning 188, **44**
Humboldt Redwoods State Park
  156-9, **31**, **122**
Humboldt State University 165
Huntington Beach 304, **372**

I

Indian Canyons 250
in-line skating
  Los Angeles 74-5
  San Diego 323
  San Francisco 103

Inspiration Point 226
insurance 383, 392
international visitors 383-5
internet access 385-6
internet resources 45
  Bay Area & Northern
    California 127
  Central & Southern California
    Coast 275
  Deserts, the 219
  food & wine 348, 349, 375
  Los Angeles 59
  San Francisco 93
  Sierra Nevada 219
  surfing 339
  Wine Country 181
  Yosemite National Park 229
itineraries 31-8, **33**, **35**, **37**, see
  also driving tours
  Bay Area & Northern
    California 128-9, **129**
  Central & Southern California
    Coast 276-7, **277**
  coastal route 34-5, **35**
  Los Angeles 64
  San Diego 276
  San Francisco 98
  Sierra Nevada & the Deserts
    220-1, **221**
  Wine Country 182-3, **183**

J

Jack London State Historic Park
  179, 203, **179**, **203**
Japanese Tea Garden 89, 103,
  18, **89**
Jedediah Smith State Park 167
Jeffers, Robinson 291
John Muir Trail 233, 342
Joshua Tree National Park 29,
  217, 256-8, **252-3**, **29**, **217**,
  343, **371**
Julia Pfeiffer Burns State Park
  294
June Lake Loop 243, **243**

INDEX

K-M

K

kayaking 340, *see also* boating, canoeing, whitewater rafting
  Healdsburg 209
  Mono Lake 242
  Monterey 287
  Point Reyes National Seashore 147
  Sausalito 141
Keys View 257
Kinetic Grand Championship 47, 160, 161, 166, 48, 126, 166
Kings Canyon National Park 236-9, **237**, 238
kitesurfing 339
Knott's Berry Farm 309
Kruse Rhododendron State Reserve 151

L

La Brea Tar Pits 73, 69, 356
La Jolla 29, 324-5, 29, 324, 339
La Petite Rive 152
Lady Bird Johnson Grove 168, 14
Laguna Beach 21, 273, 312-14, 21, 273, 312, 338
Lake Tahoe 30, 216, 222-9, **223**, 30, 216, 224, 226, 228, 342
Lassen Volcanic National Park 172, 173, 174
Lava Beds National Monument 174
Laws Railroad Museum 246
legal matters 386
Legoland 326, 327
lesbian travelers 382
  San Francisco 118
  San Francisco Pride 47
  SF Gay Pride Month 108
lighthouses 274
  Piedras Blancas Lightstation 295
  Pigeon Point Lighthouse 135-6
  Point Arena Lighthouse 150

000 Map pages
000 Photograph pages

  Point Bonita Lighthouse 140
  Point Cabrillo Lighthouse 153
  Point Pinos Lighthouse 288-9
  Point Reyes Lighthouse 147
  Point San Luis Lighthouse 295
literature 334-5, *see also* books
Litquake 49
Little Italy 317
London, Jack 179, 203
Lone Cypress 289
Lone Pine 246-7
Long Beach 74
Looff carousel 101
Los Angeles 51-86, **52-3**, **62-3**, **68**, **71**, **79**, 57, 58, 76, 84, 366
  accommodations 76-8
  activities 74-5
  drinking 81-2
  entertainment 82-4
  food 78-81
  Hollywood 19, 54-5
  internet resources 59
  itineraries 64
  planning 59
  safe travel 59, 60
  shopping 84
  sights 60-74
  tourist information 60
  tours 75-6
  travel to/from 84-5
  travel within 59, 85-6
Los Angeles County Museum of Art 72, 73
Los Feliz 67, 80, **71**
Lost Coast 172, 172
Lundy Lake 243
Luther Burbank Home & Gardens 207-8
Lyell Canyon 215

M

Madonna Inn 300, 43
Malibu 28, 28
Mammoth Lakes 244-5, 245
Manhattan Beach 70, 58, 80

Manzanar National Historic Site 246, 247
maps 386-7
Marin County 137-47, **138-9**
Marin Headlands 124, 137-40, 124
Marine Mammal Center 140
Mariposa Grove 214-15, 214
markets, *see also* farmers markets, shopping
  Los Angeles 58
  Oxbow Public Market 189-90
Marshall Gold Discovery State Historic Park 217, 248, 217, 359
McCloud 171, 173, 171
measures, *see inside front cover*
Meier, Richard 66
Mendocino 152-5, **154**, 152
Mendocino Music Festival 47
Merced River 234
metric conversions, *see inside front cover*
Mexican food 23
Mexican rule 357-8
MH de Young Fine Arts Museum 88, 102-3, 88
microbreweries 376
microbrews 374-6
Miller, Henry 294
Minaret Vista 245
Mission period 356-7
Mission District, the 91, 108, **115**
missions 25
  Mission San Francisco Solano de Sonoma 200
  Mission San Juan Capistrano 314, 357
  Mission San Luis Obispo de Tolosa 296, 298
  Mission Santa Barbara 303, 25, 358
  San Carlos de Borroméo de Carmelo Mission 291
Miwok people 229
Mojave National Preserve 260-1

INDEX

M-N

Monarch Grove Sanctuary 290
money 382, *see also* costs, *inside front cover*
Mono Lake 242-3, 370
Monterey 272, 282-8, **284**, 272, 282, 367
Monterey Bay 278-92, 287, 365
Monterey Bay Aquarium 20, 286, 20, 286, 352
Monterey Jazz Festival 48
Moon Tree 296
Morgan, Julia 297
Moro Rock 240
Morro Bay 299
Mosaic Canyon 264
motorcycle travel 392-4, *see also*
    driving tours
    driver's licenses 392
    insurance 392, 393
    rental 393
    road conditions 393
    road rules 393-4
Mt Shasta 125, 170-1, 125, 169, 171, 364
Mt Shasta City 171, 173
Mt Tamalpais 172
Mt Whitney 247
mountain biking, *see* cycling
muggings 380
Muir Beach 145
Muir Woods National Monument 122, 144, 123, 144
murals 87, 91, 99
    tour (San Francisco) 107
Musée Mécanique 104
museums, *see also* galleries
    Annenberg Space for Photography 73
    Asian Art Museum 102
    Bay Area Discovery Museum 141
    Borax Museum 263
    Broad Contemporary Art Museum 72
    California Palace of the Legion of Honor 106-7

California State Railroad Museum 248
Carriage Museum 207-8
Cartoon Art Museum 101
Charles M Schulz Museum 208
Contemporary Jewish Museum 101
Emigrant Trail Museum 228
Exploratorium 104, 106
Ferndale Museum 160
Getty Villa 66
Grammy Museum 67
Healdsburg Museum 208-9
Kinetic Sculpture Museum 160
Laguna Art Museum 313
Laws Railroad Museum 246
Los Angeles 58-9
Los Angeles County Museum of Art 72
Maritime Museum (Monterey) 285
Maritime Museum (San Diego) 317
MH de Young Fine Arts Museum 88, 102-3
Musée Mécanique 104
Museum of Contemporary Art 65
Museum of Latin American Art 74
Museum of Man 318
Museum of the African Diaspora 101
Museum of the American West 67, 69
New Children's Museum 317
Page Museum 73
Paley Center for Media 73
Petersen Automotive Museum 72
San Diego Museum of Art 318
San Francisco Museum of Modern Art 100
Santa Barbara Maritime Museum 301

Serra Museum 319
Silverado Museum 192
Surfing Museum 280
Timken Museum of Art 318
USS Midway Museum 317
Yosemite Museum 231
music 45, 335-6
music festivals, *see also* festivals
    Coachella Valley Music & Arts Festival 251
    Joshua Tree Music Festival 256
    Mendocino Music Festival 47
    Monterey Jazz Festival 48
    Reggae on the River 47
    San Francisco Jazz Festival 48
    Simon Rodia Watts Towers Jazz Festival 48
Mystery Spot 280

N
Napa 188-91
Napa Valley 16, 178, 186-202, **187**, 16, 44, 175, 178, 186, 374
Napa Valley Wine Train 176
national & state parks 371, *see also* parks & gardens, state historic parks, state reserves
    Andrew Molera State Park 293
    Anza-Borrego Desert State Park 258-9
    Big Basin Redwoods State Park 137
    Death Valley National Park 19, 261-6
    Donner Memorial State Park 228
    Emerald Bay State Park 226
    Humboldt Redwoods State Park 156-9
    Jedediah Smith State Park 167
    Joshua Tree National Park 29, 217, 256-8
    Julia Pfeiffer Burns State Park 294

national & state parks *continued*
  Kings Canyon National Park
    236-9
  Lassen Volcanic National
    Park 172
  Patrick's Point State Park 167
  Pfeiffer Big Sur State Park 293
  Prairie Creek Redwoods State
    Park 123, 169-70
  Redwood National Park 14,
    122, 168
  Robert Louis Stevenson State
    Park 196-7
  Salt Point State Park 151
  Sequoia National Park 236,
    239-41
  Yosemite National Park 17,
    214-15, 229-36
Native Americans 167, 229, 355-7
New Children's Museum 317
Newport Beach 304, **267**
North Beach 27, 91, 108
North Coast 147-74
Northern California, *see* Bay Area
  & Northern California
Northern Redwood Coast 168-70

O

Oasis of Mara 257
Ocean Beach 106, **107**
oil production 359
Old Faithful Geyser 196
Old Spanish Days Fiesta 48
Old Town State Historic Park
  319, **329**
opening hours, *see inside front
  cover*
Orange County 306-14

P

Pacific Coast Highway 15
Pacific Design Center 70

Pacific Grove 288-91
Pacific Park 61
Paiute people 229, **355**
Palace of Fine Arts 104, **104**
Palm Springs 250-5, **254**, **218**,
  255
Palm Springs Aerial Tramway
  250, **218**
Palos Verdes 70
Panum Crater 242
paragliding 343
parks & gardens, *see also*
  national & state parks, state
  historic parks, state reserves
  Arroyo Burro Beach County
    Park 303
  Auburn State Recreation
    Area 248
  Balboa Park 317
  Brown's Park 313
  Conservatory of Flowers 89,
    103
  Cornerstone Gardens 200-1
  Crissy Field 106
  Dahlia Garden 103
  Dennis the Menace Park 285
  Fetzer Vineyards Organic
    Gardens 155-6
  Golden Gate Park 88-9
  Griffith Park 67
  Heisler Park 313
  Japanese Tea Garden 89, 103
  Kruse Rhododendron State
    Reserve 151
  Luther Burbank Home &
    Gardens 207-8
  Petrified Forest 196
  Plaza de Viña Del Mar Park
    140
  Redwood Park 165
  Russ Park 160
  San Francisco Botanical
    Garden & Strybing
    Arboretum 88-9, 103
  Yerba Buena Gardens 101

passports 384
Patrick's Point State Park 167
Petrified Forest 196, **196**
petroglyphs 174
pets, travel with 387
Pfeiffer Beach 293-4
Pfeiffer Big Sur State Park 293
Piedras Blancas Lightstation 295
Pigeon Point Lighthouse 135-6,
  121
Pismo Beach 299, **299**
planning 39-49, 382
  itineraries 31-8
plants 365
Plaza de Viña Del Mar Park 140
Point Arena 150
Point Arena Lighthouse 150
Point Bonita Lighthouse 140
Point Cabrillo Lighthouse 153
Point Lobos State Reserve 291-2
Point Pinos Lighthouse 288-9
Point Reyes Lighthouse 147, **146**
Point Reyes National Seashore
  146-7, **124**
Point Reyes Station 124, 145-6
Point San Luis Lighthouse 295
population 373
Prairie Creek Redwoods State
  Park 123, 169-70
Presidio 106
public holidays 44, 383

Q

Queen Mary 74

R

rafting, *see* whitewater rafting
railroad construction 359
Real Goods Solar Living Center 156
Reds Meadow 245-6
Redwood Coast 156-68, **158**
Redwood Creek Overlook 168
Redwood National Park 14, **14**,
  369
Redwood Park **123**

redwood trees 14, 122-3, 167, 365, **31**, **122**, **123**
  Armstrong Redwoods State Reserve 206
  Avenue of the Giants 156-9
  Big Basin Redwoods State Park 137
  drive-through redwoods 159
  Humboldt Redwoods State Park 156-9
  itinerary 128, **129**
  Muir Woods National Monument 144
  Northern Redwood Coast 168-70, **158**
  Petrified Forest 196
  Pfeiffer Big Sur State Park 293
  Redwood Coast 156-70, **158**
  Redwood National Park 122, 168
  Southern Redwood Coast 156-68, **158**
Redwood National Park 122, 168
Reggae on the River 47
regional identity 372-3
robbery 380
Robert Louis Stevenson State Park 196-7
rock climbing 342, **343**
  Joshua Tree National Park 258
  Yosemite National Park 234
Rockefeller Forest 157
Russian River Area 16, 178, 202-10, **204**, **178**

S
Sacramento 248-9, **249**
Safari West 197, **180**, **200**
safe travel 379-82
Salt Point State Park 151, **151**
San Carlos de Borroméo de Carmelo Mission 291
San Diego 314-31, **316**, **320-1**, **34**, **315**, **319**, **324**, **330**, **331**
  accommodations 325-7
  Balboa Park 20

drinking 327-8
entertainment 328-9
food 327-8
itineraries 276
microbreweries 376
San Diego Zoo 20
sights 315-25
travel to/from 329
travel within 329-31
San Diego Latin Film Festival 46
San Diego Wild Animal Park 325, **325**
San Diego Zoo 20, 273, 318-19, **20**, **273**
San Francisco 87-120, **95**, **96-7**, **102**, **105**, **115**, **36**, **46**, **91**, **92**, **101**, **361**
  accommodations 108-10
  activities 98-107
  drinking 114
  emergencies 93
  entertainment 114-16
  festivals & events 107-8
  food 110-14
  Golden Gate Bridge 22
  Golden Gate Park 18
  internet resources 93
  itineraries 98
  North Beach 27
  safe travel 94
  shopping 116-19
  sights 98-107
  tourist information 94
  tours 107
  travel to/from 119-20
  travel within 119-20
San Francisco Bay Area, see Bay Area & Northern California
San Francisco Botanical Garden & Strybing Arboretum 88-9, 103
San Francisco Fringe Festival 48
San Francisco International Film Festival 46
San Francisco Jazz Festival 48, **49**

San Francisco Museum of Modern Art 100, **337**
San Francisco Pride 47
San Gregorio 135, **136**
San Luis Obispo 296-300, **347**
San Pedro 70
Santa Barbara 21, 300-6, **302**, **21**, **25**, **301**
Santa Barbara County Courthouse 301-3
Santa Cruz 278-82, **279**, **274**, **373**
Santa Monica 57, 61, **50**, **57**, **65**
Santa Rosa 207-8
Sausalito 140-3, **126**, **141**
Schulz, Charles M 208
Schwarzenegger, Arnold 362
Scotty's Castle 264, **264**
scuba diving 313, 339
sea kayaking, see kayaking
sea lions 140, 280, **287**
seals 140, 283, **324**
SeaWorld 322-3, **323**
senior travelers 382
Sequoia National Park 236, 239-41, **237**, **218**
sequoias, see redwood trees
Serra, Padre Junípero 357
SF Gay Pride Month 108
Shasta-Trinity National Forest 170
shopping 126, 366-8, see also farmers markets, markets
Shoshone people 261
Sierra Nevada 211-47, **212-13**, **221**
Simon Rodia Watts Towers Jazz Festival 48
Skidoo 264
skiing, see also snowboarding
  Lake Tahoe 30, 222
  Mammoth Lakes 244
  Mt Shasta 171
  Palm Springs 251
  Yosemite National Park 234
snorkeling 313, 339

INDEX

S-V

snowboarding, *see also* skiing
 Mammoth Lakes 244
 Mt Shasta 171
Solana Beach 304
Solvang 309, **309**
Sonoma 179, 199-202, **179**
Sonoma Barracks 200
Sonoma Coast 125, **125**
Sonoma Coast State Beach 149-50
Sonoma Valley 16, 197-202, **198**
South Bay Bicycle Trail 56, **56**
South Lake Tahoe 224-6
South Tufa Reserve 242
Southern California Coast,
 see Central & Southern
 California Coast
Southern Redwood Coast
 156-68
spas
 Calistoga 195
 Palm Springs 251
sportfishing, *see* fishing
Spreckels Organ Pavilion 318
St Helena 192-4
Staples Center 67
state historic parks, *see also* parks
 & gardens, national & state
 parks, state reserves
 Bodie State Historic Park
 241-2
 Jack London State Historic
 Park 203
 Marshall Gold Discovery State
 Historic Park 217, 248
 Old Town State Historic Park
 319, **329**
 Sonoma State Historic Park
 200
 Sutter's Fort State Historic
 Park 249
state reserves, *see also* national &
 state parks, parks & gardens,

000 Map pages
000 Photograph pages

state historic parks
 Año Nuevo State Reserve 136
 Armstrong Redwoods State
 Reserve 206
 Point Lobos State Reserve
 291-2
Stateline 224-6
Stearns Wharf 301
Steinbeck Festival 48
Steinbeck, John
 Cannery Row 283
 Steinbeck Festival 48
Stevenson, Robert Louis 196-7
Stinson Beach 145
Stovepipe Wells 263-4
Stow Lake boathouse 103
studio tours 72, 75, 335
Sumêg 167
Sunset Drive 288
surfing 24, 339, *see also* beaches,
 swimming
 Los Angeles 75
 Tourmaline Surfing Park 323
sustainable travel 369-71
Sutter's Fort State Historic Park
 249
Swanton Berry Farm 136
swimming 75, 338-9, *see also*
 beaches, surfing
 safety 381

T
Tahoe City 226-7
Tall Trees Grove 168
tech boom 360-2
television 334
theater 337
theaters
 Grauman's Chinese Theatre 67
 Julia Morgan Theater 133
 Nokia Theatre 67
theft 380
theme parks, *see* amusement parks
Tiburon 143
time 387

tipping 42
Tor House 291
tourist information 387
Tournament of Roses 46
tours 387-8
 Amtrak 25
 Los Angeles 75-6
 San Francisco 107
 South Lake Tahoe 225
 studio tours 72, 75, 335
 Wine Country 185-6
 Yosemite National Park 234
Tower of California 318
Toyota Grand Prix of Long Beach 46
train travel 390, 394
travel to/from California 43,
 389-90
travel within California 43,
 390-4
trekking, *see* hiking
Trinidad Head 167
Trinity Alps 167
Truckee 227-9
Trump National Golf Course 70
Tuolumne Meadows 231-2
Twenty Mule Team Canyon 263
Twin Lakes 243

U
Ubehebe Crater 264
Ukiah 156
Universal Studios Hollywood 54,
 72, **54**
University of California (Berkeley)
 130
US Open Sandcastle
 Competition 47
USS *Pampanito* 103-4

V
vacations 44, 383
vegetarian & vegan travelers
 350
Venice 57, 61-82, **4**, **38**, **57**
Vikingsholm Castle 226

visas 42, 384
visual arts 336-7

W

walking, *see* hiking
Walt Disney Concert Hall 65, 65, 83
Warners Brothers Studio Tour 54
Washington Tree 239
water management 370-1
Wawona 232
weather 44, 379, 380
websites, *see* internet resources, *see also* internet access
weights, *see inside front cover*
whale-watching 340-1, 340
  Bodega Bay 149
  Monterey 285
  Point Reyes National Seashore 147
whitewater rafting 342-3, *see also* boating, canoeing, kayaking
  American River 217, 248
  Trinity River 167
  Yosemite National Park 234
wildlife 364-5
  safety 381
wildlife sanctuaries, *see also* aquariums, zoos
  Arcata Marsh & Wildlife Sanctuary 165
  Marine Mammal Center 140
  Monarch Grove Sanctuary 290
  Safari West 197
windsurfing 339
wine 374-6
  festivals 349-50
  tasting 176-7, 375
Wine Country 16, 175-210, **185**, 175, 176, 177, 178, 186, 189, 202, 205, 332
  itineraries 182-3, **183**
  tours 185-6
  travel to/from 184
  travel within 184-5
  wine tasting 176-7
wine regions 375
  Foxen Canyon Wine Trail 306
  Hopland 155-6
  Napa Valley 178, 186-202
  Russian River 178, 202-10
  Sonoma Valley 197-202
women travelers 389
Wonderland of Rocks 257
World Championship Pumpkin Weigh-off 49
WWII period 360

Y

Yosemite National Park 17, 214-15, 229-36, **215**, **230**, **232**, 12, 17, 40, 211, 214, 215, 233, 234, 341, 363
  accommodations 234-5
  activities 233-4
  drinking 235-6
  food 235
  history 229
  internet resources 229
  sights 231-3
  tourist information 229
  tours 234
  travel to/from 236
  travel within 236
Yosemite Valley 214, 231, **232**, 12
Yountville 191-2
Yurok people 167

Z

Zabriskie Point 263
Zeum Art & Technology Center 101
zoos, *see also* aquariums, wildlife sanctuaries
  San Diego Wild Animal Park 325
  San Diego Zoo 318-19

INDEX

V-Z

GOING GREEN

It seems like almost everyone in California is going 'green' these days. But how can you know which businesses really are ecofriendly, and which are simply jumping on the 'greenwashing' bandwagon?

We've done our homework. All of these sights, attractions, activities, tour operators, outdoor outfitters, nonprofit organizations, festivals, restaurants, coffeehouses, shops, lodgings and transportation providers have been hand-picked by our authors for acting in harmony with sustainable tourism goals. Some top picks are involved in environmental education, conservation and clean-up. Others are locally owned and operated, helping to preserve California's homegrown arts and cultural identities, especially that of Native Americans.

We want to keep developing our sustainable tourism content. If you think we've omitted somewhere that should be listed here, or if you disagree with our choices, email us at www.lonelyplanet .com/contact and set us straight for next time. For more information about sustainable tourism and Lonely Planet, see www.lonelyplanet.com/about/ responsible-travel.

Activities
REI 379

Bay Area & Northern California
accommodations
Chanslor Guest Ranch
(Bodega Bay) 149
Costanoa (Pigeon Point) 136
Point Reyes Hostel (Point
Reyes National Seashore)
147
food
Chez Panisse (Berkeley)
134
Osteria Stellina (Point Reyes
Station) 145
Ravens (Mendocino) 154
Terrapin Creek Café &
Restaurant (Bodega
Bay) 149
sights
Fetzer Vineyards Organic
Gardens (Hopland) 155

Marine Mammal Center
(Marin Headlands) 140
Old Mill Farm School of
Country Living
(Mendocino) 153
Organic Planet Festival
(Eureka) 349
Real Goods Solar Living
Center (Hopland) 156

Central & Southern California Coast
accommodations
Adobe on Green B&B (Santa
Cruz) 281
Asilomar Conference
Grounds (Pacific Grove)
290
El Capitan Canyon (Goleta)
305
HI Hostel Obispo (San Luis
Obispo) 298
Hotel Indigo (San Diego)
326

Pacific Blue Inn (Santa Cruz)
281
Passionfish (Pacific Grove)
290
food
Deetjen's Big Sur Inn 295
farmers market (San Luis
Obispo) 296
farmers market (Santa
Barbara) 305
Montrio Bistro (Monterey)
288
Old Monterey Marketplace
288
Soif (Santa Cruz) 281
Whisknladle (La Jolla) 328
sights
Friends of the Elephant Seal
(Piedras Blancas) 283
Henry Miller Library (Big
Sur) 294
Monterey Bay Aquarium 286
Museum of Natural History
(Santa Barbara) 303

New Children's Museum (San
   Diego) 317
Point Lobos State Reserve 291
San Carlos de Borroméo de
   Carmelo Mission (Carmel)
   294
transportation
   Lil' Toot water taxi
      (Santa Barbara) 301

Los Angeles
food
   Axe 78
   Real Food Daily 78
sights
   Aquarium of the Pacific 74
transportation
   Simply Hybrid 393

San Francisco
accommodations
   Good Hotel 109
   Orchard Garden Hotel 110
   Red Victorian 110
food
   Bi-Rite Market 113
   farmerbrown 112

Greens 111
Jardinière 112
Magnolia Brewpub 111
Mission Pie 113
Namu 112
Rainbow Grocery 113
Slanted Door 112
Tataki 112
Warming Hut 106
shopping
   826 Valencia 117
   Crossroads 117
   Nancy Boy 117
   Under One Roof 117
sights
   California Academy of
      Sciences 102
   San Francisco Ferry
      Building 98

Sierra Nevada & The Deserts
accommodations
   Cedar House Sport Hotel
      (Donner Lake) 228
   Clair Tappaan Lodge (Donner
      Lake) 228

sights
   Sequoia & Kings Canyon
      National Parks 236
   Yosemite National Park 229

Wine Country
accommodations
   Creekside Inn & Resort
      (Guerneville) 206
food
   Barndiva (Healdsburg) 210
   Ubuntu (Napa) 193
sights
   Jack London State Historic
      Park (Glen Ellen) 203
   Unti (Dry Creek Valley) 204
wineries
   Benziger (Glen Ellen) 199
   Casa Nuestra (St Helena)
      189
   Frog's Leap (Napa) 186
   Michel-Schlumberger
      (Healdsburg) 189
   Porter Creek (Healdsburg)
      189
   Preston Vineyards
      (Healdsburg) 189

MAP LEGEND

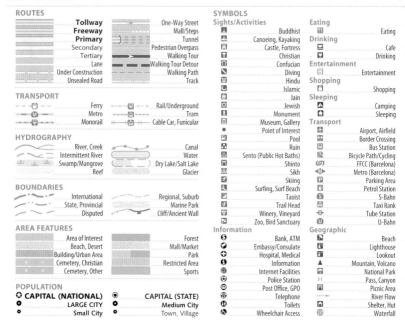

ROUTES

Tollway	One-Way Street
Freeway	Mall/Steps
Primary	Tunnel
Secondary	Pedestrian Overpass
Tertiary	Walking Tour
Lane	Walking Tour Detour
Under Construction	Walking Path
Unsealed Road	Track

TRANSPORT

Ferry	Rail/Underground
Metro	Tram
Monorail	Cable Car, Funicular

HYDROGRAPHY

River, Creek	Canal
Intermittent River	Water
Swamp/Mangrove	Dry Lake/Salt Lake
Reef	Glacier

BOUNDARIES

International	Regional, Suburb
State, Provincial	Marine Park
Disputed	Cliff/Ancient Wall

AREA FEATURES

Area of Interest	Forest
Beach, Desert	Mall/Market
Building/Urban Area	Park
Cemetery, Christian	Restricted Area
Cemetery, Other	Sports

POPULATION

CAPITAL (NATIONAL)	CAPITAL (STATE)
LARGE CITY	Medium City
Small City	Town, Village

SYMBOLS

Sights/Activities

Buddhist	
Canoeing, Kayaking	
Castle, Fortress	
Christian	
Confucian	
Diving	
Hindu	
Islamic	
Jain	
Jewish	
Monument	
Museum, Gallery	
Point of Interest	
Pool	
Ruin	
Sento (Public Hot Baths)	
Shinto	
Sikh	
Skiing	
Surfing, Surf Beach	
Taoist	
Trail Head	
Winery, Vineyard	
Zoo, Bird Sanctuary	

Information

Bank, ATM	
Embassy/Consulate	
Hospital, Medical	
Information	
Internet Facilities	
Police Station	
Post Office, GPO	
Telephone	
Toilets	
Wheelchair Access	

Eating

Eating	

Drinking

Cafe	
Drinking	

Entertainment

Entertainment	

Shopping

Shopping	

Sleeping

Camping	
Sleeping	

Transport

Airport, Airfield	
Border Crossing	
Bus Station	
Bicycle Path/Cycling	
FFCC (Barcelona)	
Metro (Barcelona)	
Parking Area	
Petrol Station	
S-Bahn	
Taxi Rank	
Tube Station	
U-Bahn	

Geographic

Beach	
Lighthouse	
Lookout	
Mountain, Volcano	
National Park	
Pass, Canyon	
Picnic Area	
River Flow	
Shelter, Hut	
Waterfall	

LONELY PLANET OFFICES

Australia
Head Office
Locked Bag 1, Footscray, Victoria 3011
☎ 03 8379 8000, fax 03 8379 8111

USA
150 Linden St, Oakland, CA 94607
☎ 510 250 6400, toll free 800 275 8555,
fax 510 893 8572

UK
2nd fl, 186 City Rd,
London EC1V 2NT
☎ 020 7106 2100, fax 020 7106 2101

Contact
talk2us@lonelyplanet.com
lonelyplanet.com/contact

Published by Lonely Planet Publications Pty Ltd
ABN 36 005 607 983

Printed by Toppan Security Printing Pte. Ltd.
Printed in Singapore

Lonely Planet and the Lonely Planet logo are trademarks of Lonely Planet and are registered in the US Patent and Trademark Office and in other countries.

Lonely Planet does not allow its name or logo to be appropriated by commercial establishments, such as retailers, restaurants or hotels. Please let us know of any misuses: lonelyplanet.com/ip.

MIX
Paper from
responsible sources
FSC™ C021741
www.fsc.org